THE NEGRO FAMILY
IN THE UNITED STATES

THE NEGRO FAMILY
IN THE UNITED STATES

E. FRANKLIN FRAZIER

Revised and Abridged Edition

Foreword by NATHAN GLAZER

Phoenix Books

THE UNIVERSITY OF CHICAGO PRESS
CHICAGO & LONDON

E
185.86
.F74
1966

99454

The University of Chicago Press, Chicago & London
The University of Toronto Press, Toronto 5, Canada

To Marie

FOREWORD

IN HIS PREFACE to *The Negro Family in the United States*, on its first publication, Ernest W. Burgess called it "the most valuable contribution to the literature of the family since the publication, twenty years ago, of *The Polish Peasant in Europe and America*." The passage of twenty-seven years has in no way reduced the stature of this classic work; on the contrary, viewing it now in the new contexts of the Negro revolution and the convulsive response to it of American society and government, we must give Frazier's study even higher praise than Burgess gave it. Written during American sociology's only golden age, it is to my mind one of the most substantial and enduring works of that age. Ironically, many efforts to establish a timeless theoretical framework for sociology and social analysis now appear to us dated and remote. This book, concretely based on the realities of Negro family life, reconstructed eclectically from personal accounts, literature, statistics and observation and direct experience, has lost nothing in immediacy and relevance.

Indeed, if anything, it has gained. As I write this introduction, the *New York Times* reports that the President and his advisers now see the Negro family as a key element in their efforts to wipe out the gap between the social, educational, and economic positions of Negro and white. Conducting a conference on the Negro family in 1965, they will have no better text than Frazier; far from being supplanted, it has scarcely been supplemented. Its major framework remains solid and structures all our thinking on the Negro family.

Indeed, Frazier's achievement is even greater than that suggested by the remarkable contemporaneity of this book. For in 1932, with the publication of *The Negro Family in Chicago* (University of Chicago Press) and *The Free Negro Family* (Nashville, Tenn.: Fisk University Press), he had already worked out the main lines of his approach. In these early works, he had to attack the crudities of contemporary sociologists and anthropologists who insisted on finding in the disorganization of the Negro family something primitive, either the "primitive" social structure of Africa or the "primitive" racial characteristics of the Negro. Frazier insisted that the social characteristics of the Negro family were

vii

shaped by social conditions, not by race or African survivals. He insisted, too, that one could not indiscriminately take statistics and statistical averages as an index of social disorganization or promiscuity or immorality. While he was more of a puritan in his sexual attitudes than some later anthropologists and sociologists more radically influenced by cultural relativism (this was true of W. E. B. Du Bois, too), he nevertheless pointed to the great differences between the illegitimacy of the rural South and the urban North. Frazier would not justify southern rural Negro family patterns as being simply an aspect of the "culture" of the group, neither better nor worse than the standards and practices of other people; but he insisted that whatever standards existed, whatever behavior we found, could be understood only in terms of the social conditions that had shaped them. The radical condemnation of Negro family life by whites reflected not only ignorance of a variety of patterns, equally well established, but an inability to see the extent to which matriarchy and illegitimacy were an adaptation to social and economic conditions, and not necessarily damaging or unhealthy adaptations—though one could make no apology for the social and economic conditions.

In *The Negro Family in the United States*, Frazier displayed the full sequence of social conditions that had shaped the Negro family. Slavery was first. In slavery the African cultural patterns were totally destroyed, and what emerged was a chaos with only fragmentary patterns and structures, easily broken and just enough to ensure the raising of slave children. But even under slavery a stable Negro family, on an American model, was built up by free Negroes and slaves living under favorable conditions. Then there was the crisis of emancipation, with the maintenance and extension of the matriarchy that had emerged under slavery as the one stable element for a good part of Negro family life. After emancipation, too, the father-centered stable families of the free Negroes were extended on the basis of the ownership of property and new occupations. Then there came a third terrible crisis in the cities of the North, a crisis as severe as those of slavery and Reconstruction, with once again the emergence of stability in the form of middle-class Negro families and the families of the new industrial working class. This is the history of the Negro family, as Frazier structured and detailed it, and it has become part of our consciousness and understanding.

Beyond praising Frazier, however, we must place him in the context of the work in the social sciences since he wrote *The Negro Family in the United States*, and ask what additional questions, what further truths, have been suggested by this new work. There are a number of areas in which to my mind significant new material has been developed that we must take into account in considering the Negro family. There is first the development, from psychoanalytically influenced anthropology, of a view of the family in which it is seen as not only the product of social causes but as itself a significant and dynamic element in the creation of culture, social character, and social structure. I refer to the work associated with such names as Abram Kardiner, Erich Fromm, Ruth Benedict, Margaret Mead, David Riesman, and Ralph Linton. Certainly, all these writers agreed, the structure of the family could be seen in terms of causes that were neither racial nor evolutionary. A specific technological and economic background, a specific social order, created a certain kind of family. That family itself, however, was the support of the social structure. Children were socialized into certain values and patterns, and they maintained a society. Sometimes the culture the family supported was sharply structured, sometimes it barely seemed to have any defined structure at all. But behind these varying social forms were family structures, patterns of child rearing.

But the critical point is that this work introduced a complication into the analysis of the family that I think was not present in Frazier's work. Frazier hoped that changes in the Negro family would result from social and economic changes. The free Negro as against the slave, the Negro farmers as against the sharecroppers, the new working class and middle class as against the disorganized lower class: all these had created better family forms, and with further economic progress the weaknesses of the Negro family would be overcome. The newer, psychoanalytically influenced social science, on the other hand, emphasized the tight web of family, personality, culture, and society, and in so doing suggested that change in the family would be enormously difficult.

There is no real contradiction between Frazier's point of view and the point of view of social scientists whose emphasis was on the family as the creator rather than the product of social forms. Yet, it was impossible to overlook the differences in emphasis.

One difference was that, from an anthropological orientation, with its strong emphasis on cultural relativism, it became difficult to make the moral judgments (and therefore the judgments concerning social action) that were relatively easy for Frazier to make. The anthropologist saw a variety of family types and cultures. Initially, this variety was explored and brought to our attention by liberal anthropologists, fighting both racism and evolutionary theories and arguing that no culture was "backward" or "primitive"—it was merely different. It is hard for us to see now how an emphasis on the tight and not easily changed web of family life, personality, and culture of a given society could be seen as progressive—for how could one intervene to change such a system?—but the point of the anthropologists was that we were probably culture-bound in emphasizing the need for this system to change in the first place and that this kind of analysis fought the racists by showing that the same racial types had radically different personalities, cultures, and societies, depending on the cultural system into which they were born.

It was not long, however, before it was clear that the potential for progressive social action in this orientation was rather limited. During World War II, the analysis of the relation between culture and personality shifted from harmless New Guinea tribes to the Germans and the Japanese, and after the war, to the Russians. The approach was also used on our own society, by scholars such as Erich Fromm and T. W. Adorno and his colleagues of *The Authoritarian Personality* (New York: Harper, 1950), to analyze the middle classes of Western society and to argue that they had a strong penchant for fascism. At this point, it was clear that national and class antagonism could be bolstered by psychoanalytic and anthropological analyses of differences as well as by racial and evolutionary analyses.

But to return to the Negro family: From this new orientation, one could also argue against Frazier that he was simply being naïve, moralistic, and culture-bound in his criticism of the Negro family. The Negro matriarchy, the acceptance of illegitimate children, the more frequent changing of spouses, the more casual discipline could be seen, not as wrong or the product of pathological conditions, but simply as culturally different, producing a different style of personality it is true but one no less valuable. Indeed, if the middle-class child—following Erich

Fromm, T. W. Adorno, and Arnold Green—suffered from some characteristic neuroses and psychopathologies, one could argue that the lower-class family, and the Negro lower-class family, was in some respects superior—it did not produce the complex of anxiety over success, cleanliness, sex, and the like. Thus, in the late thirties and early forties, we can find a good deal of work, identified particularly with the names of Allison Davis and R. J. Havighurst, which says something for the lower-class family, if not as much for the lower-class Negro family—for whatever degree of cultural relativism and anthropological romanticization we may find, there was scarcely an American social scientist from the late thirties on who was not in favor of radical changes in the political, economic, and social position of the Negroes in the United States. Nevertheless, one must see the dilemmas in the situation: to emphasize only the pathology of Negro life would lead to repulsion and perhaps even to justification of the severe patterns of discrimination and supression. To emphasize that there were virtues in lower-class life might lead to certain gains—for example, less dependence on the I.Q. test as a means of segregating Negro children. Thus, when Allison Davis emphasized that this test was culture-bound, his main objective was to modify the system of segregation by pointing to areas of achievement and fulfilment in which lower-class life might possess advantages over middle-class life. He was not arguing that lower-class Negroes did not need and demand social change. But the dilemma is apparent. If it was so good for them, why should we try to change it?

Frazier I think was more hardheaded, as well as more old-fashioned, as was W. E. B. Du Bois. It was all bad—the abandoned mothers, the roving men, the sexually experienced youth. The only thing that was good was that the mothers, in conditions that should never have existed, did their best by the children. Conditions of economic stability and social equality would change the family. And for him there was no dilemma.

And, as a matter of fact, the next turn in the development of social research in this area tended to support him. For the period of lower-class romanticization came to an end under the double impact of change in society and change in social science—and there is no question that the first was more important. The change in society was heralded by the explosion of independence movements in colonial areas after World

War II. It became impossible to persuade new nations, impatient to become strong and rich, that their traditional societies had many virtues which they should preserve. Anthropologists might convince colonial administrators that natives should be undisturbed in maintaining their equally valid approach to the organization of social life, but they could not convince the leaders of new nations, who saw in the traditional patterns simply the backwardness that made them weak in international affairs. Thus the cultural relativistic stance in sociology and anthropology went into eclipse. The question now was: How do we get development? And social scientists followed suit, now picking up their leads from Weber as well as Freud and searching for the backgrounds that emphasized ambition, achievement, work, aspiration. In this perspective, of course, the lower-class family came out rather badly—it was studied only as a mine of potential raw materials, some of which might be fashioned into the psychological material useful for achievement. Thus the New England ethnic groups—Italian, Jewish, Yankee, Irish—served as the basis for a series of studies which found that some lower-class groups seemed to take to the achievement pattern better than others (B. C. Rosen, F. L. Strodtbeck). David C. McClelland and his collaborators ransacked the cultures of the world looking for clues to this pattern of achievement.

And, meanwhile, our own colonial problem rose in seriousness to become the major domestic issue in American life. Just as the cultures and psychologies of the peoples of the world were now studied from the point of view of determining how they might be made more equal economically and politically, so we begin in a fragmentary way to study the culture and psychology of lower-class Negroes from the same point of view: What obstacles to equality are presented?

Obviously these new questions changed the perspective on the lower-class Negro family. What had been considered warmth and sensual expression and imagery now became emotional inconsistency, inability to defer gratification, and unrealistic fantasy. One presumes that beneath the varying social scientific perspectives was a single reality and that it was the points of view that were changing as we moved from the forties and fifties into the sixties, not the Negro family itself. And yet it is very likely that the family itself was changing, too. In a situation in which opportunities for economic and educational advancement were seen as largely blocked, conceivably there was an adjustment to a low-income level that permitted some degree of gratification and satisfaction. As opportunities opened, satisfaction with the long-established pre-existing level declined. Expectations rose faster than opportunities. When an all-embracing social struggle to open up more opportunities developed, engulfing larger and larger parts of the Negro community, then the new political and social situation in which the family found itself may also have changed the family. Its mood may well have changed to one of bitterness and anger.

In the shift from a view of the Negro family influenced by cultural relativism to one influenced by the paramount need for social mobility, the emphasis also shifted from the mother to the father, and in particular the absent father. Thomas F. Pettigrew, in his valuable *Profile of the Negro American* (Princeton, N.J.: Van Nostrand, 1964), has summarized the studies which suggest what disorders follow from the absence of fathers in a large percentage of Negro families: the women inevitably take over a masculine role in support and discipline; the children then have difficulty in establishing roles appropriate to their own sexes; the girls become more masculine, the boys more feminine. Even without plunging into the complexities created for psycho-social development, one must observe the problems created by the absence of a male with a stable job that creates a link to some substantial part of society, supplying, in addition to income, knowlege of some part of the work world.

We do not of course find, in this new emphasis in social science on the obstacles to economic and social change, a single unified point of view. Middle-class status is still seen as a morally ambiguous objective. We find less romanticization of lower-class life. But, as James Baldwin has said, "Who wants to be integrated into a burning house?" The middle-class job, the competition, the suburban house with its high mortgage payments, the disciplining of the children to achieve in schools which themselves come under increasing criticism (as does the society these children are being trained to enter): all this is meant by the "burning house." Frazier himself was unhappy with the Negro middle class, as he made clear as early as 1939 in his chapter in this book on "The Brown Middle Class," which prefigures the much sharper attack on the Negro middle class in *Black Bourgeoisie* (Glencoe, Ill.: The Free Press,

1957). But there is a substantial difference in the perspectives of Frazier and contemporary radical critics of middle-class objectives. Frazier was attacking the Negro middle class for living beyond its means and powers, for aping a life it did not have the political or economic strength actually to achieve. He found nothing wrong with a life that emphasized work, stable family relationships, achievement. He objected to the fact that too many in the Negro middle classes were willing to settle for the shadow of that life, rather than the substance. Radical Negro writers today attack its substance.

Inevitably, in our view of the Negro family, we will be torn between an orientation which finds something positive and unique in its distinctive features, something to be preserved and valued, and an orientation which emphasizes the elements that seem to hold back occupational advance. We find on the one hand the work of Frank Riessman, who in his book on the culturally deprived child describes a special mode of learning which is characteristic of lower-class children, and lower-class Negro children, and to which we should adapt our schools and teachers. On the other hand, we have the work of Martin Deutsch, who insists that learning cannot begin until a child has a vocabulary. For him the lower-class child does not have a different but equal culture: he has a culture deficient in some vital elements for education. There is no question which side Frazier would be on.

Nor is there any question about which side the Negro community and Negro parents are on. They want their children to read and to write and to do arithmetic as well and as early as white children. They may on occasion deny defensively that the failure of Negro children to do so has anything to do with their family background, but their concern is less to defend the cultural particularities of the Negro family—they may appreciate them less than whites—than to insist that the largest possible resources, sensitively and sympathetically deployed, be used to overcome the educational deficiencies of Negro children.

In 1964, during a conference on the Negro family held at the University of California at Berkeley, a leading social analyst and critic pointed out that most of the speakers took it for granted that the model we should attempt to set for all Negro families was the middle-class family. He himself questioned, as so many intellectuals do and for similar reasons, the worthwhileness of this goal. A Negro woman in the audience responded that it was up to Negroes to decide whether the goal was worthwhile or not: "Just give us the tickets; we'll decide where to get off."

This brings us to another striking difference between the situation in which Frazier studied and wrote and the situation we are in today. The difference is that, whatever the causes that produced the Negro family, whatever the consequences of the Negro family, Frazier expected little intervention by government in the attempt to transform the conditions of Negro life and the characteristics of the Negro family. He saw Negro advance—as did the other writers of this time—as dependent largely on Negro self-help. The Negro middle class was the creation of the Negroes themselves; the Negro working class was also based on the spirit of self-help and personal achievement in a society where it was assumed that economic advance was the responsibility of the individual. He writes (Chapter 21): "It is in those well-organized workers' families where the entire family is working in order to purchase a home or that their children may obtain an education that one finds a spirit of democracy in family relations and a spirit of self-reliance on the part of the children." Indeed, the entire Chicago school of sociologists, despite its liberalism and progressivism, shared the individualist values of the times, which assumed that government played only limited roles in shaping economic and social life and which therefore viewed social trends and developments as independent, almost natural movements, quite impervious to political influence. Thus the Chicago sociologists could study the transition of neighborhoods as different ethnic and racial groups moved through them and hardly consider whether this was good or bad, desirable or undesirable, and whether political forces could modify such movements in any way. Similarly, Frazier saw the development of the Negro family as in large measure shaped by Negro action (note his applause of a spirit of self-reliance in the passage we have quoted). Of course government had a role in establishing political equality, in maintaining prosperity, in establishing sound social and educational services—but did it have a role when it came to the structure of the Negro family? Inevitably, reflecting his times, he saw a really very limited role for government: "The very fact that the Negro has succeeded in adopting the habits of life that have enabled him to survive in a civilization based on laissez faire and competition, itself bespeaks a degree of success in taking on the folkways and mores of the white race. That the Negro has found within the patterns of the white man's culture a *purpose in life* and a *significance for his strivings* which have involved *sacrifices for his children* and the *curbing of individual desires and impulses* indicates that he has become assimilated to a new mode of life'' (my italics).

What a remarkable passage! The Negro is applauded for surviving in a society based on laissez faire and competition, for his strivings, for the curbing of individual desires and impulses, for assimilating a new mode of life. By contrast of course his failure to strive and to curb his impulses would be seen as *his* failure rather than society's failure, though society—history—would certainly have to share a good part of the blame. But from a position based on the values of striving, competition, and achievement, what perspective would Frazier have taken to a White House conference on the Negro family, devoted to the consideration of measures that would strengthen the family? Certainly these passages— written in 1939—did not reflect Frazier's final view on the role of government in reshaping the Negro family. But when we put together the terms ''government'' and ''family,'' when we place in juxtaposition the most public and formal part of our social life and the most intimate and concealed part, we obviously must pause and consider what *are* the relationships, what should be the relationships, between government and family?

We know how such relationships have developed. Government has taken on responsibility for economic prosperity; it has taken on responsibility, too, for seeing that every part of society, every group and class, shares in the prosperity. Now then, if we assume that certain conditions for sharing in that prosperity must be set—the condition of minimal education, of responsibility in work, of the achievement of limited skill—and if we then find that certain familial and social settings are not conductive to the achievement of these minimal conditions, then government becomes responsible in some measure for what goes on in the family.

There is another route by which government becomes related to family, which affects today many more Negro families than this route based on a governmental assumption of responsibility for a generally shared prosperity. Government much earlier took on a responsibility to see that no one who could not earn sufficient income starved; this then required an elaborate system of rules and regulations to determine what was a family, what was insufficient income, what was a minimal standard of living, etc. In effect, the establishment of a welfare system places today perhaps one-quarter of Negro children under the investigative and regulative eye of government and inevitably deeply influences a substantial part of Negro family life.

Through the responsibility for welfare, then, and through the newer responsibility to maintain general prosperity, government is involved with the family. But this is a hazardous involvement. Do we know enough about family life and the significance of any kind of intervention within it to sanction a large effort to restructure or reform the lower-class Negro family? I doubt it. In the nature of the case, this is an area in which not all knowledge can be or should be used for public policy. There are parts of the society that are more legitimately subject to government intervention than the family—the economy, the educational system, the system of police and courts and prisons—and we may hope to influence the family through these institutions. We are now all enamored with the possibilities of social engineering. And yet there are limits to the desirable reach of social engineering.

Daniel P. Moynihan, Assistant Secretary of Labor under Presidents Kennedy and Johnson, once reported to me a meeting of high government officials dealing with the crisis of the low-income Negro in the United States, falling ever behind the better educated middle class, white and Negro alike. He proposed as one immediate measure that might improve matters restoring two mail deliveries a day—in effect, creating fifty thousand new jobs in the postal service and perhaps fifty thousand new fathers of families for a community where they are too few. I think E. Franklin Frazier would have liked this form of social engineering, which left the structure of the Negro family to each family, but which set conditions that we know produce the opportunity for stability, better education, and higher income. While Frazier wrote his book well before these studies I have outlined which suggest the significance of the independent role of family structure in affecting the large social conditions of peoples and nations, in the end, for policy, it is his approach that is more valuable. We cannot interfere in the intimate spheres of life: we do not have the knowledge, and if we did, we should use it with restraint. We know that the family makes the social conditions. We know too that social conditions make the family. But it is the latter knowledge that is the basis of social policy. Or, as the Negro mother said, "Just give us the tickets; we'll decide where to get off."

NATHAN GLAZER

PREFACE

TO THE REVISED EDITION

THE REVISED and abbreviated edition of this book, which was originally published as a research monograph in *The University of Chicago Sociological Series,* requires some words of explanation. Since its publication in 1939, there have been numerous requests from the general reading public as well as from professional workers in the field of social work and race relations for a popular condensation of the original work. Because of his teaching and research program, the author found it impossible to undertake this task alone. He was fortunate in finding in Mrs. Bonita Valien, a trained sociologist, a person who was willing to assume under the direction of the author the major responsibility for the work involved in the revision. Therefore, at the outset, the author acknowledges with appreciation his indebtedness to Mrs. Valien who was chiefly responsible for carrying through the revision. To her fell the task of eliminating the footnotes and tables, and of revising the text where necessary in order to incorporate interesting footnotes into the body of the text.

Concerning the nature and extent of the revision and abbreviation, something more specific needs to be said. There has been no change in the organization of the materials of the book which presents a natural history of the Negro family. The appendices which contained family histories, supplementary statistical tables, and a comprehensive bibliography have been omitted from the present edition. The tables which were in the body of the book have also been eliminated and where necessary the significant facts presented in the tables have been incorporated into the text. However, in order not to detract from the readability of the book, there has been a conscious effort not to introduce statistics where it could be avoided. Although numerous footnotes have been eliminated, the important descriptive materials contained in many of them have been woven into the text.

A final word needs to be said concerning "bringing the book up to date." In a sense a book of this character cannot be "brought up to date" since it deals with social processes rather than historical events. Nevertheless, because the book deals with the evolution of the Negro family in its American setting, it was necessary to take account of the changes in the Negro family resulting from World War II. Figures from the 1940 federal census have been added to or substituted for the 1930 census figures (since the original edition of the book was published before the 1940 federal census figures were available). Moreover, both case materials and statistical data as far as they were available have been utilized to show the changes which have occurred in the Negro family as the result of the increasing mobility of the Negro population, involving for the first time a significant westward movement, and other changes in the Negro population as the result of World War II.

In acknowledging his indebtedness to those who made the present edition possible, the author hereby expresses his appreciation to the University of Chicago Press for granting permission for the book to be published in this revised and abbreviated form; to The Dryden Press for its interest in making it possible for the book to reach a larger public; to his secretary, Mrs. Kathryn L. White, for assisting in reading proofs as well as for typing the index and parts of the book; and to his wife for helping in reading proofs.

E. Franklin Frazier

CONTENTS

PART ONE:
IN THE HOUSE OF THE MASTER

    I. FORGOTTEN MEMORIES · · · · · · · · · 3

    II. HUMAN, ALL TOO HUMAN · · · · · · · · 17

    III. MOTHERHOOD IN BONDAGE · · · · · · · 33

    IV. HAGAR AND HER CHILDREN · · · · · · · 50

PART TWO:
IN THE HOUSE OF THE MOTHER

    V. BROKEN BONDS · · · · · · · · · · · · 73

    VI. UNFETTERED MOTHERHOOD · · · · · · · 89

    VII. THE MATRIARCHATE · · · · · · · · · · 102

    VIII. GRANNY: THE GUARDIAN OF THE GENERATIONS 114

PART THREE:
IN THE HOUSE OF THE FATHER

    IX. THE DOWNFALL OF THE MATRIARCHATE · · · 127

    X. THE SONS OF THE FREE · · · · · · · · · 142

    XI. RACIAL ISLANDS · · · · · · · · · · · · 164

    XII. BLACK PURITANS · · · · · · · · · · · 190

PART FOUR:
IN THE CITY OF DESTRUCTION

    XIII. ROVING MEN AND HOMELESS WOMEN · · · · · 209

XIV. THE FLIGHT FROM FEUDAL AMERICA · · · · · 225

XV. FATHERS ON LEAVE · · · · · · · · · · · 245

XVI. OUTLAWED MOTHERHOOD · · · · · · · · 256

XVII. REBELLIOUS YOUTH · · · · · · · · · · 268

XVIII. DIVORCE: SCRIP FROM THE LAW · · · · · · 281

PART FIVE:
IN THE CITY OF REBIRTH

XIX. OLD FAMILIES AND NEW CLASSES · · · · · 295

XX. THE BROWN MIDDLE CLASS · · · · · · · 317

XXI. THE BLACK PROLETARIAT · · · · · · · · 334

CONCLUSION:

XXII. RETROSPECT AND PROSPECT · · · · · · · · 359

INDEX   369

PART ONE

IN THE HOUSE OF THE MASTER

CHAPTER I

FORGOTTEN MEMORIES

On the nineteenth of April, in the year 1797, Mungo Park started with a slave coffle from the interior of Africa for Gambia on the west coast. Many of these slaves, who had been captured in intertribal wars, had not only been in domestic slavery but during their captivity had been sold on native slave markets. "The coffle, on its departure from Kamalia," wrote Park, "consisted of twenty-seven slaves for sale, the property of Karfa and four other Slatees; but we were afterwards joined by five at Marraboo, and three at Bala, making in all thirty-five slaves. The free men were fourteen in number, but most of them had one or two wives and some domestic slaves, and the schoolmaster, who was now upon his return for Woradoo, the place of his nativity, took with him eight of his scholars, so that the number of free people and domestic slaves amounted to thirty-eight, and the whole amount of the coffle was seventy-three."[1]

The coffle was followed for about half a mile "by most of the inhabitants of the town, some of them crying and others shaking hands with their relations." The entire caravan halted on an eminence in view of the town which they had just abandoned. The members of the coffle were ordered to sit with their faces toward the west, while apart from them sat the townspeople facing the town. Then the schoolmaster pronounced a long and solemn prayer, after which the principal *slatees* (free black traders) "walked three times round the coffle, making an impression on the ground with the ends of

[1] *The Travels of Mungo Park* ("Everyman's Library" [New York, n.d.]), p. 248.

their spears, and muttering something by way of charm." At the end of this ceremony the coffle began its journey to the coast.

The westward journey led through dense forests, over wild and rocky country, and past ruins of towns laid waste by the warlike Foulahs. When periodic stops were made for refreshments, the schoolmaster offered prayers to Allah and the Prophet that they might be preserved from the marauding bands that the coffle avoided from time to time. Six *jalli keas* (singing men) relieved the hardships of the journey and gained a welcome to strange towns. Some slaves attempted to end their captivity by flight, while others in desperation sought in suicide an escape from servitude. One woman who refused to eat was finally stripped and left to be devoured by wild beasts when she became too great a burden. For a day's journey the coffle was joined by another on its way to a slave market in the interior. After almost two months the coffle reached the coast where the American slaveship "Charleston" was seeking a cargo of slaves for South Carolina.

The hardships of the slaves were not ended when they reached the coast. There was still the ordeal of the Middle Passage which always took its toll in sickness and death. A dozen or so died before the ship set sail, and eleven of those weakened by sickness during the voyage died at sea. When the ship had been at sea three weeks, it became so leaky that it was necessary to release some of the slaves to assist at the pumps. The ship was forced to change its course toward the West Indies and put into Antiqua, where the ship was condemned and the slaves were sold.

There were among these slaves, so Mungo Park informs us, some who carried to the New World as part of the African heritage a knowledge of Arabic consisting chiefly of passages from the Koran. Bryan Edwards has left us the following picture of an old Mandingo servant standing beside him chanting a fragment from the Koran which he had preserved from his childhood memories:

An old and faithful Mandingo servant, who stands at my elbow while I write this, relates, that being sent by his father to visit a distant relation in a country wherein the Portuguese had a settlement, a fray happened in the village in which he resided; that many people were killed, and others taken prisoners, and he himself was seized and carried off in the skirmish; not, as he conceives, by a foreign enemy, but by some of the natives of the place; and being sent down a river in a canoe, was sold to the captain of the ship that brought him to Jamaica. Of his national customs and manners he remembers but little, being, at the time of his captivity, but a youth. He relates, that the natives practice circumcision, and that he himself has undergone that operation; and he has not forgot the morning and evening prayer which his father taught him; in proof of his assertion, he chaunts, in an audible and shrill tone, a sentence that I conceive to be part of the Alcoran, La illa ill illa! which he says they sing aloud at the first appearance of the new moon. He relates, moreover, that in his own country Friday was constantly made a day of strict fasting. It was almost a sin, he observes, on that day *to swallow his spittle*—such is his expression[2]

It was not unnatural that this slave, who had been brought to the West Indies in his youth, had retained but dim memories of Africa. In the case of older slaves, the past was not so easily blotted out. Recent students, who have a better knowledge of the cultural background of the slaves, have been able to trace many words in the language of Negroes in the West Indies, Suriname, and Brazil to their African sources. There is also impressive evidence of the fact that, in the West Indies and in parts of South America, African culture still survives in the religious practices, funeral festivals, folklore, and dances of the transplanted Negroes. Likewise, in regard to the social organization, Bryan Edwards noted that the practice of polygamy was "very generally adopted among Negroes in the West Indies; he who conceives a remedy may be found for this by introducing among them the laws of marriage as established in Europe, is utterly ignorant of their manners, propensities, and superstitions. It is reckoned in Jamaica, on a moderate computation, that not less than ten thousand of such as are called Head Negroes (artificers and others) possess from two to four wives." Even today it appears that the African pattern of family life is perpetuated in the patriarchal family organization of the West Indian Negroes.

In contrast to the situation in the West Indies, African traditions

[2] Bryan Edwards, *The History, Civil and Commercial of the British Colonies in the West Indies*; London, 1807, II, 71-72.

and practices did not take root and survive in the United States. The explanation, according to Robert E. Park, "is to be found in the manner in which the Negro slaves were collected in Africa and the manner in which they were disposed of after they arrived in this country. The great markets for slaves in Africa were on the West Coast, but the old slave trails ran back from the coast far into the interior of the continent, and all the peoples of Central Africa contributed to the stream of enforced emigration to the New World. . . .

"There was less opportunity in the United States also than in the West Indies for a slave to meet one of his own people, because the plantations were considerably smaller, more widely scattered and, especially, because as soon as they were landed in this country, slaves were immediately divided and shipped in small numbers, frequently no more than one or two at a time, to different plantations. This was the procedure with the very first Negroes brought to this country. It was found easier to deal with the slaves, if they were separated from their kinsmen.

"On the plantation, they were thrown together with slaves who had already forgotten or only dimly remembered their life in Africa. English was the only language of the plantation. The attitude of the slave plantation to each fresh arrival seems to have been much like that of the older immigrant towards the greenhorn. Everything that marked him as an alien was regarded as ridiculous and barbaric."[3]

From time to time, customs among the Negro population have been ascribed to the African background. For example, at an early period in New England, Negroes had the custom of electing governors who exercised an almost despotic discipline over local groups of slaves. This custom has been characterized as a survival of the social organization of African tribes. If we may trust the testimony of a slave that, on the plantation where he was held for a time, there was a man "who prayed five times every day, always turning his face to the east, when in the performance of his devotions," we

[3] Robert E. Park, "The Conflict and Fusion of Cultures," *Journal of Negro History*, IV, 117.

probably have a case of the survival of Mohammedan practices.[4] In the same account we have a description of a burial which might have been an African survival:

> I assisted her and her husband to inter the infant—which was a little boy—and its father buried with it, a small bow and several arrows; a little bag of parched meal; a miniature canoe, about a foot long, and a little paddle (with which he said it would cross the ocean to his own country), a small stick, with an iron nail, sharpened, and fastened into one end of it; and a piece of white muslin, with several curious and strange figures painted on it in blue and red, by which, he said, his relations and countrymen would know the infant to be his son, and would receive it accordingly, on its arrival amongst them. . . . He cut a lock of hair from his head, threw it upon the dead infant, and closed the grave with his own hands. He then told us the God of his country was looking at him, and was pleased with what he had done.

These isolated instances only tend to show how difficult it was for slaves, who had retained a memory of their African background, to find a congenial milieu in which to perpetuate the old way of life. Even before reaching the United States, slaves had often been subjected to influences that tended to destroy the significance and meaning of their African heritage. Once in the New World, they were separated from friends and acquaintances and "broken in" to the regimen of the plantation. Finally, they had to face the disdain, if not the hostility, of the slaves who had become accommodated and accustomed to the new environment.

The following newspaper account from the Atlanta (Georgia) *Daily Intelligencer*, March 9, 1859, of the reception of four native Africans on a Georgia plantation, except for the inferred detail concerning the delight of the newcomers, is probably indicative of the general attitude of the slaves toward their African background:

> Our common darkies treat them with sovereign contempt walking around them with a decided aristocratic air. But the Africans are docile and very industrious and are represented as being perfectly delighted with their new homes and improved conditions. The stories

---

[4] Charles Ball, *Slavery in the United States: A Narrative of the Life and Adventures of Charles Ball, a Black Man* (Lewiston, Pa., 1836), p. 127.

that they are brutes and savages is all stuff and nonsense. It was put in the papers by men who do not know what they are talking about. As to their corrupting our common negroes, we venture the assertion would come nearer the truth if stated the other way.

As regards the Negro family, there is no reliable evidence that African culture has had any influence on its development. In the autobiography of a slave a story is told of a slave who claimed that he had been a priest in Africa and, when through with his work in the field, assumed an attitude toward his wife similar to that of the husband in the West Indian Negro family. This might have been an instance of the survival of African customs. Concerning this slave, Ball wrote:

> [He] was a morose, sullen man, and said he formerly had ten wives in his own country, who all had to work for, and wait upon him; and he thought himself badly off here, in having but one woman to do anything for him. This man was very irritable, and often beat and otherwise maltreated his wife, on the slightest prov-ocation, and the overseer refused to protect her, on the ground, that he never interfered in the family quarrels of the black people.[5]

The slaves, it seems, had only a vague knowledge of the African background of their parents. For example, a slave brought to South-ampton County, Virginia, said concerning his father:

> My father's name was Joe. He was owned by a planter named Benford, who lived at Northampton, in the same state. I believe my father and his family were bred on Benford's plantation. His father had been stolen from Africa. He was of the Eboe tribe. I remember seeing him once, when he came to visit my mother. He was very black. I never saw him but that one time, and though I was quite small, I have a distinct recollection of him. He and my mother were separated, in consequence of his master's going further off, and then my mother was forced to take another husband.[6]

Although Austin Steward, one of the early leaders in protesting the emigration of the free Negroes to Africa, does not give the

[5] Ball, *op. cit.*, pp. 203-4.
[6] John Brown, *Slave Life in Georgia: A Narrative of the Life, Sufferings, and Escape of John Brown, a Fugitive Slave, Now in England*, ed. L. A. Chameroozow (London, 1855), pp. 1-2.

tribal origin of his ancestors, he gives real or legendary details of the circumstances under which his grandfather was captured in Africa:

> Some years ago, a woman engaged in washing clothes, near the sea coast, had a lad with her to take care of her two younger children —one a young babe—while she was at work. They wandered away a short distance, and while amusing themselves under some bushes, four men, to them strange looking creatures, with white faces, surrounded them; and when the lad attempted to run away, they threw the infant he held in his arms, on the ground, and seizing the other two children, bore them screaming with fear, to the ship. Frantic and inconsolable, they were borne to the American slave market, where they were sold to a Virginia Planter, for whom they labored sorrowfully and in tears, until old age deprived them of farther exertion, when they were turned out, like an old horse, to die; and did die destitute and uncared for, in their aged infirmity, after a long life of unrequited toil. That lad, stole from Africa's coast, was my grandfather.[7]

But in the case of Martin Delany, who was associated with Frederick Douglass on the *North Star* and who, after serving as a surgeon in the Civil War, became the first Negro major in the United States Army, we have a full account of his African origin. "His pride in birth," writes his biographer, "is traceable to his maternal as well as to his paternal grandfather, native Africans—on the father's side, pure Golah; on the mother's, Mandingo." Further details of his African racial heritage and the career of his ancestors are given in his biography:

> His father's father was a chieftain, captured with his family in war, sold to the slavers, and brought to America. He fled at one time from Virginia, where he was enslaved, taking with him his wife and two sons, born to him on this continent, and, after various wanderings reached Little York—as Toronto, Canada, was then called— unmolested. But even there he was pursued, and "by some fiction of law, international policy, old musty treaty, cozenly understood," says Major Delany, he was brought back to the United States. . . .

[7] Austin Steward, *Twenty-two Years a Slave, and Forty Years a Freeman*; *Embracing a Correspondence of Several Years, While President of Wilberforce Colony, London, Canada West* (Rochester, N. Y., 1857), pp. 336-37.

On his mother's side the claim receives additional strength. The story runs that her father was an African prince, from the Niger Valley regions of Central Africa; was captured when young, during hostilities between the Mandingoes, Fellahtas, and Houssa, sold and brought to America at the same time with his betrothed Graci. His name was Shango, surnamed Peace, from that of a great African deity of protection which is represented in their worship as a ram's head with the attribute of fire. . . .

Shango, at an early period of his servitude in America, regained his liberty, and returned to Africa.

Whether owing to the fact that the slave system was not so thoroughly established then—that is, had no legal existence,—or the early slaveholders had not then lost their claims to civilization, it was recognized among themselves that no African of noble birth should be continued enslaved, proofs of his claims being adduced. Thus, by virtue of his birth, Shango was enabled to return home. His wife, Graci, was afterwards restored to freedom by the same means. She remained in America, and died at the age of one hundred and seven, in the family of her only daughter, Pati, the mother of Major Delany.[8]

Major Delany was able to authenticate these incidents in his family history on an exploring trip to Africa in 1859 while investigating the Niger Valley as a suitable place to which emancipated Negroes might emigrate. He learned that his grandmother had been dead about forty-three years and that his "grandfather was heir to the kingdom which was then the most powerful in Central Africa, but lost his royal inheritance by the still prevailing custom of slavery and expatriation as a result of subjugation." Thus Major Delany realized the ambition which, according to his biographer, was first kindled in him by the chants of his Mandingo mother.

The case of Major Delany is unusual, in respect to both his zeal in searching out the source of his African heritage and to the definiteness of his knowledge of his African ancestry. In most Negro families where there is knowledge concerning African origins it has become a more or less vague part of the family traditions. A founder

[8] Frank A. Rollin, *Martin R. Delany: Life and Public Services of Martin R. Delany, Sub-assistant Commissioner, Bureau of Relief of Refugees, Freedmen and Abandoned Lands and Late Major 104th U.S. Colored Troops* (Boston, 1869), pp. 15-17.

of a school in the Black Belt modeled after Tuskegee tells us that his maternal grandmother came directly from Africa and spoke the African language. "It is said," he sums up his knowledge of her African background, "that when she became angry no one could understand what she said."[9] Robert R. Moton, of unmixed ancestry, goes into greater detail concerning his African progenitors, and gives the following account:

> About the year of 1735, a fierce battle was waged between two strong tribes on the west coast of Africa. The chief of one of these tribes was counted among the most powerful of his time. This chief overpowered his rival and slaughtered and captured a great number of his band. Some of the captives escaped, others died, others still committed suicide, till but few were left. The victorious chief delivered to his son about a dozen of this forlorn remnant, and he, with an escort, took them away to be sold into slavery. The young African pushed his way through the jungle with his bodyguard until he reached the coast. Arrived there, he sold his captives to the captain of an American slave ship and received his pay in trinkets of various kinds, common to the custom of the trade. Then he was asked to row out in a boat and inspect the wonderful ship. He went, and with the captain and the crew saw every part of the vessel. When it was all over they offered him food and he ate it heartily. After that he remembered no more till he woke to find himself in the hold of the ship chained to one of the miserable creatures whom he himself had so recently sold as a slave, and the vessel itself was far beyond the sight of land. After many days the ship arrived at the shores of America; the human cargo was brought to Richmond and this African slave merchant was sold along with his captives at public auction in the slave markets of the city. He was bought by a tobacco planter and carried to Amelia County, Virginia, where he lived to be a very old man. This man was my grandmother's great grandfather.[10]

But the very details of Moton's story cast doubt upon its authenticity. Du Bois, of mixed blood, has woven the slender bond between himself and Africa from a romantic story of a Bantu ancestress. Two hundred years before his birth, "Tom Burghardt had come through the western pass from the Hudson with his Dutch captor, 'Coenraet Burghardt,' sullen in his slavery and achieving his freedom

[9] W. J. Edwards, *Twenty-five Years in the Black Belt* (Boston, 1918), p. 1.
[10] Robert Russa Moton, *Finding A Way Out* (New York, 1920), pp. 3-4.

by volunteering for the Revolution at a time of sudden alarm. His wife was a little, black, Bantu woman, who never became reconciled to this strange land; she clasped her knees and rocked and crooned:

> 'Do banna coba—gene me, gene me!
> Ben d'nuli, ben d'le——.' "[11]

Similarly, traditions in other Negro families go back to African ancestors, who are identified at times with various tribes or nations. The Wrights, who for two generations have achieved distinction as educators, claim descent from a Mandingo chief. George Schuyler, who holds a unique place among Negro journalists and authors, traces his ancestry on his mother's side to Madagascar. With his characteristic skepticism, he remarks that the claim that she was a princess was "probably a lie." A physician in Charleston, South Carolina, traces the African origin of his family to his father's grandmother, the daughter of a chief in Madagascar, who was taken by missionaries to France to be educated but was stolen and sent to America, where an unsuccessful attempt was made to enslave her. Traditions in the family of a young lawyer of mixed blood in Chicago also point to Madagascar as the home of his African ancestor. A physician in the same city tells of a great-grandfather of royal blood who was purchased and freed by Quakers after he refused to be enslaved. Sometimes the particular tribal or racial identity of the African progenitor has been lost, as in the family history of a lawyer in Harrisburg whose great grandfather was simply known as an African called Brutus, who was killed when he refused to submit to slavery. The vagueness of most of these traditions concerning the African ancestry is shown in the family history of a young woman who teaches in a Negro college. She writes:

> As far back as I can go on my mother's side I can remember my great-grandmother. We are of the opinion that she was not far removed from the African group. Her parents were born, I think, in Africa. This one thing she must have told my grandfather for he told me that his people on the African side were Ebos. We didn't know what he was talking about when he told us but I have found out since about the Ebo by reading Woodson's books where he talks

[11] W. E. B. Du Bois, *Darkwater* (New York, 1920), p. 5.

about how hard it was to manage them and they stopped bringing them here as slaves. I remember that my great-grandmother was hard to manage and grandfather had to build a separate house for her. She lived to be ninety-six years old.

Sometimes the tradition is almost forgotten; all that has been transmitted is that some remote ancestor was a "native of Guinea" or from some other part of Africa.

Except in rare instances the few memories and traditions of African forebears that once stirred the imagination of the older generations have failed to take root in the minds of the present generation of Negro youth. Here and there one finds among the family traditions of college students a story of an African ancestor portrayed in more or less distinct outlines. In one story the African progenitor is bound up with the well-known legend among Negroes of the red flag that lured slaves from the African shore. A college student writes:

> As was told me, Granny's grandmother was a "Golden Nigger." She had a gold star branded on her forehead. She told Granny that one day she and some other children were playing in Africa. They sighted a red flag flying at a distance from them. They became curious as to what the red rag was and ran to it. On approaching they were grabbed by some white men and put on a ship. This ship brought them to Virginia where they were sold. She always hated anything red because that was the color that attracted her from home and people whom she never saw or heard from. She is referred to as often saying "Oh, that red rag, that red rag, that red rag brought me here."

Another student writes with more assurance a story that has the appearance of sober history:

> In the year 1771 somewhere in the heart of Africa, there was born to an African king a baby boy by the name of Lewis; this baby boy was destined to be one of my ancestors. This baby had a brother by the name of Hosea. Very little is known of Lewis' early days, and of his life in Africa, for at a very early age his father sent him to France with two bachelors who were Frenchmen. Here in France, Lewis was to receive his education and learn the ways of the French people. Lewis had no sir name, thus he took the name of the two bachelors,

who were brothers and is now Lewis De Benyard. After staying in France for only a short while these Frenchmen turned their faces towards America, and it was thus that Lewis De Benyard found himself in America. At the age of about 15 Lewis landed in America on St. Simons' Islands. He was reared on Jeckle Island and having received a rather good education was made overseer of a set of slaves in that district.

In the same tone still another student relates the details, which he received from his grandfather, of the capture in Africa and transportation to America:

> Peter, as I have it from my old grandfather, was the name of his grandfather and could remember when he was captured and carried across the "big water." It was one day during the dry season when Peter was a young boy that some natives and white men came to talk to his, Peter's, father and the other warriors of the tribe. There was much shaking of heads and finally the white men left very angry. Some days later the runners came in telling of a large army coming to destroy the village and take all as slaves. When the fighting was over, Peter, his mother and smaller brother were chained to the long line of prisoners and marched for days through the forest into the setting sun. Then one day they came at last to the "big water." Here they were bathed, treated and examined and next day put on board a big boat out in the "big water." On the trip over Peter's brother died.
>
> Then one night they were roused from their sleep and crowded on deck quietly, put into small boats and carried ashore. The next morning Peter's eyes saw a new land, different from his native village and its surroundings but he was too glad to be on ground again to worry about that. All day they stood, or sat in the hot sun but they didn't mind that for did they not have clothes again? On the voyage over they were stripped of all clothing, as I have learned, to insure a maximum of cleanliness. On the following day they were taken out in small groups and sold one at a time. Peter's mother had become ill and no one would buy her, but Peter was bought by a funny looking man with whiskers. What were they saying to him about his mother? Surely they were not angry because he wanted to stay with her. He cried and the funny man struck him with a whip. He quit crying for he didn't like that. He hadn't liked any of it, but he wouldn't stand for much beating. Not Peter! The man didn't strike any more and Peter found a friend in another of the slaves, a woman who knew his mother. They were put in a wagon and rode all day and part of the night before being unloaded and locked in a cabin. Many days passed

and Peter was now one of the workers and he could understand some of the things said to him.

Pride in purity of race has evidently kept alive the tradition of African heritage in the family of another student:

> I remember my father often boasting of the fact that he had a pure strain of Negro blood in his veins. He told me that he could trace his ancestors back to the very heart of Africa. His grandfather, who was a wonderful influence in his life, often told him tales of his great-grandfather who was a slave in the early days of slavery. He would relate very interestingly facts concerning his transportation from Africa into this country to his great-grandchildren. In this manner the tales were handed down the line until they came to me, and I guess even I will relate them to my children.

These scraps of memories, which form only an insignificant part of the growing body of traditions in Negro families, are what remains of the African heritage. Probably never before in history has a people been so nearly completely stripped of its social heritage as the Negroes who were brought to America. Other conquered races have continued to worship their household gods within the intimate circle of their kinsmen. But American slavery destroyed household gods and dissolved the bonds of sympathy and affection between men of the same blood and household. Old men and women might have brooded over memories of their African homeland, but they could not change the world about them. Through force of circumstances, they had to acquire a new language, adopt new habits of labor, and take over, however imperfectly, the folkways of the American environment. Their children, who knew only the American environment, soon forgot the few memories that had been passed on to them and developed motivations and modes of behavior in harmony with the New World. Their children's children have often recalled with skepticism the fragments of stories concerning Africa which have been preserved in their families. But, of the habits and customs as well as the hopes and fears that characterized the life of their fore-bearers in Africa, nothing remains. When educated Negroes of the present generation attempt to resurrect the forgotten memories of their ancestors, they are seeking in the alien culture of Africa a basis

for race pride and racial identification. Hence, when a young sophisticated Negro poet asks,

>What is Africa to me?

and answers with true poetic license that the African heritage surges
up in him

>In an old remembered way,[12]

we hear the voice of a new race consciousness in a world of conflict
and frustration rather than the past speaking through traditions
that have become refined and hallowed as they have been transmitted
from generation to generation.

[12] Countee Cullen, "Heritage" in *Color* (New York, 1925), pp. 36-41.

CHAPTER II

HUMAN, ALL TOO HUMAN

In America there was no social organization to sustain whatever ideas and conceptions of life the Negro slave might have retained of his African heritage. If we can rely on the report of an old Negro woman that "a slave who married a girl from a group of native Africans just received on the plantation" was required "to obtain the consent of every member of the girl's group before he was allowed to marry her,"[1] we have what might be an instance of the continued control of the clan organization in America. But such cases, if they existed at all, were rare. In the new environment the Negro's sexual impulses and wishes in regard to mating, although doubtlessly influenced to some extent by the ideas which he had acquired in Africa, were liberated from group control and became subject only to the external control of the master and the wishes and attitudes of those with whom he formed unions.

In the early days of the slave trade the first restraint imposed upon the expression of the Negro's sexual impulses was the disproportionate number of males in the slave population. It was not until about 1840 that the number of Negro women equaled that of men. To this cause were probably due the numerous cases of sex relations between Negro slaves and indentured white women. An excess of males was created where slavery tended to be a purely industrial enterprise requiring masculine labor. Under such circumstances there was no opportunity for permanency in the association between

[1] Newbell N. Puckett, *Folk Beliefs of the Southern Negro* (Chapel Hill, N. C., 1926), p. 24.

the sexes. A traveler in Louisiana in 1802 has left us his observations on the results of the absence of women in the slave population. "Those who cannot obtain women (for there is a great disproportion between the numbers of the two sexes) traverse the woods in search of adventures, and often encounter those of an unpleasant nature. They frequently meet a patrol of the whites, who tie them up and flog them, and then send them home." The casualness of the contacts, when the slaves succeeded in finding women, prevented the development of strong attachments, which result from prolonged association between the sexes.

On most of the plantations, where there was no lack of women, mating ranged from purely physical contacts, often enforced by the masters, to permanent associations, in which genuine sentiment between the spouses and parental affection for children created a real family group. There were masters who, without any regard for the preferences of their slaves, mated their human chattel as they did their stock. According to a former slave, the master in giving orders concerning their work ordered them to "get married":

> In July, Claypole told us, we must cultivate five hogsheads of Tobacco for our summer's work. Added to this, was the order for us to "get married," according to Slavery, or in other words, to enrich his plantation by a family of young slaves. The alternative of this was, to be sold to a slave trader who was then in the vicinity making up a gang for a more southern market.[2]

And, when such little consideration was shown for the personality of the slaves, the practice of setting up Negro males as stallions followed as a natural consequence when it was to the economic advantage of the master to increase his slaves. A traveler in America in the eighteenth century who observed the practice was apparently more concerned with its effect upon the fertility of the slaves than its moral consequences:

> But allowing some Justice in or at least, a great deal of Necessity for, making Slaves of this Sable part of the Species; surely, I think, Christianity, gratitude, or, at least, good Policy, is concerned in using

[2] Andrew Jackson, *Narrative and Writings of Andrew Jackson, of Kentucky* (Syracuse, N. Y., 1847), p. 8.

them well, and in abridging them, instead of giving them Encourage-
ment, of several brutal and scandalous customs, that are too much
practic'd: Such as the giving them a number of Wives, or, in short
setting them up for Stallions to a whole neighborhood; when it has
been prov'd, I think, unexceptionally, that Polygamy rather destroys
than multiplies the Species.[3]

In a world where patriarchal traditions were firmly established,
probably even less consideration was shown for the preferences of
slave women. When men of the servile class were ordered to mate,
women, who on the whole played a more passive role, had little
choice in the selection of mates.

When the sexual impulses of the males were no longer controlled
by African customs and mores, they became subject only to the
periodic urge of sexual hunger. Under such circumstances the males,
as is generally true, seized upon the woman who happened to be at
hand and with whom they had been thrown into closest contact.
Such lack of discrimination or sentiment in the selection of mates
is manifested in the case of a slave who, after leaving a "wife" in
Virginia, proceeded immediately to select one from the slave-
trader's lot of which he was a member. To the prospective buyer's
question, "Have you a wife?" he answered, "Yes, massa, I lef' young
wife in Richmond, but I got a new wife here in de lot. I wish you
buy her, massa, if you gwing to buy me."[4]

But, in many cases of sexual unions or temporary matings, individual preferences and discrimination must have asserted themselves
from the beginning. We have the following story of a slave (John
Brown) who persisted in associating with a woman on a neighboring
plantation in spite of the punishment to which he was subjected:

> As soon as he felt able to go so far, that is, in about three months,
> he made another attempt to see her, was missed, pursued and caught.
> Then Thomas Stevens swore a fearful oath that he would cure him of
> "wife hunting." If he must have a wife, there was a plenty of likely
> yellow gals on the plantation for such as he to choose from. He

[3] Cf. Ulrich B. Phillips, *Life and Labor in the Old South* (Boston, 1929), pp.
203-5.
[4] *Slavery in America, with Notices of the Present State of Slavery and the Slave
Trade throughout the World* (London, 1837), p. 128.

might have the pick of 'em. But he (Stevens) wasn't going to let his niggers breed for another man's benefit, not he: so if John couldn't get a wife off the plantation he shouldn't have one at all. But he'd cure him of Nancy any how.[5]

Likewise, women who had formed attachments for particular men sometimes resisted attempts to force them into promiscuous unions. A young mulatto girl who had been a maid and dressmaker for her mistress ran away when her master decided to give her to one of his slaves:

> She was engaged to a young man from another plantation, but he had joined one of Harriet's parties, and gone North. Tilly was to have gone also at that time, but had found it impossible to get away. Now she had learned that it was her Master's intention to give her to a Negro of his own for his wife; and in fear and desperation, she made a strike for freedom.[6]

But, on the whole, since slavery was, as Phillips has well characterized it, "a curious blend of force and concession, of arbitrary disposal by the master and self-direction by the slave, of tyranny and benevolence, of antipathy and affection," the masters either through necessity or because of their humanity showed some consideration for the wishes of the slaves in their mating. In the following letter from one master to another there is not only a recognition of the slave's preference in the choice of a mate but an indorsement of his personal qualifications for marriage:

> As my boy Reuben has formed an attachment to one of your girls and wants her for a wife this is to let you know that I am perfectly willing that he should, with your consent marry her. His character is good, he is honest faithful and industrious.[7]

Whenever the slave showed discrimination and definite preference in the selection of a mate, the purely sexual impulses and feelings

---

[5] John Brown, *Slave Life in Georgia: A Narrative of the Life, Sufferings, and Escape of John Brown, a Fugitive Slave, Now in England* (London, 1855), p. 40.

[6] Sarah Elizabeth (Hopkins) Bradford, *Harriet Tubman: Scenes in the Life of Harriet Tubman* (Auburn, N. Y., 1869), p. 57.

[7] Letter of A. R. Wright, Louisville, Georgia, to Howell Cobb at Cherry Hill in the same county, in Phillips, *Documentary History of American Industrial Society: Plantation and Frontier* (Cleveland, 1910-11), II, 45.

were transformed into something more than animal appetite. There developed in many such cases what might truly be called a period of courtship. There was rivalry between the males which often assumed the character of animal rivalry, but this was controlled by the masters in the interest of order on the plantation. But there was rivalry of another sort in which brute force was replaced by manifestations of tender feelings and attention to the wishes of the woman. If during this period of courtship there was much opportunity for the expression of tender feelings and the development of mutual sympathies, the sexual impulses of the male were further transformed. A development of this nature must have taken place in the case of a slave who wooed his future wife in an adjoining field and slyly helped her with her work. The following story which a college student has written concerning the courtship of her great-grandparents may not be true in all its details, but it undoubtedly shows under what circumstances tender feelings and sympathy became fused with the purely sexual impulses. The boy, Charles, who was his master's child, was sold with his mother when the master's wife discovered the relationship. On the plantation to which they were sold they were isolated because of their lack of sympathy with the uncouth field hands and the latter's hostility toward slaves of mixed blood.

C—— W—— had reached the approximate age of twelve when his mother died. As a boy C—— W—— showed a great deal of interest in the stables. His interest in horses was so great that often it was said of him, jokingly, that he never took part in a conversation unless the subject was horses. After he left the field labor, he became stable boy. Here he spent his entire time and enjoyed every minute of it. His mother had been his only confidant, and now that interest was transferred to Mr. B's horses. No one on the plantation particularly liked C—— W——. The slaves whispered that his white skin portrayed "bad blood." When, in the stables, his meditations were noted, the beliefs of his fellows were confirmed. His thoughts and schemes were said to be of the devil. Everyone overlooked C——-W——'s utter loneliness except a little slave girl, who worked in Mr. B's kitchen. Often, she would conceal goodies in her apron for C—— W——. She encouraged him to talk and yet never attempted to pry into the problems of his past life, unasked. In this way she won his confidence and finally his love. At times they talked for

hours. One day it occurred to C—— W—— that he had entirely
ignored the name of this benevolent person. Upon asking he found
it to be Julia—his mother's name. This proved to be an even
better reason why he should like this little slave girl. Their interests
grew more intimate and personal. Julia tried to uplift C—— W——'s
conception of life by describing to him as best she knew how her
God. He told her of his mother's life and how misfortune had fallen
her at his birth. C—— W—— even enjoyed being depressed and
despairing, for there was always Julia to comfort him. Gradually,
Julia became the most precious thing in his life. The slaves talked
and attempted to destroy Julia's friendship with C—— W——, but
to no avail.

In addition to the psychological factors that tended to modify
the slave's impulses, there were social forces in the organization of
slavery that molded his personality and subjected his impulses to
moral restraints. The plantation economy, which was more or less
self-sufficient, gave numerous opportunities for the expression of
individual talent. As Coppin relates, "Those who had musical talent
often became 'fiddlers' and some of them became quite expert with
the bow."[8] In addition, there was a division of labor that became the
basis of social distinctions among the slaves. Frederick Douglass
has left us an instructive account of the division of labor on the
plantation and the esteem in which the various occupations were
held:

> "Uncle" Tobey was the blacksmith, "Uncle" Harry the cartwright,
> and "Uncle" Abel was the shoemaker, and these had assistants in
> their several departments. These mechanics were called "Uncles"
> by all the younger slaves, not because they really sustained that rela-
> tionship to any, but according to plantation etiquette as a mark of
> respect, due from the younger to the older slaves.
>
> Among other slave notabilities, I found here one called by every-
> body, white and colored, "Uncle" Isaac Copper. Once in a while
> a negro had a surname fastened to him by common consent. This
> was the case with "Uncle" Isaac Copper. When the "Uncle" was
> dropped, he was called Doctor Copper. He was both our Doctor
> of Medicine and our Doctor of Divinity. Where he took his degree I
> am unable to say, but he was too well established in his profession to

---

[8] Levi J. Coppin, *Unwritten History* (Philadelphia, 1920), p. 48.

permit question as to his native skill, or attainments. One qualification he certainly had. He was a confirmed cripple, wholly unable to work, and was worth nothing for sale in the market. Though lame he was no sluggard. He made his crutches do him good service, and was always on the alert looking up the sick, and such as were supposed to need his aid and counsel. His remedial prescriptions embraced four articles. For diseases of the body, epsom salts, and castor oil; for those of the soul, the "Lord's prayer," and a few stout hickory switches.[9]

Undoubtedly, the most influential personalities among the slaves were their preachers. Douglass received his religious training under one of the characters whom he describes in the foregoing selection. He relates:

I was early sent to Doctor Isaac Copper, with twenty or thirty other children, to learn the Lord's prayer. The old man was seated on a huge three-legged oaken stool, armed with several large hickory switches, and from the point where he sat, lame as he was, he could reach every boy in the room. After standing a while to learn what was expected of us, he commanded us to kneel down. This was done, he told us to say everything he said. "Our Father"—this we repeated after him with promptness and uniformity—"who art in Heaven" was less promptly and uniformly repeated, and the old gentleman paused in the prayer to give us a short lecture, and to use his switches on our backs.

These preachers became the interpreters of a religion which the slaves had developed on American soil. This religion was not a heritage, as many have assumed, from Africa. In the main, if one omits the unsubstantiated statement concerning "racial temperament," Robert E. Park seems to be right in his assumption that "the reason the Negro so readily and eagerly took over from the white man his heaven and apocalyptic visions was because these materials met the demands of his peculiar racial temperament and furnished relief to the emotional strains that were provoked in him by the condition of slavery."[10]

[9] Frederick Douglass, *My Bondage and My Freedom* (New York and Auburn, 1855), pp. 30 and 31.
[10] Robert E. Park, "The Conflict and Fusion of Cultures," *Journal of Negro History*, IV, 128.

Although the house servants, because of their favored position in relation to the master class, were early admitted to the churches, it was only with the coming of the Methodists and Baptists that the masses of the slaves "found a form of Christianity that they could make their own." Often independent congregations were set up in which there was full opportunity for the development of leadership and character in a social world that was essentially the Negro's own creation. Although, partly because of this isolation, these churches did not develop moral conceptions and restraints identical to those of the masters, they undoubtedly exercised control over the sex behavior of the slaves. An observer reported:

> I perceive, also, improvement in their tempers and intercourse as husbands and wives. The last point in which improvement is to be looked for respects their morality. In this a change for the better is seen in the greater frequency of marriage, the greater permanency of the relation, and the rebuke which a growing sense of virtue administers to transgressors. If in the church, they are expelled—if out of it, they lose, in some degree, the standing which they held before among their fellow servants.

Thus the personality of the slave gradually developed in accordance with his role on the plantation and in response to the attitudes of his fellows which found expression often in forms of etiquette suitable to his status. Consciousness of his status in the little world of the plantation tended to exercise control over his behavior, including his relations with the other sex. However, the most fundamental social distinctions among the slaves were based upon the difference in status between the field hands and house servants.

Charles Lyell (in *Second Visit to the United States*, recorded in Phillips, *Documentary History of American Industrial Society, II*) made the following observations concerning the house servants: "The colored domestic servants are treated with great indulgence at Tuscaloosa. One day some of them gave a supper to a large party of their friends in the house of a family which we visited, and they feasted their guests on roast turkeys, ice-cream, jellies and cakes."[11]

[11] Charles Lyell, *Second Visit to the United States* (New York, 1849), II, 72, in Phillips, *Documentary History of American Industrial Society* II, 46.

A former slave recounts the advantages that came with his eleva-
tion to the position of a house servant:

> I was now made a house slave. My duties were to wait on the
> table and help in the kitchen. I was extremely glad of this promotion,
> as it afforded me a better chance of obtaining good food. . . . At
> this period I had a tolerably good time of it, being employed in the
> kitchen helping to cook, or waiting at the table, and listening to the
> conversation going on, I learned many things of which the field hands
> were entirely ignorant.[12]

In the social life of the slaves the superior status of the house servants
was generally recognized. Steward, a former slave, wrote:

> It was about ten o'clock when the aristocratic slaves began to
> assemble, dressed in the cast-off finery of their master and mistress,
> swelling out and putting on airs in imitation of those they were forced
> to obey from day to day
> House servants were of course, "the stars" of the party; all eyes
> were turned to them to see how they conducted, for they, among
> slaves, are what a military man would call "fugle-men." The field
> hands, and such of them as have generally been excluded from the
> dwelling of their owners, look to the house servant as a pattern of
> politeness and gentility. And indeed, it is often the only method of
> obtaining any knowledge of the manners of what is called "genteel
> society"; hence, they are ever regarded as a privileged class; and are
> sometimes greatly envied, while others are bitterly hated.[13]

The prestige of the house servants was not due entirely to artificial
distinctions and hollow pretensions. And, although it may occasion a
smile to read that the house girl from the "Big House" in "the cast-
off clothing of her mistress" was the "Lady at the Quarters," there
was often a fundamental difference between her deportment and that
of the semibarbarous field hands.

The extent to which the slaves assimilated the ideas, sentiments,
and beliefs of the whites depended upon the range and character of
the contacts between the two races. At the one extreme there were

---

[12] Francis Frederick, *Autobiography of Rev. Francis Frederick of Virginia*
(Baltimore, 1869), pp. 9 and 15.

[13] Austin Steward, *Twenty-two Years a Slave, and Forty Years a Freeman; Embracing a Correspondence of Several Years, While President of Wilberforce Colony,
London, Canada West* (Rochester, N. Y., 1857), pp. 30-32.

the impersonal relations of the slave-trader, feared and hated by every slave, who treated his human wares as utilities; while at the other extreme the personal and intimate relations between the house servants and their masters created truly human relationships. The relations of the overseer, who lacked both culture and worldly goods, to the field hands were similar to those of the trader, although the overseer was compelled to recognize individual differences among the slaves. But men and women of the master race, living in daily contact with their slaves, were bound to recognize the personality of those with whom they had often shared their joys and sorrows from early childhood. A former slave, Robert Anderson, in his memoirs, *From Slavery to Affluence,* recalls:

> The old colonel was a very easy going man, kind and generous, and loved by all the plantation people. We colored folks did what he ask us to because we liked him. He was kind to us and very seldom resorted to punishment. Almost as soon as I was able to toddle about, I would follow him over the plantation whenever he would let me. It was because of his fondness for me as a little fellow that I was given his name.[14]

At the same time intimate and personal relations between the two races permitted the development of personal antagonisms and hatred as well as feelings of affection and sympathy. Lewis Clarke, a mulatto slave, complained:

> There were four house-slaves in this family, including myself, and though we had not, in all respects, so hard work as the field hands, yet in many things our condition was much worse. We were constantly exposed to the whims and passions of every member of the family; from the least to the greatest, their anger was wreaked upon us.[15]

In the following incident recorded in the *Life and Public Services of Rev. William Washington Brown* we see how in some cases assimilation of the manners of the white destroyed the social

---

[14] Robert Anderson, *From Slavery to Affluence: Memoirs of Robert Anderson, Ex-Slave* (Hemingsford, Nebraska), 1927, p. 19.

[15] *Narrative of the Sufferings of Lewis and Milton Clarke, Sons of a Soldier of the Revolution, during a Captivity of More than Twenty Years among the Slaveholders of Kentucky, One of the So-called Christian States of North America,* (Boston, 1846), pp. 15-16.

distance that was supposed to exist between master and slave and therefore created resentment on the part of the former:

> Unconsciously he partook more or less of the forms of life, language, traits and habits of the white folks,' even to the extent that suddenly his mistress discovered that he was adopting their language entirely which she solemnly forbade. While giving ready promise to resume the plantation patois, he found it impossible.

The slave on his part was not less affected by this association, for he often developed sentiments of loyalty that withstood the severest ordeals. But, more than that, the slave tended to take over the attitudes and sentiments of his master toward religion, sex and marriage, and the other relations of life.

Where the white and black children were reared together, the process of assimilation was more thoroughgoing. Douglass attributed the purity of his speech to association with his master's son:

> I have been often asked during the earlier part of my free life at the north, how I happened to have so little of the slave accent in my speech. The mystery is in some measure explained by my association with Daniel Lloyd, the youngest son of Col. Edward Lloyd. The law of compensation holds here as well as elsewhere. While this lad could not associate with ignorance without sharing its shade, he could not give his black playmates his company without giving them his superior intelligence as well. Without knowing this, or caring about it at the time, I, for some cause or other, was attracted to him and was much his companion.

The manner in which the slave assimilated the language of the whites indicates the process by which the slave took over the ideas and attitudes of the master race. Childhood attachments, which developed during play and other activities carried on in common, created similarity of sentiment and feelings. In fact, it was often necessary for masters to interfere and define the proper relations and aspirations of the children of the two races. The following incident is related in the biography of a former slave who became an officer in the United States Army:

> Little Tommy, feeling himself the master and imitating his teacher, was found by Miss Bett giving his orders. He was told after this discovery that he was doing wrong, that he must not continue

the practice; but boy-like he persisted in doing the very thing he was forbidden to do. Allen was told that he must not play school with Tommy, but he had gotten the habit, and the spirit had entered his soul and brain, and so he continued to play school and encourage Tommy in the sport. Miss Bett finding the nursery school still doing business at the same old stand, after repeated warnings, finally decided to break it up for good. Her method was that of elimination. She told Mr. Starbird and he forthwith found another home for Allen.[16]

Lunsford Lane, who purchased his freedom and established himself as a successful merchant in Raleigh, wrote concerning his childhood:

> My early boyhood [was spent] in playing with the other boys and girls, colored and white, in the yard, and occasionlly doing such little matters of labor as one of so young years could. I knew no difference between myself and the white children; nor did they seem to know any in turn. Sometimes my master would come out and give a biscuit to me, and another to one of his own white boys; but I did not perceive the difference between us. . . . . When I began to work, I discovered the difference between myself and my master's white children. They began to order me about, and were told to do so by my master and mistress.[17]

But even after the children had grown up and assumed their respective roles as master and slave, those slaves who had lived in close association with the whites tended to identify themselves with their masters. This is evident in a recent autobiography of a former slave:

> There was a social distinction with the slaves. The house and personal servants were on a higher social plane than the field slaves, while the colored persons, who would associate with the "po' white trash" were practically outcasts, and held in very great contempt. The slaves belonging to the lower class of white folks, were not considered on the same level as those belonging to the "quality folks," and the slaves of these families were always proud of, and bragged of their connection with the better families.[18]

Where slavery developed as a patriarchal institution, a certain amount of formal religious instruction supplemented the unconscious

---

[16] Charles Alexander, *Battles and Victories of Allen Allensworth* (Boston, 1914), p. 14.
[17] *The Narrative of Lunsford Lane, Formerly of Raleigh, N. C., (Boston,* 1842), pp. 5-6, 7.
[18] Robert Anderson, *op. cit.,* p. 29.

assimilation of the white man's moral and religious ideas. In addition
to being required to be present at family prayers, the slaves were
given regular religious instruction. The master's regard for the moral
development of the slave included in some cases a close supervision
of their conduct in sex matters and marriage relations.

Nellie Arnold Plummer, the historian of a Negro family that developed considerable stability and organization under a patriarchal
household, writes as follows:

> Among Miss Sallie's slaves were great grandmothers, grandmothers,
> mothers, children, grandchildren, and great grandchildren, for she
> seldom sold any of her people. Her women were taught and required
> to be as chaste, as were her nieces. All received great care, and much
> attention from "Miss Sallie" personally, requiring them to sleep in
> the great house until their marriage. . . . .
>
> It was a rare thing, indeed, for slave girls to reach majority before
> being married or becoming mothers. Be it said to the credit of Sarah
> O. Hilleary that she taught those girls the value of a good name, and
> personally watched over them so carefully that it was known far and
> near. She allowed them to be married in her dining room instead of
> in the cabin, and, with ceremony. She always had to see and pass upon
> the man who was to marry one of her maids. She did all she could to
> impress them with the importance of being clean, honest, truthful,
> industrious, and religious.[19]

Where such care was exercised in the rearing of slave girls, it was
to be expected that some concern would be shown for the marriage
alliances which they formed. In the case referred to above, the suitors
were only allowed to visit the slave girls after they had "passed Miss
Sallie's inspection." However, even Miss Sallie believed that some
limitations should be placed upon the development of the slave's
personality, for, according to the historian of the family, "when she
found Adam [a suitor] had taught William Arnold how to read and
write, she said that had she known that Adam was a 'lettered' man
she would never have let him on her place."

Thus the male slaves became conscious of distinctions in character
and status among themselves as well as among the women. In fact,

---

[19] Nellie Arnold Plummer, *Out of the Depths or the Triumph of the Cross*
(Hyattsville, Md., 1927), pp. 19-20.

some slaves took pride in the fact that they were able to form marriage alliances with females in certain families. While the authority of the slave husband or father was always more or less limited and subject to the will of the masters, certain responsibilities were placed upon him when he assumed the marriage relationship. When a prospective husband applied for permission to marry a slave woman, her master questioned him as follows:

> I next went to her master, Mr. Boylan, and asked him, according to the custom, if I might "marry this woman." His reply was, "Yes, if you will behave yourself." I told him I would. "And make her behave herself?" To this I also assented; and then proceeded to ask the approbation of my master, which was granted. So in May 1828, I was bound as fast in wedlock as a slave can be.[20]

While the duration of marriage as well as its inception was subject to the will of the masters, there were other factors affecting its permanency. We have seen how easily slave marriages that were based upon the mere desire to satisfy sexual hunger were dissolved. Even where marriages were entered into because of mutual attraction, their permanency depended upon prolonged association between the sexes, during which common interests and strong attachments developed. For example, where husband and wife were permitted to cultivate patches as a means of supplying themselves with extra food or better clothing, co-operation for these common ends helped to strengthen the bonds between them. It seems, too, in some instances that a sort of public opinion in the slave community had some effect on the significance of the marriage bonds. It is reported that a slave woman was spoken to by her friends "about going with a man so soon after the death of her husband." Children in the slave household often strengthened the bond between husband and wife; and, though the mother was generally the more dependable parent in the family, the father often developed strong attachments for his family and took pride in his position. Where marriage and family life among the slaves achieved this high development, the organization of slavery had become a settled way of life in which the slave's interest

[20] Lane, *op. cit.*, p. 11.

in marriage and family life became a part of the expression of his
personality.

We can see to what extent such development of family life
could be achieved under favorable circumstances in the case of the
family of Pennington, who, after being released from slavery, became
a distinguished minister and received the degree of Doctor of
Divinity from the University of Heidelberg. Pennington's family
was a well-organized social group in which paternal authority was
firmly established. This was partly owing to the fact that his father,
a highly skilled mechanic, was able to provide for his family. The
extent to which a family consciousness had developed is shown in
the reaction of the family to punishment inflicted upon Pennington's
father:

> This act created an open rupture with our family—each member
> felt the deep insult that had been inflicted upon our head; the spirit
> of the whole family was roused; we talked of it in our nightly gather-
> ings, and showed it in our daily melancholy aspect. . . . . I had always
> aimed to be trustworthy; and feeling a high degree of mechanical
> pride; I had aimed to do my work with dispatch and skill; my black-
> smith's pride and taste was one thing that had reconciled me so long
> to remain a slave. I sought to distinguish myself in the finer branches
> of the business by invention and finish; I frequently tried my hand at
> making guns and pistols, putting blades in pen knives, making fancy
> hammers, hatchets, sword-canes, &c., &c. Besides I used to assist my
> father at night in making strawhats and willow baskets, by which
> means we supplied our family with little articles of food, clothing and
> luxury, which slaves in the mildest form of the system never get from
> the master; but after this, I found that my mechanic's pleasure and
> pride were gone. I thought of nothing but the family disgrace under
> which we were smarting, and how to get out of it.[21]

Thus, the very families that had achieved considerable organization
and had assimilated most completely the folkways and mores of the
whites were, in spite of their internal character, always insecure.
Despite Miss Sallie's solicitude for her slaves' welfare, at her death
slave families that had been together for decades were scattered. No
matter how far the moralization of the slave went, his group life,

---

[21] J. W. C. Pennington, *The Fugitive Blacksmith; or Events in the History of
James W. C. Pennington* (London, 1850), pp. 7-9.

including his most intimate relations in his family, could not resist the fundamental economic forces inherent in the slave system.

In this chapter we have traversed the road by which the Negro, stripped of his cultural heritage, acquired a new personality on American soil. At first his impulses knew no restraint except that imposed by the physical force of those that had enslaved him. But soon even the strongest of these impulses, sexual hunger, was modified and controlled by feelings of tenderness and sympathy toward those who shared his bondage and enabled him to escape from loneliness and isolation. Moreover, bondage could not crush out individual talent, and the division of labor on the plantation promoted mental differentiation and became the basis of differences in status. Then, too, the emergence of the slave as a human being was facilitated by his assimilation into the household of the master race. There he took over more or less the ideas and attitudes and morals and manners of his masters. His marriage and family relations reflected the different stages and aspects of this process. Where the assimilation of western mores went farthest and the development of personality was highest, the organization of family life approached most closely the pattern of white civilization. But in the end fundamental economic forces and material interests might shatter the toughest bonds of familial sentiments and parental love. Only the bond between the mother and her child continually resisted the disruptive effect of economic interests that were often inimical to family life among the slaves. Consequently, under all conditions of slavery, the Negro mother remained the most dependable and important figure in the family.

CHAPTER III

MOTHERHOOD IN BONDAGE

Strange to say, the idealized picture of the Negro mother has not grown out of the stories of her sacrifices and devotion to her own children but has emerged from the tradition of the Negro mammy—a romantic figure in whom maternal love as a vicarious sentiment has become embodied. There is plenty of evidence to give a solid background to the familiar picture—stories of cold, and often inhuman, indifference toward her own offspring and undying devotion to the children of the master race. "The devotion of the nurses of these foster-children was greater than their love for their own" is the comment of one observer, Susan Smedes, who supports her generalizations with the following instance which she has recorded in *A Southern Planter:*

> One of them, with a baby at home very sick, left it to stay with the white child. This one she insisted on walking the night through, because he was roaring with the colic, though the mistress entirely disapproved and urged her to go home to her own child, whose illness was more serious, if less noisy, than the white nursling with its colic.[1]

This seems all the more strange when we recall the universal testimony of travelers and missionaries that the love of the African mother for her children is unsurpassed in any part of the world. "Maternal affection (neither suppressed by the restraints, nor diverted by the solicitudes of civilized life) is everywhere conspicuous among

[1] Susan Smedes, *A Southern Planter*, Baltimore, 1887, p. 50.

them," wrote Mungo Park, "and creates a correspondent return of tenderness in the child." He reports the following incident:

> In the course of the day, several women, hearing that I was going to Sego, came and begged me to inquire of Mansong, the King, what was become of their children. One woman in particular, told me that her son's name was Mamadee; that he was no heathen, but prayed to God morning and evening, and had been taken from her about three years ago, by Mansong's army; since which she had never heard of him. She said she often dreamed about him; and begged me, if I should see him, either in Bambarra, or in my own country, to tell him that his mother and sister were still alive.

Likewise, we learn that in East Africa mothers offered themselves to the slave-raiders in order to save their sons, and Hottentot women refused food during famines until their children were fed.

How are we to explain this contrast between the native Negro mother and her descendants in America? Surely transportation to the New World could not have eradicated fundamental impulses and instinctive feelings.

Elizabeth Donnan, in the *Documents Illustrative of the History of Slave Trade to America*, of which she is editor, gives evidence that the dehumanizing of the Negro began before he left the shores of Africa. An official of the Dutch West India Company on the African coast wrote as follows concerning the Negro's reputed indifference to family ties where the slave trade was carried on: "Not a few in our country fondly imagine that parents here sell their children, men their wives, and one brother the other: but those who think so deceive themselves; for this never happens on any other account but that of necessity, or some great crime. But most of the slaves that are offered to us are prisoners of war, which are sold by the victors as their booty."[2]

To pregnant women who formed a part of the slave caravans motherhood meant only a burden and an accentuation of their miseries. Maternal feeling was choked and dried up in mothers who had to bear children, in addition to loads of corn or rice, on their backs during marches of eight to fourteen hours. Nor did life in the

---

[2] Elizabeth Donnan (ed), *Documents Illustrative of the History of the Slave Trade to America*, Washington, D. C., 1930, I, 441.

slave pens on the coast, where they were chained and branded and sometimes starved, mitigate the sufferings of motherhood.

In the selection of Negroes for the cargoes of the slave ships, their physical condition and their suitability for the specific requirements of the trade were the only factors of moment to the traders. When William Ellery, the father of one of the signers of the Declaration of Independence, instructed the captain of his slaver: "If you have a good Trade for Negroes may purchase forty or Fifty Negroes. get most of them mere Boys and Girl, some Men, let them be Young, No very small Children," it is unlikely that the faithful captain in obeying his orders cared much about the feelings of the Negro mothers who had to surrender their children. During the Middle Passage that followed the gathering of slaves on the coast, the last spark of maternal feeling was probably smothered in the breasts of many mothers who were packed spoon fashion between decks and often gave birth to children in the scalding perspiration from the human cargo. Then whatever was left of maternal sentiment had to undergo another ordeal in the slave markets of the New World.

Scarcely more regard was shown for the humanity of the slaves in the American markets than in those of Africa. To be sure, humanitarian sentiment was more likely to make itself felt in the American communities than among the adventurers and criminals who frequented the slave markets of Africa. Moreover, in the slave markets of Charleston and Richmond it was to the economic advantage of those who bought and sold slaves to see that infants did not die because of the lack of maternal care. But since, as a South Carolina court held in 1809, "the young of slaves . . . . stand on the same footing as other animals," the relation of mothers to their children was recognized not because of its human or social significance but because of the property interests involved in the relationship.

In some cases the affectional ties between mother and children survived the ordeals of the slave markets and the Middle Passage and were perhaps strengthened by common suffering. But the characteristic attitudes and sentiments which the slave mother developed in America grew out of her experiences with pregnancy and childbirth and her relations with her offspring in the new environment. Where slave women were maintained as breeders and enjoyed certain indulgences and privileges because of their position, the experience of pregnancy and childbirth was likely to cause them to look upon their children as the source of these favors.

The following instructions were sent to an agent for the management of a plantation in Virginia in 1759: "The breeding wenches particularly, you must instruct the overseers to be kind and indulgent to, and not to force them when with child upon any service or hardship that will be injurious to them and that they have every necessary when in that condition that is needful for them, and the children to be well looked after and to give them every spring and fall the jerusalem oak seed for a week together and that none of them suffer in time of sickness for want of proper care."[3]

On the other hand, where slave women were forced into cohabitation and pregnancy, and childbirth brought no release from labor, they might develop a distinct antipathy toward their offspring. A former slave, Moses Grandy, wrote the following concerning the treatment of women by the overseer:

> On the estate I am speaking of, those women who had sucking children suffered much from their breasts becoming full of milk, the infants being left at home; they therefore could not keep up with the other hands: I have seen the overseer beat them with raw hide, so that the blood and milk flew mingled from their breasts. A woman who gives offence in the field, and is large in the family way, is compelled to lie down over a hole made to receive her corpulency, and is flogged with the whip, or beat with a paddle, which had holes in it; at every stroke comes a blister. One of my sisters was so severely punished in this way, that labor was brought on, and the child was born in the field. This very overseer, Mr. Brooks, killed in this manner a girl named Mary: her father and mother were in the field at the time.[4]

Even under the more normal conditions of slavery, childbirth could not have had the same significance for the slave mother as for

[3] Arthur W. Calhoun, *A Social History of the American Family from Colonial Times to the Present*, Cleveland, 1917-18, I, 327.

[4] Moses Grandy, *Narrative of the Life of Moses Grandy; Late a Slave in the United States of America*, Boston, 1844, p. 18.

the African mother. In Africa tribal customs and taboos tended to fix the mother's attitude toward her child before it was born. In America this traditional element in the shaping of maternal feeling was absent. Consequently, the development of maternal feeling was dependent largely upon the physiological and emotional responses of the mother to her child.

Concerning the biologically inherited elements in the so-called "maternal instinct," L. L. Bernard writes:

> It is difficult to separate early acquirements through the imitation process from biological inheritance without considerable intensive investigation. But it is doubtful if more than the response to touch, temperature and odor stimuli from the child by fondling, holding and licking or kissing, a more or less vague unorganized emotional response to its cries, which chiefly manifests itself in movement toward the child, vague answering cries and the discharge of milk upon certain definite stimuli of pressure upon the breast, can be said to be inherited by the human mother.[5]

Generally, during the period of pregnancy, the slave woman's labor was reduced, and on the birth of a child she received additional clothes and rations. But the following letter of an overseer indicates that the needs of the mothers and their newborn children were not always promptly met:

> Charlotte & Venus & Mary & Little Sary have all had children and have not received their baby clothes also Hetty & Sary & Coteler will want baby clothes. I see a Blanket for the old fellow Sampson he is dead. I thought I wrote to you that he was dead. Little Peggy Sarys daughter has not ever drawn any Blanket at all, and when they come I think it would be right to give her the Blanket that was sent to Sampson.[6]

As soon as possible after childbirth, the mother was required to return to the fields, often taking her unweaned child along. A former slave describes the situation as follows:

[5] L. L. Bernard, *Instinct: A Study in Social Psychology*, New York, 1924, p. 326.
[6] Letter of Elisha Cain, overseer, on Retreat Plantation, Jefferson County, Georgia, to his employer, Miss Mary Telfair, Savannah, November 20, 1836, in Phillips, *Documentary History of American Industrial Society: Plantation and Frontier*, Cleveland, I, 333-34.

The bell rings, at four o'clock in the morning, and they have half an hour to get ready. Men and women start together, and the women must work as steadily as the men, and perform the same tasks as the men. If the plantation is far from the house, the sucking children are taken out and kept in the field all day. If the cabins are near, the women are permitted to go in two or three times a day to their infant children. The mother is driven out when the child is three to four weeks old.[7]

In some cases the mothers were permitted to return to the cabin in order to nurse the infant who was left either alone or in the charge of a child. "At this period," writes a former slave, John Brown, "my principal occupation was to nurse my little brother whilst my mother worked in the field. Almost all the slave children have to do the nursing; the big taking care of the small, who often come poorly off in consequence. I know this was my little brother's case. I used to lay him in the shade, under a tree, sometimes, and go to play, or curl myself up under a hedge, and take a sleep."

The following situation described by Frances A. Kemble in her *Journal* was typical of many plantations:

> It is true that every able-bodied woman is made the most of in being driven afield as long as, under all and any circumstances, she is able to wield a hoe; but, on the other hand, stout, hale, hearty girls and boys, of from eight to twelve and older, are allowed to lounge about, filthy and idle, with no pretense of an occupation but what they call "tend baby," i.e., see to the life and limbs of the little slave infants, to whose mothers, working in distant fields, they carry them during the day to be suckled, and for the rest of the time leave them to crawl and kick in the filthy cabins or on the broiling sand which surrounds them.[8]

Consequently, where such limitations were placed upon the mother's spontaneous emotional responses to the needs of her children and where even her suckling and fondling of them were restricted, it was not unnatural that she often showed little attachment to her offspring.

[7] Lewis Clarke, *Narrative of the Sufferings of Lewis and Milton Clarke, Sons of a Soldier of the Revolution*, Boston, 1846, p. 127.

[8] Frances A. Kemble, *Journal of a Residence on a Georgian Plantation*, New York, 1863, pp. 121-22.

A slaveholder, who loved "to recall the patriarchal responsibility and tenderness" which her father "felt for his poor, ignorant, dependent slaves," tells the following story to "show that the master's feelings are sometimes even deeper than the mother's":

> One of my slaves had an infant child two months old who was attacked with an affection of the windpipe. I never saw such extreme suffering; it was one continual spasm and struggle for breath. The physician visited it several times every day, but could give no relief. The poor little sufferer seemed as if it would neither live nor die. These extreme tortures lasted a whole week before it breathed its last; and my own mind was so excited by its sharp and constant convulsive shrieks, that I never left it night or day, and could not sleep, even a moment, sitting by its side; and yet its own mother slept soundly at the foot of the bed, not because she was fatigued, for she was required to do nothing but nurse the dying child.[9]

While the pathos expressed here is understandable, one would require a knowledge of the mother's experience during pregnancy and childbirth and her subsequent relations with her infant in order to decide whether her behavior was unnatural or extraordinary. However, one might ask: Why were these slave women, in the words of the same informant, "the most enthusiastically fond foster-mothers, when they [were] called upon to nurse the infant child of their owners"?

Often the relations of the foster-mother or "mammy" to her "white children" offered greater scope for the expression of the emotions and impulses characteristic of maternal love than the contacts which she had with her own offspring. The attachment and devotion which the "mammy" showed for the white children began before the children were born. The "mammy," who was always an important member of the household, attended her mistress during pregnancy and took under her care the infant as soon as it was born. Often she, instead of the mother, suckled the child and if the child was a girl, was never separated from her until she was grown. Miss Bremer has left a picture of one of these foster-mothers sitting "like a horrid specter, black and silent by the altar," during

[9] H. B. Schoolcraft, *By A Southern Lady: Letters on the Condition of the African Race in the United States*, Philadelphia, 1852, pp. 13-14.

the wedding of her foster-child from whom she "could not bear the thought of parting." If these black foster-mothers showed more maternal affection and devotion for their charges than they or their black sisters showed for their own offspring, it was due to the emotional and biological dependence that developed between them as the result of this intimate association. Moreover, where this intimate association extended over several generations and the "mammy" became assimilated into the master's household, tradition tended to define her role and to inculcate in her sentiments proper to her status.

It should not be inferred from what has been said concerning the Negro woman's devotion to the children of the master race that she never developed a deep and lasting sentiment for her own children. In the slave cabin, where she was generally mistress, she often gathered about her a numerous progeny, in spite of miscarriages and a high infant mortality. Miss Kemble enters is her *Journal*, pp. 190-91, the following information relative to the size of slave families, miscarriages, and infant mortality:

"*Fanny* has had six children; all dead but one. She came to beg to have her work in the field lightened.

"*Nanny* has had three children; two of them dead. She came to implore that the rule of sending them into the field three weeks after their confinement might be altered.

"*Leah*, Caesar's wife, has had six children; three are dead.

"*Sophy*, Lewis's wife, came to beg for some old linen. She is suffering fearfully; has had ten children; five of them are dead. The principal favor she asked was a piece of meat, which I gave her.

"*Sally*, Scipio's wife, has had two miscarriages and three children born, one of whom is dead. She came complaining of incessant pain and weakness in her back. This woman was a mulatto daughter of a slave called Sophy, by a white man of the name of Walker, who visited the plantation.

"*Charlotte*, Renty's wife, had had two miscarriages, and was with child again. She was almost crippled with rheumatism, and showed me a pair of poor swollen knees that made my heart ache. I have promised her a pair of flannel trowsers, which I must forthwith set about making.

"*Sarah*, Stephen's wife—this woman's case and history were alike deplorable. She had had four miscarriages, had brought seven children into the world, five of whom were dead, and was again with child.

She complained of dreadful pains in the back, and an internal tumor which swells with the exertion of working in the fields; probably, I think, she is ruptured."

The following entries concerning births and deaths of children were made by an overseer on a plantation in Florida, 1851.

BIRTHS ON THE PLANTATION IN 1851

Florer was confined this morning with a male Child, Jany. 27, 1851.
May 28th, Cate was delivered of a Female Child this morning.
June 4th, Martha was delivered of a male child at 12 o'clock today.
June 13th, Long Mariah was delivered of a male Child today at twelve o'clock.
August 17th, B. Mariah was delivered of a male child this morning.

DEATHS ON THE PLANTATION IN 1851

August 4th, Catherine, a child departed this life today at 2 oclock.
September 18th, one Child Departed this life today at ten oclock; by the name of Amy.
December 31. B. Mariers Child Billy died this morning.

After the day's labor in the field under an unsympathetic overseer, she could find warmth and sympathy and appreciation among her children and kinsmen. There the mother could give full rein to her tender feelings and kindly impulses. "One of my earliest recollections," writes Booker T. Washington, "is that of my mother cooking a chicken late at night, and awakening her children for the purpose of feeding them." The devotion of the mothers to their own children was often demonstrated in their sacrifices to see them when they were separated from them. Douglass' childhood recollections of his mother, who lived twelve miles from him, were of "a few hasty visits made in the night on foot, after the daily tasks were over, and when she was under the necessity of returning in time to respond to the driver's call to the field in the early morning."

It is not surprising, then, to find that slave mothers, instead of viewing with indifference the sale, or loss otherwise, of their children, often put up a stubborn resistance and suffered cruel punishments to prevent separation from them. The fact that slave families were often divided when it was to the economic advantage of the owners is too well established to take seriously the denials

of those who have idealized slavery. Washington Irving, who regarded the separation of children from their parents as a peculiar
evil of slavery, rationalized thus: "But are not white people so, by
schooling, marriage, business, etc."[10]

When Loguen's brothers and sisters were taken from his mother,
she was "taken into the room which was used for weaving coarse
cloth for the negroes and fastened securely to the loom, where she
remained, raving and moaning until morning." Another slave recounts his mother's efforts to prevent her children from being sold:

> The master, Billy Grandy, whose slave I was born, was a hard
> drinking man; he sold away many slaves. I remember four sisters and
> four brothers; my mother had more children, but they were dead or
> sold away before I can remember. I was the youngest. I remember
> well my mother often hid us all in the woods, to prevent master sell-
> ing us. When we wanted water, she sought for it in any hole or
> puddle, formed by falling trees or other wise: it was often full of
> tadpoles and insects: she strained it, and gave it round to each of us
> in the hollow of her hand. For food, she gathered berries in the
> woods, got potatoes, raw corn, &c. After a time the master would
> send word to her to come in, promising he would not sell us. But, at
> length, persons came, who agreed to give the prices he set on us. His
> wife, with much to be done, prevailed on him not to sell me; but he
> sold my brother, who was a little boy. My mother, frantic with grief,
> resisted their taking her child away; she was beaten and held down:
> she fainted, and when she came to herself, her boy was gone. She
> made much outcry, for which the master tied her up to a peach tree
> in the yard, and flogged her.[11]

When Josiah Henson's master died, and it was necessary to sell the
slaves in order to divide the estate among the heirs, he says:

> We were all put up at auction and sold to the highest bidder, and
> scattered over various parts of the country. My brothers and sisters
> were bid off one by one, while my mother, holding my hand, looked
> on in an agony of grief, the cause of which I but ill understood at
> first, but which dawned on my mind with dreadful clearness, as the
> sale proceeded. My mother was then separated from me, and put up
> in her turn. She was bought by a man named Isaac R., residing in

[10] *The Journals of Washington Irving*, ed. William P. Trent and George S. Hell-
man, Boston, 1919, III, 115.
[11] Grandy, *op. cit.*, pp. 5-6.

Montgomery county, and then I was offered to the assembled pur-
chasers. My mother, half distracted with the parting forever from all
her children, pushed through the crowd, while the bidding for me
was going on, to the spot where R. was standing. She fell at his feet,
and clung to his knees, entreating him in tones that a mother only
could command, to buy her BABY as well as herself, and spare to her
one of her little ones at least. Will it, can it be believed that this
man, thus appealed to, was capable not merely of turning a deaf ear
to her supplication, but of disengaging himself from her with such
violent blows and kicks, as to reduce to the necessity of creeping out
of his reach.[12]

We need not rely solely on the slave's word concerning the strength
of the mother's affection for her children; indirect evidence, as well
as contemporary observations, gives the same testimony. Concerning
the slave mother's attachment for her children, the remark of an
overseer in reply to another who spoke of the danger of losing slaves
when they were taken North, is significant:

> Oh, stuff and nonsense, I take care when my wife goes North with
> the children, to send Lucy with her; *her children are down here, and
> I defy all the Abolitionists in creation to get her to stay North.*

In the following accounts of a sale we learn that the mother's distress
at the separation from her child was sufficient to cause it to be
purchased with her:

> *Gambling* v. *Read*, Meigs 281, December 1838. 1837, Gambling
> sold Read, Hannah, a female slave for $1200, ... Hannah had a
> young child, (a boy, three months old,) and her distress at the separa-
> tion from it induced Read to propose to purchase it; . . . . agreed that
> he should have it for 150 dollars.[13]

The *Alexandria Gazette's* comment on the slave trade in the national
capital gives a vivid picture of the effect of selling children of the
bereft mothers:

> Here you may behold fathers and mothers leaving behind them
> the dearest objects of affection, and moving slowly along in the mute

---

[12] *The Life of Josiah Henson, Formerly a Slave, Now an Inhabitant of Canada, as
Narrated by Himself*, Boston, 1844, pp. 3-4.

[13] Helen Tunnicliff Catterall (ed), *Judicial Cases concerning American Slavery
and the Negro*, Washington, D. C., 1929, II, p. 507.

agony of despair; there, the young mother, sobbing over the infant whose innocent smile seems but to increase her misery. From some you will hear the burst of bitter lamentation, while from others the loud hysteric laugh breaks forth, denoting still deeper agony. Such is but a faint picture of the American slave-trade.

Let us return to the cabins at the quarters where the slave mothers lived with their children. A slave described the quarters where he lived as follows:

> About a quarter of a mile from the dwelling house, were the huts, or cabins, of the plantation slaves, or field hands, standing in rows; much like the Indian villages which I have seen in the country of the Cherokees. These cabins were thirty-eight in number; generally about fifteen or sixteen feet square; built of hewn logs; covered with shingles, and provided with floors of pine boards. These houses were all dry and comfortable and were provided with chimnies; so that the people when in them, were well sheltered from the inclemencies of the weather. In this practice of keeping their slaves, well sheltered at night, the southern planters are pretty uniform; for they know that upon this circumstance, more than any other in that climate, depends the health of the slave, and consequently his value. In these thirty-eight cabins, were lodged two hundred and fifty people, of all ages, sexes, and sizes. Ten or twelve were generally employed in the garden and about the house[14]

In spite of the numerous separations, the slave mother and her children, especially those under ten, were treated as a group. The following advertisement from the *Charleston* (S.C.) *City Gazette,* February 21, 1825, is typical of a sale of a group of slaves:

VALUABLE NEGROES FOR SALE

A Wench, complete cook, washer and ironer, and her 4 children— a Boy 12, another 9, a Girl 5, that sews; and a Girl about 4 years old.

Another Family—a Wench, complete washer and ironer, and her Daughter, 14 years old, accustomed to the house.

A Wench, a houseservant, and two male Children; one three years old, and the other 4 months.

A complete Seamstress and House Servant, with her male Child 7 years old.

Three Young Wenches, 18, 19, 21, all accustomed to house work.

[14] Charles Ball, *Slavery in the United States*, Lewistown, Pa., 1836, p. 107.

A Mulatto Girl, about 17, a complete Seamstress and Waiting Maid, with her Grandmother.

Two Men, one a complete Coachman, and the other a Waiter. Apply at this Office, or at No. 19 Hasell-street, Feb. 19.

Sometimes more than one family occupied a cabin. "We all lived together with our mother," writes a former slave, "in a long cabin, containing two rooms, one of which we occupied; the other being inhabited by my mother's niece, Annike, and her children." Since the slaves were rationed according to families and under some circumstances were permitted to cultivate gardens for their own use, a sort of family economy gave a material foundation to their sentimental relationships.

A typical food ration list for 1856 is recorded in the *Florida Plantation Records*, pp. 513-14, as follows:

	Meal (Pecks)	Meat (Lb.)		Meal (Pecks)	Meat (Lb.)
Chesley and family	3	6½	Maria and Pollidor	4¼	5
Simon, Phillis, B. Peggy and dren	5	7½	L. Renty, Leah and two children ...	4	7
England and family	4	5	L. Dick	1	2½
Nathan and Coatney	2	5	Brave Boy	1	2½
Isaac	1	2½	Wallace	1	2
Jacob and family .	4	7	Jim and family ...	2½	5
Esaw and Binah ..	2	5	Sucky	1	2½
O. Betty, O. Billy and family	6	9	L. Sarah	1	2
Caesar and family	4¾	7½	O. Sucky	1	2½
Prophet, Joe and Cinder	3	7	Frank	1	
Cupid	1	2½	pecks	68	119½
B. Dick and family	4	5	equal to 17 Bushels.		
Flora	1½	2½	Pounds of Meat		
Minda	1	2½			
Kate and family ..	6½	9½	Take off ½ lb. when you		
Nurse and Peggy..	2	4½	give a Pint of Syrup.		

Although the families were recognized as more or less distinct units, the fact that life among the slaves was informal and familiar

tended to bring them all into intimate relations. The orphans had
little difficulty in finding mothers among the women at the quarters.
Concerning a former slave, the biographer writes:

> Aunt Phyllis showed him tender sympathy and remarked to aunt
> Betty that it was a pity "ter-tek' dat po' child fum his sick mamma,
> and brung him on dis place whah he won't meet nobody but a pas'le
> o' low-down, good-for-nuthin' strangers." This remark attached the
> boy to aunt Phyllis and he loved her ever afterward. He loved her, too,
> because she had the same name as his mother. Aunt Phyllis was a
> big-hearted old soul, and she looked with commiseration on all who
> suffered affliction or distress.[15]

But, in spite of this seemingly indiscriminate feeling toward
children, mothers were likely to show special regard for their own
offspring. Douglass, who was among the children placed under
care of a cook, says:

> She had a strong hold upon old master, for she was a first-rate
> cook, and very industrious. She was therefore greatly favored by
> him—as one mark of his favor she was the only mother who was per-
> mitted to retain her children around her, and even to these, her own
> children, she was often fiendishly in her brutality. Cruel, however, as
> she sometimes was to her own children, she was not destitute of ma-
> ternal feeling, and in her instinct to satisfy their demands for food,
> she was often guilty of starving me and the other children.

When the mother was sold away or died, the oldest sister often
assumed the role of mother to her brothers and sisters. A former
slave wrote recently:

> When my mother was sold I had one brother, William, and three
> sisters, Silva, Agga, and Emma. My father and mother were both
> pure blooded African Negros and there is not a drop of white blood
> in my veins, nor in those of my brother and sisters. When mother was
> taken away from us, Emma was a baby three years old. Silva, the
> oldest of the children, was fourteen, and she was a mother to the rest
> of us children. She took my mother's place in the kitchen as cook
> for my boss.[16]

[15] Charles Alexander, *Battles and Victories of Allen Allensworth*, Boston, 1914,
p. 27.
[16] Robert Anderson, *From Slavery to Affluence; Memories of Robert Anderson,
Ex-Slave*, Hemingsford, Neb., 1927, p. 5.

We have spoken of the mother as the mistress of the cabin and as the head of the family. There is good reason for this. Not only did she have a more fundamental interest in her children than the father but, as a worker and free agent, except where the master's will was concerned, she developed a spirit of independence and a keen sense of her personal rights. An entry in a plantation journal represents her in one case requesting a divorce because of the burden of having so many children:

> Lafayette Renty asked for Leaf to Marry Lear I also gave them Leaf. Rose, Rentys other wife, ses that she dont want to Libe with Renty on the account of his having so Many Children and they weare always quarling so I let them sepperate.

Usually the prospective son-in-law had to get the consent of the girl's mother. A slave complained that the mother of the girl whom he sought to marry opposed him because

> she wanted her daughter to marry a slave who belonged to a very rich man living near by, and who was well known to be the son of his master. She thought no doubt that his master or father might chance to set him free before he died, which would enable him to do a better part to her daughter than I could.[17]

The dominating position of the mother is seen in the comment of a former slave on the character of her father and mother. Her father, she said, was "made after the timid kind" and "would never fuss back" at her mother who was constantly warning him: "Bob, I don't want no sorry nigger around me. I can't tolerate you if you ain't got no backbone."

Sometimes it happened that the husband and father played a more aggressive role in the slave family.

In some lists of groups of slaves bought, the father appears:

NEGROES BOUGHT FEBY, 1839

Brave Boy, Carpenter, 40 years old	Pompey, Phillis's son, 16
	Jack B. Boy & Phillis's son, 16
Phillis, his wife, 35	Chloe child do do

[17] Henry Bibb, *The Narrative of the Life and Adventures of Henry Bibb, an American Slave, Written by Himself, with an Introduction by Lucius Matlock,* New York, 1849, pp. 39-40.

Primus B. Boy's son, 21
Cato Child, B. Boy's son
Jenny (Blind) B. Boy's mother
Nelly's husband in town, 30
Betty, her sister's child who
    died—child
Affey Nelly's child,—child, 11

Louisa her sister's child who is
    dead—child, 10
Sarah, Nelly's child, 8
Jack, Nelly's carpenter boy, 18
Ismel, Nelly's, 16
Lappo Phillis & Brave Boy's, 19

I paid cash for these 16 Negroes, $640. each—$10,240.00

Henson tells the following story of his father's defense of his mother:

> The only incident I can remember, which occurred while my mother continued on N.'s farm, was the appearance of my father one day, with his head bloody and his back lacerated. He was in a state of great excitement, and though it was all a mystery to me at the age of three or four years, it was explained at a later period, and I understood that he had been suffering the cruel penalty of the Maryland law for beating a white man. His right ear had been cut off close to his head, and he had received a hundred lashes on his back. He had beaten the overseer for a brutal assault on my mother, and this was his punishment. Furious at such treatment, my father became a different man, and was so morose, disobedient, and intractable, that Mr. N. determined to sell him. He accordingly parted with him, not long after, to his son, who lived in Alabama; and neither mother nor I ever heard of him again.[18]

In some accounts of their families, former slaves included their father. For example, Steward wrote: "Our family consisted of my father and mother—whose names were Robert and Susan Steward— a sister, Mary, and myself." But generally the husband made regular visits to his wife and children. According to Bishop Heard, his father, who lived three miles away, "would come in on Wednesday nights after things had closed up at his home, and be back at his home by daylight, Thursday mornings; come again Saturday night, and return by daylight Monday morning."

The strength of the bond that sometimes existed between the father and his family is shown in such advertisements as the following:

[18] Austin Steward, *Twenty-two Years a Slave, and Forty Years a Freeman*, Rochester, 1857, p. 13.

$50 REWARD

Ran away from the subscriber his Negro man Pauladore, commonly called Paul. I understand GEN. R. Y. HAYNE* *has purchased his wife and children* from H. L. PINCKNEY, Esq.,** and has them now on his plantation at Goose-creek, where, no doubt, the fellow is frequently lurking. T. DAVIS.

When Ball escaped from slavery in Georgia, he made his way back to his wife and children in Maryland. The apparently insignificant detail in the journal of an overseer: "To Eldesteno, old ben, to see his Grand son Samuel die," is an eloquent testimony to what some men felt in regard to their progeny. On the other hand, many slaves had the same relation with their fathers as Anderson, who says that, after his mother was sold away, "I frequently saw my father after that, but not sufficient to become familiar with him as a father and son should be. A few years later he married another woman from another plantation."

Generally speaking, the mother remained throughout slavery the dominant and important figure in the slave family. Although tradition has represented her as a devoted foster-parent to her master's children and indifferent to her own, it appears that, where this existed, the relations between the slave woman and the white child were similar to the relations which normally exist between mother and child. On the other hand, pregnancy and childbirth often meant only suffering for the slave mother who, because of her limited contacts with her young, never developed that attachment which grows out of physiological and emotional responses to its needs. Nevertheless, there is abundant evidence that slave mothers developed a deep and permanent love for their children, which often caused them to defy their masters and to undergo suffering to prevent separation from their young. This is only a part of the story of the slave mother, for there was another mother who bore children for the men of the master race. To the story of this mother we shall turn in the next chapter.

CHAPTER IV

HAGAR AND HER CHILDREN

Nowhere did human impulses and human feelings and sentiments tend to dissolve the formal relations between master and slave as in their sexual association, from which sprang those anomalous family groups consisting mainly of slave mother and mulatto offspring. But it was often in these very cases of human solidarity created by ties of blood that the ideas and sentiments embodied in the institution of slavery prevailed over the promptings of human feeling and sympathy. Where sexual association between master and slave was supported by personal attachment and in many cases genuine sentiment, we find the black, and more often mulatto, woman, under the protection of her master's house, playing a double role—a wife without the confirmation of the law and a mistress without the glamour of romance. Where the slave woman was only the means of satisfying a fleeting impulse, we find her rearing her mulatto offspring on the fare of slaves or being sold at a premium on the auction block because of her half-white brood. But whether her children were doomed to servitude or nurtured under the guidance of a solicitous father, they were not unconscious of their relation to the master race.

The admonition contained in the sermon preached at Whitechapel in 1609 for the benefit of adventurers and planters bound for Virginia, that "Abrams posteritie [must] keepe to themselves," was ignored in regard to the Negro as well as to the Indian. But the added injunction that "they may not marry nor give in marriage to the heathen, that are uncircumcised" became, except in rare instances, the inexorable policy of the whites in their relation with both of the subordinate races. Intercourse between whites and Negroes began as soon as the latter were introduced into America. In the beginning the sexual association between the two races was not confined to white males and the women of the black race. Colonial records furnish us with numerous instances of bastard children by Negro men and indentured white women. Two instances of this nature are reported by Helen Tunnicliff Catterall. A case brought into the Virginia courts in 1769 by a mulatto in suing for his freedom begins thus:

> A Christian white woman between the year of 1723 and 1765, had a daughter, Betty Bugg, by a negro man. This daughter was by deed indented, bound by the churchwardens to serve till thirty-one. Before the expiration of her servitude, she was delivered of the defendant Bugg, who never was bound by the churchwardens, and was sold by his master to the plaintiff. Being now twenty-six years of age, and having cause of complaint against the plaintiff, as being illy provided with clothes and diet, he brought an action in the court to recover his liberty, founding his claim on three points.

Another case for the following year states that

> the plaintiff's grandmother was a mulatto, begotten on a white woman by a negro man, after the year 1705, and bound by the churchwardens, under the law of that date, to serve to the age of thirty-one.

There is also good evidence that intercourse between Negro males and white servant women was sometimes encouraged by white masters who desired to increase the number of their bound servants. Marriages of Negroes and whites, most of whom were indentured servants, seem to have been numerous enough to require the enactment of severe laws for their prevention. But, when the principle of racial integrity and white domination became fixed in the minds of the whites, social censure and severe penalties were reserved, with rare exceptions, for the association of Negro men and white women. Calhoun has given us the following items from the court records of Chester County, Pennsylvania, in 1698:

> For that hee . . . . contrary to the lawes of the government and contrary to his masters consent hath . . . . got with child a certain mulato woman called swart Anna. . . . .

David Lewis Constable of Haverford returned a negro man of his
and a white woman for haveing a baster childe . . . . the negro said
she intised him and promised him to marry him; she being examined,
confest the same . . . . the court ordered that she shall receive twenty-
one lashes on her beare backe . . . . and the court ordered the negroe
man never to meddle with any white woman more uppon paine of his
life.

As slavery developed into an institution, neither the segregation
of the great body of slaves from the masses of the whites nor the
mutual antagonism between the "poor whites" and the blacks was
an effectual check on the sexual association between the two races.
In the cities, especially, where the slaves were released from the
control under which they lived on the plantations, and there were
many free Negroes, association between the women of the subordinate
race and white men assumed in the majority of cases a casual and
debasing character. In fact, a traffic in mulatto women especially
for prostitution became a part of the regular slave trade in southern
cities. The following item appeared in the *Memphis Eagle and
Enquirer*, June 26, 1857: "A slave woman is advertised to be sold in
St. Louis who is so surpassingly beautiful that $5,000 has been
already offered for her, at private sale, and refused."

Prostitution of slave women became in many cases a private affair
and, when in such cases it led to the formation of more or less
permanent associations, it merged into that developed and almost
socially approved system of concubinage which was found in
Charleston, Mobile, and New Orleans. The cities were not, however,
the only places where widespread intermixture of the races occurred.
Although it is difficult to estimate the extent to which the slaveholders entered into sexual associations with their slaves, there is
abundance of evidence of both concubinage and polygamy on the
part of the master class. Moreover, although the intercourse between
the masters and slave women on the plantations assumed as a rule
a more permanent form than similar relations in the cities, the
character of these associations varied considerably. Therefore, we
shall examine the character of the different types of associations and
try to determine the nature of the family groups that grew out of
them.

In view of the relations of superordination and subordination between the two races, how far did these associations originate in mere physical compulsion? How far did the women of the subordinate race surrender themselves because they were subject to the authority of the master race? Or was the prestige of the white race sufficient to insure compliance on the part of the black and mulatto women, both slave and free? How far was mutual attraction responsible for acquiescence on the part of the woman?

All these factors were effective in creating the perplexing relationships in which men of the master race and women of the subject race became entangled. That physical compulsion was necessary at times to secure submission on the part of black women, both slave and free, is supported by historical evidence and has been preserved in the traditions of Negro families. A young man in a Negro college writes concerning the birth of his great-great-grandfather on his mother's side:

> Approximately a century and a quarter ago, a group of slaves were picking cotton on a plantation near where Troy, Alabama, is now located. Among them was a Negro woman, who, despite her position as a slave, carried herself like a queen and was tall and stately. The over-seer (who was the plantation's owner's son) sent her to the house on some errand. It was necessary to pass through a wooded pasture to reach the house and the over-seer intercepted her in the woods and forced her to put her head between the rails in an old stake and rider fence, and there in that position my great-great-grandfather was conceived.

In the family history of another college student the story of the circumstances under which the Negro woman had been forced to yield to the sexual assault by her white master had become a sort of family skeleton, well guarded because of the sensitive feelings and pride of the victim. Of her great-grandmother, our informant writes:

> As young as I was when I knew her, I remember distinctly her fierce hatred of white people, especially of white men. She bore marks of brutal beatings she received for attempted escapes, or for talking back to her master or mistress. One mark in particular stands out in my memory, one she bore just above her right eye. As well as she liked to regale me with stories of her scars, this is one she never dis-

cussed with me. Whenever I would ask a question concerning it, she would simply shake her head and say, "White men are as low as dogs, child. Stay away from them." It was only after her death, and since I became a woman that I was told by my own mother that she received that scar at the hands of her master's youngest son, a boy of about eighteen years at the time she conceived their child, my grandmother, Ellen. She belonged to a family of tobacco planters I believe, for she often spoke of tobacco, and liked very much to smoke it in an old pipe, which seems to have been almost as old as she. During the time she was carrying Ellen, she was treated more brutally than before, and had to work even harder than ever. But strange to say, after the child was born, and was seen to be white, in appearance at least, the attitude of the whole C—— family seemed to soften toward her somewhat, and after this she became a house servant and was taught to sew, and became the family seamstress.

It seems that at times resistance to the white man's passion resulted in sadistical revenge upon the women. The form of punishment administered in the following case bears this implication.

> Thomas James, Jep's second son, had cast his eyes on a handsome young negro girl, to whom he made dishonest overtures. She would not submit to him, and finding he could not overcome her, he swore he would be revenged. One night he called her out of the gin-house, and then bade me and two or three more, strip her naked; which we did. He then made us throw her down on her face, in front of the door, and hold her whilst he flogged her—the brute—with the bullwhip, cutting great gashes of flesh out of her person, at every blow, from five to six inches long. The poor unfortunate girl screamed most awfully all the time, and writhed under our strong arms, rendering it necessary for us to use our united strength to hold her down. He flogged her for half an hour, until he nearly killed her, and then left her to crawl away to her cabin.[1]

However, in many instances men of the master race did not meet much resistance on the part of the slave women. The mere prestige of the white race was sufficient to secure compliance with their desires. As Miss Kemble observed, the slaves accepted the contempt of their masters to such an extent that "they profess, and really seem to feel it for themselves, and the faintest admixture of white

[1] John Brown, *Slave Life in Georgia*, ed., L. A. Chameroozow (London, 1855), pp. 132-33.

blood in their veins appears at once, by common consent of their own race, to raise them in the scale of humanity." The following incident related by John Thompson, a former slave indicates compliance on the part of a woman who was married to a slave:

> Soon after my arrival in the family, Mr. Thomas let me to one of his sons, named Henry, who was a doctor, to attend his horse. This son was unmarried, lived a bachelor, and kept a cook and waiter. The cook belonged neither to him nor his father, but was hired. She was a good looking mulatto, and was married to a right smart, intelligent man, who belonged to the doctor's uncle. One night, coming home in haste, and wishing to see his wife, he sent me up stairs to request her to come down. Upon going up I found she was in a room with the doctor, the door of which was fast. This I thoughtlessly told her husband, who, upon her coming down a moment after, upbraided her for it. She denied it, and afterwards told the doctor. . . . The doctor was a very intemperate man. As soon as his cook told him her story, he came to his father with the complaint that I had left him without his consent; upon which his father told him to flog me.[2]

Moreover, there were often certain concrete advantages to be gained by surrendering themselves to the men of the master race that overcame any moral scruples these women might have had. In some cases it meant freedom from the drudgery of field labor as well as better food and clothing. Then there was the prospect that her half-white children would enjoy certain privileges and perhaps in time be emancipated.

Mutual attraction also played a part in securing the compliance of the woman. In many cases the intimacies that developed began in the household where the two races lived in close association. The historian of Alabama, who attempts to place the responsibility for these illicit unions upon the slave woman, refers to the seductiveness of the latter. But it appears that, aside from the prestige of the white race and the material advantages to be gained, these slave women were as responsive to the attractiveness of the white males as the latter were to the charms of the slave women. Hence, slave women were not responsive to the approaches of all white men and

[2] John Thompson, *The Life of John Thompson, a Fugitive Slave; Containing His History of Twenty-five Years in Bondage, and His Providential Escape, Written by Himself* (Worcester, 1856), pp. 30-31.

often showed some discrimination and preference in the bestowal of their favors. The following incident is from the life of Bishop Loguen's mother, who was the mistress of a white man near Nashville, Tennessee:

> When she was about the age of twenty-four or five, a neighboring planter finding her alone at the distillery, and presuming upon the privileges of his position, made insulting advances, which she promptly repelled. He pursued her with gentle force, and was still repelled. He then resorted to a slaveholder's violence and threats. These stirred all the tiger's blood in her veins. She broke from his embrace, and stood before him in bold defiance. He attempted again to lay hold of her—and careless of caste and slave laws, she grasped the heavy stick used to stir the malt, and dealt him a blow which made him reel and retire. But he retired only to recover and return with the fatal knife, and threats of vengeance and death. Again she aimed the club with unmeasured force at him, and hit the hand which held the weapon, and dashed it to a distance from him. Again he rushed upon her with the fury of a madman, and she then plied a blow upon his temple, which laid him, as was supposed, dead at her feet.[3]

The relations between the white men and the slave women naturally aroused the jealousy and antagonism of the women of the master race. Because of the patriarchal character of the family, it was probably true to some extent, as one traveler related, that "a Southern wife, if she is prodigally furnished with dollars to 'go shopping,' apparently considers it no drawback to her happiness if some brilliant mulatto or quadroon woman ensnares her husband." But, frequently, the wife visited her resentment not only upon the slave woman but upon her husband's mulatto children. In some cases white women arranged marriages for their female slaves as a means of breaking off their husband's attachment. This expedient seemingly failed in the following incident related by a former slave concerning his sister:

> Mistress told sister that she had best get married, and that if she would, she would give her a wedding. Soon after a very respectable young man, belonging to Mr. Bowman, a wealthy planter, and reputed

[3] J. W. Loguen, *The Rev. J. W. Loguen, as a Slave and as a Freeman* (Syracuse, N. Y., 1859), pp. 20-21.

to be a good master, began to court my sister. This very much pleased Mistress, who wished to hasten the marriage. She determined that her maid should be married, not as slaves usually are, but that with the usual matrimonial ceremonies should be tied the knot to be broken only by death. The Sabbath was appointed for the marriage, which was to take place at the Episcopal Church. I must here state that no slave can be married lawfully, without a fine from his or her owner. Mistress and all the family, except the old man, went to church, to witness the marriage ceremony, which was to be performed by their minister, Parson Reynolds. The master of Josiah, my sister's destined husband, was also at the wedding, for he thought a great deal of his man. Mistress returned delighted from the wedding, for she thought she had accomplished a great piece of work. But the whole affair only enraged her unfeeling husband, who, to be revenged upon the maid, proposed to sell her. To this his wife refused consent. Although Mrs. T. had never told him her suspicions or what my sister had said, yet he suspected the truth, and determined to be revenged. Accordingly, during another absence of Mistress, he again cruelly whipped my sister. A continued repetition of these things finally killed our Mistress, who the doctor said, died of a broken heart. After the death of this friend, sister ran away leaving her husband and one child and finally found her way to the North.[4]

Sometimes white women used more direct means of ridding themselves of their colored rivals. There was always the possibility of selling them. If they were not able to accomplish this during the lifetime of their husbands, they were almost certain to get their revenge when the slave woman's protector died, as witness the following excerpt from the family history of a mulatto:

My father's grandmother, Julia Heriot, of four generations ago lived in Georgetown, South Carolina. Recollections of her parentage are, indeed, vague. Nevertheless, a distinct mixture of blood was portrayed in her physical appearance. And, because she knew so little of her parents, she was no doubt sold into Georgetown at a very early age as house servant to General Charles Washington Heriot. Julia Heriot married a slave on the plantation by whom she had two children. Very soon after her second child was born an epidemic of fever swept the plantation, and her husband became one of the victims. After her husband's death, she became maid to Mrs. Heriot, wife of General Heriot. From the time that Julia Heriot was sold to General

[4] Thompson, *op. cit.*, pp. 33-34.

Heriot, she had been a favorite servant in the household, because of the aptitude which she displayed in performing her tasks. General and Mrs. Heriot had been so impressed with her possibilities that in a very short time after she had been in her new home, she had been allowed to use the name of Heriot. . . . in the midst of her good fortune, a third child was born to her, which bore no resemblance to her other children. Reports of the "white child" were rumored. General Heriot's wife became enraged and insisted that her husband sell this slave girl, but General Heriot refused.

During the winter of the following year General Heriot contracted pneumonia and died. Before his death, he signed freedom papers for Julia and her three children; but, Mrs. Heriot manoevered her affairs so that Julia Heriot and her three children were again sold into slavery. In the auction of properties Julia Heriot was separated from her first two children. She pleaded that her babies be allowed to remain with her, but found her former mistress utterly opposed to anything that concerned her well-being. Her baby was the only consolation which she possessed. Even the name Heriot had been taken away by constant warnings.

In spite of the moralizing tone of the following excerpt the incidents related are probably authentic:

Among the slaves on Mr. McKiernan's plantation were a number of handsome women. Of these the master was extremely fond, and many of them he beguiled with vile flatteries, and cheated by false promises of future kindness, till they became victims to his unbridled passions. Upon these unfortunate women fell the heavy hatred of their mistress; and year after year, as new instances of her husband's perfidy came to her knowledge her jealousy ran higher, till at length reason seemed banished from her mind, and kindliness became a stranger to her heart. Then she sought a solace in the wine cup; and the demon of intoxication fanned the fires of hatred that burned within her, till they consumed all that was womanly in her nature, and rendered her an object of contempt and ridicule, even among her own dependents.[5]

The resentment of the white woman was likely to be manifested toward the offspring of her husband's relations with the slave woman. A mulatto former slave, after remarking that white women

[5] Mrs. Kate E. R. Pickard, *The Kidnapped and the Ransomed: Being the Personal Collections of Peter Still and His Wife "Vina," after Forty Years of Slavery* (New York, 1856), p. 167.

were "always revengeful toward the children of slaves that [had] any of the blood of their husbands in them," tells of his mother's anxiety when he, because of his relation to his master, became the object of the mistress' resentment. Calhoun cites the case of a mistress who, "out of ungrounded jealousy, had slaves hold a negro girl down while she cut off the forepart of the victim's feet."

Resentment against the mulatto child was especially likely to be aroused if the white father showed it much affection. In South Carolina in 1801 a woman secured alimony from her husband on the grounds that

> he cohabited with his own slave, by whom he had a mulatto child, on whom he lavished his affection; whilst he daily insulted the complainant, and encouraged his slave to do the same. . . . . That at dinner one day, he took away the plate from complainant when she was going to help herself to something to eat, and said, when he and the negro had dined she might.[6]

The slave woman's relations with the white males sometimes aroused the antagonism of the entire household. Her relations with the sons in the family were regarded in such cases as an offense against the integrity of the family. In the incident related by Pennington we see her not only as the victim of the sexual desires of the son in the household but also as the object of the affection of her colored father who sought to save her:

> My master once owned a beautiful girl about twenty-four. She had been raised in a family where her mother was a great favourite. She was her mother's darling child. Her master was a lawyer of eminent abilities and great fame, but owing to habits of intemperance, he failed in business, and my master purchased this girl for a nurse. After he had owned her about a year, one of his sons became attached to her, for no honourable purposes; a fact which was not only well-known among all the slaves, but which became a source of unhappiness to his mother and sisters.
>
> The result was that poor Rachel had to be sold to "Georgia." Never shall I forget the heart-rending scene, when one day one of the men was ordered to get "the one-horse cart ready to go into town"; Rachel, with her few articles of clothing, was placed in it, and taken

---

[6] Helen Tunnicliff Catterall (ed), *Judicial Cases concerning American Slavery and the Negro*, Washington, D. C., 1929, II, p. 281.

into the very town where her parents lived, and there sold to the traders before their weeping eyes. That same son who had degraded her, and who was the cause of her being sold, acted as salesman, and bill of salesman. While his cruel business was being transacted, my master stood aside, and the girl's father, a pious member and exhorter in the Methodist Church, a venerable grey-headed man, with his hat off, besought that he might be allowed to get some one in the place to purchase his child. But no: my master was invincible. His reply was, "She has offended in my family, and I can only restore confidence by sending her out of hearing." After lying in prison a short time, her new owner took her with others to the far South, where her parents heard no more of her.[7]

The white wife often saw in the colored woman not only a rival for her husband's affection but also a possible competitor for a share in his property.

Catterall cites several court cases where this was the chief issue. In Kentucky in 1848 the court held that a white man's will should be rejected because he had disinherited his children. The record of the court stated that

> during the few last years of his life, ... he [the testator, who died in 1845] seems to have had no will of his own, but to have submitted implicitly to the dictation of a colored woman whom he had emancipated, and whose familiar intercourse with him, had brought him into complete and continued subjection to her influence. . . . . The gratification of the wishes of this colored woman, seems to be its leading object. The natural duty of providing for his own children . . . . was entirely . . . . disregarded.

Probably not many men of the master race became so enamoured of their colored mistresses as to disinherit their wives and children. In fact, where they showed strong attachment for their colored mistresses, attempts were made to prove mental disability. This was the contention set up by the heirs-at-law in a case in South Carolina in 1856:

> Elijah Willis, by his will, dated 1854, bequeathed Amy (his slave mistress), her seven children (some of whom were his own), and their descendants to his executors, directing them "to bring or cause

[7] J. W. C. Pennington, *The Fugitive Blacksmith; or Events in the History of James W. C. Pennington* (London, 1850), pp. vi-vii.

said persons, and their increase, to be brought to . . . . Ohio, and to emancipate and set them free." He also bequeathed and devised to his executors all the rest of his property, from the sale of which to purchase lands in one of the free states for said slaves, to stock and furnish the same, and to place said persons in possession thereof. "Elijah Willis, taking with him his negro slave, Amy, and her children, and her mother, in May, 1855, left his home (in South Carolina) . . . for Cincinnati. . . . He arrived in a steamboat, and leaving it at a landing, on the Ohio side . . . . he died between the landing and a hack, in which he was about proceeding, with his said negroes, to his lodgings." His heirs-at-law contended that the will was void under the act of 1841, and also "undertook to show insanity, fraud, and undue influence, by proving . . . . that the deceased was often under gloomy depression of spirits—avoiding society on account of his connection with Amy, by whom he had several children; that he permitted her to act as the mistress of his house; to use saucy and improper language; that she was drunken, and probably unfaithful to him; and that she exercised great influence over him in reference to his domestic affairs, and in taking slaves from his business, to make wheels for little wagons for his mulatto children, and in inducing him to take off for sale the negro man who was her husband. . . . .[8]

When the same contention was made against a will in a Kentucky case in 1831, the court held:

"The fact that the deceased evinced an inclination to marry the slave, Grace, whom he liberated, is not a stronger evidence of insanity than the practice of rearing children by slaves without marriage; a practice but too common, as we all know, from the numbers of our mullatto population. However degrading, such things are, and however repugnant to the institutions of society, and the moral law, they prove more against the taste than the intellect. *De gustibus non disputandum.* White men, who may wish to marry negro women, or who carry on illicit intercourse with them, may, notwithstanding, possess such soundness of mind as to be capable in law, of making a valid will and testament"[9]

The attempt to define as insane the devotion of white men to their colored mistresses and mulatto children was to be expected since such behavior was so opposed to the formal and legal relations of the two races and the principles of color caste. But the human rela-

[8] Catterall, *op. cit.*, II, 451.
[9] Catterall, *op. cit.*, I, 318.

tions between the two races constantly tended to dissolve the formal and legal principles upon which slavery rested. Sexual relations broke down the last barriers to complete intimacy and paved the way for assimilation. There was some basis for the belief expressed by some persons that parental affection would put an end to slavery when amalgamation had gone far enough.

Not all masters, of course, developed a deep and permanent attachment for their mistresses and mulatto children. In some cases men of the master race even sold their own mulatto children. The slave woman was often abandoned and fared no better than other slaves. Neither Booker T. Washington nor his mother received any attention or benefactions from his supposedly white father. Frederick Douglass and his mother apparently derived no advantages from his reputed relation to the master race. After Loguen's mother had borne three children for her master, his passion for her cooled, and he took a white woman for his wife or mistress. But Loguen remembered that, when he was a very small child, "he was the pet of Dave, as his father was also nicknamed, that he slept in his bed sometimes, and was caressed by him." In the adjudication of the South Carolina case cited above, a witness testified that the white father gave his mulatto children "the best victuals . . . . from the table" and that "one of the small ones got in his lap." It was the prolonged association between the master and his colored mistress and their mulatto children that gave rise to enduring affections and lasting sentiment.

Although the association between the men of the master race and the slave women was regarded as an assault upon the white family, white children of the masters sometimes manifested an affection for their mulatto half-brothers and half-sisters similar to that of their fathers. The mulatto Clarke tells us that at least one of his mother's white half-sisters respected the tie of blood when the estate was sold:

> When I was about six years of age, the estate of Samuel Campbell, my grandfather, was sold at auction. His sons and daughters were all present, at the sale, except Mrs. Banton. Among the articles and animals put upon the catalogue, and placed in the hands of the auctioneer, were a large number of slaves. When every thing else had

been disposed of, the question arose among the heirs, "What shall be done with Letty (my mother) and her children?" John and William Campbell, came to mother, and told her they would divide her family among the heirs, but none of them should go out of the family. One of the daughters—to her everlasting honor be it spoken—remonstrated against any such proceeding. Judith, the wife of Joseph Logan, told her brothers and sisters, "Letty is our own half sister, and you know it; father never intended they should be sold." Her protest was disregarded, and the auctioneer was ordered to proceed. My mother, and her infant son Cyrus, about one year old, were put up together and sold for $500!! Sisters and brothers selling their own sister and her children.[10]

All classes of whites in the South were involved in these associations with the slave women. Some have attempted to place the burden upon the overseers and the landless poor whites, the class from which they were recruited. But there is no evidence that the poor whites were more involved than the men of the master class. In fact, there was always considerable antagonism between the slaves and the overseers and the class to which they belonged. Concubinage was the privilege of those classes in the South that were economically well off. In Charleston, South Carolina, and in New Orleans, where the system of concubinage reached its highest development, wealthy bachelors included beautiful mulatto women among their luxuries. Sometimes they developed a serious and permanent affection for these women that culminated in marriage. Clarke, a mulatto, gives the following account regarding his sister:

> Sister was therefore carried down the river to New Orleans, kept three or four weeks, and then put up for sale. The day before the sale, she was taken to the barber's, her hair dressed, and she was furnished with a new silk gown, and gold watch, and every thing done to set off her personal attractions, previous to the time of the bidding. The first bid was $500; then $800. The auctioneer began to extol her virtues. Then $1000 was bid. The auctioneer says, "If you only knew the reason why she is sold, you would give any sum for her. She is a pious, good girl, member of the Baptist church, warranted to be a virtuous girl." The bidding grew brisk. "Twelve!" "thirteen," "fourten," "fifteen," "sixteen hundred," was at length bid, and she was knocked off to a Frenchman, named Coval. He wanted her to live

[10] Catterall, *op. cit.*, II, 469.

with him as his housekeeper and mistress. This she utterly refused, unless she were emancipated and made his wife. In about one month, he took her to Mexico, emancipated, and married her. She visited France with her husband, spent a year or more there and in the West Indies. In four or five years after her marriage, her husband died, leaving her a fortune of twenty or thirty thousand dollars.[11]

More often, it seems, the women developed real affection for the men; for, when they were abandoned by the white men who entered legal marriage, these women seldom entered new relationships and in some cases committed suicide.

The colored families of the aristocrats were too well known for the fact to be concealed.

According to William Goodell, a sister of President Madison was reported to have remarked to Rev. George Bourne, a Presbyterian minister in Virginia: "We southern ladies are complimented with the names of wives; but we are only the mistresses of seraglios." While Andrew Johnson was governor of Tennessee, in a speech to the newly emancipated blacks, he chided the aristocracy on their objection to Negro equality by reminding them of their numerous mulatto children in the city of Nashville:

> The representatives of this corrupt, (and if you will permit me almost to swear a little), this damnable aristocracy, taunt us with our desire to see justice done, and charge us with favoring negro equality. Of all living men they should be the last to mouth that phrase; and, even when uttered in their hearing, it should cause their cheeks to tinge and burn with shame. Negro equality, indeed! Why, pass, any day, along the sidewalks of High Street where these aristocrats more particularly dwell,—these aristocrats, whose sons are now in the bands of guerillas and cutthroats who prowl and rob and murder around our city,—pass by their dwellings, I say, and you will see as many mulatto as Negro children, the former bearing an unmistakable resemblance to the aristocratic owners.[12]

The white masters acknowledged the relationships, gave protection to their colored families, and generally emancipated them. The often-

[11] Lewis Clarke, *Narrative of the Sufferings of Lewis and Milton Clarke, Sons of a Soldier of the Revolution* (Boston, 1846), p. 75.

[12] William Goodell, *American Slave Code in Theory and Practice* (New York, 1853), p. 111.

cited case of Thomas Jefferson, who emancipated his colored children, is only a conspicuous example of the numerous aristocratic slave-holders who left mulatto descendants. Only as tradition has cast a halo about the southern aristocracy has an attempt been made to remove this supposed stain from their name.

Numerous mulatto families are traceable to the associations between slaveholders and their slave women. The family background of a mulatto who played a part in Texas politics after the Civil War is similar to that of other mulatto families whose relationship to the master race is well authenticated. From the biography of Cuney, written by his daughter, we learn:

> Norris Wright Cuney was of Negro, Indian and Swiss descent. The Negro and Indian blood came through his mother, Adeline Stuart, for whom free papers were executed by Col. Cuney, and who was born in the State of Virginia. . . . . The Caucasian blood of my father came principally from the Swiss family of Cuney's who were among the early settlers of Virginia, coming there with the Archinard family from Switzerland. About the time of the Louisiana purchase, they migrated to the new provinces and became planters in Rapides Parish. . . . . When Col. Philip Cuney came to Texas with his family, he settled in Waller County, near Hempstead, on the east side of the Brazos River. Here, in the heart of the cotton and melon belt, he maintained a large plantation and held slaves, among whom was my grandmother, mentioned above, Adeline Stuart, who bore him eight children and whom he eventually set free . . . . on May 12, 1846, my father was born at "Sunnyside," the plantation on the Brazos River owned by his father, Col. Philip Cuney. In 1853, when father was seven years of age, the family moved to Houston and the two older boys were sent to Pittsburgh to attend school.[13]

When men of the slaveholding aristocracy renounced the conventional society of their peers, withdrew to the seclusion of their feudal estates, and took as their companions mulatto women, it was natural that deep and permanent sentiment should develop between them and their colored mistresses and children. This was the case with those anomalous family groups in which the woman enjoyed the protection of her master and paramour and occupied a dignified and respected position in relation to her children and other slaves

---

[13] Maud Cuney Hare, *Norris Wright Cuney* (New York, 1913), pp. 1-4.

on the plantation. It is not surprising, then, to find in the court cases, contesting the wills of masters who emancipated their mistresses and mulatto children and left them their estates, that the fact of the woman's having "had the influence over him of a white woman and a wife" was cited to show undue influence on her part.

That such associations undermined the moral order upon which slavery rested and made possible the gradual assimilation of the Negro as his blood became more and more diluted by white blood cannot be denied. Within the intimacy of these family groups color caste was dissolved, and the children, who were often scarcely distinguishable from white, took over the ideals, sentiments, and ambitions of their white fathers. Their mothers, who were generally mulattoes and already possessed some of the culture and feeling of the master race, were further assimilated into the white group by their close association with the cultured classes of the South.

We can view this process in John M. Langston's mulatto family that originated on a large plantation in Virginia. Captain Ralph Quarles, according to his mulatto son who was elected to Congress during the Reconstruction,

> believed that slavery ought to be abolished. But he maintained that the mode of its abolition should be by the voluntary individual action of the owner. He held that slaves should be dealt with in such manner, as to their superintendence and management, as to prevent cruelty, always, and to inspire in them, so far as practicable, feelings of confidence in their masters. Hence, he would employ no overseer, but, dividing the slaves into groups, convenient for ordinary direction and employment, make one of their own number the chief director of the force.[14]

Because of these views and practices in the management of his plantation, Captain Quarles was condemned and finally ostracized. "For twenty years before his death, no white man resided upon his plantation other than Captain Quarles himself." As he spent most of his life among his slaves, naturally, as his son remarks, he found "a woman, a companion for life, among his slaves to whom he gave his affections," and made "the mother of his children."

[14] John M. Langston, *From the Virginia Plantation to the National Capital* (Hartford, Conn., 1894), p. 12.

The woman, for whom he discovered special attachment and who, finally, became really the mistress of the Great House of the plantation, reciprocating the affection of her owner, winning his respect and confidence, was the one whom he had taken and held, at first, in pledge for money borrowed of him by her former owner; but whom, at last, he made the mother of his four children, one daughter and three sons. Her name was Lucy Langston. Her surname was of Indian origin, and borne by her mother, as she came out of a tribe of Indians of close relationships in blood to the famous Pocahontas. Of Indian extraction, she was possessed of slight proportion of negro blood; and yet, she and her mother, a full-blooded Indian woman, who was brought upon the plantation and remained there up to her death, were loved and honored by their fellow-slaves of every class.

She had been emancipated by Captain Quarles in 1806 after the birth of the first child, a girl. It was after her emancipation that the three sons were born to them in 1809, 1817, and 1829.

The children were the objects of their father's affection and solicitude as well as their mother's love. The oldest boy was educated by his father, who required him to appear "for his recitations, in his father's special apartments, the year round, at five o'clock in the morning; and be ready after his duties in such respect had been met, at the usual hour, to go with the slave boys of his age to such service upon the plantation as might be required of them." This boy became so much like his father in physical and mental qualities that Captain Quarles made the significant addition of Quarles to his name. In remarking upon his father's regard for his children, the youngest son wrote:

> Could his tender care of them, in their extreme youth, and his careful attention to their education, as discovered by him as soon as they were old enough for study, be made known, one could understand, even more sensibly, how he loved and cherished them; being only prevented from giving them his own name and settling upon them his entire estate, by the circumstances of his position, which would not permit either the one or the other. He did for his sons all he could; exercising paternal wisdom, in the partial distribution of his property in their behalf and the appointment of judicious executors, of his will, who understood his purposes and were faithful in efforts necessary to execute them. Thus, he not only provided well for the

education of his sons, but, in large measure, made allowance for their settlement in active, profitable business-life.

The mother probably played no small part in the training of their children and in helping to create in them a conception of their superior status. She was described by her son as

a woman of small stature, substantial build, fair looks, easy and natural bearing, even and quiet temper, intelligent and thoughtful, who accepted her lot with becoming resignation, while she always exhibited the deepest affection and earnest solicitude for her children. Indeed, the very last words of this true and loving mother, when she came to die, were uttered in the exclamation, "Oh, that I could see my children once more!"[15]

After a long life together Captain Quarles and his mulatto mistress died in 1834.

The former, as he neared his end, requested and ordered, that Lucy, when she died, should be buried by his side, and, accordingly, upon a small reservation in the plantation, they sleep together their long quiet sleep. While the humblest possible surroundings mark the spot of their burial, no one has ever disturbed or desecrated it.

During his last sickness, Captain Quarles was attended only by Lucy, her children, and his slaves. During the two days his body lay upon its bier, in the Great House, it was guarded, specially and tenderly, by the noble negro slave, who, when his master was taken sick suddenly, and felt that he needed medical assistance, without delay, but a few nights before, hurried across the country to the home of the physician, and secured his aid for his stricken owner.

In his will of October 18, 1833, Captain Quarles left a large part of his estate, including lands and bank stock, to his three sons. According to the provisions of the will, if they desired to move into free territory the real estate was to be sold. Soon after the death of their parents the sons departed for Ohio.

This case represents the highest development of family life growing out of the association of the men of the master race with the slave women. At the bottom of the scale was the Negro woman who was raped and became separated from her mulatto child without any violence to her maternal feelings; or the slave woman who sub-

[15] Langston, *op. cit.*, p. 13.

mitted dumbly or out of animal feeling to sexual relations that spawned a nameless and unloved half-white breed over the South. Between these two extremes there were varying degrees of human solidarity created in the intimacies of sex relations and the birth of offspring. Sexual attraction gave birth at times to genuine affection; and prolonged association created between white master and colored mistress enduring sentiment. There were instances where white fathers sold their mulatto children; but more often they became ensnared by their affections for their colored offspring. Neither color caste nor the law of slavery could resist altogether the corrosive influence of human feeling and sentiment generated in these lawless family groups. The master in his mansion and his colored mistress in her special house near by represented the final triumph of social ritual in the presence of the deepest feeling of human solidarity.

IN THE HOUSE OF THE MOTHER

PART TWO

IN THE HOUR OF THE MOUSE

CHAPTER V

BROKEN BONDS

How did the Negro family fare when it left the house of the master and began its independent career in the stormy days of emancipation? What authority was there to take the place of the master's in regulating sex relations and maintaining the permanency of marital ties? Where could the Negro father look for a sanction of his authority in family relations which had scarcely existed in the past? Were the affectional bonds between mother and child and the solidarity of feeling and sentiment between man and wife strong enough to withstand the disorganizing effects of freedom? In the absence of family traditions and public opinion, what restraint was there upon individual impulse unleashed in those disordered times? To what extent during slavery had the members of the slave families developed common interests and common purposes capable of supporting the more or less loose ties of sympathy between those of the same blood or household?

Emancipation was a crisis in the life of the Negro that tended to destroy all his traditional ways of thinking and acting. To some slaves who saw the old order collapse and heard the announcement that they were free men emancipation appeared "like notin' but de judgment day."[1] Bishop Gaines, recalling the effect of the announcement upon him and his fellow slaves, wrote:

[1] Thomas Wentworth Higginson, *Army Life in a Black Regiment* (New York, 1900), p. 235.

I shall never forget the moment when I heard the first tidings proclaiming liberty to the captive. Memory holds that hour as the most beautiful and enrapturing in all the history of a life which has alternated between the experience of a debasing servitude and that of a joyous and unfettered freedom.

I was ploughing in the fields of Southern Georgia. The whole universe seemed to be exulting in the unrestraint of the liberty wherewith God has made all things free, save my bound and fettered soul, which dared not claim its birthright and kinship with God's wide world of freedom. The azure of a Southern sky bent over me and the air was fragrant with the fresh balm-breathing odors of spring. The fields and the forests were vocal with the blithe songs of birds, and the noise of limpid streams made music as they leaped along to the sea.

Suddenly the news was announced that the war had ended and that slavery was dead. The last battle had been fought, and the tragedy that closed at Appomattox had left the tyrant who had reigned for centuries slain upon the gory field.

In a moment the pent-up tears flooded my cheek and the psalm of thanksgiving arose to my lips. "I am free," I cried, hardly knowing in the first moments of liberty what and how great was the boon I had received. Others, my companions, toiling by my side, caught up the glad refrain, and shouts and rejoicings rang through the fields and forests like the song of Miriam from the lips of the liberated children of Israel.[2]

When the news was received that they were free, other slaves were bewildered as the boy who said it sounded "like Greek" to him when his mother whispered with a quiver in her voice: "Son, we have been slaves all our lives, and now Mr. Abe Lincoln done set us free, and say we can go anywhere we please in this country, without getting a pass from Marse Cage like we used to have to do."[3] Sometimes when the slaves received a formal notice of their freedom from the master, his broken authority proved an ineffectual restraint upon their rejoicing. A prominent young Negro minister recounts the story of the announcement of freedom on the plantation where his grandfather held a responsible position:

The slaves were in the fields chopping the cotton and chanting the rhythm of the day as a testimony to the drowsy overseer that they

[2] W. J. Gaines, *The Negro and the White Man* (Philadelphia, 1897), pp. 71-72.
[3] J. Vance Lewis, *Out of the Ditch: A True Story of an Ex-Slave* (Houston, Texas, 1910), p. 9.

were doing his bidding. "Massah" Ridley was on the porch of the "big house" fast asleep. The Yankees had ridden up to the mansion, and the horses put their hoofs on the low and unrailed porch as if at home. Doctor Ridley awakened quickly, surprised, startled, bewildered, perplexed, a riot of color. Some words passed between the parties, and then one of the soldiers took something from his pocket and read it. By this time "Missus" Ridley had come from the house. She too heard the story and saw her husband's eyes suffused with tears but said not a word. Doctor Ridley was trying hard to keep the tears back. He summoned Miles and spoke slowly with a tear in his voice: "Miles, call all the niggers together."

The slaves did not know the meaning of Miles' news to them, although they had heard rumors that they should sometime be free. Few could read, and none had access to newspapers. As they left the field they wondered who was to be whipped or who was to be sold or what orders were to be given. Half-startled, half-afraid, they wended their way through the fields in one silent mass of praying creatures. On seeing the Yankees they started back, but "Massah" Ridley beckoned.

The master was weeping bitterly. Finally he sobbed, "I called you together, Miles—" then he stopped. His words were stifled with sobs. The slaves were awe-stricken; they had never seen a white man cry. Only slaves had tears, they thought. All eyes were fastened on Doctor Ridley. He was saying something. "All you niggers—all you niggers are free as I am." The surprise was shocking, but in an instant in his usual harsh voice he added: "But there ain't going to be any rejoicing here. Stay here until the crop is made, and I'll give you provisions. Go back to work."

But the slaves did rejoice and loudly, too. Some cried; some jumped up and cracked their heels. Charlotte took her younger children in her arms and shouted all over the plantation: "Chillun, didn't I tell you God 'ould answer prayer?"[4]

The same writer informs us that many of the slaves left the plantation immediately. In fact, the right to move about was the crucial test of freedom. "After the coming of freedom," wrote Booker Washington, "there were two points upon which practically all the people on our place were agreed, and I find that this was generally true throughout the South: that they must change their names, and

---

[4] Miles Mark Fisher, *The Master's Slave—Elijah John Fisher* (Philadelphia, 1922), pp. 6-8.

that they must leave the plantation for at least a few days or weeks in order that they might really feel sure that they were free."[5]

Some, of course, in whom the attitude of subordination was still strong were less bold in asserting their newly acquired rights. This was the case with a Negro bishop who said:

> One day in 1865 I was plowing with a mare called "Old Jane," and I looked and saw the "Yankees." I had heard before of their coming. I took out Old Jane and went to the house about three o'clock in the afternoon. I was asked why I had come home at that hour. I told them "I was afraid the Yankees would steal my horse, so I brought her home," but that was not the cause at all. Freedom had come, and I came to meet it.[6]

A similar attitude on the part of a slave is recalled by Bishop Coppin:

> Father Jones was promptly on hand with Lincoln's proclamation, but here was no one present with authority to say to the slave, you are free; so all were in suspense.
>
> Uncle Jim Jones drove his mistress to Cecilton, and some one, a white person, told him that he was free now, and it was discretionary with him whether or not he drove the carriage back. When Uncle Jim reached home he informed every one of what he had heard. When a few evenings after that, his old master himself drove the carriage to town and was late returning, Uncle Jim, in order to make a test case, would not remain to unharness the horses, but said, in a way that his master would be sure to hear it: "There has got to be a new understanding," which "new understanding," came promptly the next morning when "Mars Frankie" approached him to know about the strange doctrine which he was preaching around the place. Poor Uncle Jim begged pardon, saved his back, and said no more about a "new understanding."
>
> He was too old to be very independent. He continued to live in the little house on the place, and work for Marse Frankie, who paid him about what he thought his services were worth. He never was able to throw off the terrible fear he always had of his master, who, by the way, was never cruel to him; but, he finally mustered enough courage to go and come at will.[7]

The spirit of submission was not so deeply ingrained in all slaves as in this old house servant. Especially was this true with the younger

---

[5] Booker T. Washington, *Up From Slavery* (New York, 1902), p. 23.

[6] William H. Heard, *From Slavery to Bishopric* (Philadelphia, 1924), p. 28.

[7] L. J. Coppin, *Unwritten History* (Philadelphia, 1920), pp. 91-92.

slaves. A former slave in Alabama remarked not long ago to the writer that the older Negroes continued to ask for passes to go to church while the younger generation took delight in going off when they chose without the pass. In many places, especially those in the path of the invading armies, the plantation organization, the very basis of the slave system, was swept away. When Sherman's army swept through Georgia, it drew after it thousands of Negroes from the plantations. Reports that have come down to us of the effects of the destruction of the established order show that in some cases even the bond of maternal affection between mother and child was severed. The hardships of the journey with Sherman were so fearful that "children often gave out and were left by their mothers exhausted and dying by the roadside and in the fields." Some of the mothers, we are told, "put their children to death, they were such a drag upon them, till our soldiers, becoming furious at their barbarous cruelty hung two women on the spot."[8] But in other cases the shock of war and emancipation that uprooted the old social order only revealed how strong were the bonds of affection between parents and children and husband and wife. For the same informant tells us that a woman with twelve children "carried one and her husband another and for fear she would lose the others she tied them all together by the hands and brought them all off safely, a march of hundreds of miles."

Other witnesses who were in a position to observe the effects of emancipation on family relations have provided similar testimony. For example, in an account which Higginson has left us of the fleeing refugees, we find that "women brought children on their shoulders; small black boys carried on their backs little brothers equally inky, and, gravely depositing them, shook hands." One who worked among the refugees noted the fact that "these people had a marvellous way of tracing out missing members of their families, and inflexible perseverance in hunting them up."[9] Numerous instances of the general disposition on the part of the emancipated Negro to rejoin his relatives who had been sold away could be cited. But we

[8] Elizabeth Pearson, *War Letters from Port Royal, Written at the Time of the Civil War* (Boston, 1906), pp. 293-94.

[9] Elizabeth Hyde Botume, *First Days among the Contrabands* (Boston, 1893), p. 154.

shall let a former slave, whose sister was sold away from the family, tell of her sister's return after emancipation.

> My sister tried to locate us and found us by inquiring from place to place. She came to the door one day and told me that she was my sister but I refused to let her in for I didn't know her and my mother had told me not to open the door to strangers, so I didn't let her in. She had to go some place and stay until my mother came home. She would come and visit us for awhile and she corresponded with us after that. I don't think I had the same feeling for her as I had with the sister with whom I had been associated all the time. There was nothing antagonistic of course but I just didn't know her, that was all. She was very fond of me though.

The strong attachment which, as we have seen, mothers showed for their children during the crisis of emancipation could be matched with many instances of deep affection between husbands and wives and between children and their parents. Witness, for example, among the refugees an old man with "his sick wife on his back, and a half-grown boy (with) his blind daddy, toting him along 'to freedom.' " Higginson cites the case of a man who refused to join the army, "saying bluntly that his wife was out of slavery with him, and he did not care to fight." But there was another side to the picture which we are able to piece together from the recollections that have been preserved. The mobility of the Negro population after emancipation was bound to create disorder and produce widespread demoralization. Thousands of Negroes flocked to the army camps where they created problems of discipline as well as of health. Some wandered about without any destination; others were attracted to the towns and cities. When the yoke of slavery was lifted, the drifting masses were left without any restraint upon their vagrant impulses and wild desires. The old intimacy between master and slave, upon which the moral order under the slave regime had rested, was destroyed forever. In describing the effects of the destruction of intimacy between the two races upon the conduct of the Negroes, Bruce writes:

> Even if, in any instance, a father and mother were to desire to instill a spirit of self-restraint into their children, they would not be led to seek, when necessary, the assistance of their former master, who

is now their employer, and who never assumes the right to intervene, unless the heedlessness or depravity of the children is displayed in injuring, destroying, or purloining his property. He has no longer authority enough to insist upon order and discipline in the family life, or to compel parents to prevent their offspring from running wild, like so many young animals. Even when he feels any interest in their moral education, irrespective of their connection with the government of his own estate, he finds it impossible to come near enough to them to win and hold their attention, for child and parent alike shrink from association with him. His advances are not cordially met. However keen his sense of moral responsibility, therefore, and however earnestly he may wish to prosecute a plan of moral education among the children of his laborers, he runs upon an almost insurmountable obstacle in his path at the very beginning, and he is generally discouraged from going any further. As far, therefore, as he is concerned, the children of the new generation receive no moral instruction at all. Under the old system, the ladies of his family often instituted Sunday-schools, to teach the young slaves the leading principles of the Christian faith, as well as general rules of good conduct; but this custom, which was the source of much benefit to the pupils, has fallen into disuse; and as there are now no points of contact between the home life of the cabin and that of the planter's residence, no social or moral influence of any kind emanates from his domestic circle to enlighten the minds of the children who live on his estate.[10]

A former slave gives in more concrete terms an account of his feelings when the prospect of freedom seemed to destroy the intimate relations between himself and his master's son.

I shall never forget, [he says] the feeling of sickness which swept over me. I saw no reason for rejoicing as others were doing. It was my opinion that we were being driven from our homes and set adrift to wander, I knew not where. I did not relish the idea of parting with my young master who was as true a friend as I ever had. There was also a very difficult problem for us to solve—we had three coon dogs which we jointly owned, and I did not see how to divide the dogs without hurting his feelings, my feelings or the dogs' feelings, without relinquishing my claims, which I was loathe to do.[11]

Promiscuous sexual relations and constant changing of spouses became the rule with the demoralized elements in the freed Negro

---

[10] Phillip A. Bruce, *The Plantation Negro as a Freeman* (New York, 1889), p. 4.
[11] J. Vance Lewis, *op. cit.*, pp. 9-10.

population. "Mammy Maria, who had left two husbands in Mississippi," writes Mrs. Smedes, "came out in the new country as 'Miss
Dabney,' and attracted, as she informed her 'white children,' as much
admiration as any of the young girls, and had offers of marriage too.
But she meant to enjoy her liberty, she said, and should not think
of marrying any of them."[12] Some of the confusion in marital relations was owing, of course, to the separation of husbands and wives
during slavery and the disorganization that followed emancipation.
This was one of the problems that particularly vexed the northern
missionaries who undertook to improve the morals of the newly
liberated blacks. Botume tells the story of a case which was finally
adjusted so that the couple settled down and lived a monogamous
life:

> One day Uncle Kit came to me greatly troubled. His wife Tina's
> first husband, who had been sold away from her "in the old secesh
> times," had come back and claimed her. "An' I set my eyes by her,"
> said the poor fellow. Tina had been brought up on another plantation
> to which husband number one had now returned. But Kit had be-
> longed to the Smith estate. So the wife went from one place to the
> other, spending a few weeks alternately with each husband. She had
> no children, so had nothing to bind her more to one than the other.
> Kit came to ask me to write a letter to Tina and beg her to come back
> and stay with him. "Fur him want to come to lib, but him shame,"
> said poor Kit. He was ready to forgive all her waywardness, "fur no-
> body can tell, ma'am, what I gone through with fur that woman.
> I married her for love, an' I lub her now more an' better than I lub
> myself." We thought such devotion should be rewarded. I expostu-
> lated with Tina over her way of living, and finally threatened to
> ignore her altogether. She seemed surprised, but replied, "I had Sam
> first, but poor brother Kit is all alone." Finally she decided to drop
> Sam and cling to Kit, "fur he, poor fellow, ain't got nobody but me,"
> she said. They lived happily together for many years. Then Tina died,
> and Kit refused to allow any person to live in the house with him,
> telling me he never liked confusion. And folks *would* talk, and "I
> don't want Tina to think I would bring shame upon she," he said.[13]

The confusion in marital relations was often brought to light
when the freedmen decided or were persuaded to enter formal

[12] Susan Smedes, *A Southern Planter* (Baltimore, 1887), p. 179.
[13] Elizabeth Hyde Botume, *op. cit.*, pp. 160-61.

marriage. "A couple came forward," so runs one account, "to be married after church, as often happens, when Sarah from this place got up and remarked that was her husband! Whereupon Mr. Philbrick was called in from the yard and promised to investigate and report. Jack said he had nothing against Sarah, but he did not live on the plantation now, and wanted a wife at Hilton Head." Marriage as a formal and legal relation was not a part of the mores of the freedmen. There was a great deal of supersitition concerning it, which probably helped to establish it in the mores of the Negroes. This is shown in the attitude of a recently married husband:

> We were passing the "negro quarters," and one of these men brought out a very young and plump baby for us to see, saying they had had "a heap of children," but it seemed as if none could live until they got married, and got their certificate. "But dis gal is boun' to live," he said.

T. G. Steward, an educated Negro minister from the North, who worked among the freedmen remarked concerning their condition:

> This whole section with its hundreds of thousands of men, women and children just broken forth from slavery, was so far as these were concerned, lying under an almost absolute physical and moral interdict. There was no one to baptize their children, to perform marriage, or to bury the dead. A ministry had to be created at once—and created out of the material at hand.[14]

Sometimes nothing short of force could get the former slaves to abandon their old promiscuous sexual relations:

> We had a case of imprisonment here last week. I learned that old Nat's boy, Antony, who wanted to marry Phillis, had given her up and taken Mary Ann, July's daughter, without saying a word to me or any other white man. I called him up to me one afternoon when I was there and told him he must go to church and be married by the minister according to law. He flatly refused, with a good deal of impertinence, using some profane language learned in camp. I thereupon told him he must go home with me, showing him I had a pistol, which I put in my outside pocket. He came along, swearing all the way and muttering his determination not to comply. I gave him lodging in the dark hole under the stairs, with nothing to eat. Next morn-

[14] T. G. Steward, *Fifty Years in the Gospel Ministry*, (Philadelphia, 1922), p. 33.

ing Old Nat came and expostulated with him, joined by old Ben and
Uncle Sam, all of whom pitched into him and told him he was very
foolish and ought to be proud of such a chance. He finally gave up
and promised to go. So I let him off with an apology. Next Sunday
he appeared and was married before a whole church full of people.
The wedding took place between the regular church service and the
funeral, allowing an hour of interval, however.[15]

On the other hand, the marriage ceremony was in many cases the
confirmation of a union that was based upon genuine sentiment
established over a long period of years. This was evidently what it
meant to the couple in the following account:

> Amongst the first persons who came forward to be married were
> Smart and Mary Washington, who had lived together over forty
> years. They were very happy when they walked away together side
> by side, for the first time endowed with the honorable title of
> husband and wife. Smart chuckled well when we congratulated him,
> saying,—"Him's my wife for sartin, now. Ef the ole hen run away,
> I shall cotch him sure." We thought there was no danger of good
> Aunt Mary's running away after so many years of faithful service.

"The colored people," wrote Bishop Gaines, "generally held their
marriage (if such unauthorized union may be called marriage)
sacred, even while they were yet slaves. Many instances will be
recalled by the older people of the South of the life-long fidelity
and affection which existed between the slave and his concubine—
the mother of his children. My own father and mother lived together
for over sixty years. I am the fourteenth child of that union, and I
can truthfully affirm that no marriage, however sacred by the sanction
of law, was ever more congenial and beautiful. Thousands of like
instances might be cited to the same effect."

When the bonds of sympathy and affection between the members
of these families were strong enough to remain unbroken after
emancipation, the subsequent struggle for existence during those
trying times tended to strengthen family ties. The first problem which
the freedmen faced was that of finding food and shelter. Du Bois
writes:

[15] Pearson, *op. cit.*, p. 95.

The first feasible plan to meet this situation was to employ the Negroes about the camps, first as servants and laborers, and finally as soldiers. Through the wages and bounty money thus received a fund of something between five and ten millions of dollars was distributed among the freedmen—a mere pittance per capita, but enough in some cases to enable recipients to buy a little land and start as small farmers. All this, however, was mere temporary make-shift; the great mass of the freedmen were yet to be provided for, and the first Freedmen's Bureau law of 1865 sought to do this by offering to freedmen on easy terms the abandoned farms and planta-tions in the conquered territory. This offer was eagerly seized upon, and there sprang up along the Mississippi, in Louisiana, and on the coasts of the Carolinas and Georgia series of leased plantations under Government direction. When the Freedmen's Bureau took charge it received nearly 800,000 acres of such land and 5,000 pieces of town property, from the leasing of which a revenue of nearly $400,000 was received from freedmen. The policy of President Johnson, however, soon put an end to this method of furnishing land to the landless. His proclamation of amnesty practically restored the bulk of this seized property to its former owners, and within a few years the black tenants were dispossessed or became laborers.

The act of 1866 was the next and last wholesale attempt to place land within the reach of the emancipated slaves. It opened to both white and black settlers the public lands of the Gulf States. But lack of capital and tools and the opposition of the whites made it im-possible for many Negroes to take advantage of this opening, so that only about 4,000 families were thus provided for.

Thus the efforts to provide the freedman with land and tools ended, and by 1870 he was left to shift for himself amid new and dangerous social surroundings.[16]

The success which attended the Negro's first efforts to get estab-lished as a free man depended, of course, to a large extent upon his character, intelligence, and efficiency, which in turn reflected his schooling during slavery. We are able to see how the freedmen got started in the following description of a freedman who, although he still retained a second wife on another plantation, settled down with his family and through his enterprise and intelligence succeeded in establishing himself as a free man:

[16] W. E. B. Du Bois, *The Negro Landholder of Georgia*, "Bulletin of the Depart-ment of Labor," No. 35 (Washington, 1901), pp. 647-48.

He is a black Yankee. Without a drop of white blood in him, he has the energy and 'cuteness and big eye' for his own advantage of a born New Englander. He is not very moral or scrupulous, and the church-members will tell you 'not yet,' with a smile, if you ask whether he belongs to them. But he leads them all in enterprise, and his ambition and consequent prosperity make his example a very useful one on the plantation. Half the men on the island fenced in gardens last autumn, behind their houses, in which they now raise vegetables for themselves, and the Hilton Head markets. Limus in his half-acre has quite a little farmyard besides. With poultry-houses, pig-pens, and corn-houses, the array is very imposing. He has even a stable, for he made out some title to a horse, which was allowed; and then he begged a pair of wheels and makes a cart for his work; and not to leave the luxuries behind, he next rigs up a kind of sulky and bows to the white men from his carriage. As he keeps his table in corresponding style,—for he buys more sugar . . . . than any other two families,—of course the establishment is rather expensive. So, to provide the means, he has three permanent irons in the fire—his cotton, his Hilton Head express, and his seine. Before the fishing season commenced, a pack of dogs for deer-hunting took the place of the net. While other families 'carry' from three to six or seven acres of cotton, Limus says he must have fourteen. To help his wife and daughters keep this in good order, he went over to the rendezvous for refugees and imported a family to the plantation, the men of which he hired at $8 a month. . . . . With a large boat which he owns, he usually makes weekly trips to Hilton Head, twenty miles distant, carrying passengers, produce and fish. These last he takes in an immense seine,—an abandoned chattel—for the use of which he pays Government by furnishing General Hunter and staff with the finer specimens, and then has ten to twenty bushels for sale. Apparently he is either dissatisfied with this arrangement or means to extend his operations, for he asks me to bring him another seine for which I am to pay $70. I presume his savings since 'the guns fired at Bay Point'—which is the native record of the capture of the island—amount to four or five hundred dollars. He is all ready to buy land, and I expect to see him in ten years a tolerably rich man. Limus has, it is true, but few equals on the islands, and yet there are many who follow not far behind him.[17]

In the foregoing instance the transition from slavery to freedom was made on the coast of South Carolina where the Union army

[17] Pearson, *op. cit.*, p. 37n.

was in control. In some places the slaves were turned out without any means of subsistence. Where families had developed a fair degree of organization during slavery, the male head assumed responsibility for their support. In fact, the severe hardships became a test of the strength of family ties. Isaac Lane gives the following account in his autobiography:

> Our owners called us together and told us we were free and had to take care of ourselves. There I was with a large, dependent family to support. I had no money, no education, no mother nor father to whom to look for help in any form. Our former owners prophesied that half of us would starve, but not so. It must be admitted, however, that we had a hard time, and it seemed at times that the prophesy would come true; but the harder the time, the harder we worked and the more we endured. For six months we lived on nothing but bread, milk and water. We had a time to keep alive; but by praying all the time, with faith in God, and believing that He would provide for His own, we saved enough to get the next year not only bread, milk and water, but meat also.

The transition from servitude to freedom took place in many places with scarcely any disturbance to the routine of life established under slavery. The story as told by one who was a participant in the change is as follows:

> There was much commotion in the quarters that Saturday afternoon. The overseer had spread the report that the master desired to meet every man, woman and child on the plantation, at the big gate on the following morning, which was Sunday. So songs were hushed, and about nine o'clock, with bated breath and inexpressible anxiety, all of the slaves waited for the coming of "Mars Dunc." We knew not what he would say.
>
> We had not long to wait. The master had breakfasted, and being assured that we were all ready, undertook the task which so many men shifted to overseer and subordinates—that of informing the slaves of their freedom. I shall never forget how he looked on that day. His matchless figure seemed more superb, if possible, than usual, and the long, gray Prince Albert coat he wore added dignity to grace. He wore a black string tie and a white waistcoat, and altogether I had seldom seen "Mars Dunc" so handsomely dressed. He walked with a sprightly step and his head was held erect and his countenance looked clear and contented.

He began his address in a calm, fatherly voice, as follows: "I have called you together to impart to you, officially, a piece of news that I myself do not regret that you receive. Three days ago Abraham Lincoln, the President of the United States, issued a proclamation whereby you are made free men and women. Some of you have been with me all your lives, and some of you I have bought from other owners, but you have all been well fed and clothed and have received good treatment. But now you are free to go anywhere you please. I shall not drive any one away. I shall need somebody to do my work still and every one of you who wants a job shall have employment. You may remain right here on the farm. You will be treated as hired servants. You will be paid for what you do and you will have to pay for what you get. The war has embarrassed me considerably and freeing you makes me a poorer man than I have ever been before, but it does not make me a pauper, and so I have decided to divide what I have with you. I shall not turn you a-loose in the world with nothing. I am going to give you a little start in life. I have made arrangements for every man and woman to receive ten dollars a piece and every child two dollars. I have also ordered that each family be issued enough food to last them a month. I hope you will be honest and industrious and not bring disgrace upon those who have brought you up. Behave yourselves, work hard and trust in God, and you will get along all right. I will not hire anybody today, but tomorrow all who want to go to work will be ready when the bell rings."

It was a pathetic scene and there was hardly a dry eye amongst us. We had watched the master so closely that I had not seen young Mars Dunc in the crowd and was surprised when he cried out, "Say, Joe, dog-gone it, I told you you would not have to go away. Come on, and let us get our dogs and make Mollie Cottontail cut a jig from the cane patch to the woods." And off to the woods we went in a jiffy.

All told, perhaps there were two hundred Negroes upon the plantation and when the big bell rang they all reported for duty. Mr. Cage, Sr., assigned Isham Stewart over the plow gang; Jeff Thomas over the hoe gang; Doc Lewis, my father, superintendent of the ditch gang—these being considered his most trustworthy men. Mansfield Williams was retained as family coachman, and the author of this book was given to understand that all time not spent in the ditch was to be at the disposal of D. S. Cage, Jr., and of his two brothers, Hugh and Albert. I ran errands and attended them when they were at school to look after the horses.

The devotion of these slaves would make a chapter of itself, but it is sufficient to say that at the writing of this book, Isham Stewart and Jeff Thomas remain upon the plantation, and but for the sarcasm of a schoolmate the author might be there, too. But that is another story and will be related in another place.[18]

Often the emancipated Negro was unwilling to continue as a tenant or a laborer; so we find the more ambitious among them undertaking to buy land:

> Miles and Charlotte worked for Doctor Ridley until the summer of 1864 when they began life anew on a farm of forty-eight acres, upon which they had made an initial payment to their former master. . . . .
>
> By 1874, Miles paid the last dollar on his farm which had furnished a home for his wife, Charlotte, his seventeen children, and his sisters-in-law, Jane and Sissey. Just when he was able to rest from his labors, he was taken ill, and in the spring of 1875 he died.
>
> There was one request that Miles made on his death-bed, after he had called his family around him, and that was for Elijah to take care of Charlotte and the farm. Although Elijah was only seventeen years old, he had shown ability in dealing with the business of the farm. Each child had an equal portion of the farm for his inheritance, and all were to contribute to the support of their mother and her sisters.
>
> However, farm life appealed less and less to all except Elijah. He contracted to buy the inheritances of the other children and assumed the care of his mother. He was able the first year to raise four or five bales of cotton and several hundred bushels of corn and potatoes.[19]

Here we have a well-organized family under the authority of the father starting out after emancipation as tenants, then later undertaking to purchase land, and finally becoming small independent farmers. The transition from slavery to freedom was made with little interruption of the habits acquired during slavery. The schooling which the father had received as a responsible person on the plantation enabled him to assume the responsibilities and duties of a free man. Upon the father's death, the responsibility for the maintenance of the family and direction of the property was passed on to the oldest son, who, in acquiring subsequently the interests of his brothers and sisters, assured the continuance of the family group.

Two general tendencies are manifest in the fortunes of the Negro family during the period of its adjustment to the state of freedom.

[18] Lewis, *op. cit.,* pp. 12-14.
[19] Fisher, *op. cit.,* pp. 8, 11-12.

First, following the collapse of the slave regime, the families that had achieved a fair degree of organization during slavery made the transition without much disturbance to the routine of living. In these families the authority of the father was firmly established, and the woman in the role of mother and wife fitted into the pattern of the patriarchal household. Moreover, in assuming the responsibilities of his new status, the father became the chief, if not the sole, breadwinner. Sometimes he acquired land of his own and thereby further consolidated the common interests of the family group. Second, the loose ties that had held men and women together in a nominal marriage relation during slavery broke easily during the crisis of emancipation. When this happened, the men cut themselves loose from all family ties and joined the great body of homeless men wandering about the country in search of work and new experience. Sometimes the women, chiefly those without children, followed the same course. But more often the woman with family ties, whether she had been without a husband during slavery or was deserted when freedom came, became responsible for the maintenance of the family group. Since often her sexual contacts continued to be of a more or less casual nature, she found herself, as in slavery, surrounded by children depending upon her for support and parental affection. Thus motherhoood outside of institutional control was accepted by a large group of Negro women with an attitude of resignation as if it were nature's decree. In the three succeeding chapters we shall follow the career of the Negro family where motherhood has been free on the whole from institutional and communal control and the woman has played the dominant role.

CHAPTER VI

UNFETTERED
MOTHERHOOD

Those who were in a position to observe the Negroes after emancipation have left vivid accounts of their demoralized family and sex relations. A quarter of a century after the Civil War one observer, Phillip A. Bruce, thought that illegitimacy was increasing on the plantations of the South. He wrote at the time:

> The number of illegitimate children born to unmarried negresses is becoming greater every year, but this, instead of being a lasting stain on their reputations or a stumbling-block in the path of their material thrift, is an advantage when regarded from a practical point of view. If these children have come to an age when they are old enough to work, then they constitute a valuable dowry to whoever marry their mothers, such women occupying somewhat the position of widows with considerable property at their command, which they confer absolutely upon their husbands at the hour of marriage.[1]

Even as late as the opening of the present century an investigator reported that it was practically impossible to compute the percentage of illegitimacy among plantation Negroes. "Of forty couples on Cinclaire," he wrote, "who reported themselves as married, and who were known well by the head overseer, only 20 were legally married in the church or by the civil authorities. This would indicate that only 50 per cent of the married persons, so reported, were legally married."[2] The high rate of illegitimacy on this plantation

---

[1] Phillip A. Bruce, *The Plantation Negro as a Freeman* (New York, 1889), pp. 19-20.
[2] J. Bradford Laws, *The Negroes of Cinclaire Central Factory and Calumet Plantation, Louisiana* (U. S. Department of Labor Bull. 38, January, 1903, pp. 102-3.

was hardly typical of conditions among the rural Negroes but probably reflected the extreme social disorganization on the industrialized plantations. At the present time illegitimacy among the rural Negroes, though only approaching this figure in relatively few isolated cases, is still high when compared with the situation among the whites.

Although we have no precise measure of the extent of Negro illegitimacy in rural communities, our most reliable sources of information indicate that from 10 to 20 per cent of the Negro children are born out of wedlock. The colored illegitimacy rate in rural areas of the southern States in 1936 was 15.4 per cent. In the rural areas of Kentucky, during the years 1920, 1924, and 1925, not more than 10 per cent of the Negro births were illegitimate, while in Maryland such births amounted to 16-18 per cent. Not only do these wide variations appear among the various southern States for which we have reports, but similar variations can be noted within the same state. A survey of rural illegitimacy in Orange County, North Carolina, for the years 1923-27 showed that about 8 per cent of the Negro births were illegitimate.[3] This was much lower than the rate for the entire Negro population in the state where the rate had mounted from 12.8 in 1921 to 17.3 in 1930. Although this increase was probably due to the movement of Negroes into urban areas where illegitimacy rates are generally higher, there are rural areas in the South where illegitimacy is more frequent among Negroes than in urban areas. For example, in the relatively isolated and stable Negro population on St. Helena Island T. J. Woofter, Jr., in *Black Yeomanry* (1930) estimates that 30 per cent of the births are illegitimate. In the Birth-Registration Area, the percentage of illegitimate birth (among live births) for the years 1940 to 1943, were 16.9, 17.6, 17.0 and 16.5 respectively.[4] These differences in illegitimacy rates, even where they are approximately accurate, are not a measure of the social significance of the phenomenon in the various communities, for statistics on illegitimacy are only an enumeration of the

[3] Wiley Britton Sanders (director), *Negro Child Welfare in North Carolina: A Rosenwald Study* (Chapel Hill, 1933), p. 282.
[4] *Vital Statistics of the United States*, Part II, Washington, 1945, p. 12.

violations of the formal requirements of the law. Only when we view illegitimacy in relation to the organization of Negro life in the South does its social significance become apparent.

In the region stretching from North Carolina to eastern Texas the majority of the rural Negro population are living under a modified form of the plantation. Although the slave quarters have disappeared and the school bell that in some cases formerly called slaves to labor now breaks the silence of the most solitary regions, Negro life follows the folkways that emancipation modified but did not destroy. Hundreds of thousands of landless peasants still look to their white landlords for meager advances in food and clothing until "the crop is made." And when the crop, which is usually cotton, is sold, the Negro "signs up" for another year. Whether he gets a new pair of overalls for himself or a new cotton dress for his wife or receives a larger or smaller "advance" at the store, all depend upon the price of cotton. Thus the ignorant Negro peasant's life moves in an orbit formed by great economic forces beyond his control or understanding.

But, in submitting to an inescapable fate, the Negro still feels that through prayer and religion he can soften his hard lot in this world or at least find compensation for it in the next. Therefore, the church remains the most important institution, enlisting his deepest loyalties and commanding his greatest sacrifices. When an old woman who eked out a living on a small "patch" that was once a part of a large plantation in Alabama said, "I plants and pray Jesus it increase," she expressed a faith that inspires the efforts of many a Negro peasant. Another woman who expressed her resignation sardonically with the remark, "Colored folk has no chance; white folks can bring back slavery if they wants," was an exception. For she had been as far as Ohio once and had seen something of the world. But the majority of these simple peasant folk are concerned less with human arrangements than with divine dispensation. Hence, their preoccupation with thoughts of God, who has brought them "through many storms" and "held back the hand of death," as a Negro prayed at the funeral of one of the leaders in his community. Death, the ever present specter, releases one from the poor habitation of the flesh and, if all acounts are right with God, permits one to enter "a building of God not made with hands."

However destitute of worldly goods one may be, he bears his lot patiently as long as he is consoled by the prospect that his burial will be attended by the pageantry for which these rural Negro funerals are noted. The lament of one old woman, "If I die today or tomorrow I ain't got a penny to bury me," voiced the despair of one who had lost the last consolation that life has to offer. Consequently, organizations for mutual aid are chiefly for the purpose of securing its members a proper burial. Even the poorest member of the community scrapes together a few pennies each month in order to pay his dues in the "burial 'sociation" or the 'nevolent." The chief appeal of the more formal and rational organizations like insurance companies is that they will enable one to be "put away right."

The advent of the insurance company is indicative of the process by which the isolation of these regions is being broken down. Concrete highways are beginning to penetrate the most remote parts of the South. Along these avenues of communication new ideas as well as new means of transportation are finding their way into these twilight zones of civilization. By means of these highways an old automobile brings a modern city as close as a town was before. A trip to the cinema in the city opens up an undreamed world of romance and adventure. Better schools are bringing in better-educated teachers to give new ideas to the younger generation. The men who can no longer depend upon cotton seek a living on the roads, at the mills, and at logging and turpentine camps, while the women go to town to work as maids or cooks. The migrations during the first World War uprooted many from the old ways of life to which they can never return. The effect of these various changes has been to destroy the simple folkways and mores and to create confusion in thought and contradictions in behavior.

Illegitimacy in a community in this area is affected by all these social and economic forces. For example, the fact brought out in a survey of 612 families in a section of Macon County, Alabama, in 1931, that 122 women in 114 of these families had had 191 ille-

gitimate children means little unless these cases are seen in relation
to the social and economic organization of Negro life. In some cases
the illegitimacy had taken place during the disorganization following
emancipation. For example, there was the case of an old woman,
who has born "Christmas Eve before Freedom Year," working with
her daughter on a "one-horse farm" which was sublet from a more
prosperous Negro tenant. Her father had been sold away from his
first wife during slavery. She was the only survivor among thirteen
children whom her father had by a second wife. When she was
fifteen, she was married to her first husband, of whom she said, "I
tried nineteen years to make a husband out of him but he was the
most no 'count man God ever made. Since I seen I could make no
husband out of him I left him." It was during the next twelve years
when, being "so glad to be free and going about," she "found her
twenty-seven year old daughter." When she decided to remarry,
according to her story, she went to the judge for a divorce, but he
told her, "If that no 'count man has been away from you twelve
years you are already divorced and can marry any time you want."
She left her second husband after seventeen years. Concerning her
break with him she said, "Me and him parted; I ain't seen nor heard
from him since. They tell me he is dead." This old woman, unlike
many others, was not converted until she was fifty-six. Although
she does not attend church regularly, she is convinced that "God
don't want nothing but pure in heart."

The career of the daughter has been similar to that of her mother.
She had three children by a man to whom she was married. After
the death of her husband she started "slipping up on the hill" to see
a man who was the father of the baby that she was expecting in a
few days. Although this woman was "moral" to the extent that she
boasted that she did "not bother any other woman's husband," she
was seemingly unconscious of the moral significance of motherhood
outside of marriage. The father of her unborn child wanted to marry
her, but she was unwilling to marry him because she did not "want
to be bothered with a husband" and was glad that her first husband
died. Instead of being ashamed of her pregnancy, she was proud of
the fact that she was to become a mother and had been congratulated

by the women in the neighborhood on her fertility. Some months later this woman with her four children and their grandmother were living apparently contented in the two-room shack with a sheet-iron covering where they had been four years. But how much longer one cannot say, for the old grandmother remarked, "Hit ain't good to stay in one place; jes gets tired; I'll be gone from here t'reckly."

This woman was not alone in her attitude toward motherhood outside of marriage. The same attitude was apparent in the case of the daughter of the sixty-five-year-old woman whose husband "jes swole up with dropsy and died." The daughter was one of three living children out of ten. The mother said that her children "jes got sick and died with fever and pneumonia." The mother and daughter were working as day laborers for fifty cents a day. Although the mother boasted that she had been married only once and had lived with her husband forty years, she remarked with seeming indifference that her daughter with a five-year-old child was not married. She added, concerning her daughter, "She started to get married, but didn't; liable to marry after while."

The daughter, on her part, appeared completely unconscious of any violation of the mores in having children outside of marriage. All that she seemed to be aware of was that she loved her child and would not be separated from it for anything because, according to her, " 'tis all the company I got back here." She was still having sex relations infrequently with the father of her child whom she had gone with "a pretty good while." The prospect of having another child did not disturb her because, as she said, "Sometimes I wants another child to match this one." But that she should marry before having another child seemed to her quite unnecessary and irrelevant to the matter of motherhood.

The attitudes of these women indicate that they regard sex relations as normal behavior during courtship which may or may not lead to marriage. When it results in the birth of a child, certain obligations are thereby imposed upon the mother. These obligations are the obligations which every mother should feel toward her offspring. The unmarried mother is as sensitive as the legally married mother to what is expected of the woman who is a mother. A certain distinction attaches to being fruitful. To say that a woman "never did find anything," meaning that she has never had a child, may imply disparagement as well as commiseration. Motherhood signifies maturity and the fulfilment of one's function as a woman. But marriage holds no such place in the esteem of many of these women. If they marry the father of their illegitimate offspring, it is not due to the fact that the woman regards it as an obligation on the part of the man. He may suggest marriage because he wants someone to make a home for him and he in return is willing to provide subsistence for his family. The woman's response to the suggestion of marriage will depend upon a number of considerations.

Often the parents may think that their daughter is too young to assume the duties of a wife. Here we should note that in many of these rural communities where relationships are sympathetic and informal and marriage and the family do not have an institutional character, the father of the girl's child is not guilty in the eyes either of her family or of the community of any offense against the integrity of her family. When a conventional social worker remonstrated with an expectant mother for not marrying the father of her child, on the grounds that she should do so in order to give the child a name, the woman naively responded: "Yes mam, I'se gwine to gi' it a name."

Thirty-three of the 122 unmarried women referred to above were daughters living at home with their children begotten out of wedlock. One of these women was one of three daughters whose parents were working a "one-house farm" for a bale of lint cotton as rental and were receiving two dollars and a half a month as an "advance" for food. They had worked on one place twelve years, but, like many of these tenants, had "jes' got tired and 'cide to move." During the previous year their former landlord had taken their cow, and they received seed from the Red Cross. When the fifteen-year-old daughter became a mother, she was expelled from church. The mother's indifference toward the action of the church was expressed in her comment: "Dey told me dey put her out of church; dat's de' rules." But, so far as she was concerned, she did not want her daughter to marry. The illegitimate child, for whom the grandmother had got a name from a piece of newspaper, was taken into the family.

Again, the woman may not want to marry because of the obligations which marriage imposes. One woman did not marry the father of her child when he proposed it to her because "he was too mean." Even when for any reason the couple do not marry, the man may continue to visit the woman and bring presents in the form of clothes for the child. Sometimes this association continues until the couple decide to marry and work on their own. Of the same 122 women, mentioned above, who had had illegitimate children, 24 were married, and 14 of these were married to the father of their illegitimate offspring. One young couple who had been married five years and was working thirty acres for "a little bale of cotton" rental had left their illegitimate child with her mother. Generally, however, the children before marriage are reared along with the other children. Whether the wife's children are his or not, the husband will take them into the family. A couple who were day laborers had a child in the family whom the woman had before marriage. He expressed his approval of the presence of the child with the explanation that, when his wife had the child, she did not belong to him. The husband may also bring his share of illegitimate children to the family group when he marries. In some cases both husband and wife may start their married life each with illegitimate children; and, as it sometimes happens, the husband may add his after marriage.

A description of one of these families in which illegitimate children have the same status as those born in wedlock will make clearer the character of these family groups, which are held together by ties of sympathy and through co-operation in making a living:

> The husband, fifty-six, and wife, forty-five have been married for twenty years. They have had eight children all of whom are living except one. Their children are grown and distributed as follows: on a neighboring plantation there are two married sons, one with eight children and the other with three, and an unmarried daughter with a child. The other three daughters are married, one twice, with children, and are living on as many different plantations. The seventh child is a son thirty-one years old who was born to the husband and wife when they first began their sexual contacts. The family group as it is now constituted consists of the husband, his wife and the husband's illegitimate twenty-three-year-old daughter with her illegit-

imate child ten months old. After the man and woman finally married, the wife had their oldest son, who was working in the mines in Birmingham, bring her husband's illegitimate daughter home. The family, including the four mentioned, is farming fourteen acres; while the husband supplements the family income by working as a carpenter's helper on a government building ten miles away. Neither the unmarried mother nor any other member of the family had any complaint to make against the father, especially since he gives the mother anything she requests for the child.

Some of the illegitimate offspring of these women are due to their relations with white men. Although there are indications that these relations are not as widespread as during slavery, they are still responsible for some of the burden which the unmarried Negro mother must bear. The case of a great-grandmother who was just managing to survive on a "small patch" is one of those instances in which the mulatto daughters of these illicit unions follow the example of their mothers. This woman had her first child when she was "in knee dresses going to school," by a white man, who, according to her story, was a county judge. She was later married but did not have any children by her husband whom she left because he had relations with her sister-in-law. However, she had a number of illegitimate children, most of whom were dead, by several men. By one man, who was married, she had six children. Concerning her relation with this man's wife, she said: "Me and his wife got along like two children; had no fuss or nothing." Her half-white daughter had a child by a white man before she was twenty. During the war the daughter, with her mulatto child, migrated to Birmingham and later to the North. The promiscuous sex relations of this woman, who "still frolics and has a beau," had resulted in syphilitic infection which was doubtless responsible for two stillbirths and three miscarriages.

Our account, so far, of illegitimacy in the rural communities in the South would seem to indicate that neither the families of the women nor the community express any moral disapproval of this type of behavior. That this is not universally true is suggested by the remark of the wife in a family that included two of her children before marriage as well as two of her husband's since marriage. She explained, concerning her illegitimate children, that she had had them before becoming a member of the church. In fact, the community expresses its disapproval of moral delinquencies almost exclusively through the church. We have previously noted cases in which the women have been turned out of church because they gave birth to illegitimate children. In those cases the discipline of the church did not appear as a very effective means of social control. As a rule, church discipline amounts to little more than a mere formality, although it may be supported by a genuinely strong sentiment on the part of few individual members. The delinquent may return as soon as she is willing to make a confession of guilt and promise to avoid such behavior in the future. These performances are seldom expressive of any contriteness of heart. As one delinquent remarked smilingly, she returned after a month and "beg' pardon."

The effectiveness of the church as an institution of control over sex behavior is dependent upon the character of the family life and other social relations in these communities. In the better-organized communities where the church and other forms of communal enterprises are supported by families with some property and traditions of regular family life, the church reflects the character of its constituents and in turn controls to some extent their behavior. But among the impoverished and illiterate peasants scattered over the plantations of the Black Belt, even the church is only a poorly organized expression of a weak community consciousness. The really important social bonds are the sympathetic ties existing between the members of the more or less isolated family groups. In some of these families the parents endeavor through strict discipline to prevent their daughters from becoming mothers before marriage. But even the strictest family discipline may prove ineffectual when it is not supported by the opinion of the community and is opposed to what is regarded as normal behavior. Since family feeling rests upon a firmer basis than moral principles, parents may ofttimes accommodate themselves to the disapproved conduct of their children, especially if the latter are grown. This was apparently the situation in the case of the family of an old couple who boasted that they had both been married only once and had been together between thirty-nine and forty years, although their daughter was living with a man near by without being married.

This family, including the husband, his wife, and their seventeen-year-old daughter, was working "a one-horse farm on halves." Unlike most of these tenants, they owned two cows and had a fair garden. Except for two years during the war when they went to Virginia to "public work" on the road, they had been farming forty years. The wife was fifteen when she married and had given birth to thirteen children, seven of whom were dead. Of the four living sons, all of whom were married, two were working in Birmingham and the other two in Louisiana. Although the mother permitted her seventeen-year-old daughter to go to picnics occasionally, she "held her foot to the fire" where boys were concerned. But this discipline seemingly had no effect upon their twenty-nine-year-old daughter who was living just across the road on a twenty-acre farm. This daughter, whose husband had left her for another woman three years previously, was apparently the head of a family of four children. A girl, sixteen, with a two-month-old illegitimate child, and a boy, thirteen, were her own children; while the fourth child was the daughter of her brother who had died in Birmingham. During the past year the mother herself had given birth to a child, presumably illegitimate, that had died.

The explanations of this woman in regard to the illegitimacy of her daughter and the man in the house are typical of the attempts on the part of some of these women to reconcile their behavior with what they know to be the dominant mores. The father of her daughter's illegitimate child, explained the mother, said that he was going to marry her daughter. In regard to the presence of the man in the house, who was probably the father of her dead child, she as well as her parents across the road explained that he was a "boarder" in the house. Nevertheless, the "boarder" was assisting the woman in farming "twenty acres on halves."

The simple folkways of these peasant folk are conflicting more and more with the ideals and standards of the larger world as their isolation is being destroyed. Moreover, the mobility of the population and the wider contacts are destroying the sympathetic relationships that were the basis of the old simple folkways. Some of these women have achieved some sophistication of outlook as compared with the older generation. The breaking-down of the isolation of these communities is probably reflected in the incidence of syphilis among the population. Wassermann examinations of one-fourth of the Negroes in this Alabama county showed positive reactions for 35 per cent of them in 1930. In some families the infection undoubtedly originated through the contacts which the men had with women in logging camps and cities. In other cases it was owing to the more promiscuous relations of the younger generation. For example, the old couple who boasted of forty years of unbroken married life were found to have negative reactions; while the reactions of their daughter and granddaughter across the road with the illegitimate child were positive.

As the women in these rural communities move about and come into contact with the outside world, illegitimacy loses its harmless character in becoming divorced from the folkways of these simple peasants. It becomes a part of the general disorganization of family life, in which the satisfaction of undisciplined impulses results in disease and in children who are unwanted and uncared for. The story of two women living in a two-room shack on a six-acre patch which they were working will show the degradation of some of these women.

> Flora, who claimed to be eighteen but was probably older, and Ora, thirty-five, were third cousins who decided to farm the "six acre patch on halves" with an "advance" of five dollars a month between them. Flora had left home four years previously when her father died. She was unable to get along with her family, consisting of her widowed mother, who had an illegitimate child, two brothers, and two sisters, one of whom also had an illegitimate child. When she was thirteen she began to have sexual intercourse with a boy with whom she continued to associate for three years. But after leaving home, she roamed about and had sexual relations with seven other men with whom she was associated for a few months or so. She was jailed for cutting one of her lovers. Her version of the story was: "Me and him just got into it in Tuskege. He just boy friend of mine. Got into fight. I cut him deep in the arm. White man who raised him had me 'rested." While she was in jail the doctor found that she had "bad

blood." Flora started going with her present boy friend, a chauffeur, when the father of her illegitimate child went off. Ora has had experiences similar to Flora's and was also found to be syphilitic. Her illegitimate eighteen-year-old child stays with her father. Ora lives in one of the rooms with her "boy friend" who visits her occasionally. Men's overalls were hanging in Flora's room, which was furnished with a broken-down bed and a table with a tin water basin. As Flora told her story, she was lying on the bed twitching and moaning with pain which, she said, was due to her ovaries because "it hurts different from female hurts on the side."

The extreme degradation revealed here contrasts sharply with those cases in which illegitimate children are taken into the girl's family or where the mother and her illegitimate offspring form a natural family group held together by maternal feeling. In cases like those just described, motherhood becomes an obstacle to women who have broken all social bonds and are seeking the satisfaction of individualistic impulses. Birth control is practically unknown to these women, although a few have a notion that there are methods for preventing conception. A twenty-four-year-old mother of two children, who was working a "one-horse farm on halves" with an old "auntie" by marriage, was a case of this sort. Her older child was by her husband who had been killed at a mill; while the younger child was by "an old sweetheart" after her husband's death. She had not married this man because "he was too mean." Since, as this woman remarked, "every one pleasures hisself who gets a chance," she wished that she knew how to have sexual intercourse without having children. Significantly enough she often went with her "boy friend" to the cinema and the dances in town and had a slightly romantic notion of sex which was uncommon among these women.

In spite of the novel ideas and new conceptions of life that are slowly penetrating these regions, the great mass of women still bear motherhood patiently; and in many cases they carry on the struggle for existence without the assistance of a man. In the following chapter we shall follow the career of the Negro mother as she has carried on this struggle alone and has thereby assumed a dominant position in family relations.

CHAPTER VII

THE MATRIARCHATE

Only women accustomed to playing the dominant role in
family and marriage relations (if we may regard the slaves as
having been married) would have asserted themselves as the Negro
women in Mississippi did during the election of 1868. We are
told that,

> if a freedman, having obtained [a picture of Grant], lacked the cour-
> age to wear it at home on the plantation in the presence of "ole marsa
> and missus" or of "the overseer," his wife would often take it from
> him and bravely wear it upon her own breast. If in such cases the
> husband refused to surrender it, as was sometimes the case, and hid
> it from her or locked it up, she would walk all the way to town, as
> many as twenty or thirty miles sometimes, and buy, beg, or borrow
> one, and thus equipped return and wear it openly, in defiance of hus-
> band, master, mistress, or overseer.[1]

These women had doubtless been schooled in self-reliance and
self-sufficiency during slavery. As a rule, the Negro woman as wife
or mother was the mistress of her cabin, and, save for the interference of master or overseer, her wishes in regard to mating and
family matters were paramount. Neither economic necessity nor
tradition had instilled in her the spirit of subordination to masculine
authority. Emancipation only tended to confirm in many cases the
spirit of self-sufficiency which slavery had taught.

When emancipation came, many Negro mothers had to depend

[1] A. T. Morgan, *Yazoo; or, on the Picket Line of Freedom in the South* (Washington, D. C., 1884), p. 232.

upon their own efforts for the support of themselves and their children. Their ranks were swelled by other women who, in seeking sex gratification outside of marriage, found themselves in a similar situation. Without the assistance of a husband or the father of their children, these women were forced to return to the plow or the white man's kitchen in order to make a livelihood for their families. From that time to the present day, as we have seen in the preceding chapter, each generation of women, following in the footsteps of their mothers, has borne a large share of the support of the younger generation. Today in the rural sections of the South, especially on the remnants of the old plantations, one finds households where old grandmothers rule their daughters and grandchildren with matriarchal authority. Sometimes their authority dates from the days following emancipation when, in wandering about the country, they "found" their first child.

It is, of course, difficult to get a precise measure of the extent of these maternal households in the Negro population. The 1940 census showed a larger proportion of families with women heads among Negroes than among whites in both rural and urban areas of the South. Moreover, it also appeared that in the Southern cities a larger proportion of Negro families were under the authority of the woman than in the rural areas. In the urban areas of southern States 31.1 per cent of the Negro families were without male heads while the proportion for rural-nonfarm areas was 22.5 per cent and for rural-farm areas 11.7 per cent. In the rural-nonfarm areas of southern States from 10 to 28 per cent of the Negro families were without male heads; while in the rural-farm areas the proportion ranged from less than one to 15 per cent. In the rural-farm areas tenant families had a much smaller proportion with women heads than owners, except in those States where a modified form of the plantation regime is the dominant type of farming. For example, in the rural-farm area of the southern States in 1940, 10 per cent of Negro tenant families and 16 per cent of Negro owner families were without male heads. Although rural areas showed a smaller proportion of families without male heads than urban areas, still it is in the rural areas of the South that we find the maternal family functioning in its most primitive form as a natural organization.

The true conjugal relation of the woman head is most often revealed in the histories of their marital experiences. The divorced, and in some cases the widowed, in published statistics are often in fact merely separations, since divorce is regarded by many of these people as an individual affair not requiring legal sanction. As we shall see below, "divorce" in one case consisted in giving the man a "scrip." On the whole, in many of the small rural communities, there is a vague notion concerning the legal requirements for divorce. One man said that he did not need a divorce from his wife because "she was in one county and me in another." Another man considered himself divorced when his wife was sentenced to jail for cutting a woman. Many of the women who were heads of families have been married and in some cases often married. They have often broken marital ties and remarried without a legal divorce. On a plantation in Alabama a woman near sixty, who worked a "one-horse farm" with her son, recounted the story of her three marriages. Her father, who had been "raised up under the hard task of slavery," had sent her as far as the fourth grade. Then her marriage career began. Of the first two husbands she said:

> Me and him separated and he divorced me. Me and the second one got married and come down here. Then he fought me when this boy [her son] was six months old. We fought like cats and dogs. One night I had to call Uncle R—— P——. He asked me for his 'vorce and I gi' it to him. I just wrote him a "scrip." I got a man to write it for him.

Her third husband, who had been dead seven years, died, according to her testimony, of high blood pressure, leakage of the heart, and kidney trouble. Another old woman had a similar story to tell. When she announced "all my children done married off," she was speaking of two sets of children—one by her husband and another by the man with whom she lived after having "divorced" her husband. According to her story, her husband had told her that he wanted a divorce, and she had replied that he was welcome to it. But as to the reason back of the breaking of the marriage bond, she exclaimed: "He didn't work to suit me, and I didn't work to suit him."

This last naïve statement concerning divorce reveals much in regard to the nature of marriage and its dissolution among these simple folk. Among these people we come face to face with marriage as it probably existed in the early stages of social development. Marriage as an institution rooted in the mores does not exist in many places. Where it has developed any degree of permanency and the couples are seemingly bound by conjugal affection, more fundamental interests than mere sentiment have been responsible in the beginning for the continuance of the association in marriage. When one woman was asked whether she was married, her reply was: "Me and my husband parted so long, done forget I was married." What marriage means to many of these women was expressed by a woman who spoke of herself as "Miss," although she had been married twice, and wanted another husband to help her work. Her first husband, whom she had married when she was fifteen, was killed by lightning after they had been together twelve years. A second husband had been dead two years, and at present she was making a living by "hoeing and fertilizing" on a place that, she said, "they tells me it was here in slavery times." Her only idea indicating preference in regard to a husband was that he must be dark, for "if he is most too light, he looks too much like white folks." But the main factor in regard to the partner in marriage was that he should co-operate with her in farming. As she remarked, "I am looking for someone to marry, so I can get on a farm and kinda rest." She had hoped that her son in Cleveland, who had served in France during the war, would relieve her from going into the field each day in the hot sun; but he had written that he was sick, and she had sent for him to come home.

Where marriage is regarded chiefly as a means of co-operation in the task of making a living and does not rest upon an institutional basis, it is not surprising to find some of these women speaking of "working with a man" as a sufficient explanation of their living together. This was the explanation offered by an illiterate buxom black woman of forty or more who had been farming "right round twenty-five acres" for two years with a man who was separated from his wife a quarter of a mile away because they "just couldn't get along and separated." She had had several children without being married, the only living one being cared for by her mother. But some of these cases of irregular unions are not the result of the naïve behavior of simple folk. We have seen in the preceding chapter how in one case both the parents of the unmarried mother and the unmarried mother herself attempted to represent the man in the house as a "boarder." Bishop Coppin related the following concerning marital relations after the Civil War and attempts on the part of the church to break up such irregular unions:

> Then there were other kinds of irregular living by Church members when there was no one to prefer 'charges and complaints,' and bring the transgressor to book. A man might be a member of the Church, and yet be 'stopping' with a woman to whom he was not married. Or, in the irregular union, the woman might be the Church member. These are cases where even Common law marriage was not claimed. Both parties going for single. The man just a 'star boarder.' But, in this general clean up at Friendship, under the new regime, such parties had to choose between getting married, or facing charges for immoral conduct. Dear old Friendship now became the Ecclesiastical Court House, as well as the Church. For any of the above named lapses, hitherto unnoticed, a member was liable at any 'Quarterly Meeting' to be called to face charges and complaints.[2]

Wherever we find this consciousness of the violation of the dominant mores or a certain sophistication, the couples will attempt to represent their union as some socially approved relationship or as conventional marriage. This was the case with a brickmason, forty-seven, who had been educated at Tuskegee Institute. He was living with a woman, twenty-two, on a "patch" of five acres for which they were paying sixty dollars rental a year. The woman was a mulatto who thought that she had some Indian blood. Her mother was farming with eight children, while her father had deserted the mother and gone to Detroit. This irregular union was especially convenient for the man, since it was outside the public opinion and

[2] L. J. Coppin, *Unwritten History* (Philadelphia, 1920), pp. 126-27.

sensure of the group with whom he spent much of his time in town.

Some of these irregular unions are due to the association between white men and colored women. The prevalence of these associations is determined by several factors. They are found more frequently in the small towns of the South than in the isolated rural regions where large numbers of Negroes have been concentrated for nearly a century or longer. The proportion of mulattoes in the Negro population is a measure of the isolation of the Negro and of the amount of contacts between the races. In Issaquena County in the Yazoo-Mississippi Basin only 10 per cent of the families were mulattoes in 1910, while in Hertford County, North Carolina, 40 per cent of the families showed mixed blood. In Hertford County, where in 1910, about 35 per cent of the women who were heads of families had had only irregular relations with men, the association between white men and colored women continued on a large scale for a long period after slavery. These irregular unions were generally formed by white men and mulatto women. According to our figures, 28 of the 108 women heads of families who had carried on irregular relations were mulattoes. In 1920 there were 19 mulattoes among the 47 women in this class. The change in these figures is indicative of an actual decrease in these types of associations; for in this community there has been a conscious effort on the part of the colored population to repress such associations and enforce conventional standards of conduct. Bishop Coppin (*op. cit.,* pp. 130-31) recites the following typical case in which a white man forced the Negro community to accept his colored concubine:

> The father being a man of means and influence, defied public sentiment, and held family number one in servile submission. But his influence did not stop there; he would have it understood that his mistress must not be Churched, but rather must be regarded as a leading spirit at the Church to which she belonged, and which he gave her means to liberally support. If he had power enough to enslave his own legitimate family, forcing even the wife into unwilling silence, and besides, to so maintain himself in society as to prevent a general protest, it is not to be wondered at, that the Colored Community, dependent, perilous, would also hold its peace.

A minister, who established a school in Hertford County and has worked there nearly a half-century, related the following concerning these associations when he began his work there:

> When I first came here I often heard mulatto women say that they would rather be a white man's concubine than a nigger's wife. The mulatto women and white men claimed that since the law did not allow them to marry and they had only one wife that it was all right. Conflict over this almost broke up P—— P—— Baptist Church. There was a scattering of families, many going north and passing for white. The feeling was such between mulattoes and blacks that they wanted me to place the mulattoes on the second floor and the blacks on the third floor of the school dormitory. I mixed them up in the school purposely and got black evangelists for the church.

Although frequently the white man was not married and lived with his mulatto concubine as his wife, this was not invariably the case. It is also true that in many instances the economic advantages which these mulatto families enjoyed were due to the provision which the white father had made for his concubine and his mulatto children. In the following document, which was furnished by a woman who was born before emancipation, we have the case of a white man with a white family as well as a colored family. In this case, the white father made no provision for his colored family:

> I wanted to be somebody and some account. I was ashamed of my back family [family background]. I hated that my mother did not marry a colored man and let me live like other folks with a father, and if he did not make much he could spend that with us. I despised my white father and his folks. I might have loved him if he had noticed and treated us like other folks. His wife died after a while, but she never fussed as I know of about his colored family. He had large children, some grown. He did not stay at home. He would have the work done by Negro slaves. He had lots of slaves and families of slaves. He must have had, with the children, fifty or seventy-five slaves in all. He was right good to them. He would eat at my mother's house. She called him "the man," and we called him "the man." He would come in at bed-time; and even before his wife died, he would come and stay with my mother all night and get up and go to his house the next morning. His children despised us and I despised them and all their folks, and I despised him. We had to work hard, get no education, and but a little to live on. He had plenty of property but

didn't give mother one thing. Her uncle gave her home and field and we had to work it.

The disgust which this woman felt toward her home life caused her to leave it and establish one based upon conventional moral standards. Referring to her home, she said, "It was so ugly and common that I meant to get married and leave that hateful place. It is true I loved the man I married; but I had as much in mind in getting married to leave that place as I had in marrying for love."

While the association between white men and colored women in this community has been on a larger scale than in most southern communities, it is similar to many other areas in the South where there has been a long history of such associations dating from slavery. Just as the phenomenon in this community has declined because of the growing sentiment against it on the part of both blacks and whites, it has decreased in other areas of the South.

Let us turn our attention to these women in their role of mothers and as heads of their families. Some of the separated and widowed in Issaquena County in 1910 had given birth to as many as twenty children or more. Even among those who had had only irregular relations with men there were women with from ten to twelve children. But the actual number of children in these families was often small because of the numerous miscarriages and stillbirths and the high infant mortality which we find among them. The following case of a woman who had two stillbirths and three miscarriages was not unusual, for some women had lost as many as nine or ten children.

This woman had no conception of her age for she thought that she might be about 20, although later she said that her husband had been dead nearly 20 years. She was living in a one-room shack, covered with sheet iron, with a daughter's illegitimate 12 year old son, and her own illegitimate 14 year old daughter. These two children were helping her to hoe and plow a "one-horse farm on halves," instead of attending school. The family was receiving an "advance" of $4.00 a month. Another daughter, who "had taken sick with a misery in the head and breast," died suddenly during the past year. The mother tried to get a doctor; but as she said concerning her landlord, "Dis white man don't gi' you doctor like talking." Although it was difficult to get a clear history of her pregnancies and children, it appeared that she had had three children while married and three illegitimate children after the death of her husband. Two of these latter children were stillborn and in addition she had three miscarriages. These stillbirths and miscarriages were evidently due to syphilitic infection since she showed a positive Wasserman reaction.

This woman and her children had been on the present location for three years; and, although she had moved away from her former landlord because she "got tired of working for nothing," she "hadn't seen a nickel for a year." With her "advance" of four dollars a month, she and the children were living on "dry meat and corn bread," with an occasional dinner of greens from her garden on Sundays. Her situation was not unlike that of many other women who were heads of families.

The struggle of these women to get a living for themselves and the children who are dependent upon them is bound up with the plantation system in the South. Most of the mothers are tenants; and many of the relatively large group of unknown home tenure are either living with their parents who are tenants or are themselves mere farm laborers. They work from year to year "on halves" or are supposed to pay a stipulated amount of cotton and receive in return an "advance" in food, and, occasionally, clothes at the store. Mothers living with their parents and mothers with grown sons to aid them are able to work larger farms than women depending solely on their own labor. Consequently, mothers with young children are generally only able to work a "patch," comprising four to six acres. The "advances" in food, which often consist of corn meal and fat bacon, are correspondingly small. They supplement this with vegetables from their gardens when the dry weather does not destroy them. As the result of this restricted diet, we find both mothers and children suffering from pellagra. Statistics indicate that eight Negroes in Macon County died in 1930 of pellagra, but we know little concerning the numerous cases that did not result in death.

One could scarcely find a more depressing picture of abject poverty and human misery than that presented by a young black woman, who had had two illegitimate children by different fathers, living in a one-room shack on a plantation in Alabama not many miles from Tuskegee Institute. The father of one child was somewhere over the creek, while the father of the other was "in Montgomery or somewhere." One child had evidently died of undernourishment and neglect. The young mother sat on a broken stool in the middle of the room furnished only with an iron cot covered with filthy rags. From her dried-up breast a baby, half-strangled by whooping cough, was trying to draw nourishment. Bare-footed and clothed only in a cotton waist and dress pinned about her, she was rocking the child as her body swayed listlessly to an inarticulate singsong tune. On the cold embers in the fireplace lay a skillet containing the remnants of corn bread made only with water, because the landlord had refused fat meat as a part of her "advance." That same morning he had driven her with blows from her sick child to work in the field.

Not all mothers with children depending upon them for support sink to the level of poverty and misery of the woman portrayed above. Although as tenants they receive no accounting from their landlords, many of them manage to get adequate clothing and food of sufficient variety to keep them in health. In the plantation area the relatively few owners are better off so far as the necessities of life are concerned. But ownership of land is not always an infallible sign of independence and comfort. The system of credit and the relations of the races in the former stronghold of slavery cause even landowning mothers to lead a precarious existence. In regions like Hertford County, North Carolina, outside of the area where agriculture is still dominated by the plantation system, homeownership signifies much more independence and comfortable living. No single crop dominates the agricultural activities; and, consequently, even during times of economic stress there may be an abundance of food for consumption. Moreover, in situations like that in the North Carolina county, where colored women have lived with white men, the struggle for existence has been relieved by the provision which the white fathers often made for their concubines and children.

The maternal family is not held together solely by the co-operative activities incident to farming; it is also a natural organization for response. Although some women, after a brief marriage career, return to their mothers' households in order to work with them at farming, many others return to the family group for satisfactions of an emotional nature. There was, for instance, a thirty-eight-year-old woman who had left her husband after five years of marriage, because, as she said, she "got tired of staying with him" and preferred to "be with mamma and them." She was working on a "two-horse farm" with her brother, who took care of her until the settlement was made at the end of the year. That she usually received nothing at the end of the year was of no importance to her as long as she lived with her mother and brother and sister. The same valuation which she placed upon the intimate and sympathetic contacts afforded by the family group was expressed by a man, when he remarked: "I'm rich; when you have mother and father, you're rich." In fact, in the relatively isolated world of these black peasants, life is still largely organized on the basis of the personal and sympathetic relations existing between the members of the various family groups.

As a rule, the mothers show a strong attachment for their children. This is evident even in the young mothers whose offspring could be mistaken for younger brothers or sisters and are frequently regarded as such. In fact, in this world where intimate and personal relations count for so much, the relation between mother and child is the most vital and is generally recognized as the most fundamental. The rumor that even a starving mother was giving up her children was received by some women as an unpardonable crime against the natural dictates of the human heart. The intense emotional interdependence between mother and child that one so often finds is encouraged by a long nursing period. According to their own testimony, some women have nursed their children until they were three or four years old. Of course, these elemental expressions of love and solicitude for their offspring are often detrimental to the welfare of the children. Many a woman who "jes lives and wuks to feed her chillen" will give her child meat and bread when it is a few days old. This is done, they say, "to strengthen their stomachs." When one mother pointed to her overfed nineteen-year-old daughter as proof of the efficacy of such treatment, she never thought of the possible relation of such treatment to the death of ten of her children during infancy.

The dependence of the child upon the mother, who is the supreme authority in the household, often creates a solidarity of feeling and sentiment that makes daughters reluctant to leave home with their husbands and brings sons back from their wanderings. During World War I Negro soldiers who had been drafted in these rural areas and sent to camps often complained in the manner of children of being torn from their mothers. The mothers on their part show equally strong attachment for their grown sons and daughters. The reason which mothers frequently give for not permitting their daughters to marry the fathers of their illegitimate children is that they were unwilling to part with their daughters. No matter how long a wandering son or daughter has been away from home, mothers rejoice in their return; and, if they hear that their children are sick, they will make great sacrifices to bring them back in order that they may have the ministrations that only a mother can give, or that they may die in the arms of the one who bore them.

As a rule, where we find mothers who do not want their children or neglect them, the sympathetic basis of family relations has been destroyed through the mobility of the population, or life and labor have made children a burden and a hardship. The isolation of these simple communities is being broken down, and "overproduction" in agriculture is sending women and girls to seek a living in town. The old relationships and traditional values are being destroyed, and new wishes, generally indicating an individualization of life-pattern, are becoming dominant. Sometimes children are left at home to be cared for by grandmothers. In spite of these changes, a large proportion of each generation of Negro mothers in these rural areas continue to bear patiently the burden of motherhood and assume responsibility for the support of their children. Their daughters still follow in their footsteps and bring their offspring to the maternal household. Then these mothers are elevated to the dignity of grandmothers, a position which gives them a peculiar authority in family relations and places upon them the responsibility for keeping kindred together.

CHAPTER VIII

GRANNY: THE GUARDIAN
OF THE GENERATIONS

During the Civil War an old slave and his wife attempted to escape from a plantation near Savannah but were caught and returned to their master. While the old man was receiving five hundred lashes as punishment, his wife collected "her children and grandchildren, to the number of twenty-two, in a neighboring marsh, preparatory to another attempt that night. They found a flatboat which had been rejected as unseaworthy, got on board—still under the old woman's orders—and drifted forty miles down the river" to the lines of the Union army. An officer who was on board the gunboat that picked them up said that "when the 'flat' touched the side of the vessel, the grandmother rose to her full height with her youngest grandchild in her arms, and said only, 'My God! are we free?' "[1]

The energy, courage, and devotion of this woman, who was nearly seventy, are characteristic of the role which the grandmother has played in the Negro family. During slavery the Negro grandmother occupied in many instances an important place in the plantation economy and was highly esteemed by both the slaves and the masters. In the master's house she was very often the "mammy" whom history and tradition have idealized because of her loyalty and affection. Because of her intimate relations with the whites, "all family secrets," as Calhoun observes, "were in her keeping; she was the defender of the family honor. The tie of affection between

---

[1] Thomas Wentworth Higginson, *Army Life in a Black Regiment* (New York, 1900), pp. 332-33.

her and her charges was never outgrown. Often she was the con-
fidential adviser of the older members of the household. To young
mothers she was an authority on first babies."[2] Age added dignity to
her position, and "her regime," as Thomas Nelson Page says,
"extended frequently through two generations, occasionally through
three." Writing of her grandmother, a former slave remarks: "She
became an indispensable person in the household, officiating in all
capacities, from cook and wet-nurse to seamstress."[3] From Frederick
Douglass, who was reared by his grandmother and grandfather, we
have the following testimony:

> I infer that my grandmother, especially, was held in high esteem,
> far higher than was the lot of most colored persons in that region.
> She was a good nurse, and a capital hand at making nets used for
> catching shad and herring, and was, withal, somewhat famous as a
> fisherwoman. I have known her to be in the water waist deep, for
> hours, seine-hauling. She was a gardner as well as a fisherwoman, and
> remarkable for her success in keeping her seedling sweet potatoes
> through the months of winter, and easily got the reputation of being
> born to "good luck." In planting time Grandmother Betsy was sent
> for in all directions, simply to place the seedling potatoes in the hills
> or drills; for superstition had it that her touch was needed to make
> them grow. This reputation was full of advantage to her and her
> grandchildren, for a good crop, after her planting for the neighbors,
> brought her a share of the harvest.[4]

The grandmother's prestige and importance were as great among
the slaves on the plantation as among the whites in the master's
house. She was the repository of the accumulated lore and superstition of the slaves and was on hand at the birth of black children
as well as of white. She took under her care the orphaned and
abandoned children. A former slave recalled that the usual scanty
fare of slaves caused her no trouble; for, she wrote, "on my various
errands I passed my grandmother's house and she always had
something to spare for me. I was frequently threatened with punishment if I stopped there; and my grandmother, to avoid detaining me,

[2] Arthur W. Calhoun, *A Social History of the American Family* (Cleveland,
1917-18), II, 284.
[3] L. Maria Child, *The Freedmen's Book* (Boston, 1865), pp. 206-07.
[4] *Life and Times of Frederick Douglass* (Chicago, 1882), p. 14.

often stood at the gate with something for my breakfast or dinner. I was indebeted to her for all my comforts, spiritual or temporal." This same grandmother, because of her dignity and the esteem in which she was held by the community, was bought and emancipated by a kindly old woman. This was done when, at the death of her mistress, she forestalled an attempt to sell her privately to a trader by insisting upon mounting the public auction block with the other slaves. Later she gathered under her care two generations of her descendants.

When emancipation came, it was often the old grandmother who kept the generations together. One who worked with the newly emancipated slaves during and after the Civil War has left us a picture of one of these old women presiding over four generations of descendants. Miss Botume writes concerning Tamar, a robust, merry-looking, middle-aged woman:

> Her mother and grandmother lived in the room with her. She also had three children, one of whom was married and lived there with his wife and baby, which baby the oldest woman was "minding." It was something to see five generations together, all apparently in good condition. At my request, Ned, the young father, took the baby, and all stood in a row. In the old vernacular they would have been called "a prime lot of niggers." I never saw a more fearless and self-contained set. They were all very black, and had been considered valuable, and they knew their own importance.[5]

The sentiments and feelings that lay beneath the quiet dignity and force of these old women are only dimly reflected in the recorded observations of those who knew them in the past. But occasionally we run across a former slave on one of the plantations of the South who forms a link between the past and the present. A grandmother who was a former slave living on a small plot of land that was once a part of a large plantation in Alabama told the following story:

> I was 77 years old this last gone February. I satisfied I'm oldern that, but that's what the white folks gied me when I was freed, but if I don't disremember, that's my sister's age. When war was declared and freedom come, I was nursing and working at the white folks house. They jest got us niggers all mixed up. I remembers well when

[5] Elizabeth Hyde Botume *First Days among the Contrabands* (Boston, 1893), p. 56.

the people was drilling ter free the slaves. That's why I knows I'm oldern that. I ain't got naire child but one son up in Ohio and he ain't a bit a use ter me. Hits hurtin' too ter raise chillen grown and they don't care 'bout you. I been married twice. I had one child by my first husband. That's my son in Ohio I was tellin' you 'bout. I had three chillen by my second husband and all dead 'cept one, that's him. My husband been dead now going on three years. I got one grandchild but hit ain't wid me. The two little orphan chillen I raised, they here wid me. I got four acres of land, me and the chillen. I let them work out fer people so they will come and plow fer us. This my own little house and four acres he left me on. My husband said he wanted his own house. I pays $3.10 fer taxes ever year. Last year, I didn't make naire bale of cotton. Hit wont a half bale. See I hafta 'vide my little land up wid cotton, corn and 'taters. I jest make 'nough ter barely pay my taxes. These little orphan chillen mother dead and father dead too. I'm they great aunt. Me being the oldest one and me being they mother's auntie and the oldest head, that's how I come by them. So me and my husband raised them chillen from leetle bit a things. Sometimes I don't git food, go widout eating all day so's ter leave hit fer them ter eat 'cause they hafta work. I been had them in school, though I has a tough time I send them.

In her explanation of why the responsibility for the care of "her chillen" falls upon her, this old woman expresses the characteristic attitude of the grandmother in her role as "oldest head" in the family. Where the maternal family organization assumes such importance as among a large section of the Negro population, the oldest woman is regarded as the head of the family. Some of these grandmothers will tell you of their courting, which sounds very much like that of their granddaughters' today. Often, instead of having been a prelude to marriage, it culminated in motherhood and the responsibilities which it imposed. Even when they married, sometimes marriage was of short duration, and the responsibility of rearing and supporting their children fell upon them. Thus it has been the grandmother who has held the generations together when fathers and even mothers abandoned their offspring.

Although one old grandmother, whose mother, a centenarian, had just died, announced, "all my chillen done married off," two grandchildren and two daughters who worked part of the time in Montgomery were looking to her for support. With the aid of her son who lived over the hill she was working a plot of land, "not quite a one-horse farm," that was once a part of a large plantation. This old woman boasted that she had been on the place forty years and on the spot thirty years. She was the mother of fifteen children, six of whom were living. In recounting her numerous miscarriages and dead children, she said: "Some come live but didn't live no time, yet three got to be big chillun walkin' 'bout befo' dey dies. One boy got to be eighteen years old. He had dat fever and from dat, spasms and spells, and from spells he fell in de fire and got burnt and never did git over hit. De other two just died with de fever." Of her six surviving children, two were by her husband from whom she separated when she found him unsuitable to work with and four by a man to whom she had never been married. One son, who was living in Montgomery when he was drafted for the war, had not been heard from for years. This son had given his illegitimate child to his mother when it was three years old. She was also taking care of her daughter's child. This daughter, who had been deserted by her husband, was working in domestic service in Montgomery with her sister. Both sisters returned to their mother and looked for support from the land when they could no longer make a living in the city. The old grandmother, who had been ill for years, had denied herself medicine and even the consolation that when she "lay down and die" there would be "something to bury" her, in order that her grandchildren might have clothes and tuition for school. As she labored on her little plot of land, she could always renew her courage and faith by glancing at a near-by dead tree that marked her praying-ground. It was, as she said, "by dat dead tree where de Lord convert my soul at nine o'clock on a Thursday. I was over dere praying; over by dat tree was my praying-ground. I know when de Lord poured his Holy Ghost around my soul. . . . . He told me to go in all parts of de world and tell what he have done for my soul."

On another "one-horse farm," for which she was paying four hundred pounds of lint cotton, a great-grandmother, who was two years and six months old when "Freedom 'clared," was living with her daughter's two grandchildren, one two years old and the other three and a half. Her daughter, who had gone to town to work as a cook and a laundress for a white family, sent something occasionally for her grandchildren. The old great-grandmother remarked concerning her granddaughter, the mother of the two children, "she ain't had ne'er a husband; dese chillen was her 'dopted chillen." The latter part of this statement turned out to mean that they, like their mother, were illegitimate. The old woman had given birth to eleven children, nine of whom were dead. Of the nine children, one was born dead; the oldest died from a fall in Montgomery; her youngest died of worms; while the others died when they were "little bits of things." Her surviving son, she said, had always been thickheaded, and, although he reached the second grade in school, he had never learned anything. With "a piece of a plow" she was making a living for herself and her great-grandchildren, the youngest of whom had a piece of copper hung about his neck to help "his teething." She had to depend upon her own efforts as she had been "kinda separated" from her second husband for two or three years. Her only consolation was that nearly a half-century ago she was converted. "I never felt," she said, "such a feeling in my life. Wouldn't go back to a life of sin for anything. Give me Jesus, if I didn't have a rag, or crumb. God got my soul." As she talked, she began to cry and added despairingly, "I'se had a hard time. Sometimes I feel like I wish I'd never been born. Jest like I travel the path of this world, may the Lord spare me to have something to eat this fall."

The Negro grandmother's importance is due to the fact not only that she has been the "oldest head" in a maternal family organization but also to her position as "granny" or midwife among a simple peasant folk. As the repository of folk wisdom concerning the inscrutable ways of nature, the grandmother has been depended upon by mothers to ease the pains of childbirth and ward off the dangers of ill luck. Children acknowledge their indebtedness to her for assuring them, during the crisis of birth, a safe entrance into the world. Even grown men and women refer to her as a second mother and sometimes show the same deference and respect for her that they accord their own mothers. In spite of the advent of the doctor, who represents the invasion of science and the rational order of civilization in the South, the "granny" is still the dependable figure who presides at the crisis of childbirth. In 1942 in rural Tennessee, 37.6 per cent of Negro life births were attended by midwives; whereas during the same year in Mississippi midwives attended four-fifths of all Negro births. (See the 1942 reports of vital statistics for these states). In some places we can see the transition from the "granny" to the doctor. As one woman remarked: "I had a midwife but got a doctor to get the afterbirth." Although custom and tradition are largely responsible for the continued use of the midwife, the expense of securing a doctor is prohibitive for the majority of these economically dependent folk.

We have the following picture from the Sea Islands of one of these grandmothers who, after becoming too old to act as midwife, has resumed her traditional role as guardian of the younger generation:

> She is seventy-four and no longer able to pursue her profession as midwife, or to engage in active work in the field. From time to time she shoulders her heavy hoe and ties up her hips with heavy cord to "gib stren'th" and does what she can. Through the migration of her daughter to Savannah, she had acquired four grandchildren to care for. The children are able to do some light work in the gathering of compost and cultivation of the crops, but there is no one to do the heavy plowing or hoeing. The land is unfenced so that the animals have to be staked out to forage and constantly watched. All of the children are visibly undernourished and it was quite an experiment at the headquarters of the study to try to fill them up with food and to see how much would be required. Incredible quantities were eaten. When she was asked in the early spring what she had on hand in way of food she said, "Few peas and some cracked corn."[6]

So far we have seen the grandmother in her role as the head of the maternal family among a primitive peasant people. She has often played a similar important role in families, maternal in organization, which have originated through the relations of white men and colored women. In the following excerpt from the family history of a young woman in a secretarial position in Chicago, we see how

[6] T. J. Woofter, Jr., *Black Yeomanry* (New York, 1930), p. 91.

one grandmother is placed at the head of the family line while the other has played the usual role of looking after her daughter's mulatto child:

> My maternal grandmother was a house-servant in a family in the northern part of Alabama at the time of the Civil War. This family owned a large plantation. My grandmother told me that she was a favorite in the house and had her way pretty much. During the third year of the Civil War my mother was born. Her father was the master of the house. My mother has always been very sensitive about her birth and has never wanted to talk about it before her children. When very small my mother was separated from her mother as the latter went to Tennessee because of the activities of the Ku Klux Klan. My mother was reared by her grandmother during the absence of her mother. When my grandmother returned from Tennessee she married a minister and had three sons by this marriage. My mother spent her childhood with the family on a farm in Madison County, Alabama. She helped to care for her three half brothers.

A mulatto dentist in a northern city, who remarked concerning his grandmother, "My grandmother always told me something that always impressed me—that no one in the family was ever convicted of a crime," was only able to trace his family back to the Revolutionary War period because of this grandmother's recollections of her own grandmother. Continuity in this family had been maintained through the female line, since the male progenitors had been white for the first two generations and died at an early age during the next two generations. The first grandmother, according to the traditions which have come down through four generations, was a free woman of color, with a considerable mixture of Scotch blood, and lived in Baltimore. She was "seven years old when the Revolutionary War started and fourteen years old when it ended," so runs the tradition. While a bonded servant for seven years, she was kidnapped, sold as a slave, and taken to Georgia. She became the mother of a child by one of the young men in her master's family just before he left home to study at Oxford. The mulatto child was reared in the house and, when grown, was placed in charge of the domestic affairs of the household. Following the example of her mother, she had a child, who was born in 1832, by a white man. This child, who was the grandmother of the dentist, remained a dominant figure in the family until her death at ninety-six years of age. Although she was married twice during slavery, the deaths of her husbands placed upon her the responsibility of rearing the children. Through her efforts her children were sent to the schools that were established for the freedmen shortly after the Civil War and were thus started on the way to culture and achievement. Similarly we find a prominent physician's mulatto wife, whose mother objected to her being reared as white by her white father, briefly tracing her family through a number of female ancestors who had children by white men. "My great-grandmother was the offspring of a white man and an Indian squaw. She had a child, who was my grandmother, by a Negro. My grandmother had two sets of children: one by a white man, and another by a Negro. My mother was one of the children by a white father." The old great-grandmother was the real head of the family. She gathered up her descendants in Kentucky and took them to the West, where, after keeping a boardinghouse for miners, she acquired money herself through investments in the mines. Later she bought homes for her children and grandchildren and sent several of them to college.

Some of the younger generation of mixed blood give the same testimony concerning their grandmothers' dominating influence in family relations. A mulatto college student, whose grandmother lived apart from her husband after attempting unsuccessfully to "subordinate him," thought that she typified the spirit of the C——— women "who have always demanded and asserted their rights, whatever may be the costs." The mother of this girl had left her husband in the South because he was apologetic when a white man struck her. This student wrote concerning her maternal grandmother:

> My favorite ancestor was my Grandma Ann. I can probably attribute this attachment to the fact that my sisters who knew her have remarked how like her I was in feature, and even tastes. I remember when as a child I would ask my mother some of the things her mother used to do when she was a little girl, and then try to do some of them myself, in an effort to be as much like her as possible. I have a very

definite mental image of what I imagine she must have been like, but I can best describe her by quoting directly from my sister. "Grandma Ann—well now there was a character. Her mother must have been a clever woman to have named her so aptly. She, too, was trained as a special maid to her mistress. She sewed and did beautiful embroidery work. Grandma did not care about and could not do housework not cooking at all. In fact, she seemed to have inherited all the characteristics of a 'Southern lady'—even to petite hands and feet. She was a staunch Presbyterian—the entire family being permitted to attend the white church, which fact attests their high standing among the whites in the community, and consequently they were 'looked up to' by the Negroes. Grandma maintained her independence until the time of her death, near the age of eighty-three." I especially remember her as being extremely thrifty. I judge that she handled the finances mostly in her family, because my mother has often evoked many a good laugh from me by relating instances where her father would have to ask her for money and she would dole it out in little bits.

The Negro grandmother has not ceased to watch over the destiny of the Negro families as they have moved in ever increasing numbers to the cities during the present century. For example, she was present in 61 of the families of 342 junior high school students in Nashville. In 25 of these a grandfather was also present. But in 24 of the remaining 36 families, we find her in 8 families with only the mother of the children; in 7 with only the father; and in 9 she was the only adult member. However, figures cannot give us any conception of the grandmother, unawed and still with her ancient dignity, watching over her children in the strange world of the city. We shall, therefore, let one who has met her daily and portrayed her in all her dignity give a final testimonial:

Great-grandmother hobbles in on crutches, her garments pinned across her chest with a safety pin, and her cap tied on with a black ribbon. But it takes more than crutches and discarded ribbons to abash a colored grandmother. In fact, they are the only grandmothers whom I have ever known to come into their own. They are still persons. They never quail before a stylish granddaughter by so much as the fraction of an inch. If they look like scarecrows, it embarrasses neither the one nor the other. Let the girl be saucy, and one look from her grandmother's dark heavy-lidded eyes hits its mark. Accustomed as I am to the spectacle of white grandmothers idealized according to

Whistler, but relegated in spite of themselves to shawls and chimney corners, these doughty old colored women, physically infirm but spiritually undaunted, who have somehow managed to keep a hold on their progeny, are impressive creatures. I even find it refreshingly rakish, that so many of our fights start over the debated reputation of an old creature muffled in a ragbag. Her girlish escapades still have the power to set her offspring fighting, and one feels that neither she nor they think less of each other for the scrimmage. No other race comes to court whose battles are waged so often in vindication of such ancient dames. And personally I never fail to derive a piquant savor from jousts of chivalry over the long dead flirtations of such bags of bones. Of all people these old women represent the eternal feminine. They have drunk of the fount of youth and have never lost its flavor. Nothing, one feels, but their rheumatism keeps them from joining in the dance of life with their great-grandchildren. Often a white woman loses her head in court and acts uncommonly silly. A colored woman never. She accepts what must be accepted, tosses or nods her head according to how the outcome suits her (they are not hard to please), and marches or hobbles out of the room as she came in, with her dignity unimpaired.[7]

Thus the Negro grandmother stands today, as of old, as the "oldest head" in the House of the Mother. How her authority has been overthrown at times and her regime supplanted by that of the Father of the House will be the subject of the following section.

[7] Eleanor Rowland Wembridge, *Life among the Lowbrows* (Boston and New York, 1931), pp. 169-70.

IN THE HOUSE OF THE FATHER

CHAPTER IX

THE DOWNFALL OF THE

MATRIARCHATE

A worker among the freedmen during the Civil War observed that many men were exceedingly jealous of their newly acquired authority in family relations and insisted upon a recognition of their superiority over women. It was not unnatural that men, whose authority over their wives and their children had been subject at all times to their master's will and limited by the woman's more fundamental claim upon her children, should have exhibited considerable self-consciousness in their new role. But it required something more concrete than the mere formal recognition of the man's superior position to give substance to his authority in the family and to create in him a permanent interest in marriage.

A former slave, who began life as a freedman on a "one-horse farm" with his wife working as a laundress, but later rented land and hired two men, recalls the pride which he felt because of his new status: "In my humble palace on a hill in the woods beneath the shade of towering pines and sturdy oaks, I felt as a king whose supreme commands were 'law and gospel' to my subjects." Whether or not these reflections after a lapse of thirty years were a true representation of the feelings of a Negro husband suddenly possessed of undisputed authority in his household, they, nevertheless, describe the condition under which male ascendancy very often became established in the family. In this family, as in other families in which we have been able to trace the process by which the Negro man acquired a permanent interest in his family and assumed a position of authority, it appears that the subordination of the woman in the economic organization of the family has played an important part. Very often, of course, it is impossible to follow the course of this development from the beginning; for, when we first meet some of these families as they emerge from slavery, the man's interest in his family has already taken root, and masculine ascendancy is a part of the family pattern. Since our immediate concern is with the vast majority of the Negro families that secured their freedom as the result of the Civil War and emancipation, we shall not include in our present discussion families of Negroes and mulattoes who were free before the Civil War. A separate chapter will be devoted to these free Negroes, for it was among them that the Negro family first acquired an institutional character. Likewise, we shall leave for separate consideration the development of family life in the more or less isolated communities comprising persons of Negro, Indian, and white ancestry, located in various sections of the country.

The transition from slavery to freedom required a change in the physical organization of the plantation that had been adapted to gang labor under the direction of an overseer. Slave row was broken up, and tenant houses were scattered over the plantation in order that each family might carry on an independent existence. Where attempts were made to organize the Negroes in squads under an overseer, whom the emancipated Negroes often called "supertender," they proved unsatisfactory because each man felt, as one plantation owner wrote, "the very natural desire to be his own 'boss,' and to farm to himself." A superintendent of a plantation in Florida wrote to the owner concerning this tendency:

> The tendency on the part of hands appears to be to break up in very small squads, as for instance a man with his wife and children; and even if he has no children, to attempt to make a crop with the help of his wife. This might be tried if the negro owned the mule. There is general dissatisfaction expressed by hands with the head men of squads. The latter, it is claimed, are too dictatorial, and do not perform their share of the labor—a great deal of truth in the latter complaint. . . . .[1]

[1] *Florida Plantation Records*, p. 193.

The new economic arrangement placed the Negro man in a position of authority in relation to his family. In some cases, of course, the woman refused to become subject to the authority of her husband. One former slave said that his mother took his brothers and sisters and went to live in Nashville in defiance of his father's decision to remain on his former master's place. A northern-born planter who went to Mississippi immediately after the Civil War found that only the "dissipated and unreliable" among the freedmen were willing to contract to work for him without their families for more than a brief period. As a rule, the men who signed contracts for a three-year period insisted that their families be included in the arrangements to work in the fields.[2] But, in contracting for the labor of the family, the father assumed responsibility for the behavior of his family and whatever went to the credit of the family was in his name. In some cases it appears that the wife was also a party to the contract. For example, a chattel mortgage reads as follows (*Florida Plantation Records,* pp. 582-83):

STATE OF FLORIDA,
JEFFERSON COUNTY,

WHEREAS George Noble Jones, has advanced to us, John Pride and Caroline his wife Forty dollars to enable us to pay for the purchase of said mule named John Bull, and whereas said George Noble Jones has advanced to the undersigned one hundred and seventy six dollars 22/100 on account of supplies, to enable us to feed and clothe ourselves and family we hereby convey to said George Noble Jones the aforesaid mule, this conveyance to be void whenever we shall pay to George Noble Jones or his representatives the aforesaid sum of one hundred and seventy six dollars 22/100 for said advances and the aforesaid sum of forty dollars on account of purchase of said mule. Witness our signature this eighteenth day of February, 1874.

JOHN   ✕ PRIDE
CAROLINE   ✕ PRIDE

Witness

   G. FENWICK JONES
   WALLACE S. JONES

  [2] A. T. Morgan, *Yazoo; or, on the Picket Line of Freedom in the South* (Washington, D. C., 1884), pp. 39-41.

The following entry in a Florida plantation record indicates the new position of the men in the family and their struggle to support their wives and children.

> Ancil's a/c shows $30 odd to his credit. He is very anxious to farm next year. He sayd his family is large and he can't suport it at 50 cts. a day. He wants you to sell him Sam Mule, the one Winter worked this year. He says he would like (as a matter of course he would) to get Sam on a credit for $100.—that he wishes to draw his wages at end of year. Edward Norris (John Henry's brother) would work with him. Ancil and Edward would plant corn in field near old burnt mill and would fence in 12 acres of tobacco house field if they got a showing. . . . . Charles wishes to pull off to himself. Barrach to work with his own family. Old Jimmy would go with Dick. Guy wants to go to himself. Isaac I think will leave Madison will make an effort to rent land.

The pioneer efforts of the freedman after emancipation reflected, as we have seen in a previous chapter, his character and training under the institution of slavery. The man who showed enough character to revolt against those in authority under slavery was often the very man who was most capable of self-direction as a freedman. Concerning a freedman of this type, his employer wrote:

> The one man on this plantation who, as a slave, gave most trouble, so much, in fact, that he was almost beyond control of the overseer, was Lem Bryant. Since he has been freed, he has grown honest, quiet, and industrious; he educated his children and pays his debts. Mr. Barrow asked him, one day, what had changed him so. "Ah, master!" he replied, "I'm free now; I have to do right."

Among the favored classes in the slave population the assimilation of the sentiments and ideas of the whites had gone far by the time emancipation came. In the histories of the families which had their origin among these favored slaves we are able to see the influence of their favored position upon their development after emancipation. In a recently published autobiography of a bishop, we can trace this development, which is typical of the elements in the Negro population, that have built up a stable family life since emancipation. The first significant fact recorded concerning the moralization of the life of the founder of this family is that he became a member of the church. Concerning this step, his son writes:

"In early life, in 1828, when he was fourteen years old he was converted to God: joined the M.E. Church, South; and immediately began to use his influence to induce others to follow in his wake, a Christian service which he dearly loved to the day of his death."[3]

This act evidently had a permanent effect upon the development of his personality, for twenty-eight years later he was licensed to preach and became a leader in the religious life of the slaves. He was typical of the more ambitious slaves, for we learn that "he was a blacksmith and for about twenty years prior to Emancipation he hired his time from his owner and was permitted to travel from plantation to plantation." Other factors were undoubtedly influential in forming his character and stabilizing his family relations:

> He was never sold himself nor was any of his children. His owner held him in such high esteem because of the kind of man that he was, that he never struck him himself nor allowed any one else to strike him. When talking about slavery it was always his proud boast to acclaim that no man ever struck him nor did he ever have an occasion to strike any man.

The very fact that this slave father engaged in semifree economic activities for the maintenance of his wife and children indicates that he had already acquired a strong interest in his family before emancipation. The author of the family history cites an incident concerning the father's devotion to his wife and children which later became a part of the family traditions:

> Perhaps no man had a stronger love for his family and his home than my father. In the maintenance of his family he was often away from home during the week working at his trade but always planned to return on Friday nights or during the day on Saturday. On one occasion, when, working in the Eastern part of Baldwin County he came to the river at the week end to go home, he found the ferryman gone and all the boats on the opposite side. There was no bridge across the river. So he saw that the alternatives confronted him: To turn back, or swim the stream. Being a splendid swimmer and know-

[3] Charles Henry Phillips, *From the Farm to the Bishopric: An Autobiography* (Nashville, Tennessee, 1932), pp. 8-9.

ing that he was expected at home, he plunged boldly into the stream and was soon with those whom he loved.

When families of this type emerged from slavery, they usually resisted the disintegrating effects of emancipation better than families which had not enjoyed such social and economic advantages. As in the case of this family, they had developed a feeling of solidarity and some community of interest under the authority and discipline of the father. After emancipation they generally rented a small farm which they worked co-operatively in order to maintain themselves. The purchase of the farm was generally a significant step in the development of the family since it meant the consolidation of the interests of the family and that the father had a permanent interest in his family. To quote again from the history of the Phillips family, which followed this typical course:

> For several years after emancipation he rented farms paying money rentals sometimes, and at other times such portions of the farm products as were agreed upon by him and the land owner. Three such farms were rented. The first, situated some three miles from Milledgeville, was rather small for his family, for, his children both boys and girls who were large enough, worked on the farm. I recall that he made four bales of cotton and garnered a large quantity of corn, sweet potatoes, fodder, peas, watermelons and other products. . . . . The rental of these three farms with the economic and frugal management of affairs, together with the experience obtained, impressed my father that the time was ripe to begin efforts to purchase for his family and himself a home and farm of their own. So, in consonance with these convictions and praiseworthy ideas, he in 1869 purchased a farm of about 200 acres on the suburbs of the town.

The purchase of a homestead stands out in the history of these families as a decisive event. When another family, already referred to in another place, was finally reunited after slavery, the father began to buy a home not far from the slave homestead where he had lived with his family from 1841 to 1851. The story of the purchase of the home, as related by the daughter and historian of the family, is as follows:

> On July 14, 1868, father bound the bargain with B. F. Guy, July 1, 1868, for a hill adjoining Riverdale, containing ten acres, more or less,

for the sum of one thousand dollars ($1,000), by paying him $344.75! This meant deprivation such as you, of this day and time, know not of—almost starvation. But for mother and sister some, if not all of us, would have been sacrificed for sheer need of the common necessities of life.

Father's journal tells me that after receiving a note from B. F. Guy saying come at once if you want the land, Adam F. Plummer went to see Guy that night, carrying with him $344.75 that he had saved and borrowed to bind the bargain. By September 26, 1868, Guy sent for another payment (as if money grew on bushes for the freed men). That evening he carried him $160.25, making $505 paid! Hard? worse than that, but the thought of being in our own home urged them on! Father, mother, sister, Henry, Julia, and Saunders worked out and gave all they could make. By January 17, 1870, father had paid the entire thousand dollars! Much to Guy's surprise. For he was a speculator.

He never dreamed that father would or could pay for it in the specified time—two years! So when it was completed in 18 months, it was indeed a wonder! Guy's neighbors had said to him: "You are ruining our country!" "How is that," said Guy. "Why selling 'Negroes land.'" Guy would reply: "Don't worry, they can't raise the money. In time, I'll take the land back."

But he didn't know the man with whom he was dealing! Guy said to father: "Never mind my payments, put up a nice house." "O no! Mr. Guy, not until I get the land paid for," said father.

Strange to say, by September, 1870 father had finished building our four-room log house, and we moved from that happy place on Calvert's land, where sister, Miranda, had returned, and where the church was started, about two or three hundred feet westward toward the B.&O. R.R., into a happier place—Our Own Home! And by March 17, 1872, every dollar that had been borrowed had been returned.[4]

The reference to the founding of the church in their old home shows the close relationships between the beginnings of the family on an institutional basis and the building-up of the church or the institution which expresses more than any other the autonomous and collective life of the Negroes after emancipation. The historian of the Phillips family writes concerning his father:

[4] Nellie A. Plummer, *Out of the Depths or the Triumph of the Cross* (Hyattsville, Md., 1927) p. 106.

One of the first things he thought of after emancipation was the importance of procuring a lot for a church. With this aim in view he approached the honorable Jesse Beal, a worthy white citizen, who gave a lot not far from the cemetery in that part of Milledgeville where the colored Baptist Church, the colored school, and the "home of the Yankee teachers" as they were called were located. It was in 1866 when this movement began and it continued without abatement till a Church edifice named Trinity was constructed.[5]

The church was under the domination of the men, and whatever control it attempted to exercise tended to confirm the man's interest and authority in the family. They found sanction for male ascendancy in the Bible, which, for the newly emancipated slaves, was the highest authority in such matters. But in the final analysis the Negro church had to accommodate itself to the folkways and mores of its constituents which had grown out of their fundamental interests.

We may turn, therefore, to another factor which, like the acquisition of property or a home, gave the man a fundamental interest in his family and placed his ascendancy on a firm basis. It was not uncommon for the more ambitious slaves, who were permitted to hire their time, to purchase their freedom and the freedom of their wives and children. Washington Irving records in his journals that on a trip down the Mississippi he saw

> a negro merchant thirty-six years old—going to New Orleans with forty dozen fowles—had canoe or boat with corn to feed them—goes down in steam-boat—gets passage for nothing from some—buys one dollar doz. sells three dollars—has followed the business twelve years—brings back nothing but money—pays his master fifty dollars a year—lays up money to buy himself free—buries it—cannot buy himself till next year—has wife and children but cannot buy them—means to go far where he can make most money, but means to see his wife and children occasionally and take care of them.[6]

The numerous court cases involving property rights in slaves who were bought or contracted for by relatives give us some idea of the difficulties which husbands and fathers experienced in securing the freedom of their wives and children. For example, in 1840 a

---

[5] Phillips, *op. cit.*, p. 10.
[6] *The Journals of Washington Irving*, ed., William P. Trent and George S. Hollman (Boston, 1919), II, 108-9.

free colored man in South Carolina was forced to pay $500 for his wife who was sickly and died after he gave notes for her. The record of the case reads:

> Doll, a female slave, had been the wife of the defendant (Bass), a free man of colour, and had been separated from him by her master, Lyles, who carried her away into North Carolina. The defendant went to North Carolina to purchase her. Lyles told him she was very sick— that she was unsound, and he had better not buy her; but he said, it was his own look out, she was his wife. Lyles then told him that, if she died before she left there, he should not pay for her, ... bargain was completed by the defendant giving his notes for $250. At the time . . . . and long before, Doll was obviously very ill . . . . of no pecuniary value . . . . declined constantly till she died. When sound . . . . offered for sale for $300. Bass was a man slow of apprehension, and easily imposed upon.[7]

But, of course, many men were more fortunate in their attempts to purchase their wives and children. For instance, a free Negro in Mississippi who emigrated to Africa with his family paid $500 for his wife and $3,500 for his six children and three grandchildren. The story of Noah Davis,[8] who enjoyed considerable freedom of movement and opportunities for earning money, will show how long some fathers labored to purchase their wives and children. The "Notice to the Public," which forms the Preface to his book states (p. 3)

> The object of the writer, in preparing this account of himself, is to RAISE SUFFICIENT MEANS TO FREE HIS LAST TWO CHILDREN FROM SLAVERY. Having already, within twelve years past, purchased himself, his wife, and five of his children, at a cost, altogether, of over FOUR THOUSAND DOLLARS, he now earnestly desires a humane and christian public to AID HIM IN THE SALE OF THIS BOOK, for the purpose of finishing the task in which he has so long and anxiously labored.

In his youth he was bound out to learn the boot and shoe trade in Fredericksburg, Virginia. The incident that led to his religious conversion was the solemn account given at a prayer meeting by

---

[7] Helen T. Catterall (ed), *Judicial Cases concerning American Slavery and the Negro* (Washington, D. C., 1929), II, 377.

[8] Noah Davis, *The Narrative of the Life of Rev. Noah Davis* (Baltimore, 1859) p. 28.

an old man of the sudden death of a young woman. It was at the church that he met his wife, who "embraced religion about the same time" as he did. His desire to purchase his freedom was due to his yearning to learn to read the scriptures:

> In my attempts to preach the gospel to my fellow sinners, I often felt embarrassed, not knowing how to read a chapter in the Bible correctly. My desires now increased for such a knowledge of the sacred Scriptures, as would enable me to read a chapter publicly to my hearers. I thought that if I had all my time at my own command, I would devote it all to divine things. This desire I think, led me more than anything else, to ask permission of my master, Dr. F. Patten, to purchase my freedom.

Concerning getting his master's consent, he writes:

> I went to him, and stated my wishes, informing him why I wanted to be free—that I had been led to believe the Lord had converted my soul, and had called me to talk to sinners. He granted my request, without a single objection, fixing my price at five hundred dollars. . . . But now I had to tell hm that I had no money, and that I desired him to grant me another request; which was, to let me travel and find friends, who would give me the money. After learning my wishes fully, he consented, told me, when I got ready to start, he would give me a pass, to go where I pleased.

After paying one hundred and fifty dollars on his debt, Davis spent four months in 1845 visiting churches in Philadelphia, New York, and Boston, where he succeeded in raising only an additional one hundred and fifty dollars. His narrative tells us of his discouragement at this time:

> I began to wonder to myself, whether God was in this matter, or not; and if so, why I had not succeeded. However, having returned home, I went to work at my trade, for the purpose of earning the remainder of the money. Having paid what I was able, toward my debt, and reserving enough to open a shop, upon my own account, my old boss, Mr. Wright, my true and constant friend, became my protector, so that I might carry on my business lawfully. In this, however, I was not very successful; but I had not been long engaged at it, before I received a communication from my white Baptist friends in Baltimore, through my pastor, Rev. Sam'l Smith, informing me that if I would come to Baltimore, and accept an appointment as

missionary to the colored people in that city, they would assist me in raising the balance of the money then due upon myself.

Davis overcame his reluctance in leaving his family that had been placed under his entire control by the widow who owned his wife and children and began his career in Baltimore. After paying for his own freedom his next step was to contract for his wife and children.

> I had now been in Baltimore more than a year. My wife and seven children were still in Virginia. I went to see them as often as my circumstances permitted—three or four times a year. About this time, my wife's mistress agreed to sell to me my wife and two youngest children. The price fixed, was eight hundred dollars cash, and she gave me twelve months to raise the money. The sun rose bright in my sky that day; but before the year was out, my prospects were again in darkness. Now I had two great burdens upon my mind: one to attend properly to my missionary duty, the other to raise eight hundred dollars. During this time we succeeded in getting a better place for the Sabbath school, and there was a larger attendance upon my preaching, which demanded reading and study, and also visiting, and increased my daily labors. On the other hand, the year was running away, in which I had to raise eight hundred dollars. So that I found myself at times in a great strait.

Davis continued to meet disappointments in the struggle to free his family. At the end of the year the value of the children had increased a hundred dollars. It was only through the kindness of a loan of two hundred dollars from a friend that he raised the six hundred dollars in cash. His final success in obtaining the freedom of his wife and two children is recounted in the following:

> Having now in hand the six hundred dollars, and the promise of Mr. Wright's security for three hundred more, I was, by twelve o'clock the next day in Fredericksburg. At first sight, my wife was surprised that I had come back so soon; for it was only two weeks since I had left her; and when I informed her that I had come after her and the children, she could hardly believe me. In a few days, having duly arranged all things relative to the purchase and removal, we left for Baltimore, with feelings commingled with joy and sorrow—sorrow at parting with five of our older children, and our many friends; and rejoicing in the prospect of remaining together permanently in the

missionary field, where God had called me to labor. I arrived in
Baltimore, with my wife and two little ones, November 5th, 1851, and
stopped with sister Hester Ann Hughes, a worthy member of the
M.E. Church, with whom I had been boarding for four years.

Davis tells how the borrowed money was repaid:

> My salary was only three hundred dollars a year; but with hard
> exertion and close economy, together with my wife's taking in washing
> and going out at day's work, we were enabled by the first of the year,
> to pay the two hundred dollars our dear friend had loaned us, in
> raising the six hundred dollars before spoken of. But the bond for
> three hundred dollars was now due, and how must this be met? I
> studied out a plan; which was to get some gentleman who might want
> a little servant girl, to take my child, and advance me three hundred
> dollars for the purpose of paying my note, which was now due in
> Virginia. In this plan I succeeded; and had my own life insured for
> seven years for five hundred dollars, and made it over to this gentle-
> man, as security; until I ultimately paid him the whole amount;
> though I was several years in paying it.

Of his continued efforts to buy the five children left in Virginia
we learn:

> I have been much hindered in my own labors, from pecuniary em-
> barrassment, arising from the sale of my children, who were left in
> Virginia—two daughters and three sons. The first of these, who was
> about to be sold, and taken away South, was my oldest daughter; and
> it was with great difficulty and the help of friends that I raised eight
> hundred and fifty dollars, and got her on to Baltimore. But I was
> soon called upon to make a similar effort to save my eldest son from
> being sold far from me. Entirely unexpected, I received the pain-
> ful news that my boy was in one of the trader's jails in Richmond, and
> for sale. The dealer knew me, and was disposed to let me have him,
> if I could get any one to purchase him. I was, of course, deeply
> anxious to help get my boy; but I began to think that I had already
> drawn so heavily on the liberality of all my friends, that to appeal
> to them again seemed out of the question. I immediately wrote to the
> owners of my son, and received an answer—that his price was fixed
> at seven hundred dollars.

The seven hundred dollars for his son was finally raised through
the generosity of the various colored congregations in Baltimore and
a loan from a friend. The other daughter, whose price was run up

by a slave-trader to over a thousand dollars, was finally purchased, through money collected in white and colored churches from friends who had bought the girl in order to prevent her from being sold South. Davis wrote the history of his life and struggles in order to raise money to buy his two remaining boys who had been sold in settling the estate of their mistress.

In order to make his wife and children legally free it was necessary, of course, for the father to emancipate them. A free Negro man gave his wife the following deed of manumission in Petersburg, Virginia, in 1837:

> Know all men by these presents, that I, Samuel V. Brown, of the town of Petersburg, have manumitted, emancipated and set free, and I do by these presents manumit, emancipate, and set free, my wife, Alice Brown a woman purchased by me from Mary Ann Vizonneau by her bill of sale dated the 24th day of June, 1831 and of record in the Hustings court of Petersburg, the said woman being called in the said bill of sale "Else Scott" and I hereby invest my said wife Alice Brown with all the rights and privileges of a free person of color which it is in my power to vest her. She is a woman of yellow complexion, five feet four inches high, and about twenty eight years old. In testimony whereof, I have hereunto set my hand and affixed my seal this 1st day of November A.D. 1837.

But, in many cases, instead of legally emancipating his wife and children, the father permitted them to continue in their status as slaves. Thus we find that many of the Negro owners of slaves were really relatives. Woodson has pointed out the fact that some husbands who purchased their wives did not liberate them immediately because they "considered it advisable to put them on probation for a few years, and if they did not find them satisfactory, they would sell their wives as other slave holders disposed of Negroes."[9] He cites the case of a Charleston shoemaker who paid $700 for his wife but sold her for $750 when he found her hard to please. Another owner of his wife meted out the same punishment when she became enamoured of a slave and gave her husband's free papers to her lover. In these cases we can see how the man's ownership of his wife

[9] Carter G. Woodson, "Free Negro Owners of Slaves in the United States in 1830" *Journal of Negro History*, IX, 41.

and children gave substance to his claim to authority in the family. In purchasing his wife and children the man not only secured authority over them, but he also acquired a fundamental interest in them since they represented the fruit of his industry and sacrifices.

In some present-day Negro families of the patriarchal type, it appears that the male ancestor's original interest and ascendancy in the family were due in part at least to the fact that he purchased his wife and children. Let us take, for example, a pioneer family in Chicago which has been prominent in the life of the Negro community for over a half-century. According to our informant, his father, who came to Chicago with a drove of cattle in 1854 and contracted to buy land, "was never treated as an ordinary slave."

> [His master] would trust him to drive his cattle into free territory and would give him a percentage of the sale. He went back to Kentucky and contracted to get his family. They had promised to let him have his family without charge but they made him buy them. He was afraid not to buy them as they would be sold South. He was compelled to pay $4,000 for his family and was thus deprived of the means of buying land.

After the father brought his family to Chicago, he was not satisfied to live within the Negro settlement. He moved to his own place on the outskirts of the city. As related by the son, the father's strict discipline of his children was exemplified in his requiring his sons to work the entire summers with him on jobs for which he contracted. Moreover, this son brought his earnings home until he was twenty-seven years old. However, because of his father's discipline and pride, the son felt that he never knew his father intimately: "He was one of those old Romans; children should be seen and not heard," was the son's concise characterization of his father, who died in the midst of his plans to secure more land for his family.

In tracing the origin and development of the Negro father's authority in family relations, we have seen how, following emancipation, this was facilitated by the economic subordination of the woman. To some extent, of course, his authority as well as his interest in his family represented a carry-over from slavery. Even in such cases, it was chiefly through the acquisition of property that his interest was established on a permanent basis. Before emancipation the father often acquired at least a proprietary interest in his family when he bought his wife and children and thereby brought them under his authority. But such families actually form a part of the nearly half-million Negroes who were free before the Civil War. In fact, it was among these free Negroes that the family was first established upon an institutional basis.

CHAPTER X

THE SONS OF
THE FREE

Among the "twenty Negars" who were brought in 1619 to Virginia in "a dutch man of warre" and sold to the colonists, there were some whose names indicated that they had been baptized by the Spaniards. It is probable that at that time the distinction between Christian and heathen or baptized and unbaptized had as much significance as the distinction between white and black at a later date. Contracts of indenture indicate that the Negroes who were brought to America during the early years of the colony were placed in the same category as the white servants. In 1625 a Negro named Brase was assigned to Lady Yardley at a monthly wage of "forty pownd waight of good merchantable tobacco for his labor and service so longe as he remayneth with her." As early as 1651 we find a Negro, Anthony Johnson, who was probably enumerated among the indentured servants in the census of 1624, having assigned to him in fee simple a land patent for two hundred and fifty acres of land.[1] The slave status, for which the colonists had no model in England, "developed in customary law, and was legally sanctioned at first by court decisions." There is a certain irony in the fact that in 1653 the same Anthony Johnson mentioned above was a defendant in a suit brought against him by another Negro for his freedom from servitude on the grounds that the latter had served "seaven or eight years of Indenture." By 1667 Negro labor had evidently become so profitable that Virginia enacted a law that "the conferring of baptisme doth not alter the condition of the person as

[1] John H. Russell, *The Free Negro in Virginia* (Baltimore, 1913), p. 25.

to his bondage or freedome." Masters, thus freed from the risk of losing their property, could "more carefully endeavour the propagation of christianity." Thenceforth color became the badge of servitude, and a Negro was presumed to be a slave.

Although it appears that Negroes who came to Virginia after 1682 as servants could not acquire their freedom after a limited period of service, the free Negro population continued to increase until the Civil War. Russell has indicated the five sources through which the free Negro population increased: (1) children born of free colored persons; (2) mulatto children born of free colored mothers; (3) mulatto children born of white servants or free women; (4) children of free Negro and Indian parentage; and (5) manumitted slaves. It is, of course, impossible to estimate to what extent the free Negro population was increased through each of these sources. Nor can we say just how much was due to natural increase. The numerous cases of offspring of white fathers and free colored mothers indicate that the free Negro population was enlarged through this source.[2] Mulattoes born of white servant women were also a significant element, for it was soon the cause for special legislative action. Virginia, in 1691, passed a law providing that "any white woman marrying a negro or mulatto, bond or free," should be banished. In 1681 Maryland had passed a law that children born of white servant women and Negroes were free. Eleven years later in the same state any white woman who married or became the mother of a child by either a slave or a free Negro became a servant for seven years.[3]

During the early years of the Republic the growth of the free Negro population was rapid, amounting to about three times that of the slave population. But after 1810 there was a distinct decline in the rate of the increase of the free Negro population, and during the next two decades there was only a small difference in the rates of growth of these two elements in the Negro population. It seems that the increase in the free Negro population of 36.8 per cent in 1830 was due to the gradual emancipation which was taking place

---

[2] Carter G. Woodson, *Free Negro Heads of Families in the United States in 1830* (Washington, D. C., 1925), Intro., p. vi.

[3] Jeffrey R. Brackett, *The Negro in Maryland* (Baltimore, 1889), p. 33.

in northern states. Beginning in 1840, the rate of increase in the slave population was greater than that of the free Negroes and, during the two succeeding decades, so far exceeded the rate for the free population that it is difficult to account for the difference.

Although the free Negro population did not grow as rapidly after 1840 as during the preceding decades, there was a steady growth in particular areas. These developments were related in part to certain fundamental changes in the ecological organization of slavery. Phillips has described the changes which had taken place in Virginia and Maryland by 1860:

> Tidewater Virginia and the greater part of Maryland had long been exhausted for plantation purposes and were being reclaimed by farmers working with much the same methods as were followed in the northern states. The large land- and slave-owners mostly followed an example which George Washington had set and divided up their estates into small units, in each of which a few Negroes worked in the raising of varied crops under the control of a white man, who was more a foreman leading the squad than an overseer driving it. Planters who adhered to the old methods were now of decayed estate, supported more by the sale of slaves than by the raising of tobacco. Incidentally, eastern Virginia and Maryland had come to have a very large number of free Negroes.[4]

The relation between these changes and the growth in the free Negro population was more than incidental. Free Negroes did not constitute a conspicuous element in the Negro population where the plantation system flourished. The Alabama black lands and the Mississippi and Red River bottoms were still calling for slaves. In Mississippi the number of free Negroes was always insignificant. The supreme court of the state held that "the laws of this state presume a negro prima facie to be a slave."

Thus we find the free Negro population concentrated in seven characteristic areas: the Tidewater region of Virginia and Maryland; the Piedmont region of North Carolina and Virginia; the seaboard cities of Charleston, South Carolina, Mobile, Alabama, and New Orleans; the northern cities, including Boston, New York, Chicago,

---

[4] Ulrich B. Phillips, *Documentary History of American Industrial Society: Plantation and Frontier* (2 vols.; Cleveland, 1910-11), I, 88-89.

Cincinnati, Philadelphia, Baltimore, and Washington; settlements in the Northwest Territory, located in Michigan, Indiana, and Ohio; isolated communities of Negroes mixed with Indians; and, finally, the Seminoles of Florida. The Tidewater region of Virginia "always had from one-half to two-thirds of the entire free negro class, although after 1830 that section contained less than one-fourth of the white people of the state." Like other elements which do not fit into the traditional social order, the free Negroes tended to become concentrated in the cities. In 1860 between a fourth and a third of the free colored population lived in the towns and cities of Virginia. The city of Baltimore had 25,680 of the 83,942 free Negroes in Maryland in 1860. A similar situation existed in Louisiana, where 10,689 of the 18,647 free Negroes lived in New Orleans in 1860. More than a third of the free Negro population of Pennsylvania in 1860 was in Philadelphia.[5] Concerning Mississippi, Sydnor found that "10 per cent of the slaves in Adams County lived in the city of Natchez, 57 per cent of the whites and 73 per cent of the free colored . . . . [while] Vicksburg contained 71 of the 104 free persons of color residing within the county."[6]

One of the most striking characteristics of the free Negro communities was the prominence of the mulatto element. About three-eighths of the free Negroes in the United States in 1850 were classed as mulattoes, whereas only about a twelfth of the slave population was regarded as of mixed blood. Although no definite information exists concerning the number of mulattoes during the Colonial period, we find that in 1752 in Baltimore County, Maryland, 196 of the 312 mulattoes were free, while all of the 4,035 Negroes except 8 were slaves. Early in the settlement of Virginia doubts concerning the status of mulatto children were the occasion for special legislation which determined that mulatto children should have the status of their mother. In Maryland, by an act of 1681, children born of white servant women and Negroes were free. By

[5] Edward Raymond Turner, *The Negro in Pennsylvania* (Washington, 1911), pp. 24-25.

[6] Charles S. Sydnor, "The Free Negro in Mississippi before the Civil War," *American Historical Review*, XXXII (July, 1927), p. 782.

another act in 1692 mulatto children through such unions lost their free status and became servants for a long term. In Pennsylvania the mulattoes followed the status of their mothers and, when the offspring of a free mother, became a servant for a term of years. The conspicuousness of the mulatto element in the free Negro population was not due, therefore, to any legal presumption in its favor.

The accessions to the free Negro class through unions of free white women and Negro men and free colored women and white men was kept at a minimum by the drastic laws against such unions. Nor can the enormous increase in the free mulattoes be accounted for by natural increase from their own numbers. The increase in the number of free mulattoes came chiefly from the offspring of slave women and white masters who manumitted their mulatto children.

John H. Russell says concerning the free mulattoes of Virginia: "The free mulatto class, which numbered 23,500 by 1860, was of course the result of illegal relations of white persons with negroes; but, excepting those born of mulatto parents, most persons of the free class were not born of free negro and white mothers, but of slave mothers, and were set free because of their kinship to their master and owner."

Charles S. Sydnor, in showing how the sex relations existing between masters and slaves were responsible for the free class in Mississippi, cites the fact that, "of the 773 free persons of color in Mississippi in the year 1860, 601 were of mixed blood, and only 172 were black. Among the slaves this condition was entirely reversed. In this same year there were 400,013 slaves who were classed as blacks and only 36,618 who were mulattoes." The predominance of the mulattoes among the free Negroes was most marked in Louisiana where of the 18,647 free Negroes, 15,158 were mulattoes.

Free Negroes concentrated in urban areas were able to get some formal education. In 1850 there were large numbers attending schools in northern cities. Boston seems to have been the most favorable city for free Negroes in regard to school attendance. In the case of the Virginia cities the absence of any returns for school attendance was due to the stringency of the laws against the instruction of Negroes. The small number reported as attending school in Charleston was doubtless attributable to the same cause. Nevertheless, it is a significant fact that the number of adults who could not read or write was almost negligible. The restrictions upon the education of the free Negro population were probably never enforced. In New Orleans the large number of Negroes in school was made up of the free mulatto class, who constituted a distinct caste in the city. Mobile, Alabama, showed up favorably in regard to the small number of illiterate adults. The absence of returns for school attendance in Savannah reflected the local sentiment against the education of Negroes. This is further attested by the large number of illiterate adults. However, in Charleston as early as 1790 the Brown Fellowship Society, organized among the free colored people, maintained schools for Negro children. Later, other societies were formed especially for the education of indigent and orphaned Negro children.

In New Orleans, where the creoles and freedmen counted early in the nineteenth century as a substantial element in society, persons of color had secured to themselves better facilities of education. The people of this city did not then regard it as a crime for Negroes to acquire an education, their white instructors felt that they were not condescending in teaching them, and children of Caucasian blood raised no objection to attending special and parochial schools accessible to both races. The educational privileges which the colored people there enjoyed, however, were largely paid for by the progressive freedmen themselves. Some of them educated their children in France.[7]

Although the colored people of northern cities like New York and Philadelphia did not support their education to the extent that they did in Baltimore and Washington, there was a class of ambitious and thrifty Negroes who paid for the education of their children. In New England education among the colored people began almost from the beginning of their enslavement but received an impetus after the Revolution. A separate school for the colored children was

[7] Carter G. Woodson, *Education of the Negro Prior to 1861,* (New York and London), 1915, pp. 128-29.

established in 1798 with a white teacher. According to Woodson, who has made a thorough study of Negro education before the Civil War, "an epoch in the history of Negro education in New England was marked in 1820, when the city of Boston opened its first primary school for the education of colored children."

The social life of the free colored groups centered for the most part about the churches and the fraternal organizations. In Boston as early as 1784 a Masonic lodge was formed with fifteen members. The first Negro church, originally called the African Meeting-House, was organized in Boston in 1805.[8] New York, Philadelphia, and Baltimore had large Negro congregations. The African Baptist church was organized in Philadelphia in 1809. Baltimore had ten congregations as early as 1835. The activity of Richard Allen, who became the first bishop of the African Methodist Episcopal church, shows how the growing race consciousness of the Negroes in Philadelphia necessitated a separate church in which the Negro could give expression to his own religious life. A similar movement for separate churches among Negroes took place in Washington as early as 1820.

In the urban environment free Negroes were able to enter a variety of occupations that afforded them some degree of economic security and independence. In the North they found themselves in keen competition with white labor. A study of the Negro population in Philadelphia in 1847 showed the occupations of 3,358 Negro males to be as follows: mechanics, 286; laborers, 1,581; seafaring men, 240; coachmen, carters, etc., 276; shopkeepers and traders, 166; waiters, cooks, etc., 557; hairdressers, 156; various, 96. There were also among the men musicians, preachers, physicians, and school-teachers. Although the majority of the 4,249 Negro women were classed as washerwomen and domestic servants, 486 were needle-women, and 213 were in trades. The lowest class of colored people who were out of employment found in "ragging and boning" a means of livelihood. A significant development in the economic life of the Philadelphia Negro prior to the Civil War was the guild of the caterers which grew up about 1840 and continued until about 1870. Through them the Negro was able to overcome the disastrous

[8] John Daniels, *In Freedom's Birthplace* (Boston, 1914), p. 21.

competition of foreign labor and find a field where the more energetic among them could achieve economic independence. The free Negroes of Baltimore became formidable competitors of the white laboring population. In spite of the prejudice in New York City against Negro labor, Negroes were engaged in skilled as well as unskilled occupations. Although in the census for 1850 they were listed chiefly as servants and laborers, some had found a place in the skilled occupations as carpenters, musicians, and tailors.

In Charleston and New Orleans the free Negro acquired a relatively secure foothold in the economic order. There were listed for 1860 among the taxpayers in Charleston 371 free persons of color, including 13 Indians, who were paying taxes on real estate valued at about a million dollars and 389 slaves. After the abortive attempt at insurrection by Denmark Vesey in 1822, a memorial was presented to the Senate and House of Representatives concerning the free persons of color. It was argued that this class constituted a menace to white society because their monopoly of the mechanical arts caused German, Swiss, and Scotch immigrants to seek homes in the West. In New Orleans, where color was not so great a bar as in many other cities, we find free Negroes in many skilled occupations. Of the occupations given for 1,463 mulattoes in 1850, 299 were carpenters, 143 cigar-makers, 213 masons, 76 shoemakers, and 79 tailors. There were listed also 61 clerks, 12 teachers, 1 architect, and 4 capitalists.[9] The property owned by the free colored people in New Orleans in 1860 amounted to about fifteen million dollars. An enumeration in 1819 of the free Negroes in Richmond County, Georgia, where they numbered 194, showed the men to be employed in boating, carpentry, harness-making, wagoning, and common labor; and the women in sewing, washing, and domestic service.

The foregoing facts give quite a different picture of the economic status of the free colored people from those accounts which represent them as a wholly dependent and debased pariah class. Undoubtedly, those observers who have reported the miserable conditions among free Negroes have been faithful in their portrayal of a portion of the

---

[9] Charles H. Wesley, *Negro Labor in The United States, 1850-1925: A Study in American Economic History* (New York, 1927), pp. 37-38.

free population. But we are primarily interested in the class of free Negroes who were able to achieve some degree of economic independence and culture which became the basis of future progress.

Dodge's description of the free Negroes in the rural sections of North Carolina refers to those in the Piedmont region; for the free Negroes in the coastal region were undoubtedly better off. He writes:

> A very few free Negroes prospered, bought larger and better farms, and even owned slaves—one as many as thirty,—which they held up to general emancipation. But generally when they bought land at all, the purchase was ludicrously small, and, in the country phrase, "so po' it couldn't sprout er pea dout grunt'n." On these infinitesimal bits they built flimsy log huts, travesties in every respect of the rude dwellings of the earliest white settlers. The timber growth being often too scant to afford fence rails, their little patches of phantom corn mixed with pea-vines—or, rather, stubs, their little quota of hulls akimbo on top—were encircled by brush fences, which even by dint of annual renewals were scarcely to be regarded by a beast of average hunger and enterprise.[10]

Turning now to the free Negro communities in the Northwest Territory, we find the settlement in Cass County, Michigan, of considerable interest. In this county in 1850 there were 389 colored persons, 19 of whom were attending school, while in 1860 the total population had grown to 1,368, among whom there were 981 mulattoes. Concerning the history of this colony, one of its descendants gives the following incidents:

> In 1847, a white Virginian named Saunders, becoming convinced that slavery was wrong, set his coloured people free, and brought them out to Michigan. In "Chain Lake Settlement" he bought a splendid tract of land nearly one mile square, gave all his people homes and spent his remaining years among them. Other masters in Virginia, Kentucky, and Tennessee also freed all or a part of their slaves, sometimes the old and infirm ones; sometimes the incorrigibles. These, with free Negroes from Ohio, Indiana and Illinois, continued to swell the population of the Settlement. Most of these people had helped to make the fortunes of their former masters. Now they were eager to accumulate something for themselves and their posterity.[11]

[10] David Dodge, "The Free Negroes of North Carolina," *Atlantic Monthly,* LVII, 24.

[11] James D. Corruthers, *In Spite of Handicap: An Autobiography* (New York, 1916), pp. 17-18.

The colony of Negroes at Wilberforce, Ohio, originated largely from the mulatto children of white planters who used to visit the summer resort at Tawawa Springs. The school which was established for these children was first taught by Yankees. According to a woman who went to school there, the planters lavished money on their mulatto children for whom money was deposited in the banks of Cincinnati. The Randolph slaves, numbering 385, were liberated by the will of John Randolph of Virginia and settled in Ohio. Their settlement, in Mercer County, was opposed by the whites, and they were compelled to move to a camp near the towns of Piqua and Troy. It seems that they never obtained possession of any of the land which was supposed to have been purchased by them.

Having considered the origin and growth of the free Negro population and its distribution in certain characteristic areas, we turn now to the story of those families which took root in these communities and developed an institutional character.

In 1830 we find the free Negro families, which had largely become concentrated in certain areas, enjoying, in the South at least, their greatest prosperity. We are indebted to the researches of Dr. Woodson for the names of the heads and the number of persons in these families. This information provides a basis for the study of the families in the different communities in which we find free Negroes. The comparatively small number of free families in Georgia were concentrated in Savannah and Augusta. An enumeration in 1819 of free Negroes in Richmond County, in which Augusta is located, gave the names, ages, and occupations of the 194 free persons of color. Although these persons were not recorded according to families, their names and ages, as well as the order in which they appeared, enable one to determine to some extent family groups. We have already seen how these persons were employed. In most cases the wife, as well as the husband, was employed. Eleven years later the total number of free Negroes had been reduced to 172, and they were recorded in the census for 1830 as members of thirty-two family groups, an average of 5.3 persons to each family. A striking fact about these thirty-two families was that a woman was the head in twenty cases. The predominance of female heads as well as the decrease in numbers may have been due to the attempted insurrection in 1819. By a comparison of the names we have been able to identify ten in the list of heads of families in 1830 who were either heads of families in 1819 or children in these families. When the large number of families with female heads is considered in relation to the fact that in 1860 there were 325 mulattoes among the 490 free Negroes enumerated for this county, it does not seem unreasonable to conclude that in many cases white men were the fathers of the children. We know that in one case the association acquired a permanent character. Among the children of this association there is a distinguished educator whose sisters became teachers and social workers, and whose children are finding a conspicuous place in the Negro world.

One of the most distinguished and forceful bishops in the African Methodist Episcopal church came of a free family residing in Abbeville County. Bishop Turner's biographer gives the following account of the former's ancestry:

> Henry M. Turner was born February 1st, 1834, near Newberry, Abbeville, South Carolina, of free parentage. While he was not a slave, he was subject to slave environments. Ownership in himself, only, excepted.
>
> He was the grandson on his mother's side of an African Prince, who was brought to this country in the latter part of the Eighteenth Century and held in Slavery, but was soon afterward set free, because South Carolina at that time was a part of a British Colony, and it was contrary to British law to enslave royal blood; hence the freedom of this young Prince was accorded.
>
> David Greer, the illustrious sire of this still more illustrious descendant, not being able to procure passage back to his native country, married a free woman near Abbeville, and planned to make this his home. To this union, aside from many other children, Sarah, his youngest daughter, was born, whom Hardy Turner wooed and wedded. From this union came Henry McNeal Turner, their first born, February 1, 1834.[12]

The tradition of royal ancestry in this family probably has no greater claim to historical accuracy than the same tradition in many other families. However, Turner's free ancestors seemingly enjoyed

[12] Henry M. Turner, *Life and Times of Henry M. Turner* (Atlanta, 1917), p. 33.

the same opportunities which other free Negroes had for advancement. Bishop Turner was taught to read and write by a white woman who took a special interest in him. The law against the instruction of Negroes in South Carolina stopped his education, and, although his mother moved to another town and employed a white teacher, a threat of imprisonment again arrested his intellectual development. According to his biographer it was this disappointment that embittered "his mind against the haters of his race and had much to do with the contempt which he showed in after years for those who opposed the progress of his people."

From what we have already learned concerning the economic status and general culture of the free Negroes of Charleston, it is not surprising that family life among a large group of them reached a high level of development. Before the Civil War some of these families had already acquired an institutional character. The stability and prestige of these families rested mainly upon the property which they were able to accumulate. This property often included slaves. Status in the free colored community was determined by the standing of the families. These families were intensely conscious of their superior status and took pride in their mixed blood, which marked them off from the great mass of black slaves. This was especially true of the free colored people who were descendants of the refugees from San Domingo during the revolution in the eighteenth century. The family of a prominent minister in a northern city, who has played a conspicuous part in Negro life, may be taken as representative of this class. The grandfather of this minister was the older of two brothers born in Charleston in 1798 and 1802. Their father was a refugee from San Domingo. The brothers, like other members of this class, were of Indian and French descent. In 1816 the older brother married the daughter of a wealthy planter, who gave his daughter a plantation and slaves as a dowry. Partly because of this dowry the son-in-law became a prosperous merchant in the city. The minister still has a deed of sale of a slave woman and her two children to his grandfather's brother in 1826. His grandfather was listed in the census of 1830 as the owner of five slaves;

while in 1860 he was listed as an Indian among the colored taxpayers of Charleston.

In the history of another family among the free colored people
of Charleston we can trace in greater detail the history of the family
from the time of the initial white mixture. Our informant, a leader
of the colored women in South Carolina, says concerning the origin
of her family:

> My great grandmother's father was a German scientist who came
> to this country and settled in Charleston. I don't know the history of
> her mother. I think her mother came from the West Indies. My
> great grandmother received an unusual education from her father.
> My daughter, H——, is named for her great grandmother, H——
> S——. My great grandmother had a school for free colored people
> before the Civil War and taught in the first free colored school estab-
> lished in Charleston after the War.

This great-grandmother, who was married to a man of French-
Huguenot descent, had a son whose estate was listed among the
free colored taxpayers in Charleston in 1860. This son married, as
was customary among the families of the free class, into one of the
old free families that were listed as free as far back as 1830. Our
informant's father, who was born in Charleston in 1845, of a
Scotchman and a mulatto woman, remarked that he was only able
to marry into this family because he had succeeded in accumulating
property. The fact that our informant's aunt occupies a home on land
which has been in the family since 1805 is an indication of the
stability of this family. Personal property in the form of a Swiss
watch one hundred and fifty years old, which has been given to the
oldest son in each generation, handmade silver spoons, and a hand-
carved mahogany table have become symbols of the continuity of
the traditions in this family.

Deserving mention are three other families in this group. There
were the Westons, who were probably the wealthiest family among
the free colored people. Then, there was the family of Henry
Fordham, one of the taxpayers in 1860, whose son, a lieutenant of
police from 1874 to 1896, married into the Weston family. The
third family, the Holloways, who trace their family back to free

people of color under George III, still have the home which has been occupied continuously by the members of the family since 1807.

In New Orleans and its environment there was, as previously indicated, a large community of free Negro families similar in some respects to those in Charleston. But, on the whole, the traditions of free families in Louisiana were different from the traditions of the Negroes and colored people in other parts of the country. The infusion of white blood, which began at a very early date, was due to the association between the Spanish and French settlers and Negro and Indian women. Because the Latin was inclined to accord the mixed-bloods a higher status than the blacks from whom they were differentiated culturally, this group acquired the position of an intermediate caste. According to Bienville, the scarcity of white women in Louisiana caused the early Canadian settlers to run "in the woods after Indian girls."[13] Apparently for the same reason, association with Negro women began on a large scale at an early date. Sometime later Paul Alliot, who was seemingly annoyed because mulattoes and Negroes were protected by the government, observed that the wives and daughters of the mixed-bloods were "much sought after by white men, and white women at times esteem well built men of color." Perrin du Lac, however, attempted to place the blame chiefly on Spaniards for the intimacy with the Negroes:

> About one-quarter of the whites are Spaniards, generally from the province of Catalonia. Poor, lazy, and dirty beyond expression, that people mingle indiscriminately with the blacks, free or slave, and are intimate with them in a manner dangerous to the colony. Those blacks, accustomed to be treated as equals or as friends, are most inclined to depart from the respect with which it is so important to inspire them for the whites.[14]

In 1785 the free colored people in Louisiana numbered 1,303. The early sumptuary restrictions on this class were made untenable when its number were augmented by thousands of fairly well-to-do and cultured mulatto refugees from Haiti who settled in New Orleans.

[13] Arthur W. Calhoun, *A Social History of the American Family* (Cleveland, 1917-18), I, 331.
[14] James A. Robertson (tr.), *Louisiana under the Rule of Spain, France, and the United States, 1785-1807* (Cleveland, 1911), I, p. 150, n. 4.

By the time of the Louisiana Purchase, this group had become an important enough element in the population to protest against not participating in a memorial to Congress concerning the status of the colonists under the new government. During the defense of New Orleans against the British in 1814 the free people of color achieved considerable recognition because of their conduct on that occasion.

In many of the free colored families in New Orleans before the Civil War, the family traditions went back to the soldiers who served in the War of 1812. The careers of representatives of these families have been described by Desdunes, who belonged to that class. Concerning Paul Trevigne, born in 1825 and whose father was a veteran of the war, he writes:

> During his youth Trevigne received a thorough and careful education. He became a teacher, a position in which he served for forty years in the Third District of New Orleans. Paul Trevigne spoke and wrote several languages and was the intimate friend of men of superior education . . . . Several of his students became officers in the Union Army where they distinguished themselves for their intelligence and bravery.[15]

Another, Eugene Warbourg, who was born in New Orleans about the same year and died in Rome in 1861, was a sculptor. Among the men who succeeded in industry was George Alces, who employed more than two hundred colored Creoles in his tobacco establishment. Probably one of the best known of these free men of color was Thomy Lafon, for whom a school in New Orleans was named, because of his philanthropies. He distributed his wealth among white and black, Protestant and Catholic. In recognition of his humanitarian interests the state legislature ordered his bust to be set up in one of the public institutions of the city.

The development of family life on an institutional basis was closely tied up with the accumulation of property in these families. It reached its highest development among those classes which had acquired considerable wealth and achieved marked stability among the petite bourgeoisie and the skilled artisans. In both cases the

[15] R. L. Desdunes, *Nos hommes et notre histoire* (Montreal, 1911), p. 90.

name and the traditions of the family were associated with male ancestors. The following is an excellent account of this class in 1830:

> By 1830, some of these *gens de couleur* had arrived at such a degree of wealth as to own cotton and sugar plantations with numerous slaves. They educated their children, as they had been educated, in France. Those who chose to remain there, attained, many of them, distinction in scientific and literary circles. In New Orleans they became musicians, merchants, and money and real estate brokers. The humbler classes were mechanics; they monopolized the trade of shoemakers, a trade for which, even to this day, they have a special vocation; they were barbers, tailors, carpenters, upholsterers. They were notably successful hunters and supplied the city with game. As tailors, they were almost exclusively patronized by the *elite*, so much so that the Legoasters', the Dumas', the Clovis', and Lacroix', acquired individually fortunes of several hundred thousands of dollars. This class was most respectable; they generally married women of their own status, and led lives quiet, dignified and worthy, in homes of ease and comfort. A few who had reached a competency sufficient for it, attempted to settle in France, where there was no prejudice against their origin; but in more than one case the experiment was not satisfactory, and they returned to their former homes in Louisiana. . . . .
>
> In fact, the quadroons of Louisiana have always shown a strong local attachment, although in the state they were subjected to grievances, which seemed to them unjust, if not cruel. It is true, they possessed many of the civil and legal rights enjoyed by the whites, as to the protection of person and property; but they were disqualified from political rights and social equality. But . . . . it is always to be remembered that in their contact with white men, they did not assume that creeping posture of debasement—nor did the whites expect it— which has more or less been forced upon them in fiction. In fact, their handsome, good-natured faces seem almost incapable of despair. It is true the whites were superior to them, but they, in their turn, were superior, and infinitely superior, to the blacks, and had as much objection to associating with the blacks on terms of equality as any white man could have to associating with them. At the Orleans theatre they attended their mothers, wives, and sisters in the second tier, reserved exclusively for them, and where no white person of either sex would have been permitted to intrude. But they were not admitted to the quadroon balls, and when white gentlemen visited their families it was the accepted etiquette for them never to be present.[16]

[16] Grace King, *New Orleans: The Place and the People* (New York, 1928) (From unpublished manuscript of Charles Gayarre quoted in this work), pp. 344-46.

The latter part of this account refers to the recognized system of concubinage or *plaçage* which existed alongside of the moral and juridic family. A writer reflecting upon these extralegal family groups has observed that these quadroon women "were, in regard to family purity, domestic peace, and household dignity, the most insidious and the deadliest foes a community ever possessed." On the other hand, a visitor to New Orleans in the fifties, looking at the system more dispassionately, regarded it as "a very peculiar and characteristic result of the prejudices, vices, and customs of the various elements of color, class, and nation, which have been there brought together." In fact, the system of *placage* was an accommodation to the legal prescription against intermarriage between white men and these colored women, who were admitted by all observers to be superior generally in grace, beauty, and culture to the white women. At the quadroon balls, to which only white men were admitted, the quadroon women were under the chaperonage of their mothers. The manner in which the men and women became associated in the extramoral family groups was described by Olmsted as follows:

> When a man makes a declaration of love to a girl of this class, she will admit or deny, as the case may be, her happiness in receiving it; but, supposing she is favorably disposed, she will usually refer the applicant to her mother. The mother inquires, like a Countess of Kew, into the circumstances of the suitor; ascertains whether he is able to maintain a family, and, if satisfied with him, in these and other respects, requires from him security that he will support her daughter in a style suitable to the habits she has been bred to, and that, if he should ever leave her, he will give her a certain sum for her future support, and a certain additional sum for each of the children she shall then have.[17]

The daughters of these quadroon women followed in some cases the pattern set by their mothers. Others entered conventional marriages and went to France to live, where their status was not affected by their Negro blood. Since the stigma of Negro blood was always an incentive to become identified with the whites, some passed into

[17] Frederick Law Olmsted, *A Journey in the Seaboard States in the Year 1853-1854* (New York, 1904), II, p. 244.

the white race by migrating to other sections of the country or freed their children of the stigma of Negro blood by bribing officials to omit the designation from their baptismal certificates. As New Orleans grew, other mulattoes, becoming lost in the anonymity of the city, even passed over into the white race in the city of their birth. On the other hand, the offspring of these extramoral associations often established conventional families and thereby became a part of the free colored caste. Inherited wealth and superior education and culture made them eligible to membership in this class which was sharply differentiated from the mass of Negroes.

Most of the free Negro families in North Carolina (Map III) were located in the Piedmont and coastal regions. However, in this state as in other states the free families were found in considerable numbers in the towns and cities. In Fayetteville in 1830 there were eighty free Negro families. It was in this city that Henry Evans, a full-blooded free Negro, planted Methodism. Another free Negro who became well known as a preacher long before the Civil War was John Chavis. Concerning his life, Bassett writes:

> He was, probably, born in Granville County, near Oxford, about 1763. He was a full-blooded negro of dark brown color. He was born free. In early life he attracted the attention of the whites, and he was sent to Princeton College to see if a negro would take a collegiate education. He was a private pupil under the famous Dr. Witherspoon, and his ready acquisition of knowledge soon convinced his friends that the experiment would issue favorably. After leaving Princeton he went to Virginia, sent thither, no doubt, to preach to the negroes. In 1801 he was at the Hanover (Virginia) Presbytery, "riding as a missionary under the direction of the General Assembly." In 1805, at the suggestion of Rev. Henry Patillo, of North Carolina, he returned to his native State. For some cause, I know not what, it was not till 1809 that he was received as a licentiate by the Orange Presbytery. . . . . He continued to preach till in 1831 the Legislature forbade negroes to preach. It was a trial to him and he appealed to the Presbytery. That body could do nothing more than recommend him "to acquiesce in the decision of the Legislature referred to, until God in his providence shall open to him a path of duty in regard to the exercise of his ministry." Acquiesce he did. He died in 1838 and the Presbytery continued to his widow the pension which it had formerly allowed him.

Mr. Chavis' most important work was educational. Shortly after his return to North Carolina he opened a classical school, teaching in Granville, Wake, and Chatham Counties. His school was for the patronage of the whites. Among his patrons were the best people of the neighborhood. Among his pupils were Willie P. Mangum, his brother, Archibald and John Henderson, sons of Chief Justice Henderson, Charles Manly, afterwards Governor of the State, Dr. James L. Wortham of Oxford, N.C., and many more excellent men who did not become so distinguished in the communities. Rev. James H. Horner, one of the best teachers of high schools the State has produced, said of John Chavis: "My father not only went to school to him but boarded in his family. . . . . The school was the best at that time to be found in the State."[18]

One of the most successful free Negroes in North Carolina before the Civil War was Lunsford Lane, who was born a slave in Raleigh in 1803. His mother was a house servant in the family of an owner of a plantation, while his father was owned by another slaveholder. He says he became conscious of his slave status when he began to work. As the result of opportunities to earn money the idea entered his mind that he might buy his freedom. He realized this ambition through money which he was able to accumulate from the manufacture and sale of pipes and tobacco of a peculiar flavor. After purchasing his own freedom for $1,000, he bought his wife and children for $2,500. As a result of a visit to the North, he was charged with violating the law against the entrance of free Negroes from other states. When he sought permission to return and pay the remainder on his family, the governor informed Lane's white friends that, although he had no authority to grant such permission, it would be safe for Lane to come quietly and leave as soon as possible. In fact, one white friend implied in a letter that the time was propitious because the people were "alive . . . . on the subjects of temperance and religion." This, however, did not prevent his arrest on the unfounded charge of having delivered abolition speeches in Massachusetts. He was ordered out of the city, but a mob made it necessary to place him in a jail for safekeeping. Upon his release, he was tarred and feathered by a mob of workingmen who were

[18] John Spencer Bassett, *Slavery in the State of North Carolina* (Baltimore, 1899), pp. 57-58.

satisfied with inflicting some form of humiliation. After he had settled for his family and was prepared to leave, his mother's mistress, affected by the separation of Lane from his mother, permitted her to accompany the family.

During the autumn of 1897, Bassett by chance noticed at a Negro fair in North Carolina a placard which read: "Horses Owned and Exhibited by Lunsford Lane." Approaching a Negro farmer, he asked: "Who is Lunsford Lane?"

"I am, sir," was the reply.

"What kin are you to the original Lunsford Lane?"

"Don't exactly know, sir; reckon he was my uncle."

"What became of him?" questioned Bassett in order to draw him out.

"Think he must 'a emigrated," the man answered.

Although Lane apparently failed to establish a family line, there were other free colored men who became the fountainhead of family traditions that have persisted to the present day. Two of these families originated among the free colored people of Fayetteville. Charles W. Chestnut, the distinguished Negro novelist, who died in 1932 in Cleveland, was a descendant of one of these families. Concerning another free family which has a descendant who is at present a dentist in Wilmington, North Carolina, Booker Washington wrote:

> A coloured man by the name of Matthew Leary is still remembered in Fayetteville who, before the war, was the owner of considerable land, a number of slaves, a brick store in the business part of the town, and a handsome residence in a good neighborhood. His sons gained some prominence in North Carolina during the Reconstruction era. Matthew Leary, Jr., went into politics and afterward became a clerk in one of the Government offices in Washington. A younger brother, Hon. John S. Leary, was the first coloured man in North Carolina to be admitted to the bar, of which he remained a respected member until he died at Charlotte, N.C. He was, I understand, at one time a member of the North Carolina Legislature.[19]

Likewise, another free colored man, James D. Sampson, who accumulated some wealth and published a paper in Cincinnati during

[19] Booker T. Washington, *The Story of the Negro* (New York, 1909) I, 206.

the Civil War, became the head of a family line in which members
of three generations have completed Oberlin College. The fourth
free family which has maintained a continuous history to the present
time is that of John R. Green, who was born in Newbern. His son,
the historian of the family, was still practicing law in Cleveland in
1933, while his grandchildren are members of the professional group
in that city.

Space will permit only a brief account of one of the free families
in Virginia which have had an uninterrupted history from the early
nineteenth century. The earliest ancestor concerning whom we have
any historical record was probably born during the American Revolution in Petersburg. However, according to Jackson, who has given
us a history of the family,

> our first real knowledge of him comes in 1804, when, for the sum of
> forty-five pounds, he purchased from Hector McNeil, a white mer-
> chant of Petersburg, "one certain piece of parcel of land situate,
> lying and being in the town of Petersburg, aforesaid, on the east side
> of the street known and distinguished in the plan of the said town by
> the name of Union Street." In 1820 this property, consisting of house
> and lot, was valued at $1,050. In the meantime he had also bought
> one lot on Oak Street, which was assessed at $131.25. This James
> Colson becomes the head of a remarkable line of descendants. When
> he died, in 1825, his property was taken over by his son, William
> Colson. The son in his early years was a barber in Petersburg, but a
> few years after his marriage to Sarah Elebeck, in 1826, he emigrated
> to Liberia in connection with the colonization movement of that time.
> In Liberia he engaged in a mercantile enterprise with Joseph Jenkins,
> who, too, came from Petersburg.
>
> William Colson was the father of three children, William, Mary,
> and James Major. The last of these particularly comes easily within
> the memory of Petersburg citizens living today. He was born in 1830
> and died in 1892. James Major is to be remembered especially as a
> fine shoemaker, whose patrons included most of the prominent people
> of the town. It is said that his skill at shoe making extended to the
> point where he could make a shoe to fit the special needs of a sore foot.
>
> James Major Colson was married in 1852 to a free woman of color,
> Fannie Meade Bolling. His wife naturally was primarily a homemaker,
> but at the same time her literary attainments were manifested in her
> production of poetry throughout her long life. This lady came along
> during the period of the hostile legislation against the education of

free Negroes. She learned to read and write at odd moments while in the employ of a white family that took great care that she should put her lessons aside in the event that company or strangers came into the home. Thus her very employers, regardless of the law, helped make it possible for her to acquire the rudiments of learning. Immediately after the war she put her knowledge to good use by taking the initiative in starting a private school on Oak Street in Petersburg.[20]

Among the numerous children of James Major Colson and Fannie Meade Colson, there were nine—three boys and six girls—who reached adult age. Six members of this family became teachers, while two of the boys entered other occupations, and one of the girls became a registered nurse. One of the boys, James Major III, who was born in 1855, received the Phi Beta Kappa key when he completed Dartmouth College. He served as a school principal and for awhile was president of the Negro college in Petersburg. When he died in 1909, he left his family a considerable amount of real estate.

Excluded from our discussion here are the free families in the cities of the North and the Northwest Territory, or the more or less isolated communities of free colored families, which were mixed to a considerable extent with Indians. Many of the free colored families in the northern cities and Northwest Territory had migrated from southern communities. Later we shall see how these families formed the nuclei of the higher social and economic classes in both northern and southern communities. But, instead of following the career of these families, we shall turn our attention to those communities of free families that were mixed with Indians.

[20] Luther P. Jackson, "Free Negroes of Petersburg, Virginia," *Journal of Negro History*, XII, 372-77.

CHAPTER XI

RACIAL ISLANDS

Although the free mulatto families have had a history different from the mass of the Negro population, they have, nevertheless, gradually become identified more or less with the Negro group and furnished many of its leaders. In this respect they may be distinguished from those families of white, Negro, and Indian ancestry, living in isolated communities in various parts of the country, that have remained outside the main currents of Negro life. Whereas the free mulatto families and their descendants have generally formed an upper class in the Negro group, the families that have formed these isolated communities of mixed-bloods have often regarded themselves as an altogether different race. In some instances their consciousness of being a different race from the Negro has expressed itself in the naïve reference to themselves as "a different kind of folk," while in other instances tradition has established their group identity under some such names as Creoles, Moors, or some corrupted Indian name of unknown origin. Moreover, so strong has been their determination to remain a distinct group that they have often permitted their children to grow up illiterate rather than send them to the public schools provided for Negroes.

The history of the Pamunky Tribe of Indians in Virginia is typical of those communities of mixed-bloods which, having originated in the association between Indians and Negroes, gradually lost their Indian character. As early as 1843 the white citizens of King William County petitioned the state legislature:

The object of the colonial assembly was to protect a few harmless and tributary Indians, but the law which was passed to secure the Indians from intrusion on the part of the same white inhabitants has unwittingly imposed upon the posterity of the same white inhabitants a great grievance, in the presence of two unincorporated bodies of free mulattoes in the midst of a large slaveholding community. A greater grievance of such character cannot be well conceived, when it is known that a large number of free Negroes and mulattoes now enjoy under a law enacted for a praiseworthy purpose peculiar and exclusive privileges such as an entire exemption from taxation, holding land without liability for debt, and the land so held properly speaking public land belonging to the Commonwealth. . . . . The claim of the Indians no longer exists. . . . . His blood has so largely mingled with that of the Negro race as to have obliterated all striking features of Indian extraction.[1]

Although we have historical evidence concerning the origin of other mixed communities,[2] in most instances we must rely upon the traditions which have been handed down in the communities concerning the Indian and white progenitors. Let us take as an example the mixed community near Indian Mound, Tennessee, which has all but vanished.

In order to reach the dwelling-place of the seven living grandchildren of the founder of the community, the author and his secretary had to leave the broad highways. We traveled country roads and drove over a muddy lane and through a half-dried-up creek. As we emerged from a thickly wooded area, an old but substantial house covered with corrugated iron suddenly appeared in the clearing. From the covered porch of the house a white-haired man with a great beard came to the gate to greet us. His bronze skin and granite-like features offered scarcely a suggestion of Negro ancestry. In fact, later, when he gave a well-chronicled story of the origin and history of his family, he made no mention of Negro blood.

[1] *Legislative Petitions, Archives of Virginia, King William County, 1843.* Quoted in J. H. Johnston, "Documentary Evidence of the Relations of Negroes and Indians," *Journal of Negro History,* XIV, 29-30.

[2] *Documents Printed by Order of the Senate of the Commonwealth of Massachusetts during the Session of the Grand Court, 1861,* No. 96, p. 10. Quoted in C. G. Woodson, "The Relations of Negroes and Indians in Massachusetts," *Journal of Negro History,* V, 50.

When we were ushered into the house, which had been standing over a century, we felt that we had suddenly been transported back to the pioneer days of the first half of the nineteenth century. About a wide fireplace in which huge logs were burning sat five old women ranging in age from seventy-three to ninety-one. They were dressed in wide and full-gathered skirts and high shoes with flat heels, while about their shoulders they wore pieces of flannel for shawls. Three of them had rags about their heads. One of the sisters was blind, and another found it difficult to recognize strangers. Beside these five sisters sat their eighty-eight-year-old brother bent with age. The features and color of all of them showed striking signs of Indian ancestry.

The remarkably agile seventy-six-year-old brother, who conducted us into the house and introduced us to his brother and sisters, recited the history of the family. As he told the story during this visit and a subsequent one, he was corroborated or corrected by his sisters, especially the youngest, who appealed to the oldest sister from time to time for confirmation of her statements:

> The oldest ancestor of whom they had any knowledge was their great-grandfather who lived in North Carolina. His son, of Irish and Indian mixture, migrated from North Carolina about 1803. After first settling in Rutherford County, he moved to the present location and took up land. It was because of this fact, they presumed, "land" was added to the family name. He was married twice—the first wife being assuredly an Indian and the second presumably of the same race. "Our color just came from the Cherokee race. We have no Negro blood in us." By his first wife he had eight children and by his second four. He was a Primitive Baptist. When he died around 1865, he left his land—about three-hundred acres—to his children.

Our informants were able to give a fairly detailed account of four generations of descendants of the founder of the community. Four of his eight children by his first wife were never married. The four remaining brothers and sisters had at least thirty-six children, nearly half-a-hundred grandchildren, and an unknown number of great-grandchildren. The daughter of the original settler by his second wife—the only one of the four children to marry—was the mother of nine children and numbered among her descendants more than a score of grandchildren. Our informants, who were the only surviving children of the founder's eighth child, had never married. Although two families representing the younger generation lived by and administered to their needs, these seven brothers and sisters were the real guardians of the ancestral homestead.

The picture so far presented of these ancient remnants of a once great clan gives one no idea of the traditions and ideals which have placed an indelible imprint upon the lives of its scattered representatives. The imprint of these traditions and ideals was visible in a family living on their own farm less than five miles from the original settlement. The father and mother had the same family name, their grandfathers having been sons of the original settler. The parents as well as their two children, a boy and a girl, looked more like Indians than Negroes or mulattoes. Their comfortable and well-furnished house was characteristic of the thrift, intelligence, and stability for which this group of mixed-bloods are noted. The father, who was the responsible head of the family, not only worked on his farm but supervised the work of white farm laborers. Although neither father nor mother had completed high school, they took a daily paper and one or two magazines and had plans for their children to get a college education.

This family, together with another family which was more definitely bound to the community, formed the last link between the almost vanished community and its scattered members in the world outside. Over the years, family after family had moved to Ohio, Illinois, and cities in Tennessee. Although the original settler's great-granddaughter remarked: "The X's don't do much corresponding, but we don't forget each other," the old solidarity which was celebrated in family reunions has been broken. The last family reunion, which was held in 1917 on the hundredth birthday anniversary of a daughter of the original settler, was attended only by the descendants living in Tennessee.

From what was learned of those who had gone beyond the borders of Tennessee, it appeared that they, like those who had remained within the state, were industrious and well disciplined. In both their religion and their morals they reflected the simple faith and the strict teachings of the older generation, whose seven living representatives still hold prayer meeting every Wednesday night and church on Sunday with one brother acting as the preacher. Although this close-knit clan, which was at the same time an isolated religious community, has slowly disintegrated, pride in family still stirs the younger as well as the older generations. One source of family pride was the fact that no member had ever been arrested or had otherwise brought disgrace upon the family name. However, it should not be inferred that this modest achievement appeared to them as a great accomplishment, for they maintained that they could only boast of the simple human virtues. With a single exception the members of the family had followed humble occupations and were known for their thrift and honesty. They had no apologies to make for the fact that only one member of the family was ever known to have finished college. This exceptional member of the family who was known only vaguely to the other members of the family, had achieved some distinction as the head of the colored division of a national welfare agency. While the attainments of this single member did not elicit special pride, they could boast that they kept in touch with the outside world through the daily paper and that the community had maintained a school from the beginning. Even the children in the only family that remained in the original settlement were instructed by their mother in reading and writing.

Although our aged informants were reluctant to acknowledge that in the early history of the community there had been opposition to intermarriage with Negroes, this was apparently the reason for the failure of many of them to find suitable mates. The cleavage between the mixed-bloods and the whites had been widened in the early history of the community when a minister of the white church made a remark about dark people attending the church. After this incident the mixed-bloods established a church of their own and ceased to bury their dead in the white cemetery. When the head of the family referred to above related this incident, he hastened to add that he and his wife, who were sending their children to the Negro school in the near-by town, did not share the feelings of the older generation but regarded themselves simply as colored people. In fact, the process by which this family is gradually merging with the Negro community shows how families from these isolated communities of mixed-bloods have gradually filtered into the Negro population. The change in attitude toward the Negro group has been effected in the case of this family and those families that migrated through contacts in the urban environment. Although visiting in the two cities of Tennessee to which the families have moved is still restricted largely to the homes of relatives, friendships have been formed with the better-situated mulatto families. These contacts have been facilitated through the Negro schools, in which the younger generation is gradually taking over the traditions and culture of the Negro group. As a result of these widened contacts, we find an increasing number of marriages with Negroes; but chiefly with those of mixed ancestry.

According to the traditions that have been preserved in this community, one member of the family migrated sixty or seventy years ago to Ohio and married into a family of the same racial mixture. This family evidently formed a part of the community of mixed-bloods in Darke County, Ohio, since the history of this latter community, as related by those living there today, includes a pioneer of Indian extraction who migrated from Tennessee. Like the community in Tennessee, the settlement in Ohio originated through the migration of free people of Indian, white, and supposedly Negro ancestry from North Carolina. The oldest living inhabitant in the community gave the following account of his family and the community:

> His grandfather was born free in Virginia. According to the story which was told by the grandfather, he was compelled to leave Virginia when the state threatened to re-enslave all free colored people who did not leave the state. A white man arranged to meet the grandfather, who was still a boy, in Greenville, Ohio. When the grandfather reached Greenville, he was taken in by the white man and later took up 160 acres of land at $1.25 per acre. After securing enough money through digging wells to purchase the land, the grandfather moved his family to the present location in 1808. This was the first family in the community.

Our next informant was the descendant of the second family that moved into the community. He began his story:

Uncle Tom B—— has told me at different times that two of the
B——'s rode in here horseback from North Carolina and at that time
they were offered a section of land for those two horses—640 acres—
and they didn't take that for that team. They took up a homestead
up here, each one of them. This country then was nothing but wilderness, no roads, just woods. I don't know how long they remained on
it and they went back to North Carolina to tell about what they discovered and what they found up here. Then they began to move and
wind their way in here. A white man asked me up here in Greenville
if a Randolph ever come in here and I told him no, no slave holder
ever come in here and bought up homesteads. My father said he had
seen wolves, bears, panthers. That well out there I expect has been
by here for 100 years and has never been known to go dry. As those
began to spread out then others began to come in here. They were
born in North Carolina. . . . . My grandfather, Richard B——, was
one of the original settlers of the community. Right up where that
well is was a log house where he settled and when he came from
North Carolina he taken up that 40 acres from the government. My
father bought this 40 acres from a man named D—— G——, a
white man, who purchased this land from the government. I can
remember when this place was about six miles square. Rev. S——'s
grandfather at one time owned 640 acres of land across where,—well,
across here over on the Indiana side. He came in here and couldn't
read nor write. He came from North Carolina.

Our first informant's racial origin was typical of other members
of the community. When this eighty-two-year-old man with blue
eyes, blond hair, and pinkish skin was asked concerning the race
of his grandfather, he answered:

Well, there is a lot of blood in our relation—Indian, Scotch-Irish,
Dutch, and a little bit nigger. Grandmother could talk Dutch just
as fast as she could talk. My grandfather was as white and whiter as
I was. Their mixture, they got in the South before they come here.

It is not strange that people with such a racial background should
have considered themselves a different race from the mass of the
Negro population. While it is true that, prior to the Civil War the
community was one of the stations of the Underground Railroad,
there was apparently scarcely any intermarriage with the blacks who
escaped from bondage. Although the present members of the com-

munity are hesitant about acknowledging that the blacks were not regarded as eligible mates, our informant admitted that they "don't marry that way somehow or another." On the other hand, it was acknowledged by a representative of one of the two families showing distinctly Negro ancestry that the community was not "so particular about real black people," and cited the following incident in support of her statement: "Once I was sitting in the church and I said to one of the girls that a certain one of the girls was married, and the first thing they said was, 'Oh, yes, she married a black man.' " Moreover, there was a story current in the community that a minister had not accepted a promotion, because his wife refused to go with him to a church of "black Africans."

Nor is it to be wondered at that many of the early families or their descendants married or passed over into the white race. In some cases members of the community take some pride in the fact that they can point to men of distinction in the white world whose families were among the mixed-bloods that first settled in the community. Many more families and individuals who have passed into the white world have left no trace of their whereabouts; and it is possible that their children do not know that they probably have Negro blood in their veins. Seemingly, individuals among the younger generation are continuing to filter into the white race, for it is possible to trace a number of them to occupations in the larger cities that are ordinarily closed to Negroes.

Although a number of the families have become merged with the white population, the traditions of the families in this settlement are bound up mainly with their achievements as a distinct racial group and in later years with the attainments of those who have found a place in the Negro world. These traditions stem from the activities of the sturdy pioneers who sought freedom in an unknown country and built up a community of independent landowners and successful farmers. Speaking of one of the early settlers, one informant said with pride:

> If Jack C—— had lived about two more months he would have been ninety years old and many a time he started from here with his wheat to Cincinnati. It took him a week to make the trip—no rail-

roads and no roads. He was considered the best teamster to pull horses from here to Cincinnati.

These pioneers built substantial homes and erected a church and a schoolhouse. A Wesleyan church, where a few families still gather, was built nearly a century ago. Before the Civil War a subscription school was maintained by the community, while the Quakers helped to establish a seminary for advanced education across the line in Indiana. At the present time, in two cemeteries bearing the names of the first two families to settle in the community, tombstones mark the resting-place of these pioneers and their descendants.

Although many families have migrated and whites have bought their farms and the younger generation especially is seeking its fortunes in the various cities of the North, there are still about sixty families in the community, including four families living in Indiana. Practically all these families are landowners, and, although the community is not so prosperous as formerly, their homes give evidence of economic well-being and a high level of rural culture. The rough log dwellings have long ago been replaced by large painted houses with shutters and glass windows. On the inside the walls are papered and hung with portraits of ancestors or pictures illustrating some biblical story. Their well-kept homes, with books, magazines, and a daily paper, bespeak the culture which has been built up in these families during several generations.

There has long been a tradition of education in the community. Before the consolidation of the local schools, there were five public schools, taught chiefly by members of local families who had received advanced training outside the community. Unlike the families in the Tennessee community, these families boast of the intellectual achievements of those who were born there. They were able to name college and high-school teachers and principals and professional men and women, who have sprung from families in the community. The two outstanding examples of the community's distinguished men were a Methodist bishop and a diplomatic representative to Liberia. But, perhaps, the man who typified best the role of these families in the Negro world was a minister who served a church in Dayton for thirty-three years. As a leader in the colored community, he became disgusted with the conditions under which Negroes lived and organized a realty company which enabled Negroes to purchase homes in desirable neighborhoods.

There are other communities of mixed-bloods in the North which are similar to this one in Ohio. For example, there is a community in the Ramapo Hills about thirty miles north of New York City. Concerning the inhabitants of this community, we shall let one of its representatives speak. She is a woman about forty, who, after taking the Bachelor's degree at Howard University, married and returned to the community to live. Our informant writes:

> On approaching the hills bordering the villages of Suffern and Hillburn one meets a type of native people quite different from those found elsewhere. Some of these resemble the Indian with their copper-colored skin and straight black hair. Others are very fair with flaxen hair and blue eyes while still others are of the Negroid type—although these latter are very much in the minority. Nor are these all. Also peculiar to this type of people are some having white hair and pink eyes, know as albinos. On becoming better acquainted with these albinos we find them possessed of rare skill and talent. Barnum and Bailey have exhibited some of this variety in their circus several years ago.
>
> More than a century ago some Boers were supposed to have been brought to this section by the English—possibly for the purpose of mining iron ore. As the story goes—among these Boers were four Johns—i.e., John De Groot, John Von Doonk, John De Vries and John Mann. Quite positive proof of this fact are the predominating names among the people at the present time; i.e. De Groat, Van Dunk, De Freese and Mann. After a time these people were visited by remnants of wandering tribes of Indians; i.e., Tuscaroras and Delawares who were travelling up from the South to join others of their tribe in central New York State. Still later were found, in this section, slaves maintained by a family of Sufferns. An amalgamation took place between these three classes of people. A slave named Jackson, was believed to have been the first of his kind to mingle with the others and as a result we find a type of people with certain peculiarities called "Jackson Whites."

Among these people, as in the case of the other two communities, there was prejudice against mingling with Negroes. The father of the author of the document quoted above, a man seventy-five years old, said that when he was a young man there was strong opposition to marriage with Negroes and that often he had heard the girls remark that they wanted "only men with white skins and blue veins." In fact, it seems that the community was divided to some extent according to color. Our informant writes:

> There are in this section two distinct types of "Jackson Whites"—one set of the white variety, living on the other side of Suffern, exhibit a great lack of intelligence as compared with their fellows of the predominating Indian and colored types.

The superior intelligence of the darker group is probably attributable to the fact that they have tended to move from the isolated hills down into the valley where they have enjoyed the advantages of wider contacts, in spite of the fact that separate schools are provided for them:

> Not all of the "Jackson Whites" remained up in the hills. Some of them moved down into the valley where the new Brook Chapel became the center. In the twentieth century we find them much more interested in what is going on in the outside world. They regularly attend the Jim-crow school provided for them by the leading white people of Hillburn, which is the only one of its kind in New York State. Most of the people work in the nearby iron and steel foundries while some engage in other occupations which are open to their kind. Still others have gone into the cities of both New York and other states where they engage in higher occupations. Quite a number of the children have graduated from the nearby High School. Some have finished from normal schools and colleges. One went so far as to receive his Ph.D.

In the early days when these people were confined to the hills, they maintained themselves by hunting and fishing, cutting lumber, and hiring themselves to near-by farmers. They were evidently a deeply religious group. The little information which is now available represents them as having a religion of "the Methodist type."

> For many years it was customary for them to hold singing and praying services at each other's homes. These were known as "class meetings" and each one always had a "class leader."

As the result of the missionary work of the Presbyterians, they later became a part of that religious organization. We have a

description of one of the religious leaders from the pen of his granddaughter, our informant:

> One of the most outstanding of these leaders was a remarkable
> character. He was once described as "being of almost gigantic stature,
> yet symmetrically moulded and with a head of more than Websterian
> grandeur and size." He would remind an observer of one of the
> priests of ancient Israel. The dark and solemn face, the snow-white
> hair hanging in abundant locks almost to his shoulders, the earnest
> deep tones of the voice, as he led the services, made a picture not soon
> to be forgotten. This worthy sage was known to all as "Uncle Sammy
> De Freese" and his name still is uttered very reverently in the neigh-
> borhood by all including the better class of whites who knew him
> or afterward learned of him. On entering the Brook Chapel, which he
> helped build, one will find a picture of this old saint.

This "old saint" belonged to an anomalous race of people whose
descendants have become scattered through New Jersey and New
York. They have gradually taken over the traditions and ways of life
of Negroes with whom they have become more or less identified.
The change in the attitudes and traditions of this group was expressed by one of them as follows:

> Formerly the "Jackson Whites" never possessed the same pride
> which one always finds among those of the true Negro race. Nor did
> they enjoy the same things common to that race. However, in the past
> few years, since some Negroes from outside have come in and owing
> to the conditions thrust upon them by the great prejudice abounding
> in their village, they have attained some of the pride which is prevalent
> among those who are segregated and set aside from others. The better
> thinking class protest against these conditions which tend toward
> making them feel the supposed superiority of the whites of the com-
> munity. They are also fast adopting the use of Negro literature and
> music.

Another group of mixed-bloods, whose racial identity has long
remained an enigma, had its origin in Delaware. There are two
traditions concerning the origin of this group. According to one
account, these people are the descendants of "Spanish Moors who,
by chance had drifted from the southern coast of Spain prior to the
Revolutionary War, and settled at various points on the Atlantic
Coast of the British colonies." The other tradition, which is probably

closer to the facts, says that they sprang from the mixture of whites, Indians, and Negro slaves, probably of Moorish origin.

While George P. Fisher was attorney-general of the state of Delaware, he had occasion to investigate the racial origin of these people. In 1857 one of them was indicted for having sold ammunition to another member of the same race in violation of the law against the selling of firearms to Negroes and mulattoes. An eighty-seven-year-old woman of the same race who was called as a witness gave in substance the following testimony concerning their origin: "About fifteen or twenty years before the Revolutionary War, which she said broke out when she was a girl some five or six years old, there was a lady of Irish birth living on a farm in Indian River Hundred, a few miles distant from Lewes, which she owned and carried on herself. Nobody appeared to know anything of her history or antecedents. Her name she gave as Regua, and she was childless, but whether a maid or widow, or a wife astray, she never disclosed to anyone. She was much above the average woman of that day in stature, beauty and intelligence. The tradition described her as having a magnificent complexion, or, as Lydia termed it, a rose and lily complexion, large and dark blue eyes and luxuriant hair of the most beautiful shade, usually called light auburn. After she had been living in Angola Neck quite a number of years, a slaver was driven into Lewes Creek, then a tolerable fair harbor, and was there, weather-bound for several days. . . . . Miss or Mrs. Regua, having heard of the presence of the slaver in the harbor, and having lost one of her men, went to Lewes, and to replace him, purchased another from the slave ship. She selected a very tall, shapely and muscular young fellow of dark ginger-bread color, who claimed to be a prince or chief of one of the tribes of the Congo River which had been overpowered in a war with a neighboring tribe and nearly all slain or made prisoners and sold into perpetual slavery. This young man had been living with his mistress but a few months when they were duly married and, as Lydia told the court and jury, they reared quite a large family of children, who as they grew up were not permitted to associate and intermarry with their neighbors of pure Caucasian blood, nor were they disposed to seek associations or alliance with the Negro race; so that they were so necessarily compelled to associate and intermarry with the remnant of the Nanticoke tribe of Indians who still lingered in their old habitations for many years after the great body of the tribe had been removed further towards the setting sun."[3]

On the whole, these people have devoted themselves to agriculture. They have built their own homes and churches and have been known by their neighbors as thrifty and law-abiding citizens. A small community of their descendants has been established across the Delaware River near Beacon's Neck in Cumberland County, New Jersey. Some of them have doubtless filtered into the white race, and at present others are gradually becoming merged with the Negro population.

By far the most important community of mixed-bloods in the North, for which fortunately, we have a well-authenticated record, is the Gouldtown settlement near Bridgeton, New Jersey. Traditions concerning the origin of this community go back to the end of the seventeenth century. The first mulattoes in this settlement are believed to have been the offspring of a Negro and the granddaughter of John Fenwick, who, having acquired from Lord Berkeley a tract of land in New Jersey, came to America in 1675. William and Theophilus G. Steward, relate:

> Among the numerous troubles and vexations which assailed Fenwick, none appear to have distressed him more than the base and abandoned conduct of his granddaughter, Elizabeth Adams, who had attached herself to a citizen of color. By his will he deprives her of any share in his estate, "unless the Lord open her eyes to see her abominable transgressions against him, me and her good father, by giving her true repentance and forsaking that Black which hath been the ruin of her and becoming penitent for her sins." From this illicit connection have sprung the families of the Goulds at a settlement called Gouldtown, in Cumberland County. Later, this same historian in a memoir of John Fenwick wrote: "Elizabeth Adams had formed a connection with a negro man whose name was Gould."[4]

[3] *The So-called Moors of Delaware: A Sketch Written by George P. Fisher which Appeared as a Communication and was Published in the Milford (Del.) Herald under Date of June 15, 1895.* Reprinted by the Public Archives Commission on Delaware, 1929.

[4] William and Theophilus G. Steward, *Gouldtown: A Very Remarkable Settlement of Ancient Date* (Philadelphia, 1914), pp. 50-51.

Although there is no record of the life of Fenwick's granddaughter with her Negro husband, the Gouldtown graveyard register tells the location of their son and his wife. The Gouldtown settlement included three other families of mulatto and Indian extraction:

> Tradition says that the Pierces originated from two mulattoes who were brought here in a vessel from the West Indies, with which the colony had early trade, vessels from the West Indies arriving at Greenwich and also coming up as far as to what is now Bridgeton. These two men were Richard and Anthony Pierce, brothers. . . . . Anthony and Richard Pierce paid the passage of two Dutch women, sisters, from Holland; their names were Marie and Hannah Van Aca. The last name speedily degenerated into Wanaca, and was made the Christian name of a son of one of them. From these descended all the Pierces of Gouldtown. They came to the colony of West New Jersey before the middle of the eighteenth century.
>
> The Murrays originated in Cape May; they claim an Indian ancestry. The first Murray of whom there is trace in the vicinity of the earliest settlements of Gouldtown, was Othniel Murray. He claimed to be a Lenapee or Siconessee Indian, and came from Cape May County. The Lenapees resided in the locality of Cohansey (or Bridgeton) and had quite a settlement at what became known as the Indian Fields, at a run still known as the Indian Field Run. This Othniel Murray married Katherine (last name unknown), a Swede. They had five children, three sons and two daughters, Mark Murray, David Murray, and Mary Murray and Dorcas Murray. From these descended all the Murrays of Gouldtown.

Another family which was of slave origin became united by marriage with the three original families:

> The Cuff family was of slave origin, though in a time quite remote; Cuff, a slave, was owned by a man named Padgett. Padgett had three daughters, and he, by some means, got into the Continental Army, in the French and Indian War, and was killed. Cuff took care of the widow, and she finally married him. He was called "Cuffee Padgett"; they had three sons, and when these went to school they were taunted by the other boys as being the sons of "Old Cuffee Padgett"; so they would have their father drop the Padgett and take the name of Cuffee Cuff. The names of these sons were Mordecai, Reuben, and Seth.

During the early days of its existence the settlement became divided into two communities, known as Gouldtown and Piercetown, because of the traditions connecting them with the families bearing these names. This division has lasted to the present day, although the cause of the cleavage is forgotten.

The outstanding tradition among the Goulds was their relationship to the founder of the colony. One of the historians of this family writes that the "Gould's tradition a hundred years ago was 'We descended from Lord Fenwick.' . . . The writer of this, now over three score and ten years of age, has heard the words from his grandparents, and other of the Goulds who were born and lived in the close of the eighteenth century." Included in the traditions of this settlement is a record of services in all the wars of the nation, with the exception of the Mexican War, from the Revolution to the Spanish-American War. Although the religious traditions of this settlement were originally different from those of the masses of Negroes who were chiefly influenced by the Baptists and Methodists, descendants of families in this settlement played a conspicuous part in the history of the African Methodist Episcopal Church which became the chief church in this community. In 1816 it is recorded that Rueben Cuff of the Cuff family, whose origin is given above, married into the Gould family and was one of the organizers of the African Methodist Church in Philadelphia. Though it is impossible to catalogue the descendants of these free families, some idea of their influence in the development of Negro life is afforded by the fact that, when the annual reunion was celebrated in 1910, there were two hundred and twenty-three living descendants from one grandson of Benjamin Gould I, whose mother was the granddaughter of John Fenwick. Their place in the history of the Negro was summarized by a distinguished descendant, himself an army chaplain and historian:

> Several of the earlier Goulds and Pierces as well as Murrays inter-married with whites, and members of their immediate offspring went away and lost their identity, they and their descendants becoming white; while from those who still maintained their identity as people of color, there have come many who have reached distinction, and in whom their native County shows merited pride, as for instance, a Methodist bishop, a chaplain in the United States regular army, a

physician, a lawyer, a distinguished dentist, teachers, writers, journalists; and in the industrial arts, carpenters, masons, blacksmiths, wheelwrights, painters, carriage builders, woolen spinners, and weavers; brickmakers, machinists, engineers, electricians, printers, factory men, sailors, ministers of the Gospel, and farmers; in fact none of its sister villages has produced—taking equality of environment—more or better or more creditable individualities than has this settlement.

In this community as in others of a similar character there has been much inbreeding. During recent years such unions have been looked upon with disfavor. At the Sunday-school picnic in 1933 one of the descendants who had come from a considerable distance told the author that he had dissuaded his cousin from marrying within the community because he thought that such marriages were responsible for a number of "queer" people among them.

Although the far-flung descendants of the families originating in this community have been a leavening element in the Negro population, the settlement itself has slowly dwindled and disintegrated during the last score or more years. There is nothing in the appearance of the modern well-kept homes, which are a part of the remnant of this vanishing settlement, on the highway from Bridgeton to Atlantic City, to make one aware of its singular history and the memories of those who gather there each year. The descendants of the original settlers no longer gather at the annual family reunions, once held in one of the original houses and presided over by the oldest living representative of the family. The family reunions have been transformed into an annual Sunday-school picnic, which gathers on the third Thursday in August. However, in spite of the fact that the main institutions in the settlement, the school and the church, have absorbed many outside families, these families have not lost their identity. The bonds of kinship are still strong, and there is a recognition of a common cultural heritage.

Now, we shall return to the South again to consider in a less detailed manner several other communities of mixed-bloods. The first of these communities is located in Columbus County, North Carolina. We do not find in the families that have remained in this community the well-authenticated and virile traditions which we found in the area described above. One of the two principal families traces its origin to a free man of color who was of white, Indian, and Negro mixture; while the other family which later intermarried with the first was of white and Negro ancestry and had become free before the Civil War. The Indian ancestry of these families is of special interest because of their proximity and relationship to the Indian community in Robeson County, which adjoins Columbus County. The Indians in Robeson County are the well-known Croatans, who claim that they are pure Indians and resent any imputation of Negro blood. The state maintains a separate normal school with white and Indian teachers for them. However, it seems from both tradition and reliable reports that are current in the colored community that at one time the ancestors of the Croatans and the free mulattoes associated freely and intermarried. These reports are borne out by the fact that families in the colored community have relatives who have married into the Indian community. These relatives, in the words of one of our colored informants, "want to slight their own people."

The Indians and those claiming to be Indians, according to reliable reports, definitely separated themselves from the mulattoes about forty years ago when white political leaders in their campaign to disfranchise the Negro gained the support of the Indian upon the promise that they would be treated as a separate race and enjoy certain educational and social privileges.

Although one of the older members of the colored community referred to his group as "the nationality in here," on the whole, the people have identified themselves with the Negro race and have forgotten the distinctions which the older generation was inclined to set up.

The following incident, related by a woman resembling an Indian, is typical of their present attitude: "One time I stopped there [Pembroke, i.e., the station in the Indian community] waiting in the colored waiting-room. One of the Croatan women said: 'What are you doing there, you are not a nigger? You don't belong in there. Let me show you where to go.' And she went ahead of me in the white waiting-room and told the man I was an Indian and did not belong in there. When she left, I went back to the colored waiting-room."

After the Indians and those who claimed to be Indians set themselves apart as a distinct race, the members of the colored community in Columbus County ceased to regard their group as a peculiar race and came to think of themselves as a part of the general Negro population. However, this was accomplished only gradually, for they still took pride in their free ancestry, calling themselves the "Old Free Issue," and held themselves aloof from the emancipated Negroes, or the "New Free Issue." One old woman described their attitude toward the emancipated blacks as follows:

> The tribe is all mixed up now more than they used to be. During the old times we had a separate feeling. We did not belong to the Negro or the whites. That's what started them to marrying first cousins. They were just freed about two miles from here. I guess you know how people just freed felt toward people of this settlement who had been free all of the time. We was what was considered the "Old Free Issue," and those just freed was the "New Free Issue." They did not have much [racial] mixture. They did not like us and we did not like them. They felt that they could not accept their inferiority.

Then, there were some who, rather than accept the status of Negroes, entered the white race. But the vast majority have become influential elements in the Negro population as the idea of their racial exclusiveness has died out. As a substantial group of land-owners, they have maintained strictly patriarchal ideals of family life and formed the backbone of Negro religious and educational institutions in their community. Moreover, they have furnished teachers and farm demonstrators in different parts of the state; while from the two principal families in the communities came two of the three men responsible for the well-known business enterprises in Durham.

The other communities of mixed-bloods to which we can give only passing attention are situated in Alabama. One of these communities is in Baldwin County, where we find a group of people who call themselves "Creoles" but are known by their white neighbors as "Nigger Creoles." Mr. Bond, who came across them while testing the Negro school children in Alabama, gives the following account of the legend concerning their origin:

> There is a legend in the countryside that the community goes back in its history to the days when the Spanish Main harbored numerous pirates and freebooters in the little inlets along the Gulf Coast. A portion of these Carib marauders, so the legend goes, maintained a rendezvous on the eastern shore of Mobile Bay, where these people now live. There is a little bay that bears the name of one of the largest families in the community, and that name belonged to a distinguished member of the piratical elect of the days of Jean Lafitte and his predecessors. To this little Eden, so the story goes, the robbers of the sea brought their spoils for division. Naturally, a considerable portion of these rewards of piracy were in the nature of feminine consignments. Their women were of all races: Negroes, Spanish, French and English. The hybridization begun in this way has produced the people here described.

The white member of Mr. Bond's party gave the test because, when it was found out that Mr. Bond was of Negro descent, he was told by the white teacher: "Well, I'll tell you; of course I'm not prejudiced, but if some of these Creoles heard that a nigger was up here giving tests to their children, I don't know what would happen."[5]

Another community of similar racial composition, which is located across the bay in Mobile County, has gradually disintegrated. Its inhabitants have intermarried with Negroes and have accepted teachers with Negro blood "if they were sufficiently light to 'pass' for Creoles, and if they were good Catholics." Social disorganization is also indicated by the cases of open concubinage between "Creole" women and white men. However, the "Creole" community in Baldwin County, which accepted Negro teachers forty or fifty years ago, has erected barriers against the Negro as a means of resisting the forces of disintegration. At the present time their homes, surrounded by whitewashed fences and well-kept yards and well-tilled fields, stand in marked contrast to the destitution and disorderliness of the plantation Negro. The high scores—above national standards—of

[5] Horace Mann Bond, "Two Racial Islands in Alabama," *American Journal of Sociology*, XXXVI, 552-67.

the school children are probably a reflection of the generally high social and economic status of this well-knit rural community which prides itself upon its race and keeps alive its traditions of a noble past.

The other "racial island" in Mobile County is composed of a group of mixed-bloods who call themselves Cajuns.

> Whether the Cajuns of Alabama bear kinship to those of Mississippi and Louisiana is a matter of question. The word itself is a corruption of "Acadian" or "Arcadian" and their derivation is claimed by the historians of Louisiana to be from those French-Canadians dispossessed by the British in the eighteenth century and immortalized by Longfellow. Not a single person could be found in the Mobile County community, however, who knew of this origin, or claimed it. They admit readily the racial heritage from the Indian, but deny as strongly as the Creoles of Baldwin County the presence of any "Negro taint."

This community of hybrids presents a depressing picture of poverty and social decay. Instead of churches supported by staunch believers, as in the case of the Catholic "Creoles," there are Baptist and Methodist missions housed in old weather-beaten, ramshackle buildings and supported by outside sources. These churches serve as schoolhouses for the children, whose backwardness surpasses even that of the Negro children on the plantations. Yet these same children are quick to inform any visitor that they are Cajuns, "Injuns an' white folks, all mixed up," and that they "ain't had no nigger blood" in them. In wretched rented cabins scattered about in the barren hill country, these people eke out a miserable existence through the cultivation of sparse upland cotton and sweet potatoes, the only crops that the soil is capable of producing. Contrasting the decay of this community with that of the "Creoles," Bond writes:

> In these Cajun communities where the families are brought in open contact with the white world the demoralization seems to be even more thorough. The Creoles simply disappear, while echoes of the Cajuns linger on in tales of licentious conduct, concubinage with both white and black men, and altogether a lingering survival of the disorganization now patent in the community, but even more raw and unpleasant when exposed to the probing of forces from two sides.

The social and economic conditions of the Cajuns are similar in many respects to the situation which two investigators found in an isolated community of mixed-bloods in Virginia.[6] According to the authors of this investigation, the Wins—the name by which they are designated in the study—started from "four fountain heads; one a white man named Brown, and the other three from Indians, named respectively Lane, Thomas and Jones," while the infusion of Negro blood came at a later date through matings with Negroes, both slave and free.

A white man named Brown married a Dolly Thomas, either a full-blood or a half-blood Indian. These two had many children, half-breeds, by the name of Brown, which children have in turn married and their descendants are now found in the Coon mountain regions of Ab County. Dolly Thomas' father, William Thomas, was known to have been an Indian and lived on the Ban River in that county. It is not known, however, from what tribe he, or the other Indians to be mentioned came, whether Cherokee from the Southern Appalachians or Powhatan from Eastern Virginia or Tuscarora from Southeastern Virginia. It is evident that they were wandering Indians as Ab County never belonged to any particular tribe of Indians. Legend has it that these Indians were travelling from their lands in the Carolinas on to Washington to see the Great Father just after the Revolutionary War and that for some reason these few stopped in Ab County. Another daughter of William Thomas married an Ed Jones, an Indian, on December 6, 1790, the official record of the marriage being found in the Ab Courthouse. This license does not state the color of the people concerned here. That fact is deduced from the statements of the people of Ab County and from the information secured from some of the older Wins. The son of this Ed Jones named Ned, and born about 1791, a half-breed, married his first cousin on his mother's side, a girl named Iders, and had a set of children named Jones, also half-breeds. These Jones have increased in number and now form at least one-half of the Win families now in the region. The name Jones is also found in Virginia in 1746 and later in what is now AC County, this region being north of the James River. This name is white and in certain parts of the county a good name. A third Indian strain comes in

[6] Arthur H. Estabrook and Ivan E. McDougle, *Mongrel Virginians: The Win Tribe* (Baltimore, 1926).

through a John Lane, a full blood Indian, born 1780, his daughter having married into the half-breed Brown family.

The descendants of these families became segregated from both the white and the Negro population because of their isolated situation in the mountains and the attitudes of the whites and Negroes. For the most part, they have carried on a precarious existence by raising tobacco, while a few have hired themselves as laborers to neighboring white farmers. Most of these people live in log houses or rough shacks on rented land. The school and chapel maintained by a missionary organization are indicative of the poverty and social disorganization in the community.

The authors attributed the economic inefficiency, the loose sex morals, and the low mental level of the people who form this group to the bad effects of racial mixture. They regarded the situation in this community as typical of the effects of the infusion of Indian and Negro blood in normal white family stocks, which consequently become the bearers of the inferior racial traits of the Negro and Indian. But we have seen from our study of families of the same racial mixture who have formed communities in both the North and the South that they have been as often as not a very thrifty class with sound morals and have furnished many of the leaders in the Negro population. Therefore, in concluding this chapter, we shall first consider some of the cultural factors which seem to offer a sufficient explanation of the economic and social status of these communities and then attempt to estimate the influence of these families of white, Indian, and Negro ancestry that have become a part of the general Negro population on the development of Negro family life.

All these communities have been influenced in their development by their geographic location. The Jackson Whites, the Wins, and the Cajuns have been restricted to the barren hill country where they have carried on a struggle to secure the barest means of existence, whereas the communities in Ohio, New Jersey, and North Carolina have had a fruitful soil to draw on and have consequently achieved a relatively high standard of living. Geographic location has also been responsible for the isolation of these groups. But, in estimating the effects of isolation, we must discriminate between the different degrees and kinds of isolation to which they have been subjected. The Jackson Whites in the Ramapo Hills of New York, the Wins on Coon Mountain in Virginia, the Indian Mound settlement in the hills of Tennessee, and the Cajuns of the Alabama hill country have been more effectively cut off from communication with the outside world than the mixed-bloods of Darke County, Ohio, or the Gouldtown folk in New Jersey. Moreover, there are more subtle ways in which these communities have been subjected to varying degrees of isolation. Although the mixed-bloods in these communities have been separated from the whites, the segregation has been, on the whole, more marked in the South than in the North. In the case of both the Ohio community and the New Jersey community there have always been beneficial contacts, sometimes inter-marriage, between the mixed-bloods and the whites. In fact, whites in both cases were influential in the establishment of their religious and educational institutions. That isolation has been responsible for the low stage of civilization in some of these communities is further borne out by the fact that many who have migrated from these areas have achieved some distinction in the white as well as in the Negro world. Naturally, we have not been able to point specifically to such persons in the white world, but we have already noted the conspicuous roles which descendants of these families have played in the institutional life of the Negro. The authors of *Mongrel Virginians* record the fact that one of the two Negroes who sat in the United States Senate came from a hybrid community in North Carolina.

In the institutional life of these communities was an additional clue to an understanding of the influence of cultural factors upon their social and intellectual development. Whereas, in the Ohio and New Jersey communities, well-developed educational and religious institutions with a century or more of history behind them, the people, also, are on a relatively high intellectual level. But, where we find institutions poorly developed, as among the Cajuns or Wins, or to a less extent among the Jackson Whites, we also find the people less capable. The relation between the culture of two of these communities and the intellectual level of their inhabitants has been presented in a striking manner in the study by Bond. He found that, on the one hand, the children of the efficient, intelligent, and thrifty Creoles, whose well-founded institutions and traditions were still intact, gave scores higher than the national norms, whereas the children of the poor, ignorant, disorganized Cajuns, of the same racial mixture, who were supported by missions and possessed scarcely any traditions, gave scores below those of the plantation Negro.

What, then, have been the contributions of those families of mixed blood that have fused with the Negro to the development of Negro family life? First among these contributions was their part in strengthening patriarchal traditions. In all these hybrid communities where it has been possible to trace family traditions, male progenitors were reported as the founders of the family lines. This was a natural consequence of the fact that these family lines were established in most instances by pioneer settlers. This was especially true of the communities in Ohio and Tennessee. The founders of these families migrated during the pioneer days of America across the mountains into the wilderness and there laid out communities. Consequently, these families have had a long history of industry and thrift and a sturdiness of character that differentiate them from the mass of the Negro population. When they have intermarried with the Negro population, they have generally married into families of mixed blood but with a different background. The families that have issued from such alliances have generally assumed a patriarchal pattern.

But these families of mixed blood have influenced the behavior of the Negro in other ways. The children in such families generally exhibit the restraint and self-discipline which have distinguished their forebears. For example, this may be seen even in their religious services which have been free from the extreme emotionalism of the Negro masses. In fact, when a Negro minister with a religious background of the masses has occasionally been assigned to these communities, he has been forced to modify his mode of preaching to be acceptable to their pattern of religious worship. It is no wonder that the descendants of these mixed families have often been regarded as queer by the general run of Negroes because they exhibited a firmness of character and a self-sufficiency unknown to their more pliable and sociable Negro associates. Although the peculiar cultural traits of these mixed families have been modified as they have increasingly mingled with the general Negro population, nevertheless, they have tended to enrich the family traditions of the Negro and give stability to his family life.

CHAPTER XII

BLACK PURITANS

Those elements in the Negro population that have had a foundation of stable family life to build upon have constituted in communities throughout the country an upper social class, more or less isolated from the majority of the population. Up until the first decade of the present century, their numbers were slowly increased by other families that managed to rise, as the favored families in the past, above the condition of the Negro masses. Generally, these families have attempted to maintain standards of conduct and to perpetuate traditions of family life that were alien to the majority of the Negro population. Where they have been few in numbers, they have often shut themselves up within the narrow circle of their own families in order not to be overwhelmed by the flood of immorality and vice surrounding them. In some places they have been numerous enough to create a society of their own in which they could freely pursue their way of life and insure a congenial environment to their children. Often, intensely conscious of their peculiar position with reference to the great mass of the Negro population, they have placed an exaggerated valuation upon moral conduct and cultivated a puritanical restraint in opposition to the free and uncontrolled behavior of the larger Negro world.

In general, homeownership since emancipation offers the best index to the extent and growth of this class of families in the Negro population. By 1890, or a quarter of a century after emancipation, 22 per cent of the families on farms had bought homes; while in the cities and small towns of the country a sixth of the families

were living in their own homes. During the next decade homeownership increased slightly in both rural and urban areas; but
after 1910 the proportion of farm families owning their homes
declined and by 1940 had reached less than 22 per cent. This
decline coincided with the rapid urbanization of the Negro and the
increase in homeownership in cities. We find in 1940 the highest
amount of homeownership among the rural-non-farm families, with
one family in three owning its home. Variations in the extent and
trend of homeownership during this period can also be observed
in the different states. However, the statistics for the various states
fail to give us any clue to an understanding of the character and role
of this favored group in the development of Negro family life. We
must see these families as a part of the communities in which they
have been a leavening element for the masses.

We shall turn first to those rural areas in the South which we
have already viewed from another standpoint. As we have seen, in
the two counties in the plantation regions of Alabama and Mississippi, there has been very little farm ownership. In 1910 only 7.5
per cent of the Negro farm families in Issaquena County, Mississippi,
owned their homes; while in Macon County, Alabama, where the
situation was slightly better, 11.3 per cent were homeowners.
However, even in the plantation region where farm ownership is
at a minimum, the mulatto families have some advantage over the
black families. The family histories of two of the mulatto owners
in Macon County will show how they are differentiated culturally
in many cases from the majority of landless black tenants.

The head of the first of these families was a mulatto, fifty-eight
years old, who was born in an adjoining county. His father, who
was born a slave, was the child of a white man. The father managed
to accumulate five hundred acres of land which his fifteen children
helped him to work. He exchanged this land for land in Macon
County a little more than forty years ago in order that his children
might be near Tuskegee Institute, though none of them ever attended
that school. The father left his land to his fifteen children, nine
girls and six boys. Three of the brothers, including our informant,
are still on the land. Our informant, who has been in the present

house forty years, is the father of eighteen children. He has kept
a careful record of his children's births in a book. Twelve of them
were by his first wife, who died in 1919, and the remainder by his
second wife, whom he married soon afterward. All the children by
his first wife are living, except two who died in infancy. His present
wife continues to cook for a white family in which she was employed
when she married. Three of the older children are married and live
in Montgomery, while the remaining thirteen continue to be a part
of the patriarchal household. The family occupies a large well-built
four-room house.

The head of this family was the superintendent of the Sunday
school connected with the Baptist church in which he has been a
deacon "for years." Because of his superior education and position
as a landowner in the community, he serves as a clerk in the church
and conducts the prayer meetings.

His farm consists of a hundred and sixty acres, fifty acres of
which are in cotton. He owns farm tools, including two sweep
stocks, two turn plows, three cotton-planters, and a mowing machine.
He also has two mules and four cows which give three gallons of
milk a day. His family enjoys a varied diet of beans, peas, peppers,
squash, collards, and cabbages from the garden. Though a land-
owner, he is nevertheless dependent upon the vicissitudes of the
agricultural and credit system of the plantation region. Although he
"came out even" in 1930, as he remarked, "back debts et us up."
The local bank foreclosed on its thousand-dollar mortgage, and
he has been making an effort to redeem his land. His two brothers
were in the same situation with regard to their holdings.

The history of another family of mixed blood, that owns one
hundred and sixty acres and rents four hundred acres of land which
is sublet to tenants, will show how the stabilizing of family relations
has been bound up with the growth of institutional life among this
favored class. The head of this family was born in 1880. According
to his story, he was the son of the mulatto daughter of a white man
and "a pure Negro excusing him being mixed with Spaniard." Both
of his parents were slaves. He was one of ten children and worked
for his father until he was twenty-one. He married as soon as he

was "emancipated" from the authority of his father. After working six years, he bought the farm in 1907. He attributed his success and desire to have a home to the example set by other colored people, particularly those at Tuskegee. He remarked:

> I guess it was the inspiration I got when I was quite a boy. You see I worked around white people and I always had the idea that I wanted something too; then I used to go to Tuskegee and see how other colored folks lived and that encouraged me to have the idea to own my own home. I felt like a man ought to own the very best home he could get. I just went to rural schools. My father farmed about a half a mile back east of here.

But we are able to get a further insight into the process by which this family has become stabilized and built up a tradition from other facts in the family history. His grandfather was one of the first deacons in the church which he helped to start right after the Civil War. He explained with considerable pride: "My grandfather was the first one to go there [the church], my father the second, I am the third, my children the fourth and I have some grandchildren who go there which make the fifth generation which practically have been going to that church."

There were seven children in the family, two of whom were boys, twenty-four and eighteen years of age, helping their father on the farm. The oldest daughter was teaching school, while two of her younger sisters were married and living away from home with their husbands. The remaining five children were living at home with their father and a stepmother whom their father had recently married after being a widower for eight years. The house, with its screened windows and rambling rose bushes and vines and potted plants on the porch, stood out in sharp contrast to the hovels inhabited by the multitudes of tenants on the surrounding plantations. Of the six tenant families—three on the rented land and the others on the owned land—five were working "on halves" with an "advance" of ten dollars a month. Although, on the whole, this landowner had been successful, during the previous year he had lost money, while during the current year his tenants for the first time had "come out in the hole."

The well-organized family of a sixty-one-year-old black land-owner, who called himself "a pure nigger," shows how, in some cases, those families with a small heritage of stable family traditions and culture create about them communal institutions to maintain and perpetuate their ideals and conceptions of life. When, upon reaching maturity, this man was "emancipated" by his father, he followed the instructions of his father, who had been a slave, and bought his first twenty acres of land. From time to time he added to it, and, with what he received from his father, he owned one hundred and twenty acres in all. He and his wife had been married forty-one years and had an only child, a son, who was born a year after they were married. This son, who was married to a woman with whom he "was raised up," had seven children. Since he was the only child, the mother had wanted him to remain with his parents; but he had reasoned with her thus: "Mamma, papa went to work and bought him a home and when my children get grown, I want them to see something I have done." So the son acquired a place about a mile away. Nevertheless, he sends his children to the school which, like the community, has been given the name of the family, because his father gave the land for its construction. Although there have been no lodge meetings since the "Mosaics went down," and "community meetings are held mighty seldom," they still get to-gether when they want to "transact any business about just one thing and another for the benefit of the school."

These families are representative of the relatively few families in the plantation area which have managed to forge ahead because of their superior family heritage and thrift. But, like the great mass of Negro tenants, they have been restricted in their development by the plantation system. Their numbers have remained practically stationary in spite of programs encouraging landownership and scientific farming. Individual thrift and a superior social heritage have, in the final analysis, been powerless in the face of the in-escapable economic forces inherent in the plantation system. Mi-gration has offered the only escape from the deadening effects of the poverty and the ignorance of the masses of tenants. The decrease, during the decade from 1910 to 1920, in the proportion of mulatto families in Issaquena County, Mississippi, is an indication of this selective migration. On the whole, it is only in those regions outside the plantation area that family life among the rural Negro population has reached a relatively high level of development with the support of an organized community. The development of the Negro family in Hertford County, North Carolina, is representative of family life in those areas outside the domination of the plantation system.

Homeownership among Negro families in North Carolina has increased steadily from 19.4 per cent in 1890 to 28.2 per cent in 1930. In Hertford County, where the proportion of Negro owners of farms has been slightly higher than the average for the state as a whole, it was practically the same as the state average in 1930. Although a relatively larger number of the mulatto families are homeowners, the black families in this county are much better situated in regard to homeownership than even the mulatto families in the plantation counties. A little more than a fifth of the black families and about a third of the mulatto families were homeowners in 1920. In this county, where 40 per cent of the families are of mixed blood, we can see how the blacks, who received their freedom as the result of the Civil War, and the mulattoes, who have had a longer history of freedom, have each contributed a stabilizing element to the family life in this community.

In this county, as we have seen, the illicit unions between white men and mulatto women, which were responsible for the large mulatto class, continued on a large scale until the opening of the present century. But there was a small group of families of mixed blood that had taken on an institutional character and conformed to conventional mores. In 1830 there were 168 free colored families in this county, 7 of whom were owners of slaves. Although it was not possible to trace the descendants of all these families, we were able to obtain fairly good histories of three families. A descendant of one of these families was able to give an account of six generations of the descendants of one of the free colored men listed in the 1830 census. From the son of another of these free heads of families, we were able to get an account of his father and his descendants. Our informant was born in the county, April 11, 1845. His mother was the daughter of a freeborn mulatto, who owned his home and was married to a free mulatto. His father, whose mother was a white woman, was also regarded for some time as a free colored person. According to our informant, his paternal grandfather fought in the Revolutionary War and drew a pension and later received a farm from the government in Tennessee, which he exchanged with a white man for land in the county. He told the following incident regarding the uncertainty concerning his father's racial identity:

> In those days the free born couldn't have a gun without license. My father had a gun and was indicted for toting a gun without license. J—— A——, a white man who owned a lot of land, told him to stand trial. He stood trial and when the case came up he denied the charge and said he was a white man. A—— rose and said he knew his white mother. A—— said, "she was a blue-eyed white woman." Did you know his father? was the next question, What did he look like? It was said that he looked like a white man. That cleared father.

Although his father was legally married to his mother, he left her after five children were born and was freed from supporting his family by proving himself a full-blooded white man. The subsequent history of this man's white descendants is interesting because it shows how whites have become identified with the Negro race in some instances. He entered an illicit union with a white woman who had had two colored children. His two white daughters by this woman identified themselves with the colored race in order not to be separated from their colored half-sisters. One of the white daughters had an illegitimate son by a white planter. Although this son was white, he was identified with the colored group and has married into the mulatto community described below. Our informant was pressed into service by the Confederate Army, but managed to escape at Edenton Bay to the Yankee fleet. He is receiving a pension at present for service rendered in the Union Army as a member of a heavy-artillery company. He was married twice, the first time in 1867, and the second time in 1902 to a girl just sixteen. By his first wife he had seven children and by his second, five. Two of the daughters by the second marriage are teachers in the county, while some of his children have gone North and entered the white race. Some of the children and grandchildren of his brothers and sisters are living in the county. He boasts of the fact that he has never been in any kind of trouble, having never had "a lawsuit or been arrested in the army or anywhere else."

The history of another of these free mulatto families will serve to show the role which these families have played as a stabilizing element in this community. This family has had family reunions for forty years or more. When the family reunion took place in 1930, there were grandchildren, great-grandchildren, and four great-great-grandchildren present in the ancestral homestead to pay respect to the memory of the founder of the family, who was born in 1814 and died in 1892, and his wife, who died in 1895 at the age of seventy-one. His only living son, eighty-four years old, who was the secretary-treasurer of the family organization, was unable to attend because of illness. The founder of the family had inherited the homestead from his father, who was listed among the free Negroes in 1830. A minister, who had founded a school in the community in 1885 and had known him intimately, described him as "an old Puritan in his morals and manners and the only advocate of temperance in the county" when he came there to work. This minister had been the first colored minister elected to the church, which the founder of the family had helped to establish in 1852 for the mulattoes.

The meeting was opened with a hymn, chosen because of its theme, "Leaning on the Everlasting Arm." The widow of a son of the founder of the family spoke of the necessity of the children's "walking in the straight path" that the founder "had cut out." Her daughter, a recent Master of Arts from Columbia University and the vice-principal of a colored high school in a large eastern city, had returned to the family reunion. Another granddaughter read, as was customary, a paper embodying the history of the achievements of the family and a eulogy of their ancestors. The program included a prayer service after which dinner was served. The ceremony was ended by a visit to the family burying-ground where there is a tombstone bearing the names of the founder and his wife and the date of their birth and death.

It was pointed out above that the mulattoes in this county have shown, until recent years, considerable prejudice toward the blacks with the result that they tended to form separate communities. In two such communities in this county, one taking its name from a mulatto family of free origin and the other from a black family of slave origin, we can see how the rural Negro family has become stabilized under the two very different sets of traditions. Information concerning the origin and history of "Whitetown," (The name of this community, as well as that of the black community, has been changed) the mulatto settlement, was given by the present head of the settlement. Our informant's father, who was born in 1801 and lived within a half-mile of the present settlement, was married twice and had eighteen children in all. The hundred acres of land which he owned were divided among the nine children, who were living at the time of his death. Our informant, who was born in 1853 and has the appearance of a white man, is still active. Although he sold his share for thirty-five dollars, he purchased more land from time to time until he acquired seven hundred acres, the size of the present settlement. The settlement became known by the name of the family around 1860. There was a school in the settlement at the time taught by a member of one of the other mulatto families. Our informant boasted of the fact that, when the "grandfather clause" was passed in order to disfranchise colored voters, he was the only colored man in the near-by town who could vote.

At present there are in the settlement ten children and thirty grandchildren of our informant. His brother, who also lives in the settlement, has six children and one grandchild. Working under the control and direction of the head of the settlement, the children and grandchildren raise cotton, corn, peanuts, peas, and tobacco. In this isolated community with its own school this family has lived for over a century. There has been considerable intermarriage between cousins. They have refused teachers appointed by the county unless they have been very light mulattoes. The family attends a church which was established by a mulatto minister for their benefit. These closely knit families have been kept under the rigorous discipline of the older members and still have scarcely any intercourse with the black people in the county. Seeing these families with their blond and red hair and blue eyes working in the extensive tobacco fields, one would take them for pure Nordic stock.

The other community, composed of black families who boast of pure African ancestry, grew out of a family of five brothers, former slaves, and is known as "Blacktown," after the name of the family. Although the traditions of this community do not go back as far as those of Whitetown, the group has exhibited considerable pride in its heritage and has developed as an exclusive community under the discipline of the oldest male in the family. The founder of the community, the father of our informant, was reared in the house of his master. According to the family tradition the master, "Major Black," was "one of the best white men in the section." Just before he died he called around him all the Blacks, who had taken his name, and said, "I have treated you all right; if I have wronged you, I beg your pardon." The old mansion, which is still standing, is inhabited by the grandson of the major. The paternal relations of slave days are maintained by the grandson and other descendants of the major. When one of the brothers of the original head of the Negro community died, a son of the major came from Norfolk, Virginia, to be present at the funeral.

The boundaries of the present community are practically the same as those of the old plantation, a part of which is rented from the grandson of the major. But most of the land is owned by this Negro family. The oldest of the five brothers was, until his death fifteen years ago, the acknowledged head of the settlement. At present the next oldest brother is recognized as the head of the community. His two sons, one of whom was our informant, have never divided their 138 acres. He and his three brothers, with their children numbering between forty and fifty and their numerous grandchildren, are living in the settlement. Twelve of their children have left the county, and three are living in a near-by town. Our informant left the community thirty-four years ago and worked at hotel work in Boston and as a longshoreman in Philadelphia, but returned after five years away because he was needed by the old folks and longed for the association of his people. One of the sons of the five brothers who founded the settlement is both the teacher of the school and the pastor of the church which serve the needs of the settlement.

These settlements are distinguished from similar clans of blood relatives in the plantation regions of the South by their higher economic status and their deeply rooted patriarchal family traditions. They represent the highest development of a moral order and a sacred society among the rural Negro population. This development has been possible because economic conditions have permitted the germs of culture, which have been picked up by Negro families, to take root and grow. This has been the case with the blacks, as well as with the mulattoes, who, on the whole, have enjoyed superior advantages. Although the mulattoes have less illiteracy, more homeownership, and comparatively fewer broken families with a woman head, the farm-owners among both classes in this county and the plantation counties as well have a larger number of offspring and more children surviving than the renters and farm laborers in either class. There has been sufficient isolation to shield these families from the disorganizing effects of industrialism and urban life but not enough to produce stagnation. But, as we have observed before, roads and automobiles are gradually destroying the isolation of these regions in the South. Some of the younger generation are venturing into the outside. During 1931 a member of the younger generation in both the black and the mulatto settlements was arrested and punished for transporting illegal liquor.

From these rural communities we turn now to the towns of the South, where amid the shacks and hovels inhabited by the mass of Negro population, a homestead here and there gives evidence of higher aspirations and some heritage of culture. Negroes in the towns and small cities of the South have been constantly drawn from the plantations to work as laborers on road construction, in the mills and the factories, and as domestics in the white families. Usually in these towns and cities there has been a small group of families who have remained segregated from the mass of the Negro population because of their superior economic and cultural status. In some of these communities there has been a single family that has stood out from the mass of the Negro population and endeavored to maintain the standards of family life that were foreign to the masses. A young woman, a teacher, who came from one of these communities tells of the life of her family in a town in Georgia. Her father was the son of a Negro woman and a white man. His white half-sisters became interested in him and helped him to enter one of the Negro colleges established shortly after the Civil War. On her mother's side there had also been some cultural advantages that raised her above the masses of the Negroes. Her maternal grandmother had been a house servant during slavery, and her children were later given instruction by the family that once owned her as a slave. One of these children, her mother, had been encouraged to attend the same school which her father attended. The courtship between her mother and father began while they were in college. Two northern white women, who became interested in her mother and sent her to the Latin High School in Boston, gave her two buildings to start a school in the town of her birth in Georgia. Her father came to teach in the same school and married her mother. The story of her mother's efforts to establish the school and her family's attempts to maintain their own moral standards in the face of the degradation of the masses was related by her as follows:

Our life around M—— was very seclusive. Nowhere to go and nobody to associate with. We were taken away for the summer for vacation to see a little of the world. When my mother first established the school there was quite a bit of opposition. They· thought it was at first a Congregational School and they sought to burn it down. She would have to sit up at night with a shawl around her shoulders to watch the buildings going up. Eventually a fire was started but some of the neighbors put it out. After it was erected they kept the children home—they were not going to have any "Congregations" in their families. The people in the community were mostly all Baptists. They said the Congregationalists were not Christians. Although the people there were thrifty and many of them owned their own homes, they had very low moral standards. Our mother and father kept us away from them. It caused hard feelings. We were not allowed to associate with the masses. There was a lot of factories there—canning factories and every child about fourteen years of age had to work. Every year about school time there would be so many illegitimate

children born to these girls. My sister and I were the only two girls
who didn't work there at the factory.

In the larger cities of the South where these families were more
numerous, they were able to create a more congenial environment
for their way of life. This was especially true of those cities where
there already existed a group of families with several generations of
free ancestry and where college communities were located. The
development of Negro family life in New Orleans and in Charleston,
South Carolina, had its roots among the colored people who were
free before the Civil War.

In New Orleans the Civil War and emancipation and consequent
industrial and social changes caused the disruption of the free
mulatto caste. Many of the free colored people who had themselves
been slaveholders were sympathetic toward the confederacy and in
some cases participated in the conflict on the side of the South. A
review of confederate troops held in New Orleans in 1861 included
a regiment of fourteen hundred free colored men. Between the
people of this class and the newly emancipated blacks there was
little community of interest or sympathy. Some of the members
of the free colored caste acquired positions of influence during the
Reconstruction Period. One of them was state treasurer from 1868
to 1879. But, when white domination was once more established, the
color line was drawn so as to include the former free people of color
and their descendants and the former slaves in the same category,
and both were subjected on the whole to the same restrictions.
Although this brought about some solidarity of interest and feeling
between the two classes, many of the descendants of the free colored
caste withdrew to themselves, refusing even to send their children
to the schools attended by colored people and Negroes of slave
ancestry. One of the members of this class wrote concerning the
broken morale of his group:

> Certain Creoles of our day are reduced to that point of moral
> impotence that they despise and repulse their kind, even their own
> parents. Instead of thinking of means of deliverance, they surrender
> to their weakness, without being able to determine what principles
> to follow or what resolutions to take, as if they wished to habituate

their natures to absolute submission or the obliteration of their individualities. They live in a stage of moral enfeeblement which re-
sembles the last stage of helplessness. In this state of deterioration
they not only care little about raising their abased dignity, but they
multiply their errors as if to increase their mortification.[1]

The rehabilitation of these families was often effected when they
became the leaders of the Negro group or when they intermarried
with the ambitious and rising families in the Negro group and
mingled their traditions with those of the latter. This was the case
with the family of one of the political leaders of the Negroes in the
South. Although he was a mulatto, his wife's family, who belonged
to the free mulatto caste, objected to their daughter's marrying him
because he was a descendant of slaves.

We can get some idea of the outlook of the free mulatto caste
from the following excerpt from the family history as related by the
daughter:

> Upon the death of my grandfather (who was a butcher and had
> been killed by his slave), my grandmother married an independent
> tobacco manufacturer. There were twelve children by this second
> marriage. He and grandma, of whom I have a picture, appear to
> be white. He looks like an old Confederate soldier. Grandma, when
> a widow, had refused to marry a man who had fought in the Union
> Army. She regarded him as responsible for losing her slaves. She
> consistently refused to salute the American flag. Once when she had
> to get a passport to go to New Orleans and was ordered to salute the
> American flag, she spat upon it and put it under her feet. She was not
> punished for this, either because she was a woman or because she
> was a beautiful woman. Until her death she regarded Abraham Lincoln
> as her enemy. Grandma strenuously objected to my father's marrying
> her daughter because my father was a descendant of slaves. All of
> her children who are living are now in the white race.

The conflict in traditions and outlook on life was further revealed
when the politician wanted their daughter to attend a Negro college
and his wife who wanted her to enter a convent. As it turned out,
the daughter, who married into the colored group and identified
herself with them, became a leader of colored women in politics.
Her daughter, who was completely identified with Negroes, married

[1] R. L. Desdunes, *Nos hommes et notre histoire* (Montreal, 1911), p. 103.

a successful businessman who has made a conspicuous success in manufacturing.

In Charleston the cleavage between the mulattoes of free ancestry and the emancipated Negroes, especially those of mixed blood, has never been as wide as in New Orleans. Doubtless, as we shall see in a subsequent chapter, there was prejudice against admitting black Negroes into the "charmed circle of aristocracy," as one of the mulattoes referred to her class. But what distinguished these families chiefly from the great mass of the Negro population was not simply their light skins. They took pride in their economic and educational achievements and more especially their culture and purity in family morals.

The emphasis which this class generally placed upon morality in family relations is exemplified in the remark of a member of one of these families that migrated from Charleston to Philadelphia because of an assault during the slavery agitation. In speaking of the attitude of the old Philadelphia families toward the mulatto families from the South, she remarked: "The people there regarded all mulatto women from the South as the illegitimate children of white men, but in the case of our family we could boast of being legitimate."

A brief sketch of the history of one of these old Philadelphia families will throw some light on the origin of the puritanical outlook of this class. The family in question traces its descent from the brother of Absalom Jones, who with Richard Allen organized the Free African Society in 1787. After he broke with Allen, he founded St. Thomas' Protestant Episcopal Church. This pioneer minister's nephew, who was the father of our informant, lived to be ninety-two years of age. As a boy he was bound out, as was customary, to a barber. Later he became the proprietor of three barber shops in the business section of the city and served a select white clientele. Our informant took pride in the fact that his father was one of the founders of the Central Presbyterian Church in 1844 and later wrote its history. He married into one of the old families, one of whose members was appointed to a diplomatic post by the government. There were sixteen children, including our informant.

Five of our informant's sisters became schoolteachers, one brother a barber, another a painter, and the remainder went into business. Our informant, who had completed over forty-three years in the Post Office as a clerk, was also the secretary of a building and loan association. He was married to a woman who belonged to one of the old families in New Orleans. They have two daughters who are schoolteachers and a son who is a manufacturing chemist. Our informant still has the eyeglasses which Absalom Jones wore and a chair in his living-room which belonged to his distinguished granduncle.

In other communities of the North where these families have settled they have formed nuclei of family groups that have striven to maintain purity in family morals as well as external forms of respectability. Their numbers have been increased constantly by families that possessed the traditions of the rural families which we have given some account of in this chapter. This small group has been the custodian of the gains which the Negro has made in acquiring culture and civilization. In taking over the manners and morals of the whites, there has been in some instances a disharmony between form and content. But, in most families, insistence upon moral conduct has been supported by genuine sentiment. Where their moral vision has been out of focus and their conscious strivings to attain culture have produced artificiality, this has been the result of their seeing themselves as if in two mirrors. They have seen themselves both in the mirror of their own race, whose ways of life they shunned and disdained, and in the mirror of the white race, in whose image they vainly would have made themselves over. On the whole, these families belong to an age that is past, or before the Negro became a dweller in the modern city.

PART FOUR

IN THE CITY OF DESTRUCTION

CHAPTER XIII

ROVING MEN AND

HOMELESS WOMEN

The mobility of the Negro population which began as a result of the Civil War and emancipation tore the Negro from his customary familial attachments. As the old order crumbled, thousands of Negro men and women began to wander aimlessly about the country or in search of adventure and work in the army camps and cities. In order to meet this situation and at the same time to insure a steady labor supply, the South enacted severe laws to curb the vagrancy of the landless Negro. Although the North through congressional Reconstruction put an end to these laws which practically re-enslaved the Negro, northern industrialists and capitalists were not willing to permit the former slaves to divide and take title to the land of their former owners. Consequently, the vast majority of the Negroes gradually settled down to a mode of life under a modified plantation system. A large number who had acquired migratory habits during the disordered period following the Civil War continued to drift from place to place. On the other hand, since Reconstruction, the migratory habits of the Negro have been constantly affected by the changing economic and social conditions in the South. It was due primarily to economic conditions that a mass movement was set in motion from Louisiana and Mississippi to Kansas and the West in 1879. But, from then until the mass migrations during the World War, the mobility of the Negro has consisted of an inconspicuous but steady stream of individuals and families migrating from the farms to lumber and turpentine camps and into the towns and cities of the North and South.

By 1910 nearly one and two-third million Negroes had migrated from the state of their birth to other states. Most of these migrants, a little over a million, had moved about in the South; while four hundred thousand had left the South and were living in the North. Most of these migrants had gone to southern cities, for we find that, whereas in the South as a whole 12.2 per cent of the resident Negro population was born in other states, 26.1 per cent of the Negroes residing in southern cities were born outside the state. These figures give us no information on migration from rural areas to cities within the same state; nor do they afford more than a partial measure of the general mobility of the southern Negro. However, in regard to the general migration to urban areas in the South, we know that a million Negroes have moved into towns and cities since 1900. Unlike migrations to northern cities, this movement "has been spread among 78 places of 25,000 and over, and 773 localities of from 2,500 to 25,000."

Among the million Negroes who deserted the rural communities of the South, there were thousands of men and women who cut themselves loose from family and friends and sought work and adventure as solitary wanderers from place to place. Some of the men had their first glimpse of the world beyond the plantation or farm when they worked in sawmills, turpentine camps, or on the roads. Some of the women had their first experience with city life when they went to a near-by town to work temporarily for a few dollars a month in domestic service. But a large number of them had become accustomed to going to town on Saturday afternoons to escape the boredom of the rural community. Then, too, these towns offered comparative freedom from the religious restraints imposed by the rural churches. In the dance halls these simple peasant folk could give rein to their repressed impulses without incurring the censure of the elders for their "sinful conduct." Even before the cinema and the radio revealed a larger outside world of romance and adventure, they could hear from the mouth of some "Black Ulysses" fabulous stories of the outside world. Once having caught a glimpse of the world beyond the dull routine of country life, these men and women were lured on to a world beyond these small towns where they might enjoy even greater freedom and more exciting adventures.

In the lumber and turpentine camps one may get a glimpse of the free sex behavior and spontaneous matings which these roving men and homeless women form during their wanderings. These camps offer greater anonymity and freedom from social control than the small towns. They bring men and women from the farms in contact with men and women who have already had some experience in the outside world. Often some black troubadour meets a simple girl in the town and lures her with his romantic tales and strange words of love to take up her abode with him in the camp. In the dozen or more hastily constructed one-room wooden structures which comprise these camps, one can find many such couples. Since these couples are drawn together by spontaneous attraction, in which physical desire usually predominates, their association is characterized by impulsive behavior. Quarreling and fighting as the result of outbursts of jealousy or slight irritations occur periodically.

The character of their association depends also on their past experiences. Men who have become hardened by their wandering life and believe that men should rule women with an iron hand often treat their temporary mates with brutality and only occasionally show any sympathy or tender feeling toward them. On the other hand, the men who have retained some of the humanity of their simple folk background may find in these women the response which their mothers once furnished. Therefore, one may find these men and women living together as married couples. The woman does the cooking and looks after her mate's clothing, while he furnishes the food and buys her a dress or gewgaw in town. But even such peaceful and happy associations are of short duration. The man or even the woman may take a "fancy" to another companion, or, when the camp breaks up, the man begins anew his wanderings. Deserted, the woman may return to her mother to seek forgiveness for her sin—the sign of which may be an illegitimate child. In other cases, the woman may follow her lover on his Odyssey.

From the lumber camp or small town the road to freedom and adventure and higher wages leads in the lower South to Montgomery or Birmingham or Memphis—"the home of the blues." These secular folk songs of the black troubadours in our industrial society record the reactions of the uprooted folk to the world of the city.[1] They tell of their disappointments and disillusionments and nostalgic yearnings for the sympathetic understanding and intimacy and security of the world of the folk which they have left behind. Handy, whose creations have captured the spirit of the urbanized peasant's disillusionment and disappointments, has embodied in the famous "St. Louis Blues" the plaint of the Negro woman who has lost her lover to the gilded city woman:

> St. Louis woman—wid her diamon' rings
> Pulls dat man roun' by her apron strings
> 'Twant for powder an' for store bought hair
> De man I love would not gone nowhere.

On the other hand, the sociologist may discover in the blues and more especially in the secular folk songs the general outlook on life and attitudes toward sex and family life of these wanderers. In fact, there is scarcely any phase of their wanderings and contacts with the urban environment that one cannot find touched upon in their songs. For example, as suggested above, some of these men take their women with them on their wanderings. The plight of one of these men whose "Georgia gal set de police" on him is told in the song which begins:

> Ain't yer heard my po' story?
> Den listen to me:
> I brung a gal from Tennessee.[2]

But as a rule these girls are dropped along the way, either to return home or probably to find a place in domestic service in the city. Other women are picked up in the city. These strange women often prove unfaithful or treacherous. An unknown wandering bard,

[1] Sterling A. Brown, "The Blues as Folk Poetry," in *Folk-Say: A Regional Miscellany*, 1930, ed. B. A. Botkin (Norman, Okla., 1930), pp. 324-39.

[2] Howard W. Odum and Guy B. Johnson, *Negro Workaday Songs* (Chapel Hill, N. C. 1926), p. 136.

who has learned that in the anonymity of city life woman cannot be trusted, sings:

> I ain't never seed her befo'
> Don't wanta see her no mo', baby
> She say, "Come on, go to my house,"
> She ain't nuffin but a roust-about, baby
> She s'arch my pockets through
> Den say, "I ain't got no need for you, baby."

In fact, one may discover in the spontaneous responses of these strange men and women to each other the beginnings of romantic sentiments among the masses in the Negro population. Although their responses are based chiefly upon physical attraction, as a rule the physical qualities have taken on a romantic value. The romantic element is not entirely lacking in even so crude a song as that of the woman who complains:

> I loves dat bully, he sho' looks good to me,
> I always do what he wants me to,
> Den he don't seem satisfied.

Whatever the physical qualities—"teasing brown" or "slick hair" or "big hips"—they indicate an awakening of the imagination which contrasts sharply with the unromantic attitudes of the peasant Negro toward sex and mating in the isolated rural communities of the South. In contrast to these crude songs, occasionally one comes across a simple song in which considerable tenderness is expressed. A good example of such songs is the following in which the woman sings of her man:

> I's dreamin' of you. . . .
> Every night.
> I's thinkin' of you. . . . .
> All right.
> I's wantin' you. . . .
> Day an' night.

In such songs one can detect the tenderness and sympathy which are responsible for those rare cases in which these roving men and homeless women in the city settle down to a quasi-family life and rear children. But usually the associations of these "tribeless" men and women, who live outside the public opinion of the Negro community, are of short duration and are characterized by bickerings over trifles, outbursts of jealousy, and violence. Often when the woman finds her lover unstable in his affection or the man discovers, in the language of this world, someone else in his "stall," the result is a stabbing or murder. In Odum's *Rainbow 'round My Shoulder* one may find a composite picture of the impulsive behavior of this group compressed in a single fictional character.[3]

The disillusionment and insecurity which these men experience in the city may bring back memories of the secure affection and sympathy of the wife or children whom they have left behind. This may bring a resolve, generally transitory and soon forgotten, to return to their kinfolk. One popular song embodies such a sentiment:

> I gotta wife, Buddie,
> With two little children, Buddie,
> With two little children, Buddie,
> Tell 'em I'm comin' home, Buddie, I'm comin' home.

So the Black Ulysses continues his wanderings from city to city. During the course of his wanderings in the South he may pick up lonesome women in domestic service who will satisfy his sexual cravings and furnish him with food and lodging for a night or two. Incidents in the career of one of these wanderers from Tennessee throw some light on the character of this mobile group. He began his sex experiences when fourteen as the result of the example and instructions of older boys. At the present time his sexual life is entirely of a casual nature. When he arrives in a city, he approaches women on the street or gets information on accessible women from men of his type. Usually, he goes up to lonely women in domestic service and wins their sympathy by telling them "hard-luck" stories of his life on the road. They take him to their lodgings, where he remains until his hunger as well as his sexual desires are satisfied, and then he takes to the road again. Occasionally, he sends a card to a woman to whom he takes a special liking, but usually he forgets them. In his own words, he tells the following story:

[3] Howard W. Odum, *Rainbow 'round My Shoulder* (Indianapolis, 1928).

My mother is dead. My mother has been dead about sixteen years. I was a year old when she died. When my mother died I stayed with my step sister. My father he has been in ———, Tennessee and I have not seen him in a year and a half. My father has been married four times and all his wives died but one. My father was working in a saw mill and a log fell on his leg. My father did not go when my mother was buried, cause of his leg. My step sister took care of me till my father's leg got well and then he took me to my aunts. When my father's leg got well he took us to my aunt and then to ———, Tennessee. My auntie raised me up.

When I left home I went up through about Birmingham, Alabama. I live here with my bother, B., my half brother. I mean he lives in Chattanooga and I am on my way there now. I have two whole sisters living and one whole brother. I have two half brothers living. My whole brother is in ——— with my father. He crippled and not got good mind. My cripple brother is 19. My sisters are one in Gordonville, Tennessee and one in Indianapolis. I went to school in Livingston. I went to school in all about eight months or nine months. You see, I'd go to school one day and the next day I would have to help my aunt wash or cut wood. I did not go to school every day.

Ever since I was nine years old, I been working for the white people, taking care of myself up 'til about nine or ten months ago. These people left and went to Chicago. I been to Chicago too. I went on a freight train. There were quite a good many people with me. That was the first time on the road. I came up here last night from Memphis. The train wrecked down in the yard, and I stayed there all night and came on in town this morning. I stayed in Memphis three days. The railroad bull run us out from Memphis. We had plans to make every state, but we got run out of there; and then I just come on through here on my way to Chattanooga. Nine months ago when I left home I went to Atlanta, Georgia. I left home on Friday afternoon and hoboed on a freight train and stayed there a week and one day. From Atlanta I went to Savannah, Georgia, stayed there one day and from there to Shreveport, Louisiana, for two days, then to Baton Rouge for four days. Then I went to New Orleans two days and then on to Chicago. I never stayed three days in Chicago. I stayed in the jungles. I went over by the New York Central Railroad and on out where the boats come in. That where I stay. Stayed there three days, then I went to Louisville, Kentucky. I wouldn't have stayed that long but I got lost. In Louisville, I just stayed here one day and came back down the L. & N. to Guthrie, Kentucky, and from there back over to Milan, Tennessee, and from there back to Jackson, Tennessee, and from there over here. When I left home I went over to

Atlanta, Georgia, and see I came through here at different times I
never stopped. There is a lot of places I have been but some I don't
remember because I was sleep or did not know what the names of
them was. I came out to California on a freight train. It took me three
days to come over to El Paso, Texas, and two days from El Paso to
San Antonio, then a day and a night to Houston and a day to New
Orleans and crossed the river and stayed in Baton Rouge and left
that night and went back to New Orleans. We sing songs as we ride
along and when we stopped we sing them. [He sang the following:]

> T.B. is all right to have,
> But your friends treat you so low down;
> You will ask them for a favor,
> And they will even stop coming 'round.

I have been arrested one time. I was held up in Livingston, Tennessee. They kept me three days and turned me aloose. I was held
up when somebody robbed a bank and they had been told the color
and everything and was told to hold up everybody that come through
there. This was over in Montgomery, Alabama. I have stole small
things. I don't reckon I would care if I was turned over to officers,
because I would have a place to stay. You see I don't have any particular place to go and stay, so I could stay there. I'd just have a
place to stay.

[Concerning first sex experience:] I was fourteen years old then.
That was how old I was when I first had that. When I go to these
towns if I have money, I can find out from some of the boys. I never
had no disease, nothing but measles, whooping cough, and something
like that. I never had nothing else. I use a rubber sometimes. My
father has syphilis. The doctor said he had it, that's how I know.

I am going to Chattanooga just to be going so I can stay the winter
over there. I have a half brother up there and I stay with him until
summer time. I try to get some work when summer comes. I don't
know just what I'll do. I work a little in winter. The fairs are going
on now and I can get a little work there. I didn't have any work to do
and my father didn't have any. I went and got with other people
and hit the road.

As these men and women wander about, they slough off the
traditional attitudes and beliefs that provided a philosophy of life in
the world of the folk. A young man who came north during the
migrations of the War period furnishes the following naïve account of
disillusionment and cynicism as the result of his experiences:

I have come up pretty tough from twelve years old on up til I got to be a man. I come up hard, you know. Sometimes, I would not know where I could get a piece of bread. Sometimes, you know, I would only have a dime, and say I believe I will git me a sack of tobacco. Then you know, I would sometimes only have a nickel and would git me a sack of tobacco and leave that bread off. Well, you know, Mama always taught me that whenever I was out and down, she would say, "Well, the Christians, honey, you always go up to the Christians and ask them to give you something to eat, and they will." Well, the Christians would always give me good advice but that was all, so I just got so I wouldn't bother with them and whenever I wanted anything I used to make it to the gamblers.

Although many solitary men and women made their way to northern cities before the War period, the number was considerably increased during and following this period. Naturally, it is difficult to get a measure of this mobile group of isolated men and women. It was not until the depression beginning in 1929, when the economic life of the rural South was disrupted and thousands of these un-attached men and women sought relief in the towns and cities of the South and North, that we have even a partial enumeration of this group. For the country as a whole, unattached Negro transients constituted from 7 to 12 per cent of the total during the nine-month period, August, 1934, through April, 1935. In the city of Chicago, to which many of these men and women were attracted, during the first six months of 1934, there were 1,648 unattached Negro men and 64 unattached women, or 15.7 per cent of a total of 10,962 unattached men and women, who sought assistance at the Cook County Service Bureau for Transients in Chicago.

A glimpse into a few case records (Chicago Service Bureau for Transients) on these men and women will give one some idea of their background and character. In one case the water boy who has served as the theme of a well-known Negro work song comes to life:

A—— was born in Alabama in 1917. When he was about five years old, his father deserted his mother. A—— has six sisters scattered about the country, the oldest sister having been "raised by some people in Birmingham." When fourteen, he worked irregularly at a sawmill in Mississippi as a water boy. A—— was seventeen when he began his wanderings. He went first to New Orleans where he had his first sex experience into which he was initiated by older boys and men. After his first sex experiences, he began going each week to prostitutes whom he paid fifty cents. From New Orleans he took the road to Birmingham; then on to Nashville, Tennessee; thence to Memphis, and wound up in Chicago. When he came to the shelter he was ragged, wore shredded shoes, and was tired and footsore. A psychiatric examination—after people in the neighborhood about the shelter complained that he was constantly exhibiting himself—showed that he was a high grade moron.

Another case is that of a normal boy twenty years old who constantly got into trouble at the shelter because he attacked southern white boys. Psychiatric examination revealed that he had developed a feeling that he was being imposed upon. This boy, who was born in South Carolina and had lost both parents at an early age, had been adopted by a childless couple. According to his story, his foster-father was very cruel, although his foster-mother treated him kindly. He ran away from home when he was ten to join a carnival and thenceforth wandered about the country. His migratory life had been interrupted during a term in a reformatory in New York.

Occasionally among these roving men one finds a Negro of West Indian origin:

W—— was born in Bermuda, November 6, 1913. His father, who was said to be a heavy drinker, brought him to N——, New York, when he was four years old. W—— has never heard of his mother since. He claimed that he was deserted a year later by his father. According to the story of the father who was found employed on a farm outside of M——, New York, he had brought the boy to the United States when his wife deserted him to live with another man. He took the boy first to N—— and later to a city in New Jersey where "he adopted the boy out" to the people with whom they lived. After going as far as the fourth grade, the boy ran away to join a circus. From the time he was sixteen until he was twenty he crossed the continent "three or four times." He said that in every city he looked in the directory in the police station for his mother's name. Eleven years elapsed before the father heard from the boy. On that occasion, the boy tried unsuccessfully to get money from his father in order to escape a two month jail sentence for larceny in a city in Michigan.

A final case is that of an illiterate, homeless woman, forty-eight years old, who had been moving about the country for twenty-five years. She was born in Louisiana and had been neglected by her stepfather. She left Louisiana with a family for whom she worked and went to Colorado. In 1914 she came to Chicago because she had heard of the high wages. Shortly afterward, she returned to Louisiana and married a man who deserted her. Then she returned to Chicago for a brief period, only to return again to Louisiana. Her stay there was of short duration because she heard that work at good wages might be obtained in Kansas City. When this venture proved unsuccessful, she returned to Chicago and sought relief. For awhile, she maintained herself by working for her landlord after the death of his wife, and by selling bottles and junk. She makes her home in a dark, dirty empty room on the first floor of a dilapidated house in the slum area of the Negro community.

A recent study of twenty thousand homeless men, 10 per cent of whom were colored, in the shelters of Chicago,[4] revealed that a large proportion of the cases represented family disorganization. A large proportion of these men, as shown in an analysis of 115 cases, had migrated from farms and villages in the heart of the Black Belt, leaving home at an average age of 16 when they had about a fourth grade education. Their movements generally constituted a criss-cross pattern, first within their own states, then becoming interstate, and finally resulting in a trip to a northern city and settlement there. This mobility was generally in connection with track labor and construction work. In addition, many Negroes secured jobs as Pullman porters, or waiters on diners. Thus enticed away from their parental home by types of labor which required mobility, these Negroes reached Chicago and here found few opportunities for employment and few relatives to assist them in their present economic crisis. Fifty-two per cent of these men claimed that they had been married; and, of these, three-fourths had simply deserted their wives.

A similar situation in regard to family disorganization was found

[4] Edwin H. Sutherland and Harvey J. Locke, *Twenty Thousand Homeless Men* (Philadelphia, 1936), p. 38.

among the 7,560 unattached Negro males registered with the Unattached and Transient Division of the Emergency Relief Bureau
in New York City. Slightly more than 42 per cent of these men were
under thirty-five years of age. A study of a sample of 522 cases
showed that, as in the case of the men in the Chicago shelters, 52
per cent had been married. However, about a third of them were
separated from their wives and another 13 per cent claimed to be
widowed, while only 5.7 per cent admitted that they had deserted
their wives or families. Only 1.5 per cent claimed that they had
secured a regular divorce. But these figures provide only an in-
adequate picture of a small fraction of the large group of unattached
men and women. Many more highly mobile solitary men and women
without the aid of relief make their living by both lawful and
unlawful means in the complex life of the city.

Generally by the time these wandering men and women reach
the northern metropolis, they have lost much of their naïve outlook
on life and have become sophisticated in the ways of the city. Their
songs are no longer the spontaneous creations of the uprooted
peasant who, disillusioned and lonely, yearns for the association
of kin and neighbors. When they sing, they sing the blues which
represent the conscious creations of song-writers who supply songs
for more sophisticated sentiments and behavior. Often the men
have learned ways of escaping the necessity of labor or have discovered ways of living by their wits. This involves gambling, dealing
in stolen goods, engaging in "numbers," and other rackets. What
is important in regard to these "tribeless" men and women is that
they have become purely individuated and have developed a purely
"rational" attitude not only toward the physical environment but
also toward men and women. Consequently, we find some of these
men maintaining themselves by exploiting women. In some of the
bright-light areas of Negro communities in Chicago, Detroit, and
New York, it is not unusual to hear these "pimps" boasting of the
size of their "stables." Thus, sexual gratification has become entirely
divorced from its human meaning and, like the women who supply
it, has become a commodity. We can get some notion of the career

of these men from the following excerpt from the history of one of them:

Z—— was born in a midwestern metropolis where he was put out of high school because of failures in his studies. Because of his athletic prowess and good looks he was taken up by a middle aged woman who owned a chain of beauty parlors. He even left home to live as a gigolo with this woman who had some means. With plenty of money in his pockets and a splendid automobile, he soon became known as a "big shot" in the underworld. When he fell in love with one of the young women employed by his paramour, the latter put him out. However, by this time he had established enough contacts in the underworld to maintain himself through a number of rackets. He continued to live with various women who supported him. This mode of living soon became a regular business. By adorning himself in synthetic jewelry and driving a high powered car, he attracted to himself women of the underworld. As he was unusually lucky in his gambling, he was able to amass a fairly large bankroll. Therefore, when news reached him that New York City was a fair field for rackets he staked his entire bankroll on the venture. He selected three pretty women and drove to the East. These women were displayed at the night clubs and the various rendezvous of the denizens of the underworld. He was accepted by the other "pimps" who maintained headquarters in one of the taverns. After a few years, he had established the proper connections and his fortune was made. He maintains a "stable" of four white and four Negro prostitutes; employs a physician to look after them; and assures them protection from the law.

As to the attitudes of the women who have broken away from their families and wandered about the country, the following bit of self-analysis and history furnished by a woman in New York City is revealing:

My name is X—— and I've been operating in Harlem for three years from a private pilch. I don't go in for everything like most of these frowsies. I'm a straight broad. If they can't be natural I don't play no tricks. None of that freak stuff for me. I don't play the streets—I mean I don't lay every pair of pants that comes along. I look 'em over first. I'm strictly a Packard broad. I only grab a drunk if he looks like his pockets are loaded with dough. If they get rough my man [pimp] kicks 'em out. When they're drunk they shoot the works. I've gotten over two hundred dollars, and so help me, the bastard didn't even touch me. He got happy just looking at me. Boy! this shape of mine gets 'em every time. I know how to wear clothes too. I've never been married. I could though. Plenty guys fell for me and wanted to take me to a preacher. They never had any real dough though, just guys. No flash, no car, no nothing, just guys. You know they lay you once and then off to a preacher. You want to know my early childhood. Well, it was hell. My mother never loved me and I never loved her. I never had a father and—I mean he never married my mother and her father never married her mother. I have a kid. Thank God, though, he's a boy. He will be able to give it and not have to take it like my mother and me. He's down South. I won't tell you where. I send him dough. He's only a kid—just five— ain't that funny? My kid, bless his soul, ain't never had a father either. I'm an only child and so is my mother and so is my kid. Having a kid, bless his soul, didn't make me go wrong. His old man was a swell guy. He sure loved me. He got drowned. He woulda married me. I loved him too. Oh, what the hell, what is love? All the guys know about love is a lay. My kid's old man and me were kids in Tennessee, well anyhow, right outside N——. We used to go to Sunday school together and to day school too. We started laying each other when he couldn't even dog water. You know how kids are. Well, we kept it up. My mother beat hell out of him and me too. Anyhow, it got good to me. He wasn't the only one who had me. We girls used to mess around a hell of a lot. I guess I was around about twelve when I really found out what it was all about. My mother said I had a white liver. I guess I have too. What the hell! She was a hell of a mother. Hell, when I was fourteen she tried to sick an old guy on me just because he had a good farm. Sure, I laid him a couple of times. He was so old though there wasn't a good one in him. He wanted to marry me. I got hell for turning him down. My kid's old man had my water on, though. Boy, he could go. I was fifteen when the kid was born, bless his soul. I worked for some damned good white people. They got hot as hell when they found I was knocked up. They sent me back home. My old lady raised some more hell. I stayed home till the kid was born, then I got mother's job. I kept having guys. I'm honest, I like it. I sure can give it and I can take it, too. I've always been good looking—that's why I'm in New York today. A guy, he was a peach, took me to Chicago. My old lady didn't care—she was also peddling her can on the sly. When this guy got me to Chicago, I finds out he's married. It made no difference. We had one ball for a hell of a long time. Then, his old lady gets wise and tries to beat hell out of me. I gave her plenty. Anyhow, we moved to a new pilch. I got a job and I meets a swell guy. I mean he was a good looking guy. Well, he started me. I was so wild about him I'd a done anything. He got me located at the Y—— Hotel. I'm still crazy about this guy when he falls for another broad—a little sick yaller gal. I beat hell out of her and he kicked hell out of me. That gal made him quit me. She must have seen him kill a chinaman. Well, I had some dough stacked away, so I get a pilch and go for myself.

Most of the tricks I turned were with colored guys. Harlem is different. Here we only turn tricks with ofays [white men]. They're quicker and they don't squawk out loud if you roll 'em. They know they're in Harlem. I got to New York with a bunch who went to work Saratoga one summer. That's some town. I made more there in a day than I did in Chi in a week. We left Saratoga when the races ended and the joints closed up. I been locked up. I beat the rap though. The funny part about it is they picked me up in a numbers raid. We don't give all of our money to our pimps. I got a guy, though, who ain't a real pimp. Sure I help to keep him. You gotta have some one for protection when you ain't working.

These cases represent, of course, the final stages of demoralization. Moreover, some of the men and women of the foregoing type are strangers to the background of the simple-minded peasant Negro from the South. But, it often happens that they are the children of migrants and, having been bred in the slum areas of northern cities, are more sophisticated than migrants from the South. The vast majority of the roving men from the South never get the "break" that would enable them to derive large incomes from preying on men and women. Many of them are reduced to the position of the itinerant bootblacks who may be seen soliciting shines at half-price on the curbs in Negro communities. Usually they manage to find a rooming-house in the Negro slum area and are able to save enough to pay a woman to stay with them for a night. Or they may find some impoverished and lonely woman with whom they live until one or the other drifts away or the association is ended in violence.

Some of the homeless women even in the large metropolis retain some of their naïveté. They may seek simply to form an association with some male in order to satisfy their desire for sexual satisfaction and companionship. On the other hand, the younger and more sophisticated ones may be adept in vice and crime. Some of the more sophisticated demand that their "daddies" keep them entertained by taking them to the cinema and the cabarets and use every art to enhance their personal attractions in order that their lovers are not lured away by some "hot mamma." Many of them take pride in the fact that they are "tough" and do not "fall" for "sentimental stuff." But, occasionally, these very same women, when memories of home are awakened, may reveal a hidden longing for the secure affection of their families or an abiding attachment to an illegitimate child that has been left along the way.

The solitary wandering men and women are in the majority of cases the debris, so to speak, thrown off by a bankrupt and semifeudal agriculture in the South. It is also true that in the process of adjustment to the urban environment in the North as well as in the South, thousands of migrants become footloose and join the hosts of wandering men and women. These men and women have not only been uprooted from the soil but have no roots in a communal life and have broken all social ties. Their mobility has emancipated them in many cases from the most elementary forms of social control. Hence, their sex behavior and family life should be distinguished from the disorganized family life of the migrants, to which we shall now turn our attention.

CHAPTER XIV

THE FLIGHT FROM
FEUDAL AMERICA

I. SIGNIFICANCE OF MIGRATIONS TO NORTHERN CITIES

The cityward movement of rural Negroes, which had sent a million migrants to hundreds of southern cities, became a great folk movement during and following the first World War, when more than a half-million migrants descended upon four metropolitan areas of the North. Whereas hundreds of Negro families and thousands of solitary men and women had slowly filtered into cities all over the South, during and following the war, thousands of Negro families and even whole communities picked up their meager possessions and fled from southern plantations to northern industrial centers. In the South the migrants from the rural areas were swallowed up in the submerged Negro communities of southern cities; but, in the northern cities, the sudden irruption of trainloads of primitive peasant folk overwhelmed the comparatively small Negro settlements. The sudden descent of this vast human tide upon a few northern cities constituted a flight, replete with dramatic episodes, from medieval to modern America.

The sudden rush of these black hordes upon northern cities was due to the demand of northern industries for workers to fill the places left vacant in the lower ranks of labor by European immigrants who had moved up in the industrial world or had gone home to fight. Hence, the majority of the migrants were attracted to the four cities which needed the type of labor that their unskilled but brawny arms and hands could supply. In the East the glamour of Harlem in New York City lured them as well as the demand for dock and factory workers; while many were drawn to Philadelphia because of the unheard-of wages in her industrial satellite towns. In the West the story of the fabulous wages paid by Detroit's automobile industry and Chicago's stockyards had penetrated the remotest regions of the Black Belt. Thus this unprecedented demand for the labor of the black peasants of the South became "a new vision of opportunity, of social and economic freedom, of a spirit to seize, even at extortionate and heavy toll, a chance for the improvement of conditions."[1]

One of the migrants who aspired to "better" his "condition in life" sent the following letter to the *Chicago Defender*:

DYERSBURG, TENNESSEE, 5/20, 1917

The Defender, Negro News Journal
MY DEAR SIR:

Please hand this letter to the Agency of the negro Employment Bureau—connected with your department—that I may receive a reply from the same—I am a practical fireman—or stoker as the yankee people call it—have a good knowledge of operating machinery—have been engaged in such work for some 20 yrs—will be ready to call—or come on demand—I am a married man—just one child, a boy about 15 yrs—of—age—a member of the Methodist Episcopal Church—and aspire to better my condition in life—Do me the kindness to hand this to the agent.[2]

But a letter from the Black Belt of Mississippi expresses more vividly the new vision of opportunity for social and economic freedom:

GRANVILLE, MISS., May 16, 1917

DEAR SIR:

This letter is a letter of information of which you will find stamp envelop for reply. I want to come north some time soon but I do not want to leve here looking for a job where I would be in dorse all winter. Now the work I am doing here is running a gauge edger in a saw mill. I know all about the grading of lumber. I have abeen working in lumber about 25 or 27 years. My wedges here is $3.00 a day 11 hours a day. I want to come north where I can educate my 3 little children also my wife. Now if you cannot fit me up at what I am

[1] Alain Locke (ed.), *The New Negro* (New York, 1925), p. 6.
[2] "Documents: Letters of Negro Migrants of 1916-1918," *Journal of Negro History*, IV, 303.

doing down here I can learn anything any one els can. also there is great deal of good women cooks here would leave any time all they want is to know where to go and some way to go. please write me at once just how I can get my people where they can get something for their work. There are women here cookeing for $1.50 and $2.00 a week. I would like to live in Chicago or Ohio or Philadelphia. Tell Mr. Abbott that our pepel are tole that they can not get anything to do up there and they are being snatched off the trains here in Greenville and a rested but in spite of all this, they are leaving every day and every night 100 or more is expecting to leave this week. Let me here from you at once.

Perhaps no city of the North held out a greater lure to the migrants than Chicago, the "home of the fearless, taunting 'race paper,'" the *Chicago Defender*. It was through this paper that one migrant was assured of the "rumour about the great work going on in the north." From as far as Miami, Florida, he wrote in 1917:

DEAR SIR:
   Some time ago down this side it was a rumour about the great work going on in the north. But at the present time everything is quite there, people saying that all we have been hearing was false until I caught hold of the *Chicago Defender* I see where its more positions are still open. Now I am very anxious to get up there. I follows up cooking. I also was a stevedor. I used to have from 150 to 200 men under my charge. They thought I was capable in doing the work and at the meantime I am willing to do anything. I have a wife and she is a very good cook. She has lots of references from the north and south. Now dear sir if you can send me a ticket so I can come up there and after I get straightened out I will send for my wife. You will oblige me by doing so at as early date as possible.

A migrant from Houston, Texas, who wrote that he "would like Chicago or Philadelphia But I dont Care where so long as I Go where a man is a man," reiterated the recurring theme of many of these letters. However, the Negro migrant in seeking to escape the control exercised by the dominant race was unconscious of the personal crisis that he had to face in the unsympathetic and impersonal environment of northern cities "where a man is a man." He was to learn in the northern city that he had not only escaped from the traditional subordination to white overlords but had also cut himself loose from the moral support of relatives and neighbors. In some cases, the amazement which the northern metropolis first provoked left little room for lonely reflections. From Pittsburgh a man wrote to his "dear Pastor and wife":

> I go to church some time plenty churches in this plase all kinds they have some real colored churches I have been on the Allegany Mts. twice seem like I was on Baal Tower. Lisen Hayes I am here & I am going to stay ontell fall if I dont get sick its largest city I ever saw 45 miles long & equal in breath & a smoky city so many mines of all kind some places look like torment or how they say it look & some places look like Paradise in this great city.

This same migrant acknowledges in his letter, "I like the money O.K. but I like the South bettern for my Pleasure this city is too fast for me." It was the loneliness of the migrant which called forth his greatest protest against the formal and impersonal relations in the metropolis. Some were overcome at first by the pageantry of the large churches such as that described by the migrant in a letter to the sister whom she had left in the South:

> I got here in time to attend one of the greatest revivals in the history of my life—over 500 people joined the church. We had a Holy Ghost shower. You know I like to have run wild. It was snow-ing some nights and if you didn't hurry you could not get standing room.

However, after a short experience with the city church many of the migrants felt as the woman who described her loneliness and failure to find status in a large city church as follows:

> When I was in the South I was always helping people, but I haven't been doing any of that work up here 'cause B—— Church is too large—it don't see the small people. I belonged to the Phyllis Wheatley Club at home and I was always helping people in my home. I seen lots of my people down here to the Armory. I was well known in my home. I saw quite a few people I knew down there. You see everybody mostly called me "Sister H——." They all knowed me. I was an Eastern Star when I was at home, but since I been here I ain't tried to keep it up. I would try and join a small church where the people would know me. 'Course I don't know so many people here. I been in B—— Church since 1920—went away and came back

and joined again. The preacher wouldn't know me, might could call my name in the book, but he wouldn't know me otherwise. Why, at home whenever I didn't come to Sunday School they would always come and see what was the matter. I would even stay away just to see what they would say, and I would say, "Why, wasn't I there?" and then they would say, "No," that they had come to see what was the matter with Sister H———. 'Course I am a good woman and a good natured woman. People crushes me a lot of time but I don't say anything I just go off and cry—just see how some people step on your feet, and crush you.

The experience of this woman is typical of many migrants who, failing to find status and appreciation in the large urban churches, seek the more intimate face-to-face association in the "store-front" churches that dot the poorer sections of Negro communities in northern cities. To what extent the Negro migrant valued his status in the church is indicated by a statement in a letter, sent by a migrant to his pastor in Alabama, that "his wife always talking about her seat in the church want to know who occupying it."

On the whole, the migrants, both in and out of the churches, are freed from the control exercised by the church and other forms of neighborhood organizations in the South. They need no longer fear the gossip of their neighbors or the disgrace of being "churched" if they violate the mores of the community. Consequently, when these primary forms of group control are dissolved and life becomes more secular, the migrants become subject to all forms of suggestion to be found in the city. Moreover, since tradition and sentiment no longer furnish a guide to living, the migrant is forced to make his own valuations of conduct and thereby develops "rational" attitudes toward his environment. For example, he learns that a "front" brings recognition, while a life lived according to the traditional virtues brings none of the rewards that the community values. Such an outlook on life easily leads to crime and other forms of antisocial behavior. But, in any case, the casting-off of traditional ways of thinking effects a transformation of the Negro's personality and conceptions of life. In the new environment new hopes and ambitions are kindled, and the Negro acquires a new sense of his personal worth and rights. In a letter to an old friend in Alabama, a migrant in East Chicago, Indiana, included in his description of the marvels of the northern cities the statement: "Oh, I have children in school every day with white children."

It was natural that these black migrants, who had long been accommodated to an inferior place in the white man's world in the South, should have been extremely sensitive to such evidences of a newly acquired equality. But, just as coming to the city had deprived the migrants of the moral support of friends and relatives, contacts and competition with whites in the North caused them to lose the provincial community and religious consciousness that had enveloped them in the South and quickened in them a racial consciousness that they had never known. Yet Negro newspapers have had a part in this process in that they have made the Negro conscious not only of his rights in the North but of the limitations under which he had lived in the South. This was quite evident in the case of a young woman migrant, perhaps not quite mentally balanced, who constantly spoke of her thirst for knowledge as a means of getting "out from under the feet of white people," and who never tired of reciting the horrors of southern oppression. Yet, it turned out that her sole source of knowledge concerning these horrors was the Negro newspaper. Likewise, numerous leaders and organizations, responding to this newly developed race consciousness and in turn accentuating it, sprang up for the purpose of fostering racial pride and racial solidarity. Even some of the old mulatto families who had enjoyed considerable freedom and equality, and at first resented the presence of the migrants, gradually identified themselves on abstract issues with the black masses from the South.

Consequently, today the urbanized Negro is giving up his fatalistic resignation to his traditional place in the world and is acquiring a certain degree of sophistication. Although competition and conflict with whites have tended to stimulate race consciousness, other forces are bringing Negroes into co-operative relations with whites. This is especially true where liberal and radical labor organizations are attempting to create a solidarity between white and black workers. Such phrases as "class struggle" and "working-class solidarity," once foreign to the ears of black workers, are the terms in which some

Negroes are beginning to voice their discontent with their present status. The sophistication of the urbanized Negro reveals itself especially in his ingenuity in escaping caste restrictions. It is not uncommon that in the anonymity of the metropolitan community, he assumes according to his color the racial character of various peoples. When his skin is light enough, he becomes a white American; if it is too dark for that, then he becomes Spanish; or, if he is darker still, he may assume the garb of a Hindu or an Arabian. However, in assuming these various protective masks in order to gain a livelihood and move about freely, the Negro's life is usually rooted in the Negro community.

The impact of hundreds of thousands of rural southern Negroes upon northern metropolitan communities presents a bewildering spectacle. Striking contrasts in levels of civilization and economic well-being among these newcomers to modern civilization seem to baffle any attempt to discover order and direction in their mode of life. On the one hand, one sees poverty and primitiveness and, on the other, comfort and civilization. In some quarters crime and viciousness are the characteristic forms of behavior, while in others a simple piety and industry seem unaffected by the currents of urban life. On the streets of Negro communities, painted and powdered women, resembling all the races of mankind, with lustful songs upon their lips, rub shoulders with pious old black charwomen on their way to "store-front" churches. Strutting young men, attired in gaudy clothes and flashing soft hands and manicured fingernails, jostle devout old men clasping Bibles in their gnarled hands as they trudge to "prayer meeting." On the subways, buses, and streetcars one sees men and women with tired black faces staring vacantly into a future lighted only by the hope of a future life, while beside them may sit a girl with her head buried in a book on homosexual love or a boy absorbed in the latest revolutionary pamphlet. Saunterers along the boulevards are interrupted by corner crowds being harangued by speakers on the achievements of the black race or the necessity of social revolution. The periodic screeching of police sirens reminds one of the score or more Negroes who daily run afoul of the law. Children of all ages, playing and fighting and stealing in the streets

day and night, are an ever present indication of the widespread
breakdown of family control. Finally, unseen but known to doctor
and nurse and social worker are the thousands who lie stricken by
disease or are carried off by death.

One may ask: "Is death or extinction, as prophesied by a southern
judge,[3] the only discernible goal toward which this bewildering
spectacle is tending, or can one discover in these contrasts among
Negroes in northern cities some order or direction?" In seeking an
answer to these questions, one cannot study the Negro population
in these cities as a mere aggregate of individual men and women,
each pursuing his own way in the strange world about him, but
as a part of the fabric of the Negro community, the social and
economic organization of which is an integral part of the larger
urban community.

II.   NEGRO COMMUNITIES IN NORTHERN CITIES

To the casual observer the location and growth of the large Negro
communities that have sprung up in northern cities seem to be due
to the prejudices of whites and the desires of Negroes or, viewed
more broadly, to historical accident. But a close study of these
communities reveals that, while race prejudice has not been altogether
a negligible factor, the general character of these Negro communities
has been determined by the same economic and cultural forces that
have shaped the organization of the community as a whole. Recent
studies have shown that the great cities or metropolitan communities
are not "mere population aggregates" but that the distribution of
their "population tends to assume definite and typical patterns."[4]
These typical patterns come into existence because of competition
for land as the population increases and the city expands. As a result
of this expansion, "a process of distribution takes place which sifts
and sorts and relocates individuals and groups by residence and
occupation."[5] The location of the Negro community, like that of

[3] "The Negro Migrations—a Debate," *Forum,* LXXII, 593-607.
[4] Robert E. Park, "The Urban Community as a Spacial Pattern and a Moral
Order," in *The Urban Community,* ed. Ernest W. Burgess (Chicago, 1926), p. 3.
[5] Ernest W. Burgess, "The Growth of the City," in *The City* (Chicago, 1925),
p. 54.

other racial and cultural groups, fits into the pattern of the larger community.

This may be seen in the location and growth of the Negro community in Chicago with a population of over two hundred thousand. According to tradition, the Negro community in Chicago goes back to Baptiste Point de Saible, a San Domingan Negro, who built a rude hut on the north bank of the Chicago River around 1779 (A. T. Andreas, *History of Chicago: From the Earliest Period to the Present Time* [3 vols.; Chicago, 1884], I, 70-71). " 'Baptiste Point de Saible, a handsome Negro, well educated and settled at Eschikagou; but much in the French interest.' This apparently unimportant fact, recorded July 4, 1779, by Colonel Arent Schuyler DePeyster, then British commander at Michilimakinac, is the initial point from which may be traced the growth of Chicago, from a single rude cabin on the sandpoint at the mouth of the river, to the magnificent city which stands today, the type of modern progressive civilization."

Although Negroes appeared in the chronicles of the early history of the city, they did not attain numerical significance until after the Civil War, when Chicago became the goal of Negro migrants from the South. From about the time of the great fire in 1871 onward, the Negro population practically doubled each decade until it reached 30,150 at the opening of the present century. Then there was a slowing-down of migration until the first World War. Because of their color and low economic status, Negroes first acquired a foothold in and near the center of the city where there was less resistance to alien elements. "The influence of land values at the business center radiates from that point to every part of the city. If the growth at the center is rapid it increases the diameter of the area held for speculative purposes just outside the center. Property held for speculation is usually allowed to deteriorate. It easily assumes the character of a slum; that is to say, an area of casual and transient population, an area of dirt and disorder, 'of missions and of lost souls.' These neglected and sometimes abandoned regions become the points of first settlement of immigrants."[6] From the slum area surrounding the central business section, the majority of the Negro population

[6] Robert E. Park, *op. cit.*, p. 6.

expanded southward along State Street. As late as 1920, 90 per cent of the Negro population was concentrated in the South Side Black Belt or the area bounded by Twelfth and Thirty-ninth streets and Wentworth Avenue and Lake Michigan. But this area could not accommodate the fifty thousand migrants who poured into the Negro community during the first World War. During normal times the Negro population had tended to move into those areas that were formerly white residential areas but were becoming rooming-house areas. This process had gone on unnoticed and without friction, until the shortage of homes for whites, created by the suspension of building operations during the war, brought a halt to the movement of the whites from these changing areas. It was then that the conflict between the rapidly expanding Negro population and the resisting whites led to the organization of property-owners' associations and, in some cases, to bombing and other forms of violence. However, neither violence nor the formation of property-owners' associations has been able to halt the expansion of the Negro community along lines in harmony with the growth of the city.

The social and economic forces which have caused a sifting and sorting of population, occupational classes, and institutions in the city at large, have effected a similar result within the South Side Negro community itself. It was possible to measure the sifting and sorting of different elements in the Negro population by dividing the community into seven zones, each about a mile in length. The process of selection and segregation was shown first in the variations in the proportion of southern-born heads of families and mulattoes and in the percentage of illiteracy in the population of the successive zones indicating the expansion of the community. In the first zone, just outside the central business district, over three-fourths of the heads of families were born in the South. The proportion of southern-born heads of families declined in each successive zone until it reached less than two-thirds in the seventh. A similar trend was observable in regard to illiteracy in the different zones. For example, in Zone I, which was definitely in the slum area, 13.4 per cent of the Negro population was illiterate, whereas in Zone VII only 2.7 per cent was in this category. As regards the proportion of mulattoes in the population of the different zones, one would expect a trend opposite to that observable in the case of nativity and illiteracy. This was found to be true with one interesting exception. In the first two zones where the most recent migrants from the South lived, only about one out of five Negro men and one out of four Negro women showed any admixture of white blood. But in the third zone the proportion mounted suddenly, one out of three Negro men and two out of five Negro women showing mixed ancestry. The concentration of mulattoes in this zone is understandable when we consider the place of this zone in the organization of the Negro community:

> Through the heart of this zone ran Thirty-fifth Street, the bright-light area of the Negro community. Here were found the "black and tan" cabarets, pleasure gardens, gambling places, night clubs, hotels, and houses of prostitution. It was the headquarters of the famous "policy king"; the rendezvous of the "pretty" brown-skinned boys, many of whom were former bell-hops, who "worked" white and colored girls in hotels and on the streets; here the mulatto queen of the underworld ran the biggest poker game on the South Side; here the "gambler de luxe" ruled until he was killed by a brow-beaten waiter. In this world the mulatto girl from the South who, ever since she heard that she was "pretty enough to be an actress," had visions of the stage, realized her dream in one of the cheap theaters. To this same congenial environment the mulatto boy from Oklahoma, who danced in the role of the son of an Indian woman, had found his way. To this area were attracted the Bohemian, the disorganized, and the vicious elements in the Negro world.[7]

In the fourth zone the proportion of mulattoes dropped to about that of the second zone, but in the fifth, sixth, and seventh zones there was a progressive increase in the proportion of mixed-bloods. In the seventh zone, where the higher social and occupational classes resided, close to half of the population had some admixture of white blood.

The tendency on the part of the higher occupational classes to move toward the periphery of the Negro community fitted into the general pattern of the community. Whereas only 5.8 per cent of the employed men and 3 per cent of the employed women in the

[7] E. Franklin Frazier, *The Negro Family in Chicago*, p. 103.

first zone were in professional and public service and the "white-collar" occupations, about a third of the employed men and women in the seventh zone were found in the same categories. The same tendency was true, although not to the same extent, in regard to Negroes engaged in skilled occupations. On the other hand, the lower occupational classes were segregated in the zones near the center of the city. The proportion of employed women was also higher in these zones than in the zones toward the periphery of the community where the higher occupational classes were concentrated. A considerable proportion of the employed women in these zones were in the higher occupational classes. Thus, viewed both from the standpoint of the character of its population and from the standpoint of its social and economic classes, the Negro community in Chicago has assumed a fairly definite spatial pattern.

If we turn from the Negro community in Chicago to the Harlem Negro community in New York City, we find that its growth has not only been shaped by the growth of the city but that the community, during its expansion, has assumed a pattern of zones similar to that of a self-contained city. Although there is disagreement concerning the historical events connected with the origin of the Negro community in Harlem, there seems to be no question that Harlem had already deteriorated as a residential community when Negroes began finding homes there at the opening of the present century.[8] The Negro real estate agent who is credited with having brought the Negro to Harlem in 1903 was merely an agent in a process which has characterized the growth of Negro communities. The movement of Negroes into Harlem provoked the usual opposition to such invasions. The *New York Herald* of July 10, 1906, reported indignation meetings "throughout the neighborhood of West 135th Street, where thirty-five white families" were to be ejected to make room for Negro tenants. At the end of the article there was the following prohetic comment: "It is generally believed by the residents, however, that the establishment of the Negroes in 135th Street is only the nucleus of a Negro settlement that will extend over a very wide area of Harlem within the next few years."

[8] Clyde Vernon Kiser, *Sea Island to City* (New York, 1932), pp. 19-20.

The subsequent growth of the Harlem Negro community has been a fulfilment of this prophetic statement. From the small Negro settlement in the block referred to above the Negro community has spread out in all directions. The radial expansion of the Negro population from the area about One Hundred and Thirty-fifth Street and Seventh Avenue may be represented ideally by drawing concentric circles about the census tract in which the intersection of these two main thoroughfares is located. The expansion of the community from the standpoint of population is shown graphically in the statistics on the increase of the Negro population in the five zones since 1910. In 1910 there were 15,028 Negroes, or 54 per cent of the Negroes in the Harlem area, concentrated in the first two zones. Negroes comprised less than a fifth of the entire population of these two zones; while in the three remaining zones marking their outward expansion they became less and less significant in the population. By 1920, Negroes constituted over three-fourths of the population of the first zone, over half of that of the second zone, and about a seventh of the population of the third. During this expansion native whites, whites of foreign extraction, and foreign-born whites were supplanted in these areas. However, the whites in the two outlying zones still resisted the expanding Negro population. By 1940 the Negro had not only taken over almost the entire first zone and increased to seventh-eights and nearly three-fifths of the population of the second and third zones, respectively, but had become a significant element—48.5 per cent—in the population of the fourth zone. Even in the fifth zone, Negroes had increased from 2.5 to 7.1 per cent.

Although the five zones indicate the general tendency of the population to expand radially from the center of the community, the Negro population has not expanded to the same extent in all directions. It has been held in check until residential areas have deteriorated and therefore have become accessible not only to Negroes but to Italians and Puerto Ricans, who live in areas adjacent to those inhabited by Negroes. In some instances white residential areas, even when surrounded by the expanding Negro population, have put up a long and stubborn resistance. This was the case with the area about

Mount Morris Park. However, when this area lost its purely residential character and brown-stone fronts became rooming-houses, the eventual entrance of the Negro was foreshadowed. Then, too, the advance of the Negro has been heralded by the location of light industries, as in the western section of Harlem where, after the establishment of a brewery doomed the area as a residential neighborhood for whites of foreign extraction, signs inviting Negro tenants began to appear. For a time the westward expansion of the Negro population was halted at Amsterdam Avenue but it appears that it may even invade the exclusive residential area on Riverside Drive.

The expansion of the Negro population coincides largely with the predominant types of structures located in the five zones. For example, the Negro population predominates in those zones where the majority of the structures are non-residential in character. But even more significant is the fact that the Negro population is concentrated in the zones where rooming- and lodging-houses comprise a relatively large proportion of the nonresidential structures. Data on the type, age, and condition of the residential structures in the five zones show the relation between the expansion of the Negro community and the physical character of the areas into which Negroes have moved. The comparatively large proportion of one-family dwellings in the third zone was due to the fact that the western section of the third zone included a large part of the Riverside Drive area. However, the most important differences between the zones in respect to residential structures appeared in the proportion of hotels, boarding-houses, and institutions which were simply classified as "other." The proportion of this type of residential structure declined sharply from 51.7 per cent in the first zone to 14.9 in the fifth. The differences in the physical character of the zones were shown more clearly in the age of the residential structures in the five zones. In the first and second zones, where 99 and 87.8 per cent of the residents, respectively, were Negroes, 90 per cent of the residential structures were thirty-five years of age and over. For the remaining three zones the proportion of older structures declined significantly except in the fourth zone, which included a large number of deteriorated tenements in the eastern section where Negroes have settled.

The relation between the condition of the residential structures in the various zones and the expansion of the Negro population was less obvious. However, the comparatively large proportion of first-class structures in the first zone indicated that this area was being rehabilitated.

The selection and segregation which have taken place as the Negro population has expanded is seen first in the variations in the proportion of grown people in the five zones. Practically four out of five persons in the first zone were adults in 1930. In the second zone the proportion of adults in the population declined to three out of four, and, in the next three zones, from about seven to six out of ten persons in the population. On the other hand, the relative number of children in the population of the five zones shows the opposite tendency. In the first or central zone only 3.8 per cent of the entire population in 1930 was under five years of age. The proportion of children in this age group increased in each of the successive zones until it reached 12.3 per cent in the fifth zone. There was also a slight increase in the proportion of females in the successive zones marking the outward expansion of the population. Although there was an excess of females in the total population of the community, the excess of females in the first zone was counterbalanced by the tendency on the part of males to concentrate there.

The tendency on the part of family groups to move toward the periphery of the community was indicated by the increasing proportion of married men and women in the successive zones. In the first zone only half of the men and women were married. From this zone outward, the percentage of both men and women increased until it amounted, in the fifth or outermost zone, to 64.2 per cent for the men and 60.1 per cent for the women. Correlated with the increase in the proportion of men and women married was the gradual decline not only in the proportion of men and women single in the successive zones but also in the proportion of widowed persons in these five zones. Interestingly enough, the proportion of men and women widowed, which undoubtedly included those deserted and separated, was highest in the center of the community where one would expect to find considerable family disorganization. Hence, the increase in the proportion of divorced men in the successive zones as one left the center of the community was understandable.

III. SURVIVAL IN THE NORTHERN CITY

The low fertility of Negroes in northern cities has seemed to confirm the pessimistic prophecies concerning their fate in the North. In an unpublished study of differential fertility in the East North Central States, Frank W. Notestein found that the mean number of children under age ten per wife for marriages of five to nine years' duration was smaller for Negroes in 1930 than for native or foreign white. The differential between Negro and white wives increased with the size of the community. However, the mean number of children under age ten per "mother" for marriages of five to nine years' duration was higher for Negroes in each type of community than for native or foreign white. Consequently, the percentage of homes with no children under age ten for this same marriage group was considerably higher for Negroes than for either of the two other racial groups. The percentage of Negro homes with no children under ten ranged from 28.5 in rural-farm communities to 52.5 in communities of 250,000 and more population. In the larger communities, especially those over 250,000 population, the mean number of children under ten per wife declined with the increase in the value of home (from paper read before the annual meeting of the American Sociological Society, Atlantic City, New Jersey, 1937).

Thompson and Whelpton have shown that there has been a marked tendency for the ratio of children to Negro women of childbearing age to vary inversely with size of city.[9] According to these authors, Negroes in large cities including Chicago and New York "were not maintaining their numbers on a permanent basis in either 1920 or 1928." The extremely low fertility of Negroes in Chicago has been demonstrated in an unpublished study by Philip M. Hauser, of the University of Chicago. However, in the case of Chicago, we have

[9] Warren S. Thompson and P. K. Whelpton, *Population Trends in the United States* (New York, 1933), p. 280.

found in a study of the Negro family that selective factors affected the relative fertility of different sections of the Negro population. For example, the ratio of children under five years to women of childbearing age was highest in the seventh zone, which was farthest removed from the center of the city. In this zone there were 276 children under five years to 1,000 women of childbearing age, or nearly twice as many as in the third zone, a bright-light area of considerable mobility and vice.

Kiser found in a study of Negro birth-rates in a health area of Harlem that the fertility of Negro women was lower than that of white women of similar or even higher occupational level in Syracuse and two other urban communities.[10] Kiser indicated in his study that the low fertility of Negroes was "due partly to selective processes with reference to residence in Harlem as indicated by higher birth rates among the colored population in other parts of the city." As a matter of fact, within the Harlem community itself important differences are revealed if the fertility of these women is studied in relation to the selective processes. It we compare the five zones by which we have indicated the expansion of the community with reference to the ratio of children to women of childbearing age, we find that both in 1920 and in 1930 there was, with one exception, a regular increase in the ratio of children from the first to the fifth zone. In 1930 the ratio of children in the fifth zone was 462, or four times that in the first zone. The exception to the general trend noticeable in the fourth zone in 1920 was probably due to the fact that at that time only a small number of economically better situated families had moved into this zone. On the other hand, the changes between 1920 and 1930 in ratio of children in the three outer zones seem to indicate that the more fertile groups have tended to settle in peripheral zones.

The relation between the fertility of Negro women and residence in the various areas of the community is shown also in the ratio of children to women fifteen years of age and over who were married, widowed, and divorced and number of births to married women

---

[10] Clyde V. Kiser, "Fertility of Harlem Negroes," *Milbank Memorial Fund Quarterly*, XIII (July, 1935), 273-85.

fifteen to forty-four. Here again we find the ratio of children increasing regularly in the successive zones marking the expansion of the Negro community. The same trend was observable in regard to birth-rates in 1930. In the first zone there were only 66.1 births per 1,000 Negro married women fifteen to forty-four years of age. But, as in the case of the ratio of children, the fertility of the women mounted rapidly, especially in the two outermost zones. The fertility of the women in the fifth zone was slightly over two and one-half times as great as it was in the first.

The significance of these variations in fertility for the survival of the Negro population is further emphasized if the number of births is compared with the number of deaths in each of the five zones. In the first zone deaths were in excess of births, and in the second they almost balanced the births. Only in the three outer zones was there an appreciable excess of births over deaths. However, the fourth zone was better off than the fifth in respect to the excess of births over deaths and the infant mortality rate. This was due to the fact that some sections of the fifth zone were slum areas. Nevertheless, these figures clearly demonstrate the influence of selective factors in the survival of the Negro in the urban environment.

From our study of the Negro population in Chicago and Harlem, it appears that Negro life in northern cities flows, in spite of its disorganization and apparent lack of direction, in the channels of a community life. This community life reflects in its organization the impress of social and economic forces within the community as well as those that shape the development of the larger urban area. In the Harlem community, which has assumed the character of a self-contained city, the community pattern is visibly manifested in the location of institutions. The concentration of institutions in the first zone or center of the community has been vividly described in a story of Negro life in Harlem. "In a fraction of a mile of 135th Street," wrote Rudolph Fisher, "there occurs every institution necessary to civilization from a Carnegie Library opposite a public school at one point to a police station beside an undertaker's parlor at another." A survey of this area revealed, first, that the economic life of the community, especially with respect to Negro business enterprises, was centered about One Hundred and Thirty-fifth Street and Seventh Avenue. Located in this area in 1935 there were 321 business establishments, not including 53 offices of Negro professional men and women. Although about two-thirds of these businesses were conducted by Negroes, whites owned the bank and more than 80 per cent of the retail food stores. Negroes controlled practically all the businesses providing personal services and other types of enterprises not requiring large outlays of capital. In this zone were also the two principal Negro newspapers and the offices of four Negro insurance companies. This area was also the focus of the political and cultural life of Negro Harlem. In 1935 five political clubs and two fraternal organizations had headquarters in this area. Besides a public library, a public school, and a health center, the Negro branches of the Y.M.C.A. and Y.W.C.A. and offices of the New York Urban League and the N.A.A.C.P. were all within two blocks of the busy intersection at One Hundred and Thirty-fifth Street and Seventh Avenue. The two large church edifices—one Baptist and the other Methodist—located in this central zone indicated the character of the area before it had acquired its present specialized place in the community. On the other hand, the six "store-front" churches on the fringe of this zone actually belonged with thirty-six such churches in the slum sections of the second zone.

Although this zone was the center of recreation for the Negro population, a number of the recreational institutions catered primarily to whites seeking amusement in Harlem. However, this was only one of the many indications of the manner in which the larger community has influenced life in Harlem, economically and otherwise. The ownership and control of Harlem housing and real estate are centered in the financial institutions downtown. The main arteries of travel—Lenox, Seventh, and Eighth avenues—running the entire length of the community, and the "satellite loops" at One Hundred and Sixteenth, One Hundred and Twenty-fifth, and One Hundred and Forty-fifth streets, not only mar the symmetry of the community pattern but bear the stamp of outside interests and control.

The poverty and disorganization of Negro family life in the urban environment only becomes intelligible when they are studied in relation to the organization of Negro communities and the social and economic forces which determine their development. Therefore, in the following chapters an attempt is made to study the various problems of Negro family life in their social setting and in relation to the organization of the community.

CHAPTER XV

FATHERS ON
LEAVE

Family desertion has been one of the inevitable consequences of the urbanization of the Negro population. In both northern and southern cities the ranks of Negro men who have deserted their families have constantly been recruited from several sources. Among the foot-loose men who drift from city to city in search of work and new experience, there are husbands and fathers who have deserted their wives and children. Many of the more stable men who left wives and families behind when they joined the migrating masses during and following the first World War later became deserters. Despite their often sincere intentions to rejoin their families and the initial loneliness which they experienced in the new world, the city with its varied interests proved fatal to family ties. Even when whole families have migrated, the community of interests and bonds of sympathy that created strong family ties in rural communities have often been unable to withstand the disintegrating forces of the city.

Although it is difficult to get a measure of the extent to which Negro men desert their wives and families, it appears from available sources of information that desertions are more frequent in Negro families than in the families of other racial groups. For example, while Negroes comprised 5.6 per cent of all the families in New York City in 1916-17 under the care of the Charity Organization Society, they furnished 11.2 per cent of the desertions.[1] A similar

[1] Joanna C. Colcord, *Broken Homes: A Study of Family Desertions* (New York, 1919), pp. 44-45.

245

situation was found in Cook County, Illinois, where, during the six years (exclusive of 1914) from 1909 to 1915, Negroes comprised 21.1 per cent of all desertion cases aided by the county agent.[2] Moreover, the large proportion of urban Negro families with women heads seems to be the result in some measure of desertions on the part of the men. It hardly seems likely that widowhood, divorce, and legal separation alone account for the large percentage of such families in the Negro group. In northern cities with a total population of 100,000 or more, from 10 to 30 per cent of the Negro families have female heads. This is higher than the proportion among either the native whites or the foreign-born whites. Within the Negro group itself, the proportion of families with female heads is higher among tenants than owners, especially in the larger cities where the bulk of the Negro population in the North is concentrated.

In southern cities the disparity between whites and Negroes in respect to the proportion of families with women heads is much greater. In the twenty-three southern cities with a population of 100,000 or more in 1930, from a fifth to a third of all Negro families had a female head. However, in most of these southern cities, the difference between owner and tenant Negro families in this regard was much greater than in northern cities. On the basis of data secured from the original census returns on such families in three cities—Nashville, Tennessee, Birmingham, Alabama, and Charleston, South Carolina—we can get some information on the general character of the families with women heads. These families represent a sample of about a sixth of the families in Nashville and Charleston and a fourth of the families in Birmingham from each of the federal enumeration districts in these cities. First, in all three cities, both in 1910 and in 1920, the proportion of female heads was smaller among the mulattoes than among the blacks. However, the proportion of families with women heads among blacks as well as mulattoes was significantly smaller in Birmingham, where half of the men were in industrial occupations, than among both mulattoes and blacks in Nashville and Charleston, where Negro men were employed chiefly in domestic and personal service. In the latter two cities from a third to two-fifths of the families had female heads,

[2] Earl Edward Eubank, *A Study of Family Desertion* (Chicago, 1916), pp. 15-16.

whereas in Birmingham approximately a fourth of both the black and the mulatto families were in this category.

In regard to the marital status of the women heads of Negro families in these cities, information from the original census returns gives a more accurate picture than one gets from the published data on the marital status of Negro women. The majority of these women—from two-thirds to four-fifths—were classified as widowed. From what is known concerning the marital status of Negro women who describe themselves as widowed, we can only assume, as in the case of the published census figures, that some of these widowed women had either been deserted or were unmarried mothers. But, in addition to the usual categories of widowed and divorced, we have been able to classify these women as to whether they were separated from their husbands or were living irregularly with a man in the household. In some cases as many as 20 per cent of the women heads of families were separated. In all likelihood, the majority of these women had been deserted by their husbands. It is also probable that some of the women who were living irregularly with men, but reported themselves as married to other men, had been deserted. In fact, it is also very likely that some women who called themselves divorced had been deserted. When these various facts are considered, it seems reasonable to conclude that, so far as these figures are representative of Negro families in southern cities, about a fifth of the families with women heads represent desertion on the part of men.

The original census returns throw some light on the general economic and social status of these women. From three-fourths to four-fifths of the black women heads of the families were employed in domestic service; whereas, among the mulattoes, not only was a smaller proportion employed in domestic service, but, apparently, a smaller proportion depended upon their own labor for a livelihood. Moreover, an almost negligible percentage of the black women were homeowners while about 10 per cent of the mulatto women owned their homes. It is also significant that practically all the homeowners among the black women heads of families as well as the mulattoes were widowed.

For Birmingham we have information on the extent of desertion among the cases handled by the Red Cross Family Service for the period 1925-29. During this period the number of colored major care cases increased from 502, or 11.2 per cent of a total of 4,468 cases, to 2,698, or 25 per cent of the 10,853 cases handled in 1929. For the years 1926-28 about 20 per cent of the colored cases were deserted women. However, in 1929 after the effects of the economic crisis began to be felt, the proportion of married couples increased, while the proportion of deserted women declined to 15 per cent. The following excerpt from the case record of a deserted woman, twenty-eight years of age and the mother of five children, living in a two-room house in an alley, for which she paid eight dollars a month, will throw some light on the character of some of these deserted women and their sexual relations:

Man's native home in Alabama. Woman did not know where he was reared. Father died a long time ago. Mother, living. No brothers or sisters. Family had very good health record. Fairly good home training, common school education. Religious and moral influences very good. Parents were farmers and he always worked on a farm.

Woman's home was LaFayette, Alabama. Father died when she was real young. Mother still living; has four brothers and three sisters. Her mother had ten children, of whom eight are living. One died with T.B. She was given a good home training; religious and moral influences not very good. Very quiet type, but was a mother before she was married. She was living away from home at the time. She was reared on a farm and had to work in the fields most of the time. Did not go to school very much. Husband was not the father of her illegitimate child, but another man.

Man and woman lived together very agreeable for a while. He provided very well for his family during their stay together. They were the parents of three children, and he deserted when the last one was a few months old, leaving her with nothing to live on. He left town with another man's wife. Woman has always been interested in her children and tried to provide for them. She seems very childish about planning for them. After her husband left, all her people left; she became the mother of another child. This man promised to support her children but after a while he left too. The neighbors helped during her confinement.

Later, it was found out where the father of her last child was living.

He was asked to support her. He sent a doctor to see one of the children who was sick. Her oldest daughter, unmarried, had a child.

Family desertion among Negroes in southern cities is in a large measure only one aspect of the disorganized family life and unregulated sex behavior of these newcomers to the city. Desertion is often found in conjunction with other types of loose sex behavior, as is apparent even in the sketchy details recorded in the case records of social agencies. Let us glance at the record of a twenty-four-year-old woman living on the outskirts of Birmingham:

> Live in Eureka, an ordinary type of Negro settlement. Immediate section composed of a row of shot-gun houses, built closely together, and the surroundings uncleanly and undesirable, but the common situation of the Negro. Two rooms all furnished, but the house unkempt and dirty. Conditions unsanitary.
>
> Woman apparently middle aged, pregnant and suffering from it. Visitor was amazed to learn she was young. Untidy, barefooted and unclean in person. Children dirty and ill. Willing to accept any assistance. Even though in pain she did not show any sign of impatience. She answered all questions readily and most frankly. She admitted her circumstances were due to her own misconduct. Was very grateful and cooperative. Reconciled to her fate but repentant and anxious to be self-supporting.
>
> Woman was born in Montgomery County, one of nine children. She lived on the farm with her parents until she was 21. Baptist. Apparently lived a clean, moral life as long as she was with her parents in the country. Came to Birmingham in 1921 to earn her living to relieve her widow mother. Father died when she was a child. Took in washings for her living and managed very nicely. Met B——, a laborer in the city, and married him in 1922.
>
> Man was born in Gunsville, Alabama. Common laborer. Lived with her for two years. Got along nicely but he became shiftless and left his wife and baby. Gave no excuses and no whereabouts. One child was born in 1923, one in 1925.
>
> Woman allowed a man to live with her in open cohabitation. He knew she had no divorce. He promised to marry her all the time. One child was born to them in 1927. He was a carpenter. He has now deserted her and the children and she is nine months pregnant. Has a mother living in the country, a tenant farmer with seven children and six grandchildren to care for already, in a three room house. A sister lived near her but she has gone to visit the mother. All the other sisters are married and have large families of their own.

When we turn from these southern cities to New York City, we find that there also desertion cases constitute a large portion of the cases of dependency handled by social agencies. An analysis of the records of the Charity Organization Society over a period of ten years from 1924 to 1934 showed that both the number and the proportion of Negro "under care" families served by this agency have increased as the economic crisis deepened. (The Charity Organization Society defines an "under care" case as "a family or person for which the agency assumes responsibility for instituting some study and treatment. This category is intended to include all cases which, as the result of the preliminary diagnosis, are accepted for care with the intention of giving the case such study and treatment as seem indicated.") In the area for which we have figures the number of Negro "under care" families increased during the four years from 1924 to 1928, although their numbers relative to all families receiving such assistance changed only slightly. However, beginning with the fiscal year 1928-29 there was not only an increase in the number of Negro families but also a decided increase in the proportion in the total number of families receiving major services. From 1931 onward Negro families constituted close to 45 per cent of the total. The slight decline in the proportion of Negro families during 1933-34 was doubtless due to the fact that the majority of dependent Negro families were cared for by the Home Relief Bureau. In fact, the records of the Home Relief Bureau offer the only adequate index to the widespread dependency in the Harlem community. In this community during the first week of September, 1935, there were 24,293 Negro families, not including unattached men and women, receiving relief from the Home Relief Bureau.

During the fiscal year 1928-29 the Charity Organization Society gave assistance to 571 Negro "under care" families in the Harlem community. After the economic crisis became more acute, the number rose to 1,547 during the fiscal year 1930-31. Of the 571 families receiving assistance during the first period, 101, or 17.7 per cent, were desertion cases; while during the latter period, 1930-31, the proportion of deserted families declined to 14.8 per cent.

The majority—about three-fifths—of the cases handled by the

Charity Organization Society represented migrants who had come to New York City during and subsequent to the first World War. Although specific information is lacking concerning the birthplace of about a third of the cases, the records simply stating that they were born in the United States, the majority of the cases were doubtless persons of southern birth. However, the records contained specific information to the effect that more than a fourth of the cases were of West Indian origin and that about 5 per cent were natives of New York City.

An analysis of the desertion cases revealed that 44 per cent of the 101 cases handled in 1928-29 were new cases; whereas 155, or 67.4 per cent, of the 230 cases handled in 1930-31 were new. Among the desertion cases there was a larger proportion of families that had come to New York City since the war than among the dependency cases as a whole. As to origin, they showed the same proportion of southern birth and West Indian background. As far as one could learn the occupational status of the deserters, they were employed chiefly in unskilled occupations and domestic service. In the case of the deserted women, we find that 65 per cent of the first group and 56 per cent of the second had been engaged in gainful occupations. In both groups nearly 90 per cent of the regularly employed women were in domestic service. Fifty per cent of the deserted women and their spouses were between thirty and forty years of age.

The case records contain information on the character of the households and the composition of the deserted families. About 9 per cent of the 101 families in the first group had one or two relatives in the household, whereas 19 per cent of the 230 families in the second group were living with one to five relatives. Moreover, there were lodgers in 6 of the families of the first group; and in 20 families of the second group. The increase in the number of families with relatives and lodgers in the household was probably the result of the effects of the depression during the later period. However, there was practically no change in the average number of children in these families, the average being 2.3 in 1928-29 and 2.2 in 1930-31. In

both groups about the same proportion of families had children
away from home and in institutions.

In Chicago, where large numbers of migrants from the lower
South have settled since the first World War, the trend of family
desertion during recent years may be studied in relation to the economic and cultural organization of the Negro community. Here, as in
other cities, family desertion generally comes to the attention of both
private and public welfare agencies in connection with dependency.
From 1921 to 1927 the number of Negro desertion or nonsupport
cases that came before the Court of Domestic Relations increased
almost 100 per cent. In 1927 there were 813 cases, or 19.5 per cent
of the 4,168 cases handled by the court.[3] In the same city an
examination of the records of the United Charities for the period
1921-28 showed that the proportion of Negro families receiving
major services increased suddenly from about a tenth in the first
two years to a little more than a fifth of all cases during the last
five years. According to the reports of the Chicago Urban League,
the sudden increase in the proportion of Negro families seeking
assistance from the United Charities coincided with a marked increase in unemployment among Negroes in 1924. Of the Negro
cases handled by this agency during the seven years indicated, less
than half were reported as deserted families. A check of the records
of the United Charities showed that this agency had handled 750
Negro cases of family desertion during the two and a half years from
January 1, 1926, to June 30, 1928. Social agencies experience great
difficulty in ascertaining the true marital condition of migrant Negro
families. For example, of the 248 Negro cases—129 major service
and 119 minor service—in the case records of the Central District
of the United Charities during January, 1927, marriage was verified
in 70 cases; an unsuccessful attempt was made to verify 55 cases;
and marriage was unverified in 122 cases, one case being classified as
unknown.

Two-thirds of these cases were located in the South Side community. However, they were very unevenly distributed; and, what is
of importance to us here, when on the basis of these cases desertion

[3] E. Franklin Frazier, *The Negro Family in Chicago* (Chicago, 1932), p. 148.

rates were calculated for the seven zones marking the expansion of
the community, the rates showed a distinct downward trend. Although there were only nine cases in the first zone, these cases
amounted to 2.5 per cent of the families in that area. The first zone,
which was just outside the Loop, was an area of extreme physical
deterioration and social disorganization and was fast becoming
depopulated. The one hundred deserted families in the next zone,
which was similar in character to the first zone, constituted 2.6 per
cent of the resident families. These relatively high rates coincided
with the high dependency rates—eight families out of one hundred
being supported by charity—in the first two zones. In the third zone
there was a slight decline in the desertion rate, although there were
other signs of family disorganization. The third zone was, in fact,
the bright-light area of the Negro community, there being little
family life and considerable vice in the area. The Negro in this
area was likely to exhibit greater sophistication in city ways. Therefore, it is not surprising that the nonsupport rate, based upon cases
brought before the Court of Domestic Relations, showed an increase
over the rates in the first two zones where the less sophisticated
migrants from the South lived.

A significant decline in the desertion rate did not appear until the
fourth zone, which was distinguished from the first three zones in
several respects. First, the rate of homeownership reached the average
for the city, whereas in the first zone no families owned their homes,
and in the second and third zones the rate of homeownership was
below the average for the city. Then, too, both the dependency and
the illiteracy rate declined sharply in the fourth zone. In this zone
illiteracy was about one-sixth as high as in the first zone, and the
dependency rate was almost half that in the third zone.

The decline in the desertions in the next three zones was even
more significant. From eleven in each 1,000 resident families in the
fifth zone, the rate declined to two in the seventh. The gradual disappearance of this form of family disorganization coincided with
increasing stabilization of family and community life. This was
indicated, first, by the significant increase in homeownership in
these three zones. The rate of homeownership mounted rapidly from

8.3 and 11.4 per cent in the fifth and sixth zones to 29.8 in the seventh. Then there was a decline in the proportion of migrant families in these three areas, in conjunction with an increasing proportion of mulattoes in the population. The higher economic status of the inhabitants of these zones was indicated by the fact that there was an increasing proportion of men and women in professional occupations and a smaller proportion of women employed. Along with desertions, both dependency and nonsupport tended to vanish.

When one examines the records of the social agencies concerning these deserted families, they read very much like the records which were quoted from Birmingham, as witness the record of the United Charities on a deserted woman living in the second zone:

> Mrs. G. in office asking assistance because Mr. G. had deserted her in June. Mrs. G. was born in Port Gibson, Mississippi, and moved to Missouri in 1924. She went to school in Mississippi to the 8th grade. She met her husband in St. Louis and knew him 10 months before marriage. They came to Chicago directly after marriage. Her husband was a good provider, but abused her, beating her and quarrelling continually. He is big headed. This caused the separation. He does not drink, but is very hard to get on with, as he is continually fighting. She thinks he has gone off with O—— W——, a woman who lived next door. She does not know how long he has been friendly with her. He left her in June but stayed at 29—— Cottage Grove Avenue until the first of August, when she last saw him. She does not know where he is now. She went to C.D.R. in August, swearing out a warrant for him but the officers were unable to find him.

Family desertion on the part of Negro men and its relation to the organization of the Negro community in Chicago presented the same picture in the 1940's as in the 1930's. This has been shown in those sections of Drake and Cayton's *Black Metropolis* dealing with the family life of the lower class in the community.[4]

More intimate documents, such as life and family histories, secured from these deserted women and their former husbands, furnish a wealth of information on their inner lives, their attitudes,

[4] St. Clair Drake and Horace R. Cayton, *Black Metropolis* (New York, 1945), pp. 385-86.

wishes, and conceptions of life, and how these have been affected by the urban environment. In many cases these broken families were once well adjusted to the simple rural southern community, where the sympathetic relationships existing between the members of the family were supported by the church, the lodge, and the customs of the community. But in the city, with its many attractions and conflicting standards of behavior, divergent interests are developed and individualistic wishes become dominant. But, despite these various forces in the urban environment, the sympathetic ties sometimes draw the deserters back to their families. The behavior of Negro deserters, who are likely to return to their families even after several years of absence, often taxes the patience of social workers whose plans for their families are constantly disrupted.

In many cases, of course, the dissolution of the simple family organization has begun before the family reaches the northern city. But, if these families have managed to preserve their integrity until they reach the northern city, poverty, ignorance, and color force them to seek homes in deteriorated slum areas from which practically all institutional life has disappeared. Hence, at the same time that these simple rural families are losing their internal cohesion, they are being freed from the controlling force of public opinion and communal institutions. Family desertion among Negroes in cities appears, then, to be one of the inevitable consequences of the impact of urban life on the simple family organization and folk culture which the Negro has evolved in the rural South. The distribution of desertions in relation to the general economic and cultural organization of Negro communities that have grown up in our American cities shows in a striking manner the influence of selective factors in the process of adjustment to the urban environment.

CHAPTER XVI

OUTLAWED
MOTHERHOOD

Not many years after the Civil War a woman presented, as typical of the demoralized family and sex relations of the newly emancipated Negroes in southern cities, the following picture:

> The shanty is black within and without through age and weather, but more through dirt and grime; and the decaying floor is filthier than the ground outside, though that is a sink. There is no chair or stool—nothing to sit upon but the wreck of a bedstead, which holds a nest of what was once straw, a feather pillow which trots of itself, and rags of wool and cotton which are equally smutty and frisky. The only bit of furniture besides a small table, and three children are rubbing off the slime of it with potato skins left yesterday—for they get a meal some days—and these parings furnish their only today. Under the table is a battered wash-dish in which they stir their hoe-cake, when they can get any, and a broken skillet in which to bake it; but wood is scarce to them, and only now and then can they steal a bit. A black woman sits on a log, with half-a-dozen small specimens of humanity about her, and of all shades of black, brown, and yellow. She has eight children, and was married once, but only two of the children belonged to her husband. "Where is your husband?" "Is he living?" you ask. "Dunno, missis, don't care; he may go to de debbil fur all I knows and cares." Two of the children are partially blind through measles, and a third is a cripple. The oldest daughter is married, and with her husband and child lives at home; and the second daughter, a very black and bright girl of fifteen, has a yellow baby, which knows no father; and all this numerous family live in one small room, and all sleep together. The three mothers are all members of the Methodist church.[1]

[1] E. B. Emery, *Letters from the South, on the Social, Intellectual and Moral Condition of the Colored People* (Boston, 1880), pp. 9-10.

In the foregoing picture of Negro illegitimacy in a southern city we have all the factors involved in the general problem: poverty, ignorance, the absence of family traditions and community controls, and finally the sexual exploitation of the subordinate race by the dominant race. Moreover, this description could be matched today by cases in southern cities where the sexual behavior of Negroes has been influenced by similar social forces. But, of course, such cases of illegitimacy, involving the degree of poverty, social disorganization, and personal demoralization represented in the description are not typical. Then, too, it is very probable that illegitimacy is not so widespread among the Negroes today as during the years following the Civil War.

It is impossible to draw any conclusions from available statistics concerning either the volume or the trend of illegitimacy among Negroes. In the Registration area, the proportion of illegitimate births among Negroes increased from 120.1 per 1,000 total births in 1917 to 165.2 per 1,000 in 1943.[2] The statistics on Negro illegitimacy in the District of Columbia have been used more frequently than any other source as a basis of generalization on the problem. In 1878, 9.8 per cent of the Negro births were illegitimate; but, during the next year, the percentage of illegitimate births mounted suddenly to 17 per 100 live births. By 1881 a fifth of the births were illegitimate, and the percentage fluctuated between a fifth and a fourth until 1910. Although after 1910 there was on the whole a downward trend, after 1929 the rate mounted steadily until it has reached its former level of 20 per cent. Then following World War II the rate rose suddenly to 25 per cent. The same is true of a few northern and southern cities for which there are statistics on Negro illegitimacy extending as far back as 1900. In Baltimore Negro illegitimacy declined slightly from 26.2 per cent at the opening of the century to 21.5 in 1929. During the same period in Mobile, Alabama, the rate has fluctuated considerably. At the beginning of the present century it was close to 27 per cent but declined to 11.3 per cent in 1912. However, the rate suddenly mounted the next year

[2] U. S. Department of Commerce. Bureau of the Census, *Vital Statistics of the United States* (Washington, 1945), p. 12.

and reached 27 during the first World War; then it declined to 23 per cent. However, in Hartford, Connecticut, where there have been comparatively few Negro births, the illegitimacy rate has declined on the whole during the present century despite the influx of Negroes during and since the war. In Sommerville, Massachusetts, where the Negro population has remained small, there have been only six illegitimate births scattered over a period of thirty years. Since 1900 the proportion of Negro illegitimate births in Evansville, Indiana, according to the health records, has fluctuated considerably. At the opening of the century the proportion of illegitimate births was about 14 per cent; but, after declining until it reached 9 per cent in 1906, it increased again and, after fluctuating about 20 per cent, reached 30.8 per cent in 1929.

Records of Negro illegitimacy for shorter periods in several northern and southern cities may also be cited. In Richmond and Norfolk, Virginia, the rate has remained close to 20 per cent since 1920. However, in Birmingham, Alabama, the rate has mounted from 12 to 16 per cent since 1918. The rate in Philadelphia since 1920 has closely paralleled that in Birmingham, Alabama; whereas in Trenton, New Jersey, since 1916 it has increased from 10 to 18 per cent. In Chicago it was found that from 10 to 15 per cent of the Negro maternity cases in the Cook County Hospital for the six years 1923-28 were unmarried mothers. In New York City in 1930 there were 379 Negro illegitimate births according to the records of the health department and 434 according to data of the social service agencies.[3] On the basis of these figures, the Negro rate was between 5 and 6 per cent.

Generally, when attempts have been made in the past to fathom the causes of the persistence of a high rate of illegitimacy among Negroes, especially in cities where the race has made perceptible progress economically and educationally, students have gloomily attributed it to some inherent moral degeneracy of the Negro. Hoffman, writing at the close of the last century, concluded that statistics of crime and illegitimacy furnished proof that "neither religion nor education has influenced to any appreciable degree the moral

[3] Ruth Reed, *The Illegitimate Family* (New York, 1934), pp. 119-20.

progress of *the race*" and that "*the race* as a whole has gone backward rather than forward." This opinion was not so harsh as that of the northern-born mulatto who climaxed his denunciation of the loose sex habits of Negroes with the assertion that "illegitimate motherhood is rather a recommendation in the eyes of a prospective husband."[4] Even as late as 1930 a writer, who has often proposed colonization as the only means of saving America from the moral menace of the Negro, regarded the high Negro illegitimacy rate in the District of Columbia as "one of the manifest measures of the indifferent success achieved upon the part of the white, during this long contact in mediating the ideals, the morals, of Christianity" to the Negro.[5]

Although illegitimacy is from five to ten times as high among Negroes as among whites, these opinions concerning the moral degeneracy of the Negro obviously reflect the various attitudes of the writers rather than provide explanations of the Negro's behavior. Shannon's antipathy toward the mulatto was probably responsible for his absurd argument that the Negro's attitude toward illegitimacy is the result of false ideals of equality which are encouraged in the District of Columbia. It is scarcely necessary to point out that in most of the northern cities, where the Negro enjoys far more equality than in the District of Columbia, the illegitimacy rates are much lower. But, as a matter of fact, there are relatively few white fathers of colored illegitimate offspring. In Chicago, for the two-and-a-half-year period beginning January, 1926, there were only six white and one Mexican father among the 235 cases in the records of the Cook County Hospital. Dr. Reed in her study of the situation in New York City found that, among "the 962 cases in which the Health Department had data for the race or color of the father as well as of the mother, there were only 18 instances of race crossing reported. Fifteen of these were instances of Negro women who had white fathers of their children, while three were white women who had Negro fathers of their babies." Although statistical data of a conclusive nature are

---

[4] William Hannibal Thomas, *The American Negro: What He Was, What He Is, and What He May Become* (New York, 1901), p. 179.

[5] A. H. Shannon, *The Negro in Washington: A Study in Race Amalgamation* (New York, 1930), p. 111.

lacking, from what we know of racial mixture in the South, the social and economic subordination of the Negro has been more fruitful of illegitimacy than the enjoyment of equality.

The reaction of Thomas, a cultured mulatto from New England, simply expressed his revulsion of feeling toward the disorganized Negroes of the South with whom he was identified by custom and public opinion. Similarly, many white investigators have been shocked and disgusted when they discovered in some cities that three-quarters of a century after slavery a quarter of the Negro births were illegitimate. But what these investigators fail to realize is that the constant flow of simple peasant folk from rural districts to the poverty and disorganization of city slums constantly re-creates the problem of unmarried motherhood.

That most of the unmarried Negro mothers are newcomers to the city is revealed in various studies. In New York City in 1930 about a fifth of the Negro women who became unmarried mothers were nonresidents. This was about 3 per cent less than among white women who seemingly seek the anonymity of the city more frequently to escape the censure of their home communities. However, a more significant fact relative to their migration to the city appears in regard to the birthplace of the unmarried mothers and the length of their residence in the city. Of 447 unmarried mothers for whom information was available coming before social agencies during the years 1922-23 in New York City, 70 per cent were born in southern states or in the West Indies.[6] Three-fourths of the women born in the South had been in New York City less than five years. A similar situation was found in regard to unmarried Negro mothers in Chicago, where about 80 per cent of them were born in the South and over half of them had been in the city less than five years. Moreover, life-histories and case records revealed that many of the unmarried mothers had wandered, with or without their families, about the country before settling in the cities where they gave birth to their illegitimate offspring. A large proportion of the unmarried mothers are comparatively young. Of the group of 300 unmarried mothers studied in Chicago, 50 were under seventeen years of age,

[6] Ruth Reed, *Negro Illegitimacy in New York City* (New York, 1926), p. 49.

and 165, or 55 per cent, were under twenty. In the group studied in New York City, 56 per cent were under twenty years of age. Although their sex delinquency is due in part to the lack of parental supervision, it often represents the persistence in the urban environment of folkways that were relatively harmless in the rural community. In their behavior one can often see exemplified the truth of Sumner's observation that, "so long as customs are simple, naïve, and unconscious, they do not produce evil in character, no matter what they are. If reflection is awakened and the mores cannot satisfy it, then doubt arises; individual character will then be corrupted and the society will degenerate."[7]

Many of the unmarried Negro mothers in our cities have never known normal family life. Case records of 235 unmarried mothers in Chicago showed that less than an eighth had come from normal families. In a third of the 235 cases the father or mother was dead, the parents were divorced or separated, or one or the other parent had deserted the family. This is typical of cases in other cities. In Washington a thirty-year-old unmarried woman, born outside of Atlanta, Georgia, told the following story of her family background and how she happened to come to the city:

> My mother died when I was a year and six months old. I would have been happy if I'd died then too. An old lady named Miss Mariah took care of me. She explained to me about my mother. My father died when I was seven years old. She took care of me till I become twelve, going into my thirteenth, when she died. Ever since I been taking care of myself, butting about. I didn't have no one to teach me, send me to school and give me an education. Some white people taught me a lot of things. It's funny how you can get such a few favors out of colored people. I had never seen a train till I was leben. It like to scared me to death. [A girl friend who] had been to New York and Washington and was home when Miss Mariah died took me to her house after the burial. She told me all about the city. I begged her to bring me with her.

Since these unmarried mothers are a part of the great army of poorer migrants who go to the city, they are naturally found in the deteriorated and disorganized sections of the Negro community. In

[7] William Graham Sumner, *Folkways* (New York, 1906), p. 420.

our study of illegitimacy in the city of Chicago, it was found that illegitimacy was closely tied up with the organization of the Negro community. For example, the highest rate of illegitimacy was found in the first zone, which was in the slum area just outside the central business district where the poorer migrants from the South first settled. In this zone 2.3 per cent of the mothers of childbearing age were unmarried mothers. The rate declined in the successive zones until it reached two-tenths of 1 per cent in the seventh or outermost zone. One needs only to read the description of one of the neighborhoods in which illegitimacy flourishes to see to what extent the environment in which these women live influences their sex behavior. An unmarried mother, just fourteen years of age, gave the following description of the building where she met her "beaux":

> That building where my cousin lives at now is terrible. I remember one time they shot crap from one o'clock at night on up till in the morning. You know what—that building ain't nothin' but for . . . . [female homosexuals]. I heard so much about . . . . [female homosexuals] so one day I asked my cousin what was a . . . . [female homosexual] and so she said she would show me some of them. She said it was two . . . . [female homosexuals] in that building and they got to fighting and one pulled the other's clothes off. I tried to get her to tell me what a . . . . [female homosexual] was but she never did tell me. Some of them women in that building was a hustling. You know, they sell themselves. A man go up there, you know, and then they charge them $2.00. Men used to go up there all the time. There was an old woman there who used to come up to my cousin's and she said to me one day, "Say, honey, when are you going up to my house and sleep with me?" She used to pat me down, and I turned around to her and one of the men in the house told her to let me alone I was a little girl. I remember one time all the girls and boys were out there in front of her house and she said for us all to go inside she couldn't make no money out there with all of us around. Police used to go up there and raid the place all the time. One night I was looking out the window and the patrol backed up to the door and I called L—— right away she ran and locked up the trunk. She said, "I got to get rid of this moonshine." They didn't come in my cousin's. They took men and women out of that building—some just had step-ins on and some of the men were bare foot. That place was so bad. I learned too much down there. Well, I'm glad that I did learn what I did for I can keep out of trouble from now on.

The account which this sexually precocious girl furnished concerning her surroundings shows clearly that it is needless to postulate a "compelling sexual appetite," as McCord has done, as an explanation of the conduct of girls who live in such an environment.[8] We often find in the life-histories of the unmarried mothers that their first interest in sexual knowledge has been aroused by the play groups in these disorganized areas. Consequently, their attitudes toward sex as well as their behavior reflect the attitudes of the groups in which sexual knowledge gives them status. We can see the influence of the play group in the following document written by a young unmarried mother:

> One day a girl friend of mine told me that a boy name D——
> W—— said that he seen me and another girl coming out of the
> bathroom with two boys. The next day I seen him I asked him he
> said that he did not say it. Every day I began to see him more. One
> day he asked me to go with him I said yes. Every day I would come
> home with him. All the girls was jealous of him they used to tell me
> that he go with another girl. He said that he did not I believe him.
> One hot summer night I was in Ellis Park on 37th I met D——. I
> asked him where did he live he said 36—— Cottage Grove, last fl.
> After a while along came a girl name L—— B—— and her boy
> friend. We all sat out in the Park a while He asked me if I would
> let him have it I said no The girl and boy kept on telling me to go
> head it won't hurt you I said I was afraid After a while I did. After
> he took me home the next night I did it again. One Sunday I was in
> the show I met him After the show him and is boy friend and a girl
> I don't know who she was but the boy is name J—— G——. We
> went over to his house. J—— started the radio. We dance a while
> The boys turn out the light I and D—— went in the other room.
> After that he taken me home I began to love him very much I thought
> it was no body like him.

The contacts which the unmarried mother has with the man who is the father of her child is often of a very casual nature. In many instances they know only the first name of the man. Because of the anonymity afforded by the city, married men are often responsible. Dr. Reed found that about a fourth of the fathers of illegitimate

[8] Charles H. McCord, *The American Negro as a Dependent, Defective and Delinquent* (Nashville, Tenn., 1914), p. 106.

offspring, concerning whose marital status information was available, were married. The city streets, as well as the moving-picture houses, theaters, and dance halls, provide occasions for contacts which often lead to illegitimacy. The following is an excerpt from the life-history of a naïve newcomer to the city:

> We just got acquainted ourselves and how I got acquainted was I got lost. I was on 7th Street to a five and ten cent store. He was coming down the street. I stop him and asked him how to get back home. I was shamed to tell him I couldn't read the names on the car. I just guess he considered the matter and took me home. Then he asked me could he come to see me. I stopped him on the corner cause I didn't know what the lady would say. He asked me where I lived, if I had a friend, about my people, and he showed me different places. He asked to call to see me and take me to the movies. I was 14 and had never been to a show. First time he come to see me he took me to the show. I can remember it just as good. It was a love picture about a boy falling in love with a poor girl. After the show he took me to a cafe. We had sandwiches and tea. I don't drink nothing, I ain't never drunk nothing. Then he taken me back home.

The detail concerning the romantic element in the picture suggests the manner in which the city environment gives a new definition of sex. Although the majority of the unmarried mothers have never gone beyond the eighth grade, they are often influenced in their attitudes toward sex by the printed page. As a rule the literature with which they are acquainted is restricted to such magazines as *True Stories* and *True Confessions*. Significantly enough, one girl recounted in her life-history a story from one of these magazines that centered about the romantic career of an unmarried mother.

Naturally, the vast majority of the unmarried mothers come from the lower economic strata in the Negro population. Their parents or, where they are dependent upon their own labor, they themselves are engaged in domestic service or, as in a city like Chicago, in unskilled labor. Often where young unmarried mothers are living with their parents, very frequently with only a mother, they are without parental oversight because of the employment of the mother. However, many of these working mothers make sincere efforts to control their daughters' behavior; but, because of vicious surroundings and the freedom which the city affords, their diligence is often of no avail. As one widowed mother in Chicago sadly remarked concerning her wayward daughter, "I talk and talk and teach, and, when I have done all I know how to do, I can do no more. Children in these days are a heart break."

The experience of unmarried motherhood for some of these girls is sometimes the beginning of a series of such experiences. Of the 379 unmarried Negro mothers studied by Dr. Reed, 47 had had two children; 10, three children; 8, four children; and 4 as many as seven or more. In our study of 300 unmarried mothers in Chicago the case records revealed that about 13 per cent of them had had more than one child. That more unmarried mothers do not have several illegitimate children is hardly due to their reformation but to the fact that they acquire knowledge about birth control and abortions. Nor should it be overlooked that venereal diseases play some part in preventing conception. On the whole, the unmarried mothers in the city exhibit less of the elemental maternal sympathy toward their children which one finds in rural communities in the South. In the alleys of southern cities as well as in the tenements in northern cities, the unmarried mother sometimes kills her unwanted child by throwing it in the garbage can. Yet one finds cases of unmarried mothers who show a natural sympathy and affection for their offspring that is reminiscent of the isolated communities in the rural South. In this connection one's attention is called to Dr. Reed's study that showed that, whereas only a third of the illegitimate white children are taken care of in the home of their mother or a relative, three-fourths of the offspring of unmarried Negro mothers receive such care. This difference reflects to some extent the persistence of the traditional folkways in the urban environment.

Of course, Negro illegitimacy is not merely the persistence of naïve peasant folkways in the urban environment. Undoubtedly, much of the illegitimacy issues from social disorganization and results in personal demoralization. Some of the unmarried mothers are themselves illegitimate; and it appears in some cases, at least, that they have simply imitated the loose behavior of their mothers. Nor can one overlook the fact that a few of the older women who have illegitimate offspring are already married. These women are conscious of having violated the established mores. The same may be said of the young girls who attempt in various ways to avoid exposure. As a rule, the older women attempt to deceive the social agencies by pretending that they are married.

It happens occasionally that an unmarried mother has lived over a period of years with the father of her illegitimate offspring. She may even represent herself to the community as well as to her children as a married woman. In such cases her efforts to conceal her real relation to the father of her children may spring from the desire to protect the status of her children in the community.

As typical of such women, we might cite the case in Washington of a forty-four-year-old unmarried mother, without any formal education, from a rural community in Maryland. She married when she was thirteen years old, but was deserted three years later when her husband went to Florida to work. After coming to Washington, she took up with a man by whom she had three children. When this man deserted her and married, she began living with another man by whom she also had two children. She went by the name of the second man and brought up her first set of children to believe that their father was dead and the second set that she was legally married to their father. When this woman had to apply for relief, she reported herself as having been married to these men; but, after the social worker found no record of her marriages, she explained her attempted deception in the following letter:

I want to explain something to you that I didn't tell you this morning as the questions were too embarrassing to answer and I didn't want my children to know how things were with me as I really couldn't help how things were at the time, so now I am telling you the truth. I were not married to Johnson or North but having these children couldn't be helped for the sake of my health. Jones was my only real husband and that can be found out in X . . . . , Maryland. Like many others I didn't realize what a record it would make and what all of this would really mean, but as I am not doing any of these things now I hope you can straighten this out without any further embarrassment, but for the sake of my children and my church please let me keep the name NORTH as we were to be married on the 20th of the month when he suddenly died on the 17th of June, 1934. Every other thing I have told you was true except that part of things.

Although a son and a daughter by the first man are married and are seemingly living conventional lives, the younger daughter has unconsciously followed in the footsteps of her mother.

Our analysis of Negro illegitimacy has revealed that it is a problem most entirely of the naïve and ignorant peasant folk who are newcomers to the city. Occasionally, a girl with some education and a good family background will be found among the cases in the social agencies. But among Negroes, as among whites, when women and girls who have the advantage of education and economic security and the protection of family become pregnant as a result of extramarital sex relations, they are generally shielded both from the censure of society and from the scrutiny of social agencies. It is, of course, different with the great mass of simple peasant folk who are without these economic and cultural resources. During the course of their migration to the city, family ties are broken, and the restraints which once held in check immoral sex conduct lose their force. However, in some cases where the rural folkways concerning unmarried motherhood are in conflict with the legal requirements of the city, the persistence of these folkways in the urban environment will create social problems. Illegitimacy, like other forms of family disorganization, tends to become segregated in the poorer sections of the Negro community located in the slum areas of our cities.

CHAPTER XVII

REBELLIOUS YOUTH

The disorganization of Negro family life in the urban environment, together with the absence of communal controls, results in a high delinquency rate among Negro boys and girls. However, among Negroes, as among whites, boys are much more frequently brought before the courts than girls. For example, in 1945 there were 15,058 Negro boys and 3,823 Negro girls dealt with as delinquent cases in 88 courts serving areas with populations of 100,000 or more.[1] However, during World War II there was a greater increase in delinquency among Negro girls, as among white girls, than among boys.[2] Since the misconduct of Negro girls has been considered to some extent in connection with the problem of unmarried motherhood, our attention here will be directed mainly to the misconduct of Negro boys which may be dealt with under the law.

Negro boys and girls are younger on the whole than the white boys and girls handled by the courts. Moreover, available studies indicate that the rates of delinquency for both Negro boys and Negro girls are distinctly higher than for white boys and girls. This has been true over a long period. For example, in New York City 20 years ago the Negro rate was about three times the white rate; while in Baltimore it was more than four times the white rate. The same was true of a number of other northern and southern cities.[3] In 1945 there

---

[1] U. S. Children's Bureau. *Social Statistics. Juvenile-Court Statistics, 1944-1945.* Supplement to Volume II of *The Child* (Nov. 1946 Supplement).

[2] Elsa Castendyck and Sophia Robison, "Juvenile Delinquency Among Girls." *The Social Service Review*, Vol. XVII (Sept., 1943), 253-64.

[3] T. J. Woofter, Jr., *Negro Problems in Cities* (New York, 1928), p. 227.

was still a disproportionate number of Negro boys and girls among those brought before the courts because of juvenile delinquency. In New York City, about 35 per cent of the delinquent boys and 42 per cent of the delinquent girls were Negroes.[4] Likewise, in the District of Columbia where Negroes constituted an estimated 35 per cent of the population, Negroes contributed 73 per cent of the delinquents.[5]

It is difficult to detect any significant trend in juvenile delinquency among Negroes for the country as a whole. A study by the Children's Bureau of trends in delinquency based upon rates calculated for 10,000 boys of juvenile court age indicated that juvenile delinquency among Negroes fluctuated considerably. For example, the rate declined on the whole in the District of Columbia during the period 1927 to 1933; while in New York City the rate almost doubled during the same period. But even the trends observable in the various cities throw little or no light on the problem of Negro delinquency. In order to get an understanding of the problem, it is necessary to study the delinquent boy or girl in relation to his or her family and community setting.

The facts brought out in a study of Negro juvenile delinquency in Nashville, Tennessee, will enable us to get some understanding of the social factors which are responsible for delinquency in southern cities. During the period from 1925 to 1929, the number of Negro boys brought into the juvenile court in Nashville fluctuated considerably, whereas the number of Negro girls declined from 98 to 68. The number of Negro delinquents brought to court during this period was only slightly in excess of their relative numbers in the population of the city. However, in 1932 the number of delinquent boys increased to 324 and the number of girls to 83. This increase might have been due to the apprehension of more delinquents when the Negro probation force was enlarged. In 1929 about 70 per cent of the boys and 63 per cent of the girls were from twelve to fifteen years of age. Nearly a half of the boys were charged with stealing;

[4] U. S. Children's Bureau, *op. cit.*, p. 10.
[5] Washington Criminal Justice Association, *Crime in the Nation's Capital.* Washington, D. C., May 1946, p. 7.

whereas the majority of the girls were charged with incorrigibility and disorderly conduct. It should be added that these Negro delinquents were apprehended as ordinary criminals and brought to court by the police much more frequently than the white delinquents.

The complaint of a deputy sheriff against a ten-year-old offender gives some notion of the demoralization of childhood represented in these delinquency cases:

> This boy was brought in on a state warrant charging tippling and the boy admits that he sold a pint of whisky for the people for whom he was working, to some man he did not know, for $1.50 and gave the money to the people for whom he worked. H. made an investigation of the boy's home and found conditions deplorable. The boy's mother does not live there but at the place where she works. The boy lives with a married sister whose home is filthy and unsanitary and an unfit place to live. The boy does not have supervision. He will not tell the truth and is badly in need of supervision.

In the charges brought by police officers against a fifteen-year-old boy, who was sentenced to the Children's Detention Home for a year, one can see to what extent these homeless children in the slum areas of southern cities are subjected to all types of vicious influences:

> The proof is that he, S. P., A. W., and two other men were all in one bed together on Sunday morning, March 3, and were engaged in lewdness. They admit they were guilty of lewdness. The boy is not going to school and has not been at home in weeks. He lives in this room where the officer caught all this lewdness at 7 A.M. The boy has heretofore been at the C.D.H. for larceny. He is delinquent and a truant.

But more often these boys are picked up for acts of theft ranging from petty stealing to burglaries. The record of a boy only eleven years of age charged with larceny states:

> The boy's father came in court and made complaint that the boy would not work or go to school but was stealing all around the neighborhood and was teaching the small boys with whom he associates to steal. His mother brought him to court this day and made the same complaint and both request that he be committed to the S.T.A. From the statements of both parents and after talking to the boy the court is satisfied that he is a truant and delinquent and is stealing.

Often these young lawbreakers are schooled in crime by older boys or men or even members of their families. This was evident in the case of the eight-year-old-boy charged with housebreaking and larceny:

> Policeman B. found a raincoat and two pairs of shoes in the home of this boy and arrested him. The boy admits that he and his uncle C. B. went to the home of F. about 12 o'clock at night and the uncle took a watch and chain and the boy a raincoat and the shoes home with him. The boy says that they broke in the house. The boy's uncle got away and he does not know where he is.

Sometimes boys as young as eleven or twelve are apprehended as members of criminal gangs engaging regularly in housebreaking and thefts. The extreme youth of the boys caught in such delinquencies is indicative of the general lack of parental control among some elements of the Negro population. In the complaint of the aunt against her wayward twelve-year-old nephew we get a hint of the broken homes from which so many of these delinquents come:

> This boy was brought into court by his aunt; she states that the boy's mother is dead, that his father does not provide for the boy, that she has reared him since he was one year old, that he will not work nor go to school and associates with bad company and she can no longer control him and wants the court to take the custody of him. She promises to clothe him.

In fact, only 67 of the 176 delinquent Negro boys brought into court in 1929 came from families in which both parents were living together. In 37 other cases, although both parents were living, they were separated, chiefly because of the desertion of the father. Fifty-nine boys came from homes where either the mother or the father was dead; and 13 had both parents dead. The home situation was even worse in the case of the 68 delinquent girls; only 15 of them came from normal families.

The charge of incorrigibility against 50 of these girls involved five specific offenses: sex delinquency, truancy, ungovernability, running away, and continued association with vicious companions. In 27 cases there was sex delinquency ranging from initial sex experiences to promiscuous relations and prostitution. Truancy, which was often associated with sex delinquency, was found in 23 cases. Although ungovernability was found as the sole offense in 7 cases, in 9 other cases it was associated with sex delinquency, truancy, and running away. Fourteen of the 15 girls who were charged with running away were most frequently guilty of sex offenses, while the 5 girls charged with association with vicious companions were generally guilty of the other four offenses. A view of the type of family background from which some of these girls come is given us in the following excerpt from the story given by a girl charged with incorrigibility:

> I never want nor expect to return home again, never. I guess I haven't a home anyway. I asked my adopted father to never come out here to see me. He wouldn't get me any clothes then because I said I didn't want to see him. He said if I didn't want to see him I sure couldn't have any of his money or anything his money bought. When I left home to come here I told that woman he lived with that the last thing I intended to do was to poison both of them. I might change my mind though.
>
> My own mother and father are dead. I liked my adopted father all right while my adopted mother was living. They were like real parents to me. When my adopted mother got sick and stayed for a while papa began running around with this woman that he is living with. One of my chums put me on to it. This woman lived next door to her and she used to see him going there. As soon as mama dies he took this woman in. It wasn't more than a week after mama died. I told him that he ought to be ashamed, and I said so much to him that he slapped me. He never had hit me before, and think, hit me about that hoar, I never would eat at the same table with them. After she came there to live I would leave for school at 6 o'clock in the morning, and I wouldn't come home until late at night. I hated to go home. I promised to poison both of them and they believed me. They tried to get Miss R. to put me in the C.D. Home a long time before she sent me. Miss R. said she didn't blame me for not wanting to stay around them. They would throw up to me about my real mother, that she had had four children and never been married. I never heard anything about this till this woman came.

In some cases the delinquent behavior of these girls has not only been taken over from their parents or other adults but represents their response to what is held up to them as their expected role in life. A woman who called the probation officer for aid in managing her thirteen-year-old niece described the latter as follows:

> But I know Mary. I ought to when I have had her every since she was five months old. I know I understand her. She is exactly like her mama. Her mama is my baby sister, but the truth is the truth. She had Mary when she was only 15 by an old nigger that didn't have a dime to his name. He run off and she never heard of him again after he got her in trouble. I kept her in my house until Mary was born, and treated her good and helped her with the baby. Then when Mary was five months old this gal ups and runs off with another nigger and I ain't laid eyes on her from that day to this. Mary has never seen her mama to remember. So this gal has just done like her mama. I understand alright.

This girl's aunt was reputed to have once been a prostitute and was known to be engaged at the time of the complaint in bootlegging. Her neighbors described her as "just another whore" and claimed that she had forced her niece to "hustle" in order to get money for food and clothing.

Occasionally, delinquency on the part of these girls is the result of the gradual breaking-down of standards that have been built up in the rural environment. This is shown in the following document, which was furnished by a seventeen-year-old girl. Moreover, this document is of particular interest because it shows that, although the girl's immediate family was broken by desertion on the part of the father, in the rural community the children were integrated into the larger family group. However, when the girl came to live in the urban environment, the absence of a normal family life became the means by which she was led into sex delinquency:

> From the time that I can remember anything my mother and we children were living with our grandfather who had a farm out at ———— Tennessee. I was happy and so were my brothers I remember and sisters until grandpa would begin fussing. I remember how he used to fuss long before I remember what he would be saying. I would know that something made him mad. Soon my mother married again to a man who had pretty good money for a country farmer. Then mama moved away to a town about seven miles from us. All of us cried and begged her to take us but she wouldn't. She said grandpa and grandma had helped raise us up to where we was then and that

we was just the size where we could be of help to them, and said that now we could help pay grandma and grandpa for the expenses they had been at for us. She said our father had never done anything for us. That was the first time I had heard her say anything about our father to remember. I guess when grandpa would be fussing he would be saying something about him, but I didn't know it. Anyhow I wondered how he looked and asked grandma about him but she wouldn't say much. But before I was much larger I tooked and asked grandma about him and found out that papa quit my mama about four months before my youngest brother was born and came here with another woman. This woman use to come to the house when mama and papa was living together and tried to be so nice to mama. Mama really didn't know that papa and this woman was going together.

Grandma said when one of mama friends told her about it she got mad at her. Not long after this papa pretended that his oldest brother was at the point of death in the city, and that he had to go at once. He didn't come back again until my baby brother had been born and was six years old. He didn't know papa and was scared of him like he would be of any other strange man. When my baby brother saw him he said "Oh there is Jimmy Holloman." He really didn't know papa. Then papa got mad about that. That night my brother had earache and was crying. Papa got mad about this and said that he needed a whipping for keeping up all that racket. Grandpa told him if he laid his hand on the child he would kill him dead. Papa left the. next day and didn't come no more until grandpa had been dead a long time. Mama had married and we were all large children. He came to visit his sister and brother who lived at home. Folks use to say that I looked exactly like his sister, Aunt Molly. But Grandma didn't like that because she said that Aunt Molly was nothing but a slut. She was married but she had had ten children and wasn't but two of them her husband's. The other eight had stray daddies. We didn't know how to act toward him and none of us would call him papa. We would just begin talking and wouldn't call him anything. He stayed a month. He swore that he wasn't married but he got a lot of letters while he was there. He went to fishing one day and me and my sister went into his things and found some things that almost made both of us faint. We found first two letters from two children of his that he had in ———— a little town not far from here. They were thanking him for sending them some stockings and other clothes. The oldest one of these children was a boy and we found out after we come here that this boy was almost as old as my youngest brother. The other was a girl. We couldn't speak for a while after we read these letters. There was a letter from their mama too. She said in that letter something I will never forget the longest day I live about people calling her a fool for still being crazy about him but that as long as she was satisfied they could go to hell. My grandma and grandpa had said so many times that papa was nothing but a nasty, stinking, low down nigger, who was too lazy to work and take care of a family. I don't know why we ought to have been surprised to find out more of his dirt but we were. I dreaded for him to come back from fishing and hoped that he would soon go home. There he was sending this woman and those bastards things when he hadn't send us hardly $20 worth the whole while that he had been away.

Later, the girl came to the city to live with her father and step-mother. Her story continues:

I hated so bad to live in the place in which they were living. It was an apartment flat with three families living up stairs and three downstairs. Brother said that he had heard that not a one of the couples was married. He didn't believe that papa was married to this woman either. They played cards all day Sunday. This made me sick because grandma had never allowed us to go to dances let alone play cards. I had to sleep in the same room with papa and his wife. Brother slept in a cot in the kitchen. There wasn't but two rooms. Papa and this woman would often wake us up in the night doing their business. I wouldn't let on that they woke me up. The springs would squeak and this woman wouldn't let that noise do but I could hear easy enough. This made me sick again I never heard such at grandma's house and I looked down on that kind of stuff. My sister came and we just lived through it. Sister and I dreaded for night to come. We hated papa more and more.

The two sisters and their brother continued to go to church as they had done in the country. This caused their father to ridicule them about their "country" habits. Tension between the father and the children continued to become more acute until finally there was an open break in which the children engaged in a fist fight with their father. As the result, the girls were put out of the home and reported to the court as being incorrigible. Instead of sending them to the detention home as the father requested, the court put them on probation to their brother. When their brother married, they were without a home. The girl who was charged with sex delinquency because of her conduct described below, and sent to the detention home, ends her story with the following comment:

After I had seen so much out of my father, and my brother had changed so I just seemed to slip. When I began living on the place I would have one day off. I didn't have any place to go. My boy friend invited me to spend my off-time over at his place. Everybody sows their wild oats at some time or other in their lives. I don't believe that I am guilty of any sin because I am going to marry this feller.

Let us turn our attention from this southern city to New York City, where, as we have seen, Negro juvenile delinquency rates suddenly jumped in 1928 to 342 per 10,000 boys as compared with 170 in 1927. In 1930 there were for all the boroughs 839 Negro children, or 11.8 per cent of the total of 7,090 children, brought before the Children's Court. When delinquents from all agencies were considered, there were 1,065 Negro children, or 10.3 per cent of the total of 10,374 children. However, the proportion of Negro delinquents among the delinquents in both groups varied in the different boroughs. The rate was highest in the Manhattan borough, where Negro delinquents before the Children's Court comprised 26 per cent of the total; whereas, in the borough of Brooklyn, Negro cases comprised only 5.4 per cent of all the delinquents before the court.

For our purposes here, we shall consider Negro boys and girls arrested because of delinquency and neglect in the Harlem area during the years 1930-34. On the whole, the number of Negro boys and girls arrested for delinquency declined after 1930, although the figures for 1934 indicated that the number of delinquents was mounting again. This was especially noticeable in the case of the delinquent girls.

The vast majority of the Negro delinquents were between ten and sixteen years of age; only about 3 per cent of the boys, except in 1930, being under ten years of age. However, if the children arrested because of neglect are considered separately, we find that the vast majority were under ten years of age.

When we analyze the offenses for which these boys and girls were arrested, we find that, as in Nashville, the chief offense of the boys was larceny and burglary; whereas 50 per cent of the girls were charged with incorrigibility. Thus, in 1934 about 30 per cent of the delinquent boys were charged with larceny and 10 per cent with burglary. Among the more serious offenses charged against the boys, assaults and holdups ranked third and fourth, respectively; whereas sex offenses held second place among the girls. Two boys were charged with homicide in 1931 and one with the same offense in 1932. Although there was no change in the rank of these various offenses among either boys or girls during the five years, the proportion of boys arrested for larceny and burglary increased appreciably, while the proportion for assaults and holdups declined slightly. A study of delinquent and neglected Negro children in New York City in 1925 showed a different distribution of offenses for the boys. According to that study, the most common charges against Negro boys were disorderly conduct and desertion of home; whereas approximately 85 per cent of the Negro girls were charged with desertion of home and ungovernable and wayward conduct. The most common charges against the whites were stealing and burglary. Thus, our figures indicate that the charges against Negro boys are at present similar to those against white boys. The majority of the less serious crimes were indicative of the lack of recreational facilities and programs for the children of the Harlem community. For example, in 1934 eleven of the boys were charged with hitching on trolleys and twenty-seven with stealing rides on the subways. On the other hand, the comparatively few boys charged with selling on the streets or shining shoes most likely reflected the general poverty of the families in the area.

The relation of juvenile delinquency to the organization of the Harlem Negro community is not so apparent as in Chicago, where, as we shall see, it is definitely related to the economic and cultural organization of the Negro community. In Chicago the percentage of Negro delinquent cases among the cases brought before the juvenile court has steadily increased since 1900. In that year 4.7 per cent of all cases of boys before the court were Negro boys. The percentage of Negro boys increased for each five-year period until it reached 21.7 in 1930. Naturally, these figures do not include all cases of delinquency; in fact, they do not include all the cases of arrests for delinquency. For example, in 1927 there were 1,503 boys arrested for juvenile delinquency, although only 342 cases were taken into the court.

The marked increase in the proportion of Negro cases has coincided with the increase in the Negro population during and since the first World War. However, what is more important is that this increase has followed the settlement of the Negro migrant in areas characterized by a high delinquency rate.

Shaw, who has shown in a number of well-known studies the relation between delinquency and community disorganization, makes the following statement: "It is interesting to note that the main high rate areas of the city—those near the Loop, around the Stock Yards and the South Chicago steel mills—have been characterized by high rates over a long period. Our data are based on records that go back thirty years, and the early and late juvenile court series show conclusively that many of the areas have been characterized by high rates throughout the entire period. It should be remembered that relatively high rates have persisted in certain areas notwithstanding the fact that the composition (racial) of population has changed markedly."[6]

The Negro, like other groups marked off from the general population because of color and low economic and cultural status, has found a dwelling-place in the deteriorated area just outside the Loop.[7] In the zone nearest the center of the city, the juvenile delinquency rate, based upon arrests, was over 40 per cent. From a physical standpoint this area showed extreme deterioration and gave evidence of the expansion of the central business district. On the one hand, there were dilapidated houses carrying signs of rooms for rent at fifteen and twenty cents a bed, junk shops, markets with stale meat, and crowded Negro quarters with filthy bedding half-visible through sooty and broken window panes. On the other hand, new motorcar salesrooms furnished signs of the future role which the regenerated area would play in the organization of the city. In keep-

[6] Clifford R. Shaw, et. al, *Delinquency Areas* (Chicago, 1929), p. 203. See also Clifford R. Shaw and Henry D. McKay, *Juvenile Delinquency and Urban Areas* (Chicago, 1942).

[7] Sophonisba P. Breckinridge and Edith Abbott, *The Delinquent Child and the Home* (New York, 1912), p. 153.

ing with the general character of the area, all organized community life had disappeared, and the inhabitants were, on the whole, remnants of broken families and foot-loose men and women. In 1921 the men in the county jail who claimed residence in this area comprised over 9 per cent of the adult males living in the area.

Although the delinquency rates in the next three zones were lower than in the first zone, they were still comparatively high. About three out of ten boys from ten to seventeen years of age were arrested for juvenile delinquency in these zones. The significant drop in the delinquency rate appeared in the fifth zone, where only 15 per cent of the boys of juvenile-court age were arrested for delinquency. In the sixth zone the delinquency rate continued to decline sharply, and in the seventh zone only 1.4 per cent of the boys were charged with delinquent behavior.

The decline in delinquency coincided with the decline in dependency, family desertion, and illegitimacy in the seven zones indicating the expansion of the Negro population. The rates were high in those areas that were characterized by physical decay and the lack of organized community life. In these areas the customary forms of social control, as represented by the family and the simple folk culture of the migrants from southern communities, tended to break down or to disappear altogether. Consequently, some of the fairly well-organized families lost control of their children who took over from boys or gangs patterns of delinquent behavior which were characteristic of these areas. The children from the numerous broken families, and whose mothers had to carry the entire burden of supporting their families, easily drifted into delinquency. In the third zone, where prostitution and other types of criminal behavior flourished, not only were the children subjected to the criminal influences in the neighborhood, but they were also influenced by the criminal behavior of their parents. The decline in the delinquency rate in the areas toward the periphery of the community coincided with the increasing stabilization of family life and the disappearance of various forms of social disorganization.

What we have observed in regard to juvenile delinquency in the Negro community in Chicago is characteristic of other cities, in the

South as well as the North. Though the process of selection which is apparent in the economic and cultural organization of Negro communities is less pronounced and not so well defined in some cities, the incidence of juvenile delinquency is closely tied up with the organization of the community. Juvenile delinquency flourishes in those areas where the Negro, because of his poverty and cultural backwardness, is forced to find a dwelling-place. In the slum areas of Negro communities, because of the numerous broken homes and the employment of the mother, the children lack parental control which is sometimes able to offset the influence of the vicious environment. Negro families with higher aspirations who are able to achieve some economic security are constantly escaping from the deteriorated slum areas. They move as far as they are able into the areas where the more stable families and substantial elements in the Negro population live and maintain orderly community life. This selective process is the outcome of the rigorous competition which Negro families must face in the modern urban environment, and their success or failure depends largely upon their cultural as well as economic resources.

CHAPTER XVIII

DIVORCE: SCRIP FROM
THE LAW

For a long time there has been a great divergence of opinion concerning the frequency of divorce among Negroes. Over half a century ago Commissioner of Labor Wright in his report on marriage and divorce stated, on the basis of the opinions of "clerks of courts and others in a position to judge with fair accuracy," that "it is probably true that in nearly all of the states . . . where the colored population is very dense, nearly if not quite three-fourths of the divorces granted were to colored people."[1] Likewise, the census report twenty years later stated that "statements of court officials and of divorce lawyers in those sections of the South where the negro constitutes a considerable element of the population tend to show that the divorces granted to colored persons form from 50 to as high as 90 per cent of all divorces."[2] These opinions were apparently confirmed by the 1900 census data on the marital conditions of whites and Negroes in the southern states. "These figures," as Lichtenberger points out, "show that while the ratio of marriages to population was greater among white people in both divisions and in all but three States—South Carolina, Mississippi, and Louisiana—the States having the highest percentages of Negro population, in both divisions, and in all the States without exception, the ratio of divorces to population was greater, and in several instances much greater, for the colored than for the white." However, the Bureau of the Census did not

[1] *Marriage and Divorce in the United States, 1867-1886* (Washington, 1897), p. 132. Cf. J. P. Lichtenberger, *Divorce: A Social Interpretation* (New York, 1931), p. 123.

[2] *Marriage and Divorce, 1867-1906*, Part I, p. 20.

accept these facts as final proof of the current opinions. They called attention, first, to the fact that "the number of divorced persons as returned at the census of 1900 was probably grossly deficient, because many divorced persons, sensitive in regard to their marital condition, reported themselves as single or widowed." Therefore, they concluded, since this tendency was possibly "greater among the whites than among the colored, . . . the figures for the two races would not be exactly comparable."

Some years previously, Professor Willcox in his study of divorce had questioned the accuracy of Commissioner Wright's statement. He pointed out, first, that "an a priori argument against the opinion quoted may be derived from what is known of divorce in other parts of the world. It is not the poorest and most ignorant classes that frequent the divorce courts: their poverty and ignorance prevent."[3] Then, he proposed, first, that a comparison be made between the percentage of Negroes in the total population of the various southern states and the number of divorces granted in these states. This comparison failed to show any relation between these two phenomena. Actually, the four states with the lowest percentages of Negroes— West Virginia, Kentucky, Oklahoma, and Texas—had the highest divorce rates. Professor Willcox went farther and made a study of counties in the seven states with the highest percentages of Negro population and found that "in all of the states but Arkansas the divorce rate was less in the black counties than in the white." Even this could not be regarded as decisive proof, inasmuch as it was possible that in the counties predominantly white, where there was a strict enforcement of laws regarding marital relations, the divorce-rate might have been swelled by the black litigants. Professor Willcox's carefully worded conclusion that, "on the whole, it seems probable that the average Negro divorce rate is rather below that of the southern whites, but is increasing much more rapidly, and in a few localities or states may have already reached or passed it," was probably true.

However, Professor Willcox was describing the situation in the

[3] Walter F. Willcox, *The Divorce Problem: A Study in Statistics* ("Studies in History, Economics and Public Law,") Vol. I (New York, 1897), p. 30.

South where the Negro population was predominantly rural. Even present-day statistics on the situation in Mississippi, where almost seven-eighths of the Negroes live in rural communities, indicate that the divorce-rate is lower among Negroes than among whites. For the period 1928-34 the ratio of divorces to marriages among Negroes was not only lower than the ratio for whites but declined while the white rate remained practically stationary. For the years 1928-30 there were 8.4 divorces per 100 marriages among Negroes, whereas during this same period the rate for whites increased from 12.3 to 13.7. During the next four years the rate for Negroes declined from 6.0 to 4.4 while the white rate remained unchanged.

It is not unlikely that in rural communities, such as those inhabited by the Negroes in Mississippi, the divorce-rates among Negroes are lower than among whites. As we have seen, in the rural community the Negro's social relations are based upon sympathy and sentiment and are regulated by custom and folk beliefs. When it comes to severing his marital ties, he has only vague or erroneous ideas concerning the meaning of divorce. It is regarded not as an institutional affair but as a personal matter in which one or the other partner in the marriage relationship may give the other a "divorce" or a "scrip" and thereby free themselves from their marital obligations. Unlike divorce, marriage in even the most primitive rural community is supported by the mores or is regarded at least as a relationship which must be initiated by a minister who represents the authority of the church, if not the vaguer authority of the law.

But, when the Negro migrates to the city, he learns that the stern impersonal authority of the law demands that he go through some legal procedure if he is married and desires to enter a new marriage relation. His naïve reaction to the rational and impersonal organization of the urban environment with its written records and legal formalities is often the same as that voiced by the unmarried mother, whose letter was quoted in a previous chapter. When the social worker confronted her with the fact that she had had children without being married, she wrote a letter stating that she did not realize that her immoral conduct would be recorded against her. The Negro migrant's uncertainty and lack of appreciation of the legal status of divorce is typified by a deserted woman in Nashville who had remarried. In explaining why she got a divorce, she said, "I got a divorce and married again. Some of the people [in her neighborhood] said that I didn't have to get a divorce, but I didn't want to have no trouble, so I got one before I married." The same attitude was expressed by a young woman who came to Chicago from Mississippi following the first World War. She married a young man whom she had known for two months at the night school which they attended. After many conflicts arising out of jealousies and disagreements over whether she should work and whether he should have a hand in the cooking, they separated within six months. In speaking of her plans to remarry, she said, "Some day, I am planning to marry somebody. They [her neighbors and acquaintances] told me that after you are separated three years, you didn't have to get a divorce, you could go on and marry." However, she wanted to be certain in order not to run the risk of violating the law.

The unstable family and marital relations of the Negro in the city, together with his fear of punishment in case of forming bigamous relations, provide a partial explanation of the discovery by Professor Ogburn that Negroes, on the basis of an analysis of the 1920 census for five states, sought divorces more frequently than whites.[4] The 1910 census indicated that, in a third to two-fifths of the Negro families in some southern cities, the husband or wife or both had been married more than once. Although statistics are not available for recent years, it seems reasonable to assume that there is still considerable remarriage. Consequently, the Negro in the city probably resorts to the divorce court frequently in order to avoid being punished. The statistics on the percentage of divorced persons in the Negro population indicates that he is resorting to court more frequently than in the past. Between 1920 and 1930, in practically every city with 10,000 or more Negroes, there was an increase in the percentage of divorced persons in the Negro population. A study of divorce in the county in which one of these cities—Omaha, Nebraska —is located, revealed that 89, or 8 per cent, of the 922 cases of

[4] Ernest R. Groves and William F. Ogburn, *American Marriage and Family Relations* (New York, 1928), p. 372.

divorce were colored, although Negroes comprised only 5.3 per cent of the population.[5]

An analysis of the reports from the Bureau of Vital Statistics of the state of Virginia will enable us to compare whites and Negroes in the cities of that state in regard to divorce rates for the nine-year period 1923-31. First, it appears that the relative frequency of divorces among Negroes in the various cities coincides with the frequency among whites. For example, in Danville, where both the white and the Negro rates have been extremely low, the Negro rate has declined on the whole as the white rate has declined. On the other hand, in Norfolk and Newport News, with their highly mobile population, both the Negro and the white rates have been higher than in Richmond, where the white and Negro population are more stable. However, in all four cities during the nine years the Negro rate has been significantly lower than the white rate. Naturally, one cannot draw any conclusions from these figures for Virginia cities concerning divorces in other cities, especially in the North.

Nevertheless, the causes for which divorces were granted to Negroes seem to throw some light on the family situation responsible for divorces among a large class of Negroes in the urban environment. The outstanding cause of divorce among Negroes in all these cities was desertion. Whereas among the whites adultery was given as the cause in about a fourth to a half as many cases as desertion, among the Negroes adultery figured as the cause in only from a twelfth to a tenth as many cases as desertion. For example, in Newport News in 1930 there were twenty-nine divorces granted to Negroes. Of this number, twenty-four were granted for desertion— eleven to men and thirteen to women. It is also significant that divorces for desertion are granted to Negro men in almost the same proportion of cases as to Negro women.

Although desertion here refers to the legal cause and not the real cause of divorce, from what we know of Negro family life in the urban environment, it probably describes fairly accurately the real nature of the break in conjugal relations that leads to divorce. As

[5] T. Earl Sullenger, *A Study of Divorce and its Causation in Douglas County, Nebraska* (University of Nebraska Bulletin, March, 1927), p. 9.

we have seen, many of the Negro migrants secure divorces in order "to have no trouble." In such cases they are simply endeavoring to avoid the penalty that is administered by an authority that finds no support in their own attitudes and sentiments. Since they generally live in a world of mobility and more or less anonymity and have no roots in a community life, divorce has no significance so far as their status and social relationships are concerned. Consequently, divorce is not a means of severing an institutional or legal relationship but signifies a legalized form of desertion. When the Negro woman gives desertion as the cause, she is probably describing the real situation in a large majority of cases. But the Negro man, who has often deserted his wife, will give desertion as the cause because it is accepted as a legal cause, and his wife may have no knowledge of what is occurring. In some cases the man, who is generally more sophisticated in the ways of the city than the woman, may get a divorce without his wife understanding what is happening. This was the case with a young woman from New Orleans who appeared before the Court of Domestic Relations in Chicago in order to find out if she had been legally married and, if so, whether her husband could divorce her without her consent. Her suspicions had been aroused by her neighbors whom she had informed that she had received a summons concerning a divorce which her husband had torn up with the remark that there was "nothing to it." As it turned out, the woman had been legally married, and her husband, taking advantage of her ignorance, was getting a divorce in order to marry another woman.

Here, of course, we are discussing the unstable and disorganized elements in the Negro population. Among this group, the same factors which are responsible for desertions give rise to divorce. The simple family organization which was based upon habit and sympathy and supported by the customs of the rural community goes to pieces in the urban environment. In some cases where a man is a drunkard and abuses his wife or fails to support his family, the woman who has to support the family may get a divorce in order to free herself and children from his interference in the family. This was the case with a thirty-nine-year-old mother in

Nashville who, with the aid of the small earnings of her eighteen-year-old son, was struggling to support herself and a daughter of fourteen. Concerning the reason she divorced her husband, she stated simply: "He was too darn mean to me. He was just a drunkard. When he had money he wouldn't help the children. It was up to me to care for them. I got tired of that foolishness, so we got a divorce. After the divorce, I just stayed here and worked for my children."

In other cases, the man or woman may attempt to solve his or her marital difficulties by leaving the home and taking up his or her abode with another man or woman without marrying. This is easy in the Negro slum areas where there is no community opinion to oppose such conduct. Often, when the man or woman is discovered living in such relationships, violent quarrels result. Then the man or woman who has deserted may realize that the only way to win in the tug of war is by getting a divorce. A woman in Chicago remarked that she finally surrendered and gave her husband a divorce after he had deserted her four times and had taken up his abode with another woman. From what one may learn of the married life of many such persons who apply for a divorce, a period of violent conflicts, chiefly over "outside" men and women, usually precedes the application for divorce.

On the other hand, the increase in the percentage of divorced persons in the Negro population of the various cities may indicate a growing recognition of the institutional or legal character of marriage. This is probably true of the growing numbers of laborers, semiskilled, skilled, and domestic workers who have acquired some stability in the urban environment. They have not only acquired some sophistication in the ways of the city but have also become accustomed to regulating their lives according to its laws. Of even greater importance is the fact that they have become incorporated into the institutional life of the Negro community, especially the churches and the lodges and have contacts with schools through their children. Since this class often takes considerable pride in being law-abiding citizens, when it becomes necessary to break their marital ties, they seek legal means. In fact, to some of the people in this group, to marry without a divorce would constitute not only a violation of the law but a sin. Consequently, divorce, because of its effect upon the status of the individual in the organization of the community and the relations of the family, acquires a new meaning.

It appears, however, that divorces occur frequently among the more intelligent and ambitious members of this group who, because of educational advantages, are constantly drawn into the growing new middle class in the Negro community. This produces considerable social mobility in the Negro population and consequently affects marital relations. Marriage unions among this group are usually formed on the basis of romantic attraction and are rooted neither in the traditions of the Negro nor in established class traditions. The permanence of such unions depends mainly upon the development of a community of interests between the husband and wife. But it often happens that, after the glamour of romance has faded, the partners to these unions are drawn apart by diverse interests. The diversity of interests may result from the attraction of other men and women, or from different modes of living, or separation because of occupational advantages. When the couple has married young, the man especially may acquire new interests and a different outlook on life from that of his wife. Or in other cases, the wife may seize an opportunity to enter upon a career of her own and thus destroy the pattern of family life which the man has been accustomed to. One cannot say whether divorces occur more frequently among this class than among the less sophisticated and semiliterate Negro in the lower occupational classes. At any rate, divorces among this group generally have a different sociological significance. They are more or less a part of the process by which the Negro who has risen from the masses in the urban environment achieves increasing self-consciousness and attempts to make rational adjustments to a changing world.

Since the first World War Negro newspapers have featured, in the style of sensational journalism, the divorces of the more prominent members of the new Negro middle class. Despite the multiplicity of causes which are given for the divorces among this class, they reflect on the whole the absence of established class traditions in regard to family life and give evidence of conflicting patterns of life on the part of the parties to the divorces. It appears that divorces occur more frequently among those members of the middle class who have risen from the lower strata in Negro life than among representatives of the older families. The respresentatives of the older families generally exhibit the traditional attitude against divorce and prefer to suffer conjugal infelicity rather than to air their disagreements in the divorce courts or acknowledge their marital failures before the Negro world.

A document furnished by a young schoolteacher whose parents were divorced will give us some idea not only of the nature of the family difficulties that lead to divorce among this class but also of the attitude of the family toward divorce and the effects of divorce upon the family. Our informant's family had lived very happily in a small town where her father was a successful physician. In order to afford their daughter better educational opportunities, the family moved to a large city where Negro business was undergoing considerable growth. There her father found that he could supplement his income from his practice by joining the staff of a Negro insurance company. As his income increased, he provided his family with a comparatively luxurious home and afforded them the usual advantages of successful middle-class families. However, his business connections required him to spend much time away from home. Because of the change in their mode of living, his wife began to chafe and constantly demanded clothes and various forms of entertainment. The former harmony and understanding between the parents were undermined, and the mother began to nag her husband. This only made matters worse, and according to our informant: "Soon gossip came to my mother's ears of another woman. My father would come in late and I could hear them fuss far into the night. My mother told me nothing of all this. What I knew I found out by 'listening in' on these arguments at night and on long conversations between my mother and my cousin."

Then her father went on a trip and took her and his secretary along. Although his daughter saw nothing to arouse her suspicions, when her mother became furious she says that it was then that she "found out who the other woman was." Relations between her father and mother became more strained, and after a year of bickerings her father moved from the home, and her mother applied for a divorce. Although a temporary divorce for six months was granted, there was no healing of the breach. Finally, because of the censorious attitude of the community, her father went back to the small town to practice medicine; and her mother who refused alimony maintained a smaller home for herself and her daughter. Her daughter describes her reaction to the divorce as follows:

> Up to that time I thought that love between man and woman was very sacred and that the few fusses Mother and Dad had around home were just thrown in with the pleasant things to keep marriage from growing monotonous. I thought that if two people ever loved each other my mother and father did. The last year they were together made me realize it was not "all roses"; but the final divorce thoroughly disillusioned me. I knew that the only thing my mother did was to quarrel with Dad; but my father had been untrue to mother. Naturally I sympathized with Mother more than with Dad. I began to believe all men were the same way. I felt that if after all the years my mother and father had been living together, he could do as he had done, no man would ever mean anything to me. Our friends say that the affair has made me sensitive. That is true.

As indicated in the foregoing case, divorces on this social and economic level in the Negro population are similar to divorces among the white middle class. They involve none of the lack of sophistication which one finds among the poorer Negro migrants. Moreover, divorces among this class affect the status of the family in the community. In fact, it appears that, as the Negro rises in the scale of civilization and the Negro population becomes more differentiated, divorces may even increase. In the absence of established traditions along occupational lines, many mismatings will inevitably occur. For example, some of the divorces among prominent members of the new Negro middle class have resulted from the fact that the husband's pattern of life as a teacher or scholar has conflicted with his wife's ideas of consumption and social ambitions.

Divorce, unlike desertion and other forms of family disorganization, is not simply the result of the impact of urban life upon the simple family organization of the Negro which was molded in the rural folk community. Although among the less stable elements in the Negro community divorce becomes in many cases merely a legalized form of desertion, among other elements it is indicative of a growing recognition of the institutional and legal character of marriage and divorce. But, in addition, many divorces show the influence of the increasing social mobility which has resulted from the occupational differentiation of the Negro population. While these new classes are in the process of formation, fixed patterns of behavior and traditional control of conduct will be lacking. Consequently, divorces among urban Negroes not only reflect the influence of the traditional folk culture of the Negro but also show the effects of the new class formations.

IN THE CITY OF REBIRTH

CHAPTER XIX

OLD FAMILIES AND
NEW CLASSES

W hen, during a discussion of changes in Chicago, a member of one old family remarked to a member of another that "the old families are never in the newspapers" and received the sympathetic rejoinder that "these people are struggling to get where we were born," they were expressing their partly genuine and partly affected contempt for the new classes that were coming into prominence in the large Negro community. Although these old families had shown a similar contempt for the migrants who came during earlier periods, they had never felt their position menaced as they did when the masses of ignorant, uncouth, and impoverished migrants flooded the city during the first World War and changed the whole structure of the Negro community. The earlier migrations had caused little change in the status of the Negro in the city; but, when the Negro community was overwhelmed by the black hordes from the southern plantations, new barriers were raised against the Negro. The older residents, especially those who had prided themselves upon their achievements and their culture, literally fled before the onrush of the migrants. Some of the mulatto families moved into white neighborhoods. But, as we have seen, the vast majority of the older residents who formed the upper class moved to the periphery of the Negro community.

Within the Negro community itself changes were rapidly taking place which affected, even more fundamentally, the status of these older families. In the past the more ambitious and intelligent among the migrants had become incorporated into the small group of upper-class families, and the simple class division had remained largely as it was. But, with the sudden growth of the community during the War, the older class division was being blotted out by the differentiation of the community along occupational lines. Negro workers became a significant factor in the basic industries. Many of the leaders of the migrants had followed the migrating masses, and still other leaders in new occupations were coming to the fore to serve the needs of an awakened people. The emergence of occupa tional classes gave birth to new distinctions, while within these classes new ideals and patterns of family life were created. What was taking place in Chicago was an intensification on a large scale of a process that was going on in the urbanized Negro population all over the country.

Before the rapid urbanization of the Negro population, during and after the first World War, Negro communities were divided on the whole into two main classes. The upper class was made up of a small group of families who, because of their higher standards of morality and superior culture, were differentiated from the great mass of the population. The existing occupational differentiation of the population had not become the basis of social distinctions and standards of living. The small group of upper-class families represented the whole range of occupational classes.[1] The Negro professional man had not long since made his appearance in Negro communities. "When I was, perhaps, ten years old," writes James Weldon Johnson concerning Jacksonville in the eighties, "a strange being came to Jacksonville, the first colored doctor." As a rule the upper class evolved out of the few better-situated families with similar standards and congenial ways of life. Johnson's reminiscences concerning his boyhood playmates show a stage in this evolution which was typical of the process in Negro communities:

> In the house on the lot adjoining us on the north lived the two little Ross girls, who looked white but were not. They went by the lovely pet names of "Sing" and "Babe." Sometimes my brother and I went over to their yard to play and sometimes they came over to

[1] W. E. B. Du Bois, *The Negro in the Black Belt: Some Social Sketches* (Bulletin of the Department of Labor, No. 22, (Washington, 1902).

ours. But the playmates that had our mother's unqualified approval lived at a considerable distance. We used to go across town to play with Alvin and Mamie Gibbs, whose father was steward on one of the steamboats that then plied the St. Johns River; with Sam and Charlie Grant, sons of the pastor of Ebenezer Church and with Carrie, Fred, and "Trixie" (a boy) Onley, whose father was a contractor and builder. The houses of these playmates were very much like our own; that of the Onleys was, perhaps, a bit more pretentious.[2]

When he returned to Jacksonville in the nineties, he found that this group had developed into an exclusive social class. His description of this class continues:

Now, I found that there was a social life which had a degree of exclusiveness. There were many more homes that were comfortable and commodious; and entertainment among those who went in for society had become largely a private matter. The women who were leaders in affairs social were sharply divided into two groups: a Chautauqua group that took up culture and serious thinking, and gave mild entertainments; and a group which put more stress on the mere frivolities, gave whist parties and house dances, and served a punch of more than one-half of one per cent strength. Certainly, in my boyhood the well-to-do colored people gave entertainments of one sort or another in their homes, to which they invited those with whom they associated, but I don't think there was such a thing as "society." "Society" was one of the new things I found. I also found that the men had gone in for it. There had been organized a social club called *The Oceolas*, which gave two or three dances each winter. . . . In the Oceola Club a man's occupation had little or nothing to do with his eligibility. Among the members were lawyers, doctors, teachers, bricklayers, carpenters, barbers, waiters, Pullman porters. This democracy, however, was not exactly laxness; I knew of one or two cases in which, for one reason or another, the possession of money failed to force entrance. On one point, this black "society" was precisely like Southern white "society"—anyone belonging to an "old family," regardless of his pecuniary condition or, in fact, his reputation, was eligible.

In previous chapters we have already learned something of the background of the old families referred to in the foregoing quotation. Here we want to consider the general culture, ideals, and out-

[2] James Weldon Johnson, *Along This Way* (New York, 1934), p. 41.

look on life of these old families who constituted the Negro upper
class and to study the effects of the effacement of this class by the
new occupational classes which have emerged since the opening of
the present century.

These families, as we have noted, were more or less isolated from
the great mass of the Negro population. As far as possible they
sought residence in neighborhoods outside the Negro areas. In both
northern and southern cities we find them living close to or within
the white neighborhoods. Sometimes a single block of a street normally occupied by whites would be occupied by a small group of
these families. For example, in Baltimore during the first years of
the present century in one of these blocks there were three families
of caterers, a physician's family, a schoolteacher's family, the family
of a successful grocer, and several families that, though not belonging
to this class, were struggling to maintain high standards of family
life. These last three families were struggling to give their children
an education that would make them eligible for admittance into the
upper class. Although cordial relations existed between the families
that had "arrived" and the families that were "rising," there was
consciousness on both sides of the differences in social status. Between
the old families and the families on a smaller side street and in a
near-by alley, there was no intercourse whatever. However, between
the families that were rising and one or two families in the alley
and on the side street that were also struggling to improve themselves, there were sympathetic relations in spite of a certain social
distance that was generally maintained between them.

The process of differentiation has, of course, been going on since
emancipation. In 1877 a colored citizen of Washington wrote a satire
entitled "Washington's Colored Society" in which he described the
three classes which had appeared as follows:

> The first class consisted as it does now of Negroes, who were slaves
> in the District of Columbia befo' de wah and who obtained their
> liberty by paying the *master* class more than they were really worth.
> The second or middle class consisted as it does now to a large extent
> of Negroes, who took advantage of the emancipation proclamation of
> a gentleman named Abraham Lincoln, sometime President of the

United States. The third or poor class consisted of all Negroes as it does now, who never had any master but who were only nominally free at best, and were in an immeasurably worse condition than either of the former when they were in bondage. . . . The upper class (i.e.) all Negroes who bought their freedom or were set free before the war of rebellion undertook at an early day in the history of the Negroes of the District of Columbia to mark out the boundary and the habitation not only of the "Free niggers" but also of those who but for the kindness of Mr. Lincoln might possibly have been grovelling in darkness and superstition to a greater extent than they are today. The objection raised against this last named class seemed to have risen from the fact that the prolific and inventive genius of the immortal Ben Butler had transformed them into "Contraband of war" a technicality—which shows not only wisdom and humanity but marvellous sagacity and hind sight. A Negro therefore who worked and bought himself from those whose only right to his carcass was the thief and robbers right considered himself more valuable intrinsically, than the Negro whose liberty was given him at the demands of justice. . . . The contrabands (i.e.) those Negroes who were set free by virtue of the Emancipation proclamation were as I have said in the preceding chapter an industrious hard working and to a large extent frugal and economical people. They were however not unlike other Negroes, they were by no means immaculate, were given to bad habits just as other Negroes were and occasionally one could be found with two wives on his hands and several sets of children. Considering the infamous system pursued by their Christian owners in the matter of increasing the earth's population, they could not be expected to possess the highest moral character any more than their late owners. Aside from the very few imperfections in the physical and spiritual anatomy of the contraband, he was a model working man, a faithful and good citizen, a devoted husband and father—and the owner of right smart horse sense. He did not care much for 'highfalutin' things which meant nothing, but was constantly and eagerly in search of the realities that make life possible and enjoyable. He took no pleasure in attending card receptions simply because the white folks had them nor in substituting French for English in saying good-bye to a friend, because he couldn't. The poor class or the free "nigger" as they were called drew the line on all newcomers, giving as their reason for so doing that they were old citizens, and entitled to the precedence. This theory, however, has since been knocked into a cocked hat, as it has been shown that the old citizen with a few honorable and noteworthy exceptions were entirely unequal to the emergency. One of their chief characteristics being a love for every-

thing that smacks of the customs and usages of day before yesterday.
The old citizen is decidedly aristocratic in his air and manners and
though he followed the humble occupation, tonsorial and physiog-
nomical artist and white washer in chief to some of the "fust" families
in Washington, it does not lessen my respect for him provided his
head isn't too large for his hat. He has seen Daniel Webster, Henry
Clay, Ben Wade and Joshua R. Giddings. He used to shave these
great luminaries, which is the only consolation that the memories of
departed days can now give him. He considers his existence and his
experiences as being particularly beneficial to mankind, why or how
nobody seems to know . . . (manuscript document by John E. Bruce
in the Schomburg Collection, New York Public Library).

In this community, as in Negro communities in other cities, the
old established families were of mulatto origin and took considerable
pride in their "blood." This pride was based upon their white
ancestry. The author of the satire on "Washington's Colored Society"
makes the following strictures on those who boast of white ancestry:

There is another element in this strange heterogeneous conglomera-
tion, which for want of a better name has been styled society and
it is the species of African humanity which is forever and ever
informing the uninitiated what a narrow escape they had from being
born white. They have small hands, aristocratic insteps and wear
blue veins, they have auburn hair and finely chiselled features. They
are uneducated as a rule (i.e.) the largest number of them, though
it would hardly be discovered unless they opened their *mouths* in
the presence of their superiors in intellect, which they are very careful
not to do. In personal appearance, they fill the bill precisely so far
as *importance* and pomposity goes—but no farther. They are opposed
to manual labor, their physical organization couldn't stand it, they
prefer light work such as "shuffling cards or dice" or "removing the
spirits of Frumenta from the gaze of rude men" if somebody else
becomes responsible for the damage. Around the festive board, they
are unequalled for their verbosity and especially for their aptness in
tracing their ancestry. One will carry you away back to the times of
William the Silent and bring you up to 18 so and so, to show how
illustrious is his lineage and pedigree. His great, great grandfather's
mother in law was the Marchioness So and So and his father was ex-
Chief Justice Chastity of S.C. or some other southern state with a
polygamous record. Another will tell you all about his folks, their
habits, temperament and disposition and their keen sense of honor.
They never brooked an insult in their lives—oh no. They flourished in

the days when it was not considered a healthy pastime to call
a white man a *liar*—his half brother Col. Slaughter had a private
cemetery set apart for him by the state of "Guwgegia" for the reception of all those who so far forgot themselves as to offend him by
questioning his veracity or by offering an insult to any of his lady
friends. With the possible exception of the Immortal *Don Quixote*,
Col. Slaughter was the most gallant knight that ever shot a pistol or
drew a dagger in defense of that noble creature—woman. Gallantry
unlike intelligence is transmitted from generation to generation,
why this is thusly I am unable to conjecture. Hence the narrator of
the wonderful exploits of Col. Slaughter—and by the way a blood
relative—too, will take pains before the end of his story to inform
you that he has the blood of the Slaughters of Murderville in his
veins and that he's a b-a-d man when he's started. These misguided
unfortunates are exceedingly sensitive or affect to be so anyhow,
they are the most exacting class to be met with in the whole range
of Washington Colored Society.

A descendant of one of these families recounts the fact that her
grandmother constantly exhorted both her children and her grandchildren to maintain decorum and the highest standards of morals
with the reminder that they were descended from the X's, a well-
known aristocratic white family of Virginia. The same pride in
white ancestry was displayed by an old established mulatto family in
a northern city who defended their claim to equality with whites
and pre-eminence among Negroes on the ground that they bore in
their veins the blood of an aristocratic senator and a Spanish noble-
man. This pride in white ancestry has usually been based upon
the belief in the superior hereditary qualities of their white
ancestors and has been associated with a disdain of poor white
people. Although this latter attitude has been chiefly characteristic
of old established mulatto families in southern communities, we find
Du Bois as a child in a faraway town in New England exhibiting
the same attitude. He writes: "I cordially despised the poor Irish and
South Germans, who slaved in the mills, and annexed the rich and
well-to-do as my natural companions." Du Bois, who says he was
born "with a flood of Negro blood, a strain of French, a bit of
Dutch" but thanks God for no "Anglo-Saxon," says concerning
his grandfather: "Always he held his head high, took no insults,

made few friends. He was not a 'Negro'; he was a man!" In regard to his grandfather's ancestry, he writes:

> Louis XIV drove two Huguenots, Jacques and Louis Du Bois, into wild Ulster County, New York. One of them in the third or fourth generation had a descendant, Dr. James Du Bois, a gay, rich bachelor, who made his money in the Bahamas, where he and the Gilberts had plantations. There he took a beautiful little mulatto slave as his mistress, and two sons were born: Alexander in 1803 and John, later. They were fine, straight, clear-eyed boys, white enough to "pass." He brought them to America and put Alexander in the celebrated Cheshire School, in Connecticut. Here he often visited him, but one last time, fell dead. He left no will, and his relations made short shrift of these sons. They gathered in the property, apprenticed grandfather to a shoemaker; then dropped him.[3]

Although there is no way of estimating the incalculable effects of biological heredity even in those families that can substantiate their claim to descent from aristocratic whites, nevertheless, traditions concerning aristocratic descent have left their mark upon the behavior and outlook on life of these families.

What, then, are some of the traditions which these old mulatto families have preserved respecting descent from aristocratic or prominent families? Let us begin with the family history of a prominent professional man's wife who for years was a sort of arbiter in the "society life" of a Negro community in the North. She gives the following account of her white ancestry:

> My father was a general in the Civil War and a lawyer. He played a prominent part in the building of the Union Pacific Railroad and became a multimillionaire. He educated me and brought me up in the family with his white grandchildren as he was quite old. His greatest desire was that I should not be identified with colored people. He travelled about a great deal in a private car and always took me with him. He wanted me to be adopted by his oldest daughter who was in Mexico. He had the greatest horror of my being married to a Negro. Many a time I have heard him say that he would blow my brains out rather than see me married to a Negro. I was about eight years old when they were talking about adopting me. My mother had no objection and I would have always preferred living at the "Big

[3] W. E. B. Du Bois, *Darkwater* (New York, 1920), pp. 8-9.

House" but she objected to the legal adoption. I was the child of his old age and looked like him—he was sort of swarthy. Even after I married a colored man and he had disinherited me—he was inclined to become reconciled to me but he died during a stroke.[4]

Naturally, the white ancestors are more remote where a mulatto caste has grown up and the mulatto families have intermarried. In Charleston, as we have seen, some of the old mulatto families traced their descent from some of the French refugees from Haiti who sought an asylum in Charleston and other cities along the Atlantic coast. The same is true of some of the old families in the North. For example, an old family in Chicago traced its family line on one side to a United States senator who was a member of a distinguished Kentucky family:

> My father was the grandson of Senator C. However, he was reared by his colored grandfather and took his name. He had two brothers and one sister. One brother had blonde hair and blue eyes and disappeared some years ago presumably into the white race. My other uncle married into the D. family, an old Philadelphia family, one member of whom was in the diplomatic service. As they had no children, they adopted a girl who is a teacher in Philadelphia. She is very aristocratic and moves in a very restricted circle.

There are families who claim even more distinguished white ancestry than senators and governors. For antiquity of family line, a prominent physician, who is engaged in health work among Negroes in the country, could claim first place. In letters which he has from the English branch of his family, the history of the family name is traced back to the time of the Roman occupation of Britain. However, this physician only claimed actual knowledge of an English grandfather who had a child, his own father, by a mulatto woman in Missouri in 1861. Next in age of lineage was the tradition preserved in the family of a social worker and teacher in New York City that her grandmother, who was born in Holland, could trace her ancestry back to William of Orange. Then, there are families who claim descent from presidents of the United States. A schoolteacher, whose great-grandfather was a missionary in Trinidad and.

---

[4] A. H. Shannon, *The Negro in Washington* (New York, 1930), p. 87.

built a church in Baltimore, said that this pioneer in the religious life of the Negro was supposed to have been a cousin of his white benefactor who was a president of the United States. Another teacher, in an old town in Virginia, whose parents were also teachers, claimed that her great-great-grandmother on her mother's side was the daughter of a distinguished president and lived to be a hundred and four years old. An old clergyman and teacher with two sons and a daughter who have obtained higher degrees from northern universities modestly stated that his great-grandfather was said to be the son of a president of the United States who was also one of the signers of the Declaration of Independence. From this same president the principal of a colored high school in a city in New Jersey claims descent. Three other widely separated families claimed descent from a less distinguished president. One was the family of the wife of a college professor in a southern city; another was an outstanding clergyman in a northern city; and a third was a supervisor of county schools in the South, whose brother is a distinguished Episcopal prelate.

Some years ago the following news item appeared on the front page of the *Afro-American* (January 28, 1933):

DESCENDANT OF 9TH PRESIDENT DIES AT NINETY

FAUNSDALE, ALA.—Mrs. Mary Davis (affectionately called "Aunt Mary"), who died recently at her homestead at the age of 90, widow of Philip M. Davis, who died 25 years ago, was known and loved by all races for her lofty ideals, thrift and industry. In her prime Mrs. Davis was a dressmaker, catering to the wealthy people of this section. She was the daughter of Margaret Willis and Oliver Harrison who was a descendant of William Henry Harrison, ninth President of the United States and third son of Benjamin Harrison, a signer of the Declaration of Independence. All her life Mrs. Davis lived within the family circle of the white Harrisons and Stickneys, Warrens and Collins. The family ties were lasting. A younger white descendant of the Harrisons cared for her and followed her to the grave. Mrs. Davis was the mother of 13 children.

Then follows a list of these children who are prominent in the educational, economic, political, and civic life of the Negro in various parts of the country.

Of course, the vast majority of these old families who claim aristocratic ancestry do not assert that they are descended from presidents or other such distinguished people. They simply trace their families back to the landowning aristocracy. The following document is typical of the traditions which have been preserved by the majority of these families concerning white ancestry and the cultural advantages which such ancestry has afforded them. From the family history of a college student, we have the following:

> The oldest ancestor of my family that I know is my great grand-father, W. P., a Mississippi slave owner. He was quite rich owning a great deal of property near Lauderdale, Miss. My great grandmother, A. R., a very beautiful young woman, was one of his mulatto slaves. These were my great grand parents on my fathers side. A. R. had five children for W. P. The third child, a boy named W. H. P., was born in Tuscaloosa, Ala. He was the favorite child of his father, and lived in what was termed the "big house." All of his training from the standpoint of books was personally supervised by his father and his father's white wife. He was never considered a slave, his color, hair, and features were those of any white man. He had a half brother who was a leading physician in the South, and the relationship was not concealed. In later years, it was from this uncle that one of W. H. P.'s sons, (my father) received his first inspiration to become a physician.

It was quite natural that families that placed so much value upon their white ancestry should have excluded from marriage and intimate association the unmixed Negroes. However, in estimating the role which a light skin and white blood have played as a bond of sympathy between these families or as a means of entering the upper class, there has been a tendency to oversimplify the problem. To outside observers it has often appeared that color was the only distinguishing mark of this class, and it alone made an individual or family eligible for entrance into it. But, as we shall see, color was only one factor, and it symbolized other factors. For example, although there was considerable prejudice on the part of the old mulatto families in Charleston against association with the blacks, nevertheless at least two black families were generally accepted as belonging to the upper class. This was owing to the fact that these black families could boast of free ancestry and were as well situated economically as the mulatto families. On the other hand, although these black families were members of the exclusive church to which the mulattoes belonged, there was still some resistance to admitting them into the most intimate associations. A member of one of the old mulatto families frankly confessed that black families of free origin were always referred to within the circle of the mulatto families by a whispered epithet which designated them as a peculiar kind of free persons of color. Moreover, although these black aristocrats were received by the mulattoes on formal occasions, they knew instinctively, as it were, that they should not seek a marriage alliance with the mulatto and that they were not expected at the intimate social functions although they received invitations. Although the mulatto families in Charleston have modified their attitudes toward dark Negroes during recent years, even within the last two decades some of them still exhibited, in regard to dark Negroes, the attitude described in the following document:

> There were three Negro families in our block and immediate vicinity, the R.'s, S.'s, and our family, the T.'s. The S.'s were an aged black widow, who sold vegetables and charcoal, and her crippled son and two young grandsons, with whom she lived. The rest of the people of the community were Irish-Catholics with the exception of the L.'s and M.'s, wealthy Jews. To these whites we were considered thrifty, intelligent, progressive Negroes, but under their breath, "niggers." But to the R.'s, a very fair, "blue blood" Charleston, family we were inferior and far below them in social status. Although more members of my family had been to high school and college, and our home was more pretentious than theirs, they were obsessed with the idea of being our superiors. They were of an old free, mulatto Charleston family, who had been there for years and years, while we were upstarts in Charleston, who had lived there for just about twenty years or so. We were members of the Methodist church; whereas the R.'s were members of the high tone St. Marks Episcopal Church, where for many years nothing darker than an octoroon attended.
>
> The R.'s had six children, whereas there were eight in my family. However, their children were of the same age as the six younger ones in my family. When we first moved into the community after my father's death, the children of the two families made attempts to

become friendly, but the R.'s forbade their children to associate with us. So deeply did their parents instill in them the idea of their superiority that they would turn up their clothes to us, thumb their noses at us, call us "niggers," and act in a manner that would typify the behavior of the lowest Georgia "cracker" to a Negro. The relation existing between the children of these two families was not the desire of the children of either family. The children simply accepted the instructions of their parents. When Mrs. R. scolded Jimmy for playing marbles with me, my mother reprimanded me also. Naturally she would not accept the belief that her child was inferior, or perchance endanger her self-esteem by having it thought that she desired the association and consequent recognition of the R. family. When we played ball with some of the white kids of the community, Jimmy R. would always have to leave if one of us were in the game. If Oscar, the little black-skinned grandson of Mrs. S. were there, it was all right, since his family accepted their inferior status. Mrs. S. did their washing, and I should add, ours also. Then, too, we had the same family physician. Oscar would run their errands and receive some of Jimmy's old clothes. But the R.'s referred to us as "nappy-haired niggers," and well do I recall my mother telling us not to mind "those half white asses, they have no sense and little education." With pride Mother pointed to the educational achievements of her children. It appeared that the R.'s rigid family pattern, with its ultra exclusiveness, made for deterioration. Not any of the children have gone higher in school than the eighth grade, and it took them twelve years to do that.

The R. children never walked on our side of the street, that is, in front of our door. When they wanted to go to Mrs. S.'s little shanty, they would walk on their side and cross in the middle of the block to reach her home. Not even has death been able to bring about the slightest communication between the families. When Jimmy died at the age of 17, we sent no condolences. Although when I finished high school, Mr. R. spoke to me for the first time, the separation still goes on. We live on one side of the street, and they live on the other. An insurmountable barrier separates us—social caste. But, interestingly, the children of the two families have met in other cities; for example, in New York. There the barriers were broken down and my brother took one of the R. girls to many dances. In Charleston that could never have happened.

The same type of caste sentiment, in which prejudice against the dark-skinned Negro finds expression, has existed among groups of mulatto families in other communities. However, it should be pointed out that this attitude has been bound up with a pride in family background and a consciousness of the superior culture of this group. Mulattoes, who were without family background or other attainments, were generally not accepted into this mulatto caste. Moreover, the prejudice of this group against the unmixed Negro did not necessarily involve repugnance toward the individual black Negro. It was more a question of social status and traditions.

A member of an old mulatto family reports that when her mother thought that she was falling in love with the black poet, Dunbar, her mother immediately told her that, no matter how great a poet Dunbar was, a person as black as he could not become a member of their family. Where the question of social status has been involved, mulattoes have even refused to present a black mother to their friends or have concealed pictures of black relatives. But the very fact that a mulatto's mother was black indicated that there was marriage outside the caste or that the mulattoes were the children of white fathers and the family had not been integrated into the mulatto caste.

When these closely knit mulatto communities have disintegrated and individuals and families have become scattered, they have tended to lose their prejudice against the black Negro. This has been true in recent years, especially in the large urban communities where the Negro along with other people wins a place, not because of family status but through competition. Of course, individual mulattoes may retain their prejudices against the black, but it will no longer have the support of a caste. In such cases his white skin will become the means whereby he gains economic advantages and satisfies individual wishes. He may not go downtown with a black Negro because he may be indentified and lose his job or be subjected to insults and discrimination. Or the light skin of the mulatto woman especially may acquire a purely symbolic value for the black man who has won his way up in the world. But in such cases the light skin is no longer the distinguishing mark of a caste or even of a class which is open to those who achieve success.

Next to "blood," which in the majority of instances meant white ancestry, these families have taken pride in their cultural attainments which have distinguished them from the masses and have been the basis of their ascendancy in the Negro world. As a mark of their superior culture, they have endeavored first to speak the uncorrupted language of the cultured whites. By this external mark of culture they have often endeavored to emphasize their superiority to the ignorant plantation Negro or city slum-dweller. It was among this class that much opposition was expressed to the dialect poems of Dunbar.

The language spoken by this group showed the influence of intimate contacts with the whites as well as educational advantages. In the North these old families have for several generations had more or less close contacts with the whites not only as servants but in the schools and other institutions. In their childhood they have become acquainted with the best literature, and, since this was regarded as a mark of culture, they placed considerable emphasis upon this aspect of the white man's culture. Naturally, this behavior has not been mere imitation or affectation but has unconsciously become habitual and incorporated into their general behavior. It has simply been part of the process by which northern Negroes have been able to assimilate more of the white man's culture than their southern brothers. On the other hand, in the South where the old families have ceased to have intimate contacts with the whites, they have been compelled to draw on their own cultural resources which were acquired through contacts at an earlier period. Conseqently, this aspect of their cultural heritage has been cultivated to a large extent in the Negro colleges. It was from this class that the majority of the students were recruited for the colleges and academies that were established by northern white missionaries after the Civil War. These schools gave the student much more than a formal education, inasmuch as the white missionaries from New England lived in close personal contacts with the students and encouraged their aspirations to attain social equality and cultural identity with the whites. This education was very much the same as the classical education of the day. The students were drilled in English literature and grammar and given fundamental instruction in the ancient classics because of its supposed disciplinary value. Through such influences the culture of this group was maintained and enriched.

In the South these old families took over patterns of behavior which were associated with the ideal of the southern lady and southern gentleman. Consequently, the man was expected to be lavish with his money, courteous toward women of his class, to defend the honor of his home, and to philander as a gentleman would. The woman was expected to remain chaste and be under the chaperonage of her parents, preserve a certain delicacy and modesty, and to show none of the coarser qualities of the black women, who were often her servants. Naturally, when such ideals and valuations had a slender economic basis, they led to habits of consumption that made them appear improvident and thriftless. In fact, many of the sons of these mulatto families with a small competence wasted their resources because of their ideals of what was proper and thereby caused the dissolution of these families. Then, too, the fact that the heads of some of these families, possibly to a larger extent in the North than in the South, derived their income from such positions as steward and head waiter in clubs and hotels made their standards of consumption appear ludicrous.

But all this does not mean that the culture of this group was a hollow pretense or a mere caricature of white civilization. Of course, if one evaluates critically the depth and genuineness of their cultural heritage, the seamy side becomes apparent. But these people were not, as they have been represented, crude field Negroes who had acquired a smattering of Greek or Latin and Shakespeare. The classical tradition on which they were fed was the cultural tradition of the period. From this tradition many of them drew real inspiration and mental nourishment. In the English and ancient classics they often discovered a philosophy of life and a guide to their behavior. But, because of their isolation, their cultural heritage became ingrown and highly formalized. Therefore, even the most superficial aspects of their culture were often supported by the deepest sentiment. In their social life, social ritual and social graces were often observed with a moral earnestness. And, when one views their creative efforts, their performances appear naïve and pitiable. One needs only to read the poetry which this group produced to realize how far their sorry imitations encouched in stilted language and burdened with classical references fell below accepted literary standards. Or if one takes a peep into their "literary societies" in which the frail vines of their culture were watered, there is certainly cause for amusement. These societies have about them an atmosphere of artificiality and aloofness from the real world. But, despite the apparent hollowness of their traditions concerning aristocratic blood and their naïve pride in their cultural heritage, these traditions and beliefs shaped their morals as well as their manners.

For a long time these old established families were able to maintain their ascendancy in the Negro group and to preserve their traditions of family life behind the walls of caste sentiment. But when the isolation in which they lived was broken down by the social and economic changes in American life in general and by the increasing mobility of the Negro, they found their secure and privileged position menaced. Their ascendancy was challenged by the new economic classes that were coming into existence as the result of the increasing differentiation of the Negro population. To meet this menace not only to their privileged position but also to their standards of morals and family life, they have often retreated farther within their own circle and cried "O tempora, O mores." A young professional woman who is a member of one of these old southern families wrote the following bitter complaint against the degradation of morals which had taken place as the result of the impact of new economic classes on the traditional social structure in her community.

There was a time when A. could boast of many aristocratic and cultured families. Men who have made places for themselves in the world have come from these old families. X. and Y. are representative of the kind of character that A. of a generation ago afforded. That day has passed into oblivion; and the select people who remain are those of that generation. When my mother married, she sent out five hundred invitations in the city. I doubt that I could send fifty to such intimate friends as those to whom my mother's were sent. There just simply isn't any "society" in A.

The large group that stands in the front rank of A.'s society is composed of the "rat" type. "And how did the 'rats' push to the front ranks?" you ask. Social standards began to drop about twenty-seven years ago when several professional men—a doctor and a lawyer, in particular, who now live in Chicago—in the interest of their professions, opened their homes to the entertainment of persons regardless of their social standing. Several years ago, a bootlegger and speakeasy proprietor brought his wife to the city. She was very pretty, except for the dark and sunken rings about her eyes from dissipation. In six months' time, she led A's "exclusive social set." And sad to say, there were some young people who if they had stayed together could have made up a small élite social group. But being afraid that they would not enjoy all the real social life, they "let down the bars," became intimate with the bootlegger's wife and visited her home. I live at home through my vacation without contacts, for the best is too bad. I am not snobbish; I am stating facts. If I were to attend a dance, my escort and the men I dance with would be men with "reputations." It seems that nobody will bar the undesirable. Perhaps nobody can. As for me, I do not entertain. There are some young people who themselves are nice and congenial, but whom I cannot afford to entertain in my home. Those whom I once could have entertained have permitted themselves to become victims of this social degradation, thereby rendering themselves undesirable and unfit now.

The attitude expressed in this document is typical of the attitude of this heretofore privileged group in other Negro communities. Their protest against the degradation of morals and manners has not been entirely without foundation. There was often cause for genuine contempt for the crudeness and exhibitionism of those who had suddenly acquired prominence because of their education and relatively high economic status in the Negro community. They appreciated the fundamental difference between a man or woman without a background of culture and normal family life who had secured a formal college education—and that often in an inferior Negro college—and the man or woman with a background of several generations of stable family life and civilized conduct. Consequently, they resented the pretensions of a doctor or businessman who often revealed in his ungrammatical speech, vulgar manners, and ostentatious home a lack of the fundamentals of true culture.

In some instances these old families have sought a refuge in their memories and nurtured their children on their past achievements. Within the narrow circle of a few select families, they have lived a life that was reminiscent of a world that had vanished. Even today where they continue to live in isolation, their quaint mode of dress and constrained manners often give their exclusive social gatherings the atmosphere of an animated museum.

The satirist of "Washington's Colored Society" wrote that the "fust" families in 1877

> had all the habits and customs of the day before yesterday hanging to them and about them as tenaciously and persistently as the barnacles on seashells. They live in old fashioned homes way uptown, downtown and across town. They dress in the same style that their illustrious predecessors did half a century ago. It was from this class that the mother of George Washington procured nurses for her distinguished and immortal son—now called the "Father of his country." All the leading white washers, coachmen, *valets* and servants in *ordinaire* were furnished the "fust families" of the white race from this class, half a century ago. Those of them now living in Washington wouldn't be caught dead with an ordinary Negro. . . . The most of their company consists of antiquated old white people, many of whom are near death's door. The "fust families" of Washington Colored Society—keep a servant, two dogs, a tom cat and a rifle that saw service in 1776. They are pensioners provided they or their ancestors lived with the "bloods" of their day and generation. . . . There is more family pride to the square inch in the hide of the "fust families" than there are fleas on a dog's back. To marry their children out of the circle in which they have been accustomed to mingle is decidedly out of the question and contrary to both their religious and social views. It has been said, whether truthfully or falsely I know not, that the species of misguided humanity with whose characteristics I am dealing, secretly hope to become absorbed by the white or Caucasian race.

Their children, overburdened and hedged about by outworn traditions, have proved poor competitors in the struggle with the ambitious representatives of undistinguished families in the new world of the modern city. But, on the whole, these old families, being unable to resist the march of events, have gradually intermarried or merged otherwise with those elements in the Negro community who have made their way to the top of the new class structure. Their cultural heritage, though modified, has contributed to the stability and character of the emerging Negro middle class.

The extent to which the differentiation of the Negro population has progressed during the present century is indicated in a general way by the changes since 1900 in the proportion of Negroes in the broad occupational divisions. The most important change has occurred in the field of agriculture. From 54.6 per cent in 1910, the percentage of Negroes employed in agriculture declined to 36.1 in 1930. Although from 1910 to 1920 the percentage employed in manufacturing increased from 12.6 to 18.2, there was practically no change during the next decade. However, the increase in the proportion employed in transportation, trade, and the extraction of minerals continued up to 1930. This was also true for professional occupations; but not true in regard to clerical and public services, where there were slight losses in 1930 as compared with the gains observable in 1920. These figures indicate that the shift from agricultural occupations between 1910 and 1920 resulted in increases in all the other occupations, except domestic service, whereas during the next decade the workers who shifted from agriculture were absorbed in domestic service.

The changes in the occupational status of the Negro have, of course, come about as the result of urbanization. Therefore, in order to get a better view of these changes, we shall consider some of the results of a study of the occupational status of the Negro in 1920 in fifteen cities—six northern, six southern, and three border cities. Moreover, the results of this study enable us to get a more accurate picture of the social and economic differentiation of the Negro population than the broad occupational divisions in the census. Beginning with the professional group, we find that the northern cities have relatively more men in professional services than the southern and border cities. The fact that the proportion of women in professional occupations in the northern cities did not exceed that in the southern and border cities was due to the large numbers of teachers in the separate school systems in these cities. It is also important in comparing these cities to note that the composition of the professional class in northern cities was quite different from the same class in southern cities. For example, in Atlanta and Birmingham, about 52 per cent of the professional class was composed of clergymen; whereas in Boston and New York, clergymen comprised only 11.2 per cent of the professional classes.

Similar differences between northern cities, on the one hand, and border and southern cities, on the other, appeared in respect to the other occupational classes. All northern cities showed a smaller percentage in public service than southern and border cities; with the exception of the District of Columbia, where the federal government affords considerable employment. This was doubtless due to the participation of the Negro in the political life of northern cities and the absence of a rigid color bar. The same situation was true in regard to clerical occupations. However, when we come to those engaged in trade, we find that, although only Chicago, where numerous Negro enterprises have sprung up to serve the demands of the large Negro community, showed as large a proportion in this class as the third highest southern city, all the northern cities, with the exception of Cleveland, exceeded the other southern cities. Before comparing these cities with reference to the various classes of industrial workers, it should be noted that with the exception of Richmond, where large numbers of Negro women are employed in the tobacco industry, the percentage of women employed in domestic service was significantly higher in southern cities than in northern cities, with the exception of Philadelphia. On the other hand, the proportion of Negro men in domestic service was conspicuously higher in northern cities than in both border and southern cities.

Taking first those employed as laborers, we find that southern and border cities had on the whole a larger proportion of both male and female workers in this class than northern cities. The same situation was found in the case of men in semiskilled occupations. The border and northern cities, with the exception of Seattle, had a larger proportion of Negro women in semiskilled occupations than the southern cities. However, the northern cities had a larger proportion of women in skilled occupations. The proportion of men in skilled occupations in each of six northern cities was matched by one of the southern cities, the border cities making a poorer showing than either southern or northern cities.

Although the occupational differentiation of the Negro population has progressed considerably during the present century, the emergence of these new socioeconomic classes has been too recent to effect a crystalization of distinctive patterns of behavior for each of these classes. Each class reflects more or less the broad undifferentiated cultural background in which it is rooted. In the absence of class traditions, imitation and suggestion play an important role, and there is much confusion in respect to standards of behavior and consumption. Therefore, the following chapters upon the family of the middle class and the urban proletariat deal with family forms and types of family behavior which are in the process of becoming crystallized in the urban environment.

CHAPTER XX

THE BROWN MIDDLE
CLASS

The Negro middle class signalized its achievement of self-consciousness in the organization of the National Negro Business League in 1900 under the leadership of Booker T. Washington. This organization was the culmination of a movement fostered by Negro leaders, which had its beginning in the eighties and nineties. The belated evolution of this class as well as its mental isolation was revealed in the resolutions of the leaders gathered in Atlanta in 1898. These resolutions contained a naïve profession of faith in individual thrift and individual enterprise in a world that was rapidly entering a period of corporate wealth. Hence, today when the economic foundations of the Negro middle class are explored, as was done in a fundamental study of banking, they are found insubstantial and insecure. However, here we are primarily concerned not with the economic basis of this class but rather with the traditions, mores, and patterns of behavior that determine the character and organization of its family life.

Concerning the growth and character of Negro business during the present century, Doctor Harris writes:

> The actual growth in Negro business is shown by the fact that in 1898, Dr. W. E. B. Du Bois' careful investigation showed only 1,900 enterprises, while in 1930 there were 70,000. This growth was paralleled by an increase in the number of Negroes in white-collar occupations, a large number of whom were employed in Negro enterprises and in other specifically racial undertakings. In 1920 there were 34,434 Negro stenographers, bookkeepers, advertising and insurance

agents, salesmen and clerks in stores, and floorwalkers and inspectors. In 1930 the number in these occupations had increased to 59,301. In 1920, Negro bankers, brokers, real estate agents, retail and wholesale dealers and undertakers numbered 26,822, but in 1933 the number had increased to 35,833.

The largest number of successful business ventures conducted by Negroes has been in the field of personal service—restaurants, beauty parlors, barber shops and funeral parlors. Here racial discrimination is general. For this reason, Negro businesses have been described as "defensive enterprises," the product of racial segregation. Few, if any significant or large commercial and industrial enterprises have been organized.[1]

The middle-class group, whose family life we are considering, includes, in addition to those in business enterprises and white-collar occupations, men and women engaged in professional pursuits and employed in responsible positions in public service. In limiting the new Negro middle class which has emerged in recent years to these four occupational classes, we have omitted representatives of other occupational classes who maintain similar standards of behavior and are sometimes accepted socially by members of the middle class. But here we are dealing with an economic class composed of certain occupational groups that may be identified statistically.

In the last chapter we have considered the size of these four occupational classes in the gainfully employed population of fifteen cities in 1920. Since 1920 significant changes have taken place in the size of the occupational classes comprising the middle class. Since the occupational classification for 1940 was different from that used in 1920, we shall consider only those having the following employment status: professional and semi-professional, proprietors and managers, and clerical workers. Moreover, we shall consider only the eleven cities with 100,000 or more Negro population in 1940 and Louisville, Kentucky. In the four southern cities—Atlanta, Birmingham, Memphis and New Orleans only slightly more than two per cent of the Negro men were in professional and semi-professional occupations; and only between one and two per cent were proprietors or managers of businesses. Likewise, there was only a

[1] Abram L. Harris, *The Negro as Capitalist* (Philadelphia, 1936), pp. 53-54.

small proportion—two and a half to five per cent—in clerical occupations. Those who were in clerical occupations were employed by Negro schools or Negro businesses. In the border cities—Baltimore, Washington, D. C., St. Louis, Missouri, and Louisville, Kentucky, there was a slightly larger group proportionately in professional and semi-professional occupations. Moreover, in Baltimore, St. Louis and Louisville, the proportion in business was larger. The most important difference between southern and border cities was revealed in regard to those in clerical occupations. This was especially marked in Washington where nearly ten per cent of the men were in clerical positions. The relatively large proportion in clerical positions was the result of the opportunities for employment provided by the government.

However, it is when we consider the northern cities that we are able to see the effects of larger employment opportunities upon the growth of the middle class. In New York City and Chicago between three and four per cent of the Negro men were in professional and semi-professional occupations; and in New York City five per cent of the men were proprietors and managers of businesses. For all four northern cities—New York City, Chicago, Philadelphia and Detroit—a much larger percentage of Negroes were in clerical occupations than in any southern or border city with the exception of Washington. In fact, in New York City and Chicago a slightly larger proportion were in clerical occupations than in Washington. Thus on the basis of our occupational definition of the middle class, from six to eight per cent of the Negroes in southern cities; nine to twelve per cent in border cities; and 10 to 20 per cent in northern cities comprise this class.

The family life of the middle class as well as its ideals and aspirations and even its physical characteristics reflect the different elements in the Negro population from which it springs. Physically, the middle class shows that it is comprised largely of men and women of mixed ancestry. Two decades ago Reuter found after a detailed study of leaders in practically every sphere of Negro life that the vast majority were of mixed blood. Of the 4,267 men and women included in his study, 3,239 men and 581 women were of mixed blood; whereas only 414 men and 33 women were full-blooded Negroes. A study of the grandparents of 311 persons listed in *Who's Who in Colored America: 1928–1929*, throws light on the ancestry of some of the representatives of this class. The information given by those who returned questionnaires on their families, appears, in view of what has been learned concerning the background of the Negro, to be representative of the upper-class Negro. First, it should be pointed out that the persons answering the question-naires had more information concerning their maternal grandparents than concerning their paternal grandparents and that information was lacking in the smallest number of cases for their maternal grandmothers. In regard to the color and status of their grandparents, we find that a relatively larger proportion were free and of mixed blood. Then, too, in conformity with our knowledge of the relative proportion of mulattoes in the free and slave population, we find that, except in the case of their maternal grandmothers, a large proportion of the grandparents who were slaves were black. On the other hand, the vast majority of the grandparents who were free were of mixed blood. As one would expect, a fairly large number of the grandfathers were white; but it is of interest to note that twenty-six reported that their grandmothers were white.

Data on the white, mulatto, and free ancestry of these persons indicate roughly the element in the middle class which springs from the old established mulatto families. These old families, with their fairly well-developed family traditions, constitute a stabilizing and conservative influence in the middle class. Because of their past history, they place great value upon culture and respectability. More-over, to some extent they are responsible for the continued emphasis upon a light skin among members of the middle class who regard success in one's occupation together with a good income as of more importance than membership in an old family. A man who through success in business or in his profession has a secure economic position may marry a fair daughter of one of these old mulatto families in order to consolidate his social status. As a black college professor who had risen from the black proletariat remarked concerning his blond wife who came from an old family: "You see my wife. I married her so that there would be no question about the status of my family. She has the right color and, more than that, comes from an old family." Thus, a fair skin in conjunction with and as a symbol of family status becomes a value in the new middle class. In a study of the members of the National Negro Business League, Reuter has shown the tendency of the men in this group to select wives of the same or lighter color.

However, in considering the marriage of men to women of the same or lighter color, one should take into account the process by which the men, especially, of the lower and darker strata of the Negro population ascend into the middle class. In a study of 1,051 Negro physicians, only 2.9 per cent reported that their fathers were physicians. Practically a fifth reported that their fathers were farmers; 5.2 per cent that their fathers were laborers; and 5.8 per cent that their fathers were barbers and cooks.[2] Likewise, in a study of students attending Negro colleges, it was found that only a fourth of the students came from families where the father was in professional, business, and clerical occupations.[3] Although the majority of students in Negro colleges show an admixture of white blood,[4] the boys are on the whole darker than the girls. Many of these boys have left their black families on the plantations to make their way up in the world through the attainment of an education. In choosing wives, they naturally make their selection from among their college associates or daughters of established families, both of whom are likely to be of fairer complexion. Nor should it be forgotten that the same applies to the woman of dark complexion who, because of personal achievement and family background, may be married to a man with fair skin. Thus color loses its caste basis as represented by the older mulatto families, and a brown middle class seems to be emerging.

In view of the diverse cultural backgrounds from which the

[2] Carter G. Woodson, *The Negro Professional Man and the Community* (Washington, 1934), pp. 81-82.

[3] Ambrose Caliver, *A Background Study of Negro College Students* (Washington, 1933), p. 68.

[4] E. B. Reuter, *The Mulatto in the United States*, pp. 271-73.

middle class springs, it is inevitable that there would be considerable confusion of ideals and patterns of behavior. The brown middle class that is coming into being has sloughed off in many cases the traditions of the mulatto families as well as the folk culture of the masses. Personal achievement in the way of often meager educational attainments and economic success is becoming the chief requirement for admission into this class. There has not been sufficient time for class traditions to be built up, and, in the absence of class traditions, suggestion and imitation play an important role in the determination of behavior. For example, one may find members of the middle class who, while boasting of aristocratic and conservative family background, claim to be emancipated intellectuals, defend questionable stock manipulation by holding companies, and join movements to release radicals. Within the same person, philistine, bohemian, and creative attitudes strive for expression and seek a congenial social environment.

In the absence of traditions along occupational lines, the various occupational classes strive to maintain standards of consumption set up by the economically better situated members of the middle class. These standards in turn have often been copied from the wealthy upper white middle class. In pointing out the difference between the standards of consumption of Negro and white physicians, Professor Kelly Miller once stated that he could indicate the cars in front of Freedmen's Hospital owned by Negroes by simply placing a mark on the more expensive ones. Since standards of consumption are regarded as an index to success in business and the professions, they determine to some extent the status of individuals and families in the middle class. Therefore, among this class there is much striving, involving debts on houses, clothes, and furniture, to maintain an appearance of wealth. A woman writes the following story concerning herself:

> I came from a family that people call rather "well-to-do"; I had been accustomed to have everything I wanted as a child, and all thru my school days I was accustomed to many elaborate social affairs and lovely clothes, as well as extensive travel.
>
> Against my parents' wishes, I married a fellow who was earning a

small salary and could not give me the home, the lovely furniture, a pretty car, pretty clothes, etc., that I had always had. We moved into a neat little home and he began buying; our furniture was very nice but not what I wanted; later we got a Ford but I wanted a Dodge. Gradually, I became more and more dissatisfied with the things which he could not give and as I look back over it now I see that I was constantly nagging about not being able to entertain, to travel, to dress, to "put on the show" that my friends did.

One day my husband said to me "I love you better than I do my own life and from now on I am going to see if I can't give you every thing you want." I did not know then the real import of these words. About a month afterward he told me that he wanted me to have my own car and that he would keep the Ford. I was delighted when he sent out a pretty Dodge coupe—all for me. I did not question how he got it but was satisfied that he knew what he was doing. When we had been married about two years he said he wanted to refurnish our little love nest. I was overjoyed when I saw the lovely furniture brought in and the old furniture carried out. Still I did not question. My next desire was a new home; he felt that he could not give me just what I wanted, so I continued to "nag." For a good while I was dissatisfied—wanting the home which he said he could not afford. Spats occurred frequently—conflicts continuously. Finally he said "I'll give you the home you want—just give me time." It was during this "time" that I heard that he was gambling and had been gambling for some time. The home was being built when I asked him if he ever gambled. Truthfully and frankly, he told me that my wants had been so many and so heavy that it was for that reason that he started it. I eventually had the things I wanted but since then I've always regretted the ways the accommodation was brought about.

Striving to maintain an appearance of high standards of consumption often leads, as in the foregoing case, to illegal practices. Consequently, one reads from time to time of Negro physicians being arrested or sent to prison for illegal practices or dealing in narcotics. Negro newspapers play up from time to time the criminal conduct of Negro businessmen who have been apprehended in their efforts to get rich. These criminal activities are often, from what we know of the persons involved, the result of efforts to maintain standards of conspicuous consumption that are out of proportion to the economic resources of this class.

Naturally, much of the conspicuous consumption of the middle class is devoted to social life. This is due especially in the South to racial segregation which prevents participation in the life of community. But, even when this fact is taken into consideration, the Negro middle class spends a relatively large amount of their time and resources on social life. This often appears incongruous in view of the fact that this class depends almost solely upon salaries or upon fees derived from the meager earnings of Negro workers. Hence, the surprise of a white social worker when she learned that her colored associate was in "society" and entertained lavishly. The same ideals are apparent in the leisure-time activities of a large proportion of the unemployed wives in the middle class. Since they possess on the whole only a superficial "culture," they spend very little time in reading or, where opportunities exist, in attending the theater, art galleries, or public lectures. Their lives revolve on the whole about the activities of the small social world of their class. Usually they belong to numerous clubs that engage in card-playing, eating, and gossip. In fact, the social life of the more conservative elements is little more than a dull routine of card parties. However, among the younger elements who still restrict their leisure to the Negro world, the dullness of their lives is relieved by dances, periodic alcoholic sprees, and gambling.

Homeownership is one aspect of middle-class standards of consumption that makes for stability in family life. Although in many cases the middle-class families spend beyond their means on their homes, which are often "show places," this is partly due to the fact that, when they seek decent homes, they are forced to inherit the homes of the wealthier white middle class. Of 1,775 college students studied by Caliver, 78 per cent said that their parents owned or were buying their homes. However, a larger percentage of middle-class families represented by the students owned their homes than the families of the lower occupational classes. Ninety-three per cent of the families of students whose fathers were in business owned their homes; 85 per cent of those in professional occupations; 83 per cent of those in clerical occupations; and only 68 per cent of the unskilled. As we have seen in the Negro community in Chicago, homeownership was highest—29.8 per cent—in the zone where a third of the men were engaged in middle-class occupations.

The property relations of the middle class embrace more than ownership of homes. This partly accounts for the fact that, on the whole, the economic outlook of the middle class is conservative. As Woodson has shown in his study, not only a large percentage of the lawyers but a large proportion of the physicians are engaged in business in addition to their professional duties. About 40 per cent of the physicians were connected with various kinds of business enterprises, in some cases their business activities being their major interests. The conservative attitude of the physicians is shown by the fact that a discussion of socialized medicine is strictly outlawed in some local Negro medical societies. Although this attitude is partly due to the influence of the more prosperous members of the profession, this attitude is shared largely by the less prosperous members who hope by some means to increase their incomes. Only during the depression, when a goodly number of the younger Negro physicians were forced to seek relief, did there develop among a relatively few members of the profession a receptive attitude toward socialized medicine. But, on the whole, professional men and women and the small businessmen with whom they are allied array themselves with the conservative forces in the community. In the South they have been allied with the skeleton of the Republican party organization, and in the North they have joined with whichever of the older political organizations has most to offer in terms of concrete rewards. This is especially true of the Negro lawyer who engages in business more frequently than the physician and utilizes his political connections as a means of increasing his income.

In the South, where the Negro middle class is less differentiated, it is even more conservative, on the whole, than in the North. A young Negro minister was warned by a businessman who was a large contributor to the church attended by the middle class in a southern city not to make any reference in his sermon to the fact that he had been in Russia and to avoid letting anyone know that he had been there. The businessman explained to the young minister that they were capitalists and therefore would not tolerate any references to a country that had overthrown capitalism.

This conservatism is due in part to the fact that in the South the middle class is more isolated, and its vested interests are in a rather restricted field. For example, in Durham, North Carolina, where there is a number of comparatively large and old business enterprises whose leaders have exercised considerable control in the Negro community, one finds an extremely conservative middle class. These enterprises are controlled by members of the second generation of families that have been connected with these institutions since their foundation. And the third generation has already begun to find employment in them. The younger generation has taken over not only the technique but the psychology of the modern businessman. Their efforts are directed not only toward maintaining certain standards of living but toward expanding their businesses and invading new fields. They support the same theories of government and morality as the white middle class. Their pleasures are the pleasures of tired businessmen who do not know how to enjoy life. They are leading laymen in the churches and help to support schools and charities. Middle-class respectability is their ideal—an ideal that reflects in a large measure their assimilation of American standards of behavior.

Although the middle class is probably on the whole the most race-conscious element in the Negro group, the more conservative elements are not eager to see the walls of segregation broken down unless it will improve their own status. Many of the conservative elements in the middle class are opposed to the indiscriminate admission of Negroes—the less respectable workers—into public places on equal terms with the whites. This sentiment was expressed by a colored newspaper editor who remarked to a white man that "the white people draw the line at the wrong point and put all of us in the same class." Moreover, behind the walls of racial segregation, where they enjoy a sheltered and relatively secure position in relation to the lower economic classes, they look with misgivings upon a world where they must compete with whites for a position in the economic order and struggle for status. Hence, much of their racial pride is bound up with their desire to monopolize the Negro market. They prefer the overvaluation of their achievements and position behind the walls of segregation to a democratic order that would result in economic and social devaluation for themselves.

Professor W. Lloyd Warner in an article entitled "American Caste and Class," *American Journal of Sociology,* XLII, 237, says that, because of the fact that the Negro forms a subordinate caste in the South, many of the members of the upper (middle) class are unstable and are always "off balance." This, he feels, is probably due to the fact that they "are constantly attempting to achieve an equilibrium which their society, except under extraordinary circumstances, does not provide for them." It appears to the present writer that this is an untenable hypothesis and that a study of Negro communities reveals that the reverse is true. The members of the Negro upper (middle) class achieve on the whole "an equilibrium" within their own society. A relatively few intellectuals may constantly be in conflict with caste restrictions, but they are usually severely censured by the middle class. It is in the North where the status of the members of the middle class is not fixed and where they do not enjoy a privileged position behind the walls of racial segregation that one may find considerable instability in personality organization.

Middle-class Negro families reflect in their organization and behavior the diverse economic and social backgrounds in which they are rooted. This may be seen first in the various patterns of relationship between husbands and wives. In the economically better-situated families the woman generally depends upon her husband's support, especially if she comes from one of the old mulatto families in which it is traditional for the wife not to work. Moreover, this is especially true in the South, where leisure on the part of the woman is more or less a sign of superior social status among middle-class Negroes. An analysis of families in Charleston, Birmingham, and Nashville, taken from the federal census for 1920, showed that in each city a larger percentage of the mulatto wives than of the black wives were not gainfully employed. The difference between the two groups was small in Birmingham, where large numbers of Negro workers are engaged in industrial occupations. We have seen that in the seventh zone of the Negro community in Chicago, where the middle-class families were concentrated, only a third of the married women were employed and that a third of the employed women were engaged in the white-collar and professional occupations. Dr. Herskovits found in his study of New York Negroes that the wives of the small businessmen, foremen, and minor officials in government services, did not work.[6] However, a check of sixty-five families who are members of the exclusive social clubs in Washington, D.C., revealed that forty-nine of the wives were employed. It appears that middle-class wives work more frequently in border and northern cities where there are opportunities for desirable employment and that they are motivated by the desire to supplement their husbands' income in order to maintain certain standards of consumption.

Although the woman's economic role in the family determines, on the whole, her status in the family or marriage group, there are other factors that help to influence her position. In the South, especially among the conservative middle-class families, the economically dependent wife is, on the whole, subordinate to her husband who generally desires that his wife show strict regard for conventional standards of conduct. He, himself, somewhat in the spirit of the southern gentleman, may enjoy considerable freedom and in some cases may even have outside affairs. These affairs are excused so long as they do not become a public scandal and thereby threaten the integrity of the family. He is usually so strict a censor of his wife's conduct that he will not permit her to smoke; and he would consider himself a liberal if he permitted her to indulge in smoking in the privacy of their home. Such attitudes are responsible for the hypocrisy and the extreme emphasis upon respectability which one often finds in the middle class. On the other hand, despite her economic dependence, the wife may have a dominant position in the family because traditionally the Negro woman has played an important role in family relations. Moreover, sometimes in the very families where the mulatto wife of a successful business or professional man is merely an object of pleasure and display, the husband may be a slave to her whims and extravagances. Among

[6] Melville J. Herskovits, *The American Negro* (New York, 1928), p. 56.

this group often the highest compliment that is paid a husband is that he is "her veritable slave and worships his wife." Then, too, in the North, where a successful black man has signalized his achievements by marrying a mulatto woman, he may be regarded as not considerate of his wife if he goes places with her where she otherwise might be taken for white. On the other hand, we may find middle-class wives who are economically the mainstay of their families submitting to extreme domination by their husbands. Where such is the case, there is usually an excess of middle-class women who are willing to pay this price in order to have a husband who belongs to the professional or business class.

Because of the fact that a large proportion of the middle class are salaried persons and there are few or no children in the families, relations between husband and wife, especially where both are employed, tend to be equalitarian, and a spirit of comradeship exists. This tendency is growing as occupational differentiation increases and the various occupational groups develop their own patterns of behavior and thus free themselves from standards set by the few wealthier members of the middle class. On the other hand, there is a fringe on the middle class—generally childless couples—whose behavior approaches a bohemian mode of life. Husband and wife, both of whom are employed, not only enjoy the same freedom in their outside associations and activities but, because of their so-called "sophistication," indulge in outside sexual relations. Although these people usually boast of their emancipation form traditional morality, it often appears that their actions are not based upon deep convictions. Their behavior is doubtless due to imitation and suggestion that play such an important role in the world of the city.

Available figures on the size of the middle-class families indicate that there are relatively few children in these families. However, when the 1910 census figures on children born and living in families in Charleston, Nashville, and Birmingham were analyzed according to occupational classes, there were no significant differences between the various occupations. It is probable that at that time the fundamental economic and cultural differences in the Negro population coincided more nearly with the color divisions in the Negro population, and variations in the number of children were more a matter of survival than of voluntary restriction of families on the part of the upper or mulatto class. For example, it was found that, although mulattoes had only a slightly smaller proportion of families with no children born than blacks and both groups had the same average number of children born, a larger percentage of the black families in Charleston and Birmingham had lost one or more children than mulatto families. Since the blacks had lost on the average one more child than the mulatto families in Nashville, where the same proportion of families in both groups had lost children, there was in Nashville as well as in the two other cities a larger number of children on the average in mulatto families than in black families. On the other hand, twenty years ago, when Professor Kelly Miller made a study of the families of fifty-five colored faculty members at Howard University, he found that, whereas they came from families averaging 6.3 children, they themselves had on the average only 1.6 children. Practically the same average was found in 1933 for seventeen colored faculty members at Fisk University, where the average was 1.5 children per family. A comparison of the number of children in the families from which 327 persons listed in *Who's Who in Colored America: 1928–29* came, with the number of children of 174 of those who were forty-five years of age and over, showed that the entire group came from families averaging 5.5 children, whereas the 174 families had only 2.3 children per family. In the spring of 1937 the writer made a study of the colored faculty members at Howard University similar to that made by Professor Miller. The 114 teachers replying to a questionnaire came from families averaging 5.1 children; whereas they themselves had on the average only 0.8 child. If we consider only those teachers who had been married ten years or more, the average was 1.1 children per family. It is important to point out that about 60 per cent of those replying indicated that they had voluntarily restricted the size of their families.

In Woodson's study of the Negro professional man, he found that 85 per cent of the physicians were married and that 87.9 per cent of those married had had children. Of those having had children, only 31.9 per cent had children living. About a fourth of those with children living had one child; 22.6 per cent, two children; 10 per cent, three; 6.7 per cent, four; and 1.8 per cent, five. About five-sixths of the lawyers reported themselves as married, and 54.7 per cent of those married reported that they had children living. Of those with children, 17.2 per cent had one child; 19.2 per cent, two children; 11.4 per cent, three; 3.6 per cent, four; and 0.5 per cent, five children. In the sixty-five families referred to above as members of the Washington colored élite, it was found that in thirty-six of the sixty-five families, there were no children and that there was a total of only forty-three children, or less than 0.7 of a child per family. Fourteen of the twenty-nine families with children had two children each and the remaining fifteen families one child each. Although some of these families were probably not completed families, the couples had all been married eight years or more.

When one considers the treatment of children in middle-class families, the observation made by Park thirty-five years ago that "where the children are few, they are usually spoiled" holds today. This is especially true of the comparatively well-to-do families in which the indulgence of the children's whims and extravagances is tied up with their desire for conspicuous consumption. It is not uncommon to find college students from middle-class families boasting of their parents' fine homes and expensive cars and vying with one another in expending money on clothes and other forms of conspicuous consumption. In fact, many of the middle-class Negro families send their sons and especially their daughters to certain Negro colleges where they feel that their children will have contacts with the sons and daughters of middle-class families and enjoy the so-called "cultural" environment of these colleges. Although it is also true that some middle-class families who desire that their children have contacts with whites send their children to the more exclusive white schools, other families, realizing that their children must live largely in the Negro world, send them to the Negro colleges that have middle-class traditions.

In fact, since education is the chief means by which the Negro escapes from the masses into the middle class, it is not surprising that the colleges uphold middle-class traditions. Of course, this is not the only reason, since privately supported colleges draw their incomes from the philanthropy of wealthy whites. But the very atmosphere of Negro colleges breathes the spirit and aspirations of the Negro middle class. In the very college where the middle-class aspirations were formulated and published abroad in 1898, there has been established a chair with the specific aim of training business leaders for a segregated Negro economy. It is hoped by this means to foster the spirit of business enterprise and overcome the handicap which Negro college men and women experience in being excluded from apprenticeship in white business establishments. However, middle-class ideals are inculcated in more subtle ways. For example, Negro colleges give little attention to plays dealing with Negro folk life but place much emphasis upon plays which appeal to middle-class whites and provide fashion shows from time to time in which middle-class standards of consumption are held up for emulation. So deeply are middle-class attitudes ingrained in Negro college students that some of these future members of the brown middle class regretted that the Scottsboro boys were poor and black and expressed the opinion that the predicament in which the Scottsboro boys found themselves could not possibly be the fate of "cultured" Negroes.

The vast majority of Negro college students, those from the lower occupational classes as well as those from middle-class homes, aspire to enter middle-class occupations. Studies of the vocational choices of Negro college students indicate that the majority of them plan to enter the teaching profession. In the vocational choices of Negro college students and the occupations which they enter, one can detect the cause of the "softness" of the Negro middle class. In the middle-class atmosphere of the Negro college, the students coming from working-class homes lose their stamina and often prefer any kind of charity that will enable them to ape the middle-class students to making their way through toil. The boys from middle-class families are often as spoiled as their sisters. When they reach college, they regard educational discipline chiefly as a means of preparing themselves for such salaried positions as teaching or social work where in either case their incomes may be derived from the community or philanthropy. Thus, because of their family background and education, they are unfitted for life in a world of competition. In fact, it generally turns out that they are more or less excluded from the competition of the world at large. Hence, their "softness" and sentimental outlook on life reflects the security which they find in occupations the incomes of which come from the state or philanthropy.

The future of the Negro middle class will depend, of course, upon the role of this class in American economic life. There are no grounds for the belief that this class will find a secure economic base in a segregated economy with its Negro captains of industry, managers, technical assistants, and white-collar workers. However, it seems that this class will increase mainly through the entrance of Negroes into white-collar occupations, especially wherever the number of such occupations is increased by an extension of municipal or state functions, and the Negro is permitted to compete on equal terms with whites. In fact, the Negro middle class is increasing in the very northern cities where Negroes are permitted through political power to compete with other races for positions under state control. Hence, the Negro middle class is becoming almost entirely a class of professional and white-collar workers. As racial barriers break down, the Negro middle class will become assimilated with the salaried workers in the community. Consequently, they will cease to think of themselves as a privileged and "wealthy" upper Negro class and will regard themselves as other intellectual workers. Their standards of consumption and the character of their family life will reflect these changes in status and outlook on life. The democracy which is apparent in the relations of a growing number of married men and women who earn their living will become the rule in this group of workers.

CHAPTER XXI

THE BLACK
PROLETARIAT

Whsen the brown middle class was becoming articulate during the last decade of the past century, there were widespread misgivings concerning the future of the black worker in American economic life. In fact, the Negro leaders who proposed the development of a segregated Negro economy justified their program partly on the assumption that Negro enterprises would secure the employment of black workers. In the South, where at the close of the Civil War a hundred thousand black mechanics outnumbered white mechanics five to one, by 1890 Negro artisans had as a result of white competition and trade-union exclusion lost their once secure position in southern industry.[1] In the North the black worker was confined to domestic and personal service, and his appearance in industry from time to time was generally in the role of a strike-breaker. It was not until the first World War that the black worker secured a footing in the industries of the North.

For the entire period from 1890 to 1920 the proportion of black workers in the crafts remained practically constant in the South. However, in the North, where the Negro population had increased during the war, the black worker had by 1920 made significant gains in industry. In securing a foothold in northern industry, the Negro worker not only had to meet the prejudice of white workers and to overcome the employers' preconceptions concerning his efficiency but he also had to adapt himself to the discipline of modern industry.

[1] Sterling D. Spero and Abram L. Harris, *The Black Worker* (New York, 1931), pp. 32-33 and 159-60.

His success in overcoming the preconceptions of the employers was due to the fact that they found in the black industrial reserve a reliable labor supply. According to the general testimony of employers, the workers have gradually adjusted themselves to the discipline of modern industry. Even in the South, where caste sentiment restricts the competition and the mixing of black and white workers, economic forces inevitably tend to throw workers of the two races into competition.

We have already seen to what extent occupational differentiation had progressed by 1920 in fifteen cities. We shall consider briefly the size of the occupational classes which comprised roughly the black proletariat of eleven cities with 100,000 or more Negroes in 1940, and Louisville. In Atlanta a fourth of the employed Negro men were engaged in common labor; while in Birmingham, Memphis, and New Orleans about a third of the employed Negro men were so employed. Only two and a half to five per cent of employed Negro men were in domestic service. In Atlanta three out of ten employed Negro men were in service occupations, i.e., employed as porters, elevator operators, et cetera, while in the other three cities 14 to 20 per cent were employed in such occupations. Between a fifth and a fourth of employed Negro men in Atlanta, Memphis, and New Orleans were engaged in semi-skilled industrial occupations; while in Birmingham a third were so employed. In all four cities only from 9 to 10 per cent of the employed Negro men were in skilled occupations. In the four border cities—Baltimore, Washington, D. C., St. Louis, Missouri, and Louisville, Kentucky—the occupational status of Negro men was very similar to that in southern cities. In fact, in Baltimore 43 per cent of the employed Negro men were engaged in common labor; and in all four border cities a smaller proportion of employed Negro men—five to six per cent—were employed in skilled occupations. On the other hand, in the four northern cities the employed Negro men were better off than in the southern cities. In New York City only 13 per cent of them were engaged in common labor. Only from one to three per cent of the employed Negro men were in domestic service; while about the same proportion as in southern and border cities were in service occupations. In New York City, Chicago, and Philadelphia, a fifth of employed Negro men were in semi-skilled industrial occupations, while nearly 30 per cent were engaged in similar occupations in Detroit. The first three cities had about the same proportion of employed Negro men in skilled occupations as southern and border cities, but in Detroit nearly a seventh of the employed Negro men had acquired the status of skilled workmen.

From the standpoint of general culture, patterns of behavior, and outlook on life, Negro workers in domestic and service occupations are by no means a homogeneous group. In the past, many of the old established families of free ancestry as well as the cruder elements from the plantation depended upon this type of employment. A large section of the present middle class has its roots in this same class of workers. Both during slavery and after emancipation it was through domestic and personal service that the Negro was brought into intimate contacts with the white race and was thereby able to take over elements of white civilization. Of course, such contacts often resulted in crude and bizarre imitations of white culture; but, where Negroes were employed over long periods, some times several generations, in the white families of culture, they unconsciously assimilated white ideals and standards of behavior. Moreover, when within their own families and within their more or less exclusive community life these ideals and patterns of behavior became a part of their traditions, they were supported by sentiment and acquired significance in their lives. However, the elements in the Negro population with such a background have rapidly risen, especially through education, into the middle class. Other elements in the Negro population have taken their places. In fact, each successive wave of migrants from the farms and plantations of the South brings workers seeking employment in domestic and service occupations into the urban environment.

Consequently, one finds in domestic and service occupations today Negroes with a solid background of civilized behavior and a high degree of intelligence as well as the illiterate and crude field hand with a plantation background. Usually the cruder and less efficient workers have been employed at a dollar or two a week by the poorer whites in the South. On the other hand, the more competent and more civilized reflect the discipline and influence of their contacts with the cultured whites. In a study of domestic workers in Washington, D.C., it was found that 30 per cent of the female applicants for domestic service had seventh- or eighth-grade education.[2] There were also among the 9,976 applicants for the academic years 1920-22, 17 male and 159 female students who had attended high school; 75 female normal-school students; 13 male and 126 female college students. However, it appears that, as a rule, Negroes who have obtained a high-school education do not enter domestic service but use it as a means of completing their education. The older workers in domestic and service occupations who have some background of culture and stable family life are often identified with the institutions supported by the middle class. For example, in Nashville, among 32 male members of a small Congregational church attended mainly by persons of middle-class status, there were 3 members engaged in domestic service. These families undertake to maintain middle-class standards and endeavor to fit their children for middle-class occupations. Caliver found in his study of 1,877 Negro college students that 191, or 10 per cent, came from families in which the fathers were engaged in domestic and service occupations.[3] But the vast majority of the more stable domestic workers with the cultural background of the Negro folk attend institutions and live on a plane more suited to their small earnings.

On the other hand, the less stable elements lead an existence in which the faults of the gentleman and the peasant find expression. They are improvident, and their behavior is governed by imitation and suggestion. Since many of them see white people only during their leisure, their behavior often shows the influence of the "sporting complex." Thus, the less stable as well as the better-situated workers in domestic and service occupations seldom have a real working-class consciousness. It has only been in northern cities where their relations

[2] Elizabeth R. Haynes, "Negroes in Domestic Service in the United States," *Journal of Negro History*, VIII, 400-401.

[3] Ambrose Caliver, *A Background Study of Negro College Students* (Washington, 1933), p. 68.

with their employers have been more impersonal that they have been disposed to identify themselves with industrial workers.

Although a large proportion of the black semiskilled workers and laborers come from the same rural background as the domestic workers, they are, on the whole, cruder than the domestic worker. But, on the other hand, the more stable and especially the organized unskilled workers are more likely to think of themselves as workers and are less disposed to imitate the behavior of middle-class whites. Especially is this true of the great body of black longshoremen who have had a long history of unionism and have exhibited considerable working-class solidarity. Likewise, among miners and steel and stock-yards workers, the development of working-class consciousness has been influenced by their experiences in industrial struggles, including, of course, co-operation with white workers. But certain influences in the Negro community itself tend to perpetuate, even among in-dustrial workers, a middle-class outlook. For example, in the churches and schools, Negro leaders often hold up to black workers middle-class ideals and conceptions of life and thus influence to some extent their allegiance to the working class and their valuations.

The difference in outlook between many Negro workers in domestic and service occupations and the black artisan or industrial worker whose conceptions of life and behavior have been fashioned by working-class traditions is shown in the following document:

> At that time, father had become the outstanding stone mason and bricklayer of the town, surpassing even Bill S—— [white] from whom he "stole" his trade. On excursions father would take us to the houses he was building and to the bridges that were in process of construction and my youngest sister and I would be awestruck with the wonder of it all. Dad would allow us to climb in and about the houses and he would show us how to mix mortar, handle the trowels, etc. I remember how he used to love his tools and when folks would come to the house to borrow them, we wouldn't let anyone have them.
>
> So it was very early that we acquired a deep and abiding respect for the people of the working class because we were and are part and parcel of them. We were taught early by both our parents to respect personality as it showed itself through constructive labor. The men who worked for Dad, the mechanics as well as the laborers, we thought of as constructive forces in the community. It was probably because

of these ideas that we regarded with pride all the male members of the family.

The standard set by the Negro leaders in the community was, we thought, false. The inclination was to set on a pinnacle the Negroes who were of the professional class. There weren't many, very few in fact, and probably because of this rarity was there much abject worship. You see, father and my uncles were all rated throughout as expert workmen and mother, who had learned the trade of hairdresser (that is the manufacture of hair ornaments), had enjoyed the reputation of the best worker in the finest shop in Pittsburgh, in her time. That was before her marriage. Everything my father and mother did helped to confirm our judgment that the people of the professional class were only a different kind of skilled worker and respect for them and their opinion came to being only in so far as they were masters of their trade.

Because our family on mother's side of the household was very well known and respected, our relationship with the elite of the white group was casual and usual. But, although we were often in the homes of the most wealthy, mother took care that our house while comfortably furnished, was in keeping with our economic status. It was simply but tastefully furnished. This was quite different from the standards prevailing among our Negro friends, who thought we were queer because we didn't imitate the houses of the wealthy in point of view of appointments. They also thought we were queer because we dressed in ginghams and percales and wore flat but well made shoes and lisle stockings. I thought the G—— girls [wealthy white girls] very beautifully dressed, but there never was any envy in this admiration for mother had always taught us that the important thing was to "dress within our means" and to look "clean" and "tidy." Even our Sunday clothes were simple and very often I have had to say when I was twitted about my simple clothes, "Well, anyway my father is an expert mechanic and yours is nothing but a servant for white people," or "I am sure I look as well in my ginghams as you look in satin." These statements always ended the arguments.

We did have a piano—and a very good one because mother thought that there should be entertainment in the house and she believed in the cultural influences of music. While many colored people had big houses, expensively furnished, we were the only "colored" children who belonged to the private library. There was no public one and mother had to pay for cards. We always had three cards, one for each two of us. As to politics, I can remember only that father thought a man was a good candidate if he sympathized with the aims and aspirations of the working class group. I remember him voting against

J—— for mayor because he owned the H—— Coal Mine and didn't allow the union to enter and forced the employees to buy at the company store. Discussions outside of the house between father and his friends, who were mainly white mechanics, we listened to and I believe my interest in the proletariat was generated in these early years.

We have often laughed at what mother called the "antics" of the J——'s. They had recently become wealthy and I suppose their emulation, inaccurate as it was, of the old wealthy group reminded us of the same sort of thing among the Negro working class. Their striving, we thought ridiculous and somehow we always knew when Mrs. J—— was "trying to get in" with the D——'s [the élite] or changing her house furnishings to look like theirs. We always knew, too, that Mrs. S——, the Negro barber's wife, was dressing well to look like A—— D——, and was buying curtains "exactly like the G——'s." Our home, although distinctive, was much like that of father's friends. We had books and magazines, and games like the W——'s and the atmosphere of the home in no way bespoke emulation of the wealthy.

Although this document is representative of only a comparatively small group of skilled black workers, it is indicative of the process by which this class is attaining working-class ideals and traditions.

Before considering the family life of the black worker, let us pause to see how he is housed. In southern cities one can easily recognize the areas inhabited by the black working class. For example, in Lynchburg, Virginia, it was found that 60 per cent of the Negro families lived on dirt streets and 78 per cent on streets with dirt sidewalks.[4] As to the living conditions in the unsubstantial and weather-beaten frame houses on these streets, we can get some idea from the fact that 63 per cent of the families lived in homes that were not more than half-heated. Although the median number of rooms per colored family was three, the median number of bedrooms was two. Consequently, it is not surprising that, in a fourth of the families, bedrooms were also used for living-rooms, and in about 45 per cent of the families these rooms served the double function of bedroom and laundry. In only about a fifth of the families were the bedrooms used exclusively for sleeping.

[4] Benjamin Guy Childs, *The Negroes of Lynchburg, Virginia* ("Publications of the University of Virginia" (Charlottesville, Va., 1923), pp. 39-40.

The housing of the black worker in the city is, of course, tied up with his general economic and cultural status. This becomes apparent when one studies the residence of black workers in relation to the organization of the Negro community. For example, in Chicago it was found that, in the detiorated section of the Negro community where the migrants from the South settled, 56 per cent of the employed males were common laborers; 12.4 per cent, semiskilled workers; and 17.7 per cent, in domestic service. In the report on the Negro following the race riots of 1919, the description of the houses in this area was given as follows:

> With the exception of two or three the houses are frame, and paint with them is a dim reminiscence. There is one rather modern seven-room flat building of stone front, the flats renting at $22.50 a month and offering the best in the way of accommodations to be found there. There is another makeshift flat building situated above a saloon and pool hall, consisting of six six-room flats, renting at $12 per month, but in a very poor condition of repair. Toilets and baths were found to be in no condition for use and the plumbing in such a state as to constantly menace health. Practically all of the houses have been so reconstructed as to serve as flats, accommodating two and sometimes three families. As a rule there are four, five and sometimes six rooms in each flat, there being but five instances when there were more than six. It is often the case that of these rooms not all can be used because of dampness, leaking roofs, or defective toilets overhead.[5]

In the next zone, where the houses were slightly better, there was an increase in the proportion of skilled workers in the working population. In fact, the proportion of common laborers declined regularly in the successive zones which marked the expansion of the Negro population and on the whole increasing improvement in housing facilities. In the seventh zone, which was primarily a middle-class area, only a seventh of the workers were laborers. This was the same as the proportion of skilled workers in the population of this area.

But, despite the selection which fixes the abode of black workers in the Negro community on the basis of the economic and social

[5] Chicago Commission on Race Relations, *The Negro in Chicago* (Chicago, 1922), pp. 185-86.

status, their homes even in better areas are usually unsuited to their incomes and unfavorable to normal family life. When black workers seek better living-quarters, they are compelled to occupy houses or apartments that were built for middle-class white families, and, because of the competition for housing quarters within the Negro community, they are forced to pay higher rentals than the former white occupants. That such is the case has been shown in a number of studies. For example, Reid found in a study of 2,326 Negro families in Harlem that in some cases the rentals charged Negro tenants when they moved into apartments vacated by whites amounted to almost a 100 per cent increase over what the whites had paid. As a result, 48 per cent of the Negro tenants were paying more than 40 per cent of their monthly earnings in rentals. These findings were similar to the findings in a study of West Harlem, where Negro tenants paid nearly a third of their income as compared with approximately a fifth of the tenants' income for the whole city. The typical annual income for this section was $1,300, of which $480 went for rent.[6]

In order to pay these exorbitant rents, the black worker is generally forced to take in roomers. Reid found 3,314 lodgers in the 2,326 apartments which he studied. A study of 100 migrant families in Philadelphia, almost all of whom were workers, showed that 24 of the families supplemented their incomes by rentals from lodgers. In a more comprehensive study, including every tenth 1920 federal census family in Chicago, Miss Graham found that, out of 3,339 families, 2,361 possibly had some additional source of income. Of these 2,361 families, 824 were keeping roomers, 294 had relatives employed, and 1,611 were sharing their homes. As many as 350 of these families secured incomes from at least two of these sources.

In the organization and life of the black worker's family, one can see the influence of these various economic and social forces. Already we have seen to what extent workers' families in cities are dependent solely upon the mother for support. Negro families that

[6] Carey Batchelor, *What the Tenement Family Has and What It Pays for It: A Study of 1,014 Tenement Families Showing Income, Rent and Housing Conditions* (New York: United Neighborhood Clubs, 1928).

are broken through desertion are not only almost entirely working-class families but seemingly come more frequently from the unskilled and common laborers. For example, during the fiscal year 1930-31, out of 129 desertion cases handled by the Charity Organization Society in which the occupation of the husband was given, 45, including 11 chauffeurs, were in domestic service and another 45 were employed in unskilled labor. However, various studies indicate that in a large percentage of the families in which the husband is present the women must also assist in the support of the family. Only 33 of the 100 migrant families in Philadelphia, referred to above, depended solely upon the father's earnings. In 52 of these families the mother contributed to the family income. Reid found in his study of 2,326 families in Harlem that 53.5 per cent of the wives were employed and that less than 10 per cent of the employed women added more than twenty dollars per month to the family income. Miss Graham found in her study of Negro families in Chicago that 1,500, or 51.6 per cent, of the 2,904 women heads of families with husbands were employed. Some of the workers' wives who are forced to supplement the earnings of their husbands are engaged in their homes at such work as making lamp shades or artificial flowers. For example, let us take the wife of a steel worker. His wife reported that he had been working irregularly since the preceding September, making about $50 a month. The family, consisting of husband, wife, and a schoolboy of sixteen, lived in a six-room apartment over a store for which they paid a monthly rent of $75. Sometimes they sublet one room; and when they could secure more roomers, they sublet a second room. The wife was earning $15 to $23 a week making parts of artificial flowers. She was working about sixty hours a week in the home on these flowers, and in addition making a commission on work she allowed one of the roomers to do. She had been doing this kind of work for three years and said it was "getting on her nerves," but she could not stop on account of the irregularity of her husband's employment.[7]

It appears from a study of the employment of married Negro

[7] Myra Hill Colson, "Negro Home Workers in Chicago," *Social Service Review,* II, 407.

women in seventy-five northern and southern cities of 100,000 total population or more that the employment of the wives of black workers is dependent upon the extent to which Negro men find employment in industry. By comparing the percentage of Negro married women employed with the proportion of Negro males employed in manufacturing and mechanical industries, it was found that the proportion of married women employed tended to decline as the proportion of Negro males employed in industry increased.

The status of the husband and wife in the black worker's family assumes roughly three patterns. Naturally, among the relatively large percentage of families with women heads, the woman occupies a dominant position. But, because of the traditional role of the black wife as a contributor to the support of the family, she continues to occupy a position of authority and is not completely subordinate to masculine authority even in those families where the man is present. As indicated above, the entrance of the black worker in industry where he has earned comparatively good wages has enabled the black worker's wife to remain at home. Therefore, the authority of the father in the family has been strengthened, and the wife has lost some of her authority in family matters. In fact, among some classes of black workers whose wives are restricted to the home, masculine authority is harsh or even brutal. Wives as well as children are completely subject to the will of the male head. However, especially in southern cities, one may find that the black worker's authority in his family may be challenged by his mother-in-law. In the following document, written by a woman who worked her way through college, one can get an idea of the conflict which often arises when the husband opposes his authority to the traditional authority of the wife's mother in the family. This document also throws light on the conflict which even may be found in workers' families between the mulattoes and the Negroes of unmixed blood:

> My mother and father were in high school when they became infatuated with each other and ran away. Before they had a chance to marry, my grandmother located my mother, and both my grandfather and grandmother persuaded her against marrying him. My grandfather argued that he had no profession other than wanting to be a

preacher. He prophesied that he would never be a good preacher and never would have anything. My grandmother argued that he didn't have anything, never would have anything, that nothing was known of his family and beside that, he was a black man. Mama would not listen to any of this. She said that she would run away from any school to which they sent her if they would not permit her to get married.

My grandmother and father gave her a very expensive church wedding in the same church in S. where we are now members. My grandfather would not be present at the reception or the wedding. My mother married my father and went to southern Louisiana to his home. There she found that he was not from the ideal family as she had pictured him being at school. There she found out there were many things about his family of which he never spoke. Mama found that his family did not have the status in the community that hers had in S.; for her father was known as Professor W., her mother was active in community life, church work, clubs, etc. Besides her family was considered one of the old blue blood families of S. and Mama was considered then as one of the most beautiful girls in S. This grieved her very much but as she had gone against the will of her parents she made the best of it. Papa went about his career as an ("unprepared") minister. My mother could never get him to see that pastoring small churches with small pay didn't mean anything. She could not get him to see that if he would complete his trade as a carpenter rather than trying to be a minister he would have more economic stability. Mama often quotes papa as saying, "I know my business; I'm my own boss; I know the Lord has called me to preach." He continued to be sent from one small Methodist church to another.

Of the four girls the other three have perfectly straight and curly hair. Mine is not. I was often referred to as being a duplicate of my father's hair and my mother's figure. My mother is fair, black hair with Jewish facial features. My father is black with typical Negro features. (After I went to live with my aunt), she constantly reminded me that I was the daughter of a trifling black man who cared nothing for his children. She gave me everything nice in the line of clothes, toys, and education, but I resented her speaking of my father as she did. I resolved firmly then that I would always love my father. I realized however, that I was dependent and accepted my lot. Finally, one day I told my aunt that the things she did for me were very nice, but I would like to go to work for myself. Deeply in my mind I resented her doing these things for me and at moments when she was angry she would remind me how dependent I was and would say the most cutting things about my father. She would also say that I was just his image including hair and color. She would not consent for me to go to work.

As my mother did not send me back to my aunt and my sister was well, the three of us decided that something had to be done. We decided that we would rent a house and live independently. The sister next to myself was old enough to go to school and the baby sister was placed in kindergarten. My older sister and I decided to work before and after school while my mother continued to work as ticket agent at a downtown theatre on the colored entrance. During this time my father was still carrying on his career as a preacher in the southern part of Louisiana. We had lost all hopes of his ever coming to us and being a real father. One day when I came home from high school where I was a freshman, I found my father sitting on the porch. I hardly knew him for I had not seen him since I was seven years of age and I was then fourteen years of age.

My grandmother was very discourteous to him, but he ignored it all. When mama came from work the same afternoon she too was surprised to see him. The two younger sisters did not know him at all. My older sister did not express her feeling toward him, one way or the other. Mama immediately told him of her plan to move away from her mother and live alone. He then told his plan. He had saved enough money to start buying a home. He said that he had laid preaching aside and was going to live permanently in S. if she wanted to, or, if she did not want to live with him, he would take the children with him. Mama decided that it would be better that both mother and father have us. She stopped her mother from meddling in our family affairs.

My father has about completed paying for his home now in S. Mama does not work at all. Both the younger sisters are in school. One is now in the eighth grade and the older sister in the sixth. My oldest sister has been married but her husband is now dead. She has her own home which was given to her by her husband's people. She has two children five and seven years of age. She is a graduate of the high school in S. Her highest ambition is to educate her children and help me educate our two younger sisters as well as help me to look after mama and papa when they become unable to look after themselves.

As my father was so late in settling down in life, his responsibilities were too heavy for him to do anything toward giving me a college education, although it was his greatest desire that I have one. From the time that I lived with my aunt until the present time I have realized what it means to be dependent. As I have already been thrown on my own resources at an early date, I did not dread working my way through college. I have observed that my father did not take advice nor prepare for the future as he should have done, but, I am attempting to profit by his mistake. At the present time my home is on a fairly normal basis. Both mama and papa are active in their churches. Papa is now lumber foreman at a lumber mill in S. Our status in the community is that of ordinary church-going people. Among the older families and best circles my sister and I are spoken of as Mrs. X——'s [grandmother] granddaughters.

The following excerpts from the history of a laborer's family, furnished by his son, shows the important role of the wife even in those worker's families where the father is the acknowledged head and has a fundamental interest in his family:

At the time of my parents' marriage, my father was only a laborer in the town and he never advanced beyond this stage. My mother was a cook and washwoman. My father had left his father's farm as soon as he reached manhood; my mother had left the farm at the age of 17. I do not know the circumstances under which my parents first met. A little more than a year after their marriage their first child, a son, was born. On December 20, 1901, the first daughter and second child made her appearance. In 1904, March 2, our brother joined, and in 1907 a second daughter was born. Five years later, the fifth and last child was born, but she lived only three days.

From 1899 to 1914, my parents lived in the same three room house about three blocks from the railway station in a town of about 1,500 people. In 1912 my mother who was the more thrifty, and the business manager of the family, bought four lots in a new section of the town in which the new school for Negroes was to be built. She employed a Negro contractor to draw a plan for a house of 5 rooms and a hall. When this was done, mother bought the lumber. At our request my brother and I were employed by the contractor to work for him in the construction of the building. During our employment the contractor taught us much about carpentry. After the construction of the house had been completed my brother and I, realizing that a well had to be dug, requested Mother to allow us to dig as much of it as we could. This she permitted. For our labor she gave us (together) 50¢ a foot. We dug until we struck water, and then the job was turned over to a professional well-digger, who finished it.

In 1914, we moved into the new house, where my parents lived until their deaths in 1927. For 22 years, 1899 to 1921, my father worked regularly as a laborer for two families, a physician's and a merchant's. His weekly wages from the two families ranged from

$6.00 to $10.00. For about the same time my mother cooked out and took in washing, receiving for her labor from $3.00 to $10.00 per week. As soon as we children became old enough we (boys as well as girls) did as much of the washing and ironing as we could. The training I gained enabled me to spend 7½ years in boarding school and spend only $3.65 for laundry during that time. At the age of ten I was hired out to a family to be the companion and guardian at play of their three little sons. For 4 years, before and after school hours, and in the summer I worked for this family, receiving $1.75 plus meals per week. From April, 1914, to October, 1915, I was cook at the local hotel. From that time until August, 1916, I worked on the farm of a white man, receiving per month $13.00 and the mid-day meals. The other children were never hired out, except to pick cotton.

As soon as each child reached 10 years of age he was allowed to keep a portion of what he earned during each week. As he grew older and his earnings increased, the percentage he received increased. Each child deposited his savings in his own name in the local bank. By August, 1916, I had saved $69.00, and had bought enough clothes to last me the school term of 1916-17, my first year in boarding school. Mother taught us how to plan our spending, how to make choices when our money was scarce, and the value of keeping on hand what she called an "emergency sum."

Although mother did most of the planning for the family, my father's task was to buy the food and fuel, look after the chickens, garden and potato patch, keep up the premises, and provide medical care. It was mother's duty to look after the children's clothes, pay the taxes and insurance, buy the furniture and other household articles, and look after the schooling of the children. Although there was this general division of responsibility, there was mutual interest in each other's tasks and cooperation in meeting obligations when necessary and expedient. In the home each child had specific duties, but all of us were taught to cook, sew, quilt, mend clothes, wash and iron, and buy a week's supply of groceries.

My father was a very quick-tempered man, so he left most of the disciplining of the children to mother. Frequently, mother would gather us about her and talk to us, advise us how to get along in the world, and urge us above everything else to be fair to our fellowmen, and respect their rights. A kindly woman, gentle and sympathetic, my mother hated a quarrel and never, to my knowledge, engaged in vulgar gossip in the presence of her children. She was an advocate of patience and tolerance, and often said, "It is better for you to suffer unjustly than to cause another to suffer; rather than wrong another, run the risk of being wronged."

Contrary to popular opinion, there are, on the whole, relatively few children in the families of black workers, though, as we have seen, the number varies according to residence. In the 100 migrant families studied in Philadelphia, there were only 1.73 children on the average to the family and in over a fourth of the families there were no children. This was practically the same as the average for the 1,576 families in Harlem, in which there was an average of 1.8 children per family. In 268 of these Harlem families there were no children; and in 448, only one child. In the study of every tenth census family in Chicago there was on the average only one child per family. However, 60 per cent of the 2,930 married male heads of families had no dependent children; 29.9 per cent had one or two children; 5.2 per cent, three children; and only 149, or 5.1 per cent, more than three children.[8] These findings are similar to the author's which showed that there were actually slightly more children under fifteen years of age to women of childbearing age in the seventh zone, where middle-class families were concentrated, than in the first and second zones, occupied chiefly by workers' families of southern origin.

The treatment of children in workers' families is influenced by both economic and social factors. For example, the neglect of children among this class results in part from the fact that a large proportion of the mothers are employed. According to reports from 374 working mothers in Harlem, 129 left their children with relatives or friends; 56 left their children to take care of themselves; 41 left their children at home; and 80 instructed their children to remain around the school or in the streets or to go to the library. In the Chicago sample, 23.2 per cent of the women in families with children under fourteen years of age were employed outside the home. But, since some of these families were parts of composite households, it is probable that a third of the children had the supervision of a woman during the absence of the mother. Of course, the neglect of children is not due entirely to economic causes. Among the less stable and more primitive workers, the ill-treatment accorded children results from

[8] Clyde V. Kiser, "Birth Rates and Socio-economic Attributes in 1935," *Milbank Memorial Fund Quarterly*, XVII (April, 1939), 136-41.

the disorganization of the Negro in the city. But, even among some of the poorest families, the mother's whole affectional life may be centered upon a son or daughter. In fact, her attitude often presents a striking contrast to that of the father. But the children of the workers are seldom as spoiled as the children in middle-class families. In fact, it is in those well-organized workers' families where the entire family is working in order to purchase a home or that their children may obtain an education that one finds a spirit of democracy in family relations and a spirit of self-reliance on the part of the children. In the following document, written by the daughter of a mechanic, one can get a good picture of the character of the stable family among the better-situated skilled workers:

> My Mother and my Father began their married life in Savannah, Ga., in 1910. They lived with my Grandfather and Father's four sisters in the big house. Mother did not get along with the sisters as they attempted to look down on her in many ways. She caused Father to start buying a small house of their own, and they moved into it. Grandfather was good to Mother and during those early days of her married life, she learned to care for him. Later when Grandfather came to S—— [a northern city], Mother was able to return his kindness because he lived with us a year. Mother and her sister-in-laws made a bad start which was almost impossible to correct.
>
> Mother found many things which tended to put their marriage on the rocks at the start. Her personality and traditions were so different from Father's. She was a quiet, home loving person with no desires for dances, parties, and good times. But Father was just the opposite in those days, he loved to dance, go to all night parties and run with the fast crowd. He was bored staying home after working hours. Mother used to tear his shirts off of him to keep him home, but he still went. Even after they were married a year he continued to find more pleasure outside the home. I was a baby then. Mother often told how she used to walk the floor many nights with me, while Father was out with his crowd. When she was about to give up and go home to her folks, a great crisis came in Father's life which changed everything for the good.
>
> It was on an Easter morning when Father was converted and was baptized in the Baptist church. He swore then, never to go back to worldly things such as dances, cards, and fast life. He vowed to be a different man, and from that day he was changed. He became a member of B. E. Church, and began to find new friends and

associates. Grandfather said his attitude towards his work in the blacksmith shop was even different. Although Mother was Methodist she joined Father's church for she was determined to make their marriage a success.

Then the war came and Father did not want to be sent over to fight so he decided to move away. Then too the blacksmith business was slowly dying. There was a chance to make money up North, so Father planned to move. When he left, Grandfather gave up his shop and stayed home because he had enough to live off the rest of his life. Father moved to S—— [a northern city] and found work there. He sent for Mother and me. I was only four but I can remember that trip perfectly. We all lived with some friends of Father's for a while, but it was expensive living with them. We rented a small house in a down town section of the city where the Negroes lived. We lived there for five years. Father worked hard and saved his money. Mother made all of my clothes for school because I started school my second year in S——. It used to be very cold there then, and Mother being fresh from the South, thought I would freeze to death, so she used to pile me up with clothes. However, I was never sick a day during those days.

Our family lived down in the Negro section of S——, until Father had the house in Savannah paid for, then we moved up on "the hill," where the better class Negroes lived. Mother and Father joined the small Baptist Church on "the hill," and I went to Sunday School there. By moving up into this new district, I had a better chance in school because there were not half as many Italians and Jews in the new school. There were also fewer colored children and the teachers were far nicer. Father worked hard to keep the family up economically, and Mother did her share in the home to keep things balanced. My family did very little socializing. They went to church socials and parties where the church minister was always present. They never went to dances or card parties, and in fact, Father never bothered about those things after his conversion, and Mother had never cared for them. There was complete oneness between Mother and Father then, just as it is today. When I was a senior in Junior High my brother was born, A.B.C., 3rd. I will never forget how ashamed I was to have a baby brother at that age. A baby spoiled our home for me because Mother could never go anywhere, and we used to be such pals.

A great crisis came to our family in 1926 when Father lost his job as a mechanic which he had with a packing company. He had been with that firm since he first moved to S——. He looked everywhere for work and found none so he decided to go to New York City, and look about. He found work there so he lived with one of his sisters, and sent us money to keep up our expenses in S——. We were still renting a house and Mother managed to pay the rent and live off what Father sent so that we did not have to touch our bank account. Then one night Father was taken desperately ill, so much so that my aunt had him sent to the hospital that very night. He was so ill that the doctors thought he could not tell what was the matter with him. They thought he had gotten drunk and was sick from it, but when my aunt said he never touched liquors they became more serious over his condition. The next morning the hospital doctors called for specialists from all the leading hospitals in the city of New York. They examined and made x-ray pictures of Father and concluded that he had gastric-ulcers, and would die before the day was out unless he was operated on. He was too sick to care, but he asked them to telegraph Mother and have her come at once, and then to operate on him. Father said he gave up everything, and asked God to guide the doctors. We came to New York as soon as possible. I will never forget how bad my father looked when I saw him in that high white bed propped up on stilts. Mother and I prayed with Father and then left the hospital. We went to the hospital day and night until he was pronounced out of danger. Then I returned to S——, and left Mother and little C. in New York.

One week after I arrived home I received word that the family would be home. I never can forget how happy I was to hear that Father was well again, and would be home. We lived one year off of our savings account until Father was good and well. Mother went out to work two days a week to help keep up the expenses of the home. During all that time we never missed the payment of the rent and there was always plenty of food. We did not buy many clothes and I made over things for Mother and myself. We could always buy things for my little brother at a small price. So we didn't suffer. Father got employment at the S.F.I. Company as a porter, after he was pronounced by the family physician as in good health. Mother gave up her days work and stayed home. She kept very busy planning and learning to cook as the doctors said Father's food should be cooked. She had always cooked as southerners do and it was hard for her to learn to cook over again. I was taking cooking in high school then so it was easy for me to help her. I taught her all I knew, and then we studied how to neutralize acids, as Father could never have acid foods again. Those were busy, happy days when we were being restored to normal conditions again.

After Father had been on the new job a year we started buying our home. We bought a two family house with plenty of front lawn, forces in our economic system which affect the life of the white worker. In the last section we have seen the extent to which the depression has made the black worker dependent upon relief in the city. Some measure of the decline in the incomes of black workers is afforded by a study of 2,061 households in a section of Harlem in New York City. It was found that the incomes of skilled workers suffered the greatest proportionate decrease, their median income declining from $1,955 in 1929 to $1,003, or 48.7 per cent. The decline in the income of semiskilled and unskilled workers whose median incomes in 1929 were $1,941 and $1,599, respectively, amounted to 43 per cent. The decline in the black worker's earning power and unemployment did more than years of agitation to make him conscious of his position as a worker. In his struggle for adequate relief and a living wage, the black worker began co-operating more and more with the white worker and consequently regards his problems less as racial problems.

Thus one of the main results of the urbanization of the Negro population in recent years has been the emergence of a black industrial proletariat. Though many urban Negro workers must still seek a living in domestic and personal services, the number of skilled as well as semiskilled workers and laborers is growing. These industrial workers are acquiring a new outlook on life and are dominated less by the ideals and standards of the brown middle class or workers in domestic and personal services. It appears that, as the Negro worker becomes an industrial worker, he assumes responsibility for the support of his family and acquires a new authority in family relations. Moreover, as the isolation of the black worker is gradually broken down, his ideals and patterns of family life approximate those of the great body of industrial workers.

CONCLUSION

CHAPTER XXII

RETROSPECT AND PROSPECT

Our account of the development of the Negro family in the United States traverses scarcely more than a century and a half of history. Yet, during that comparatively brief period, from the standpoint of human history, the Negro, stripped of the relatively simple preliterate culture in which he was nurtured, has created a folk culture and has gradually taken over the more sophisticated American culture. Although only three-quarters of a century has elapsed since the arrival of the last representative of preliterate African races, the type of culture from which he came was as unlike the culture of the civilized American Negro today as the culture of the Germans of Tacitus' day was unlike the culture of German-Americans.

Thus our first task has been to discover the process whereby his raw sexual impulses were brought under control not only through the discipline of the master race but also by association with his fellows. Next, we have undertaken to study the character of the restraints upon sex and family behavior which have evolved as a part of the Negro's folk culture. Our final task has been to analyze the process by which a favored few have escaped from the isolation of the black folk and gradually taken over the attitudes and sentiments as well as the external aspects of the culture of the dominant race.

When the Negro slave was introduced into American economic life, he was to all intents and purposes, to use the words of Aristotle, merely an "animate tool." But, as in all cases where slavery exists, the fact that the slave was not only animate but human affected his relations with his masters. To the slave-trader, who had only an economic interest in the slave, the Negro was a mere utility. But, where master and slave had to live together and carry on some form of co-operation, the human nature of the slave had to be taken into account. Consequently, slavery developed into a social as well as an economic institution. The lives of the white master class became intertwined with the lives of the black slaves. Social control was not simply a matter of force and coercion but depended upon a system of etiquette based upon sentiments of superordination, on the one hand, and sentiments of submission and loyalty, on the other. Thus the humanization of the slave as well as his assimilation of the ideals, meanings, and social definitions of the master race depended upon the nature of his contacts with the master race. Where the slave was introduced into the household of the master, the process of assimilation was facilitated; but, where his contacts with whites were limited to the poor white overseer, his behavior was likely to remain impulsive and subject only to external control.

Yet, social interaction within the more or less isolated world of the slave did much to mold his personality. Although in some cases the slaves retained the conception of themselves which they had acquired in their own culture, their children were only slightly influenced by these fading memories. Consequently, their personalities reflected, on the whole, the role which they acquired in the plantation economy. Individual differences asserted themselves and influenced the responses of their fellow-slaves as well as their own behavior. The large and strong of body and those of nimble minds outstripped the weak and slow-witted. Some recognition was shown these varying talents and aptitudes by the slaves as well as by the masters. Within the world of the slave, social distinctions appeared and were appreciated.

When the sexual taboos and restraints imposed by their original culture were lost, the behavior of the slaves in this regard was subject at first only to the control of the masters and the wishes of those selected for mates. Hence, on the large plantations, where the slaves were treated almost entirely as instruments of production and brute force was relied upon as the chief means of control, sexual relations were likely to be dissociated on the whole from human sentiments and feelings. Then, too, the constant buying and selling of slaves prevented the development of strong emotional ties between the mates. But, where slavery became a settled way of life, the slaves were likely to show preferences in sexual unions, and opportunity was afforded for the development of strong attachments. The permanence of these attachments was conditioned by the exigencies of the plantation system and the various types of social control within the world of the plantation.

Within this world the slave mother held a strategic position and played a dominant role in the family groupings. The tie between the mother and her younger children had to be respected not only because of the dependence of the child upon her for survival but often because of her fierce attachment to her brood. Some of the mothers undoubtedly were cold and indifferent to their offspring, but this appears to have been due to the attitude which the mother developed toward the unborn child during pregnancy as well as the burden of child care. On the whole, the slave family developed as a natural organization, based upon the spontaneous feelings of affection and natural sympathies which resulted from the association of the family members in the same household. Although the emotional interdependence between the mother and her children generally caused her to have a more permanent interest in the family than the father, there were fathers who developed an attachment for their wives and children.

But the Negro slave mother, as she is known through tradition at least, is represented as the protectress of the children of the master race. Thus tradition has symbolized in the relation of the black foster-parent and the white child the fundamental paradox in the slave system—maximum intimacy existing in conjunction with the most rigid caste system. Cohabitation of the men of the master race with women of the slave race occurred on every level and became so extensive that it nullified to some extent the monogamous mores. The class of mixed-bloods who were thus created formed the most important channel by which the ideals, customs, and mores of the whites were mediated to the servile race. Whether these mixed-bloods were taken into the master's house as servants, or given separate establishments, or educated by their white forebears, they were so situated as to assimilate the culture of the whites. Although a large number of this class were poor and degraded, fairly well-off communities of mixed-bloods who had assimilated the attitudes and culture of the whites to a high degree developed in various parts of the country. It was among this class that family traditions became firmly established before the Civil War.

Emancipation destroyed the *modus vivendi* which had become established between the two races during slavery. Although the freedmen were able to move about and thereby multiply the external contacts with the white man's world, many of the intimate and sympathetic ties between the two races were severed. As a result, Negroes began to build their own institutions and to acquire the civilization of the whites through the formal process of imitation and education. Then, too, despite their high hopes that their freedom would rest upon a secure foundation of landownership, the masses of illiterate and propertyless Negroes were forced to become croppers and tenants under a modified plantation system. In their relative isolation they developed a folk culture with its peculiar social organization and social evaluations. Within the world of the black folk, social relations have developed out of intimate and sympathetic contacts. Consequently, the maternal-family organization, a heritage from slavery, has continued on a fairly large scale. But the maternal-family organization has also been tied up with the widespread illegitimacy which one still finds in these rural communities. Illegitimacy among these folk is generally a harmless affair, since it does not disrupt the family organization and involves no violation of the mores. Although formal education has done something in the way of dispelling ignorance and superstition, it has effected little change in the mores and customs of these folk communities.

The stability and the character of the social organization of the rural communities has depended upon the fortunes of southern agriculture. Up until the opening of the present century, the more ambitious and energetic of the former slaves and their descendants have managed to get some education and buy homes. This has usually given the father or husband an interest in his family and has established his authority. Usually such families sprang from the more stable, intelligent, and reliable elements in the slave population. The emergence of this class of families from the mass of the Negro population has created small nuclei of stable families with conventional standards of sexual morality all over the South. Although culturally these families may be distinguished from those of free ancestry, they have intermarried from time to time with the latter families. These families represented the highest development of Negro family life up to the opening of the present century.

The urbanization of the Negro population since 1900 has brought the most momentous change in the family life of the Negro since emancipation. This movement, which has carried over a million Negroes to southern cities alone, has torn the Negro loose from his cultural moorings. Thousands of these migrants have been solitary men and women who have led a more or less lawless sex life during their wanderings. But many more illiterate or semi-illiterate and impoverished Negro families, broken or held together only by the fragile bonds of sympathy and habit, have sought a dwelling-place in the slums of southern cities. Because of the dissolution of the rural folkways and mores, the children in these families have helped to swell the ranks of juvenile delinquents. Likewise, the bonds of sympathy and community of interests that held their parents together in the rural environment have been unable to withstand the disintegrating forces in the city. Illegitimacy, which was a more or less harmless affair in the country, has become a serious economic and social problem. At times students of social problems have seen in these various aspects of family disorganization a portent of the Negro's destruction.

During and following the First World War, the urbanization of the Negro population was accelerated and acquired even greater significance than earlier migrations to cities. The Negro was carried beyond the small southern cities and plunged into the midst of modern industrial centers in the North. Except for the war period, when there was a great demand for his labor, the migration of the Negro to northern cities has forced him into a much more rigorous type of competition with whites than he has ever faced. Because of his rural background and ignorance, he has entered modern industry as a part of the great army of unskilled workers. Like the immigrant groups that have preceded him, he has been forced to live in the slum areas of northern cities. In vain social workers and others have constantly held conferences on the housing conditions of Negroes, but they have been forced finally to face the fundamental fact of the Negro's poverty. Likewise, social and welfare agencies have been unable to stem the tide of family disorganization that has followed as a natural consequence of the impact of modern civilization upon the folkways and mores of a simple peasant folk. Even Negro families with traditions of stable family life have not been unaffected by the social and economic forces in urban communities. Family traditions and social distinctions that had meaning and significance in the relatively simple and stable southern communities have lost their meaning in the new world of the modern city.

By accelerating once again the cityward movement of Negroes, World War II brought within the orbit of urban civilization a larger sector of the Negro population. It is estimated that about a quarter of a million Negroes were attracted to the cities of the West where there had been relatively few Negroes. In the urban areas of the West as well as in the cities of the North, the Negro family faced the same economic and social problems. During the war period the Negro family enjoyed considerable economic security. But in its adjustment to an urban way of life, the Negro family revealed the same weakness in organization which was revealed during other periods of initial contacts with city life. There was considerable family desertion on the part of fathers and husbands; there was an increase in illegitimacy and juvenile delinquency. Consequently, World War II did not cause the Negro family to face new problems; it caused new strata of the Negro population to face the same problems of family adjustment which had been faced by former migrants to the city.

Although the problems facing the Negro family were the same as those it faced during and following the first World War, the impact of these problems on the Negro family were different. Be-

cause of the opportunities for employment, including the service of
men in the armed forces, Negro men and women were more able
to support their families. There was considerable upgrading of
Negro workers partly because of the Presidents Committee on Fair
Employment Practice and perhaps more especially because of the
manpower shortage. The improved economic status of the Negro
did not always bring greater stability to the family since children and
even wives were often able to escape their dependence upon the
father and husband in the family. However, the economic basis of
family life was made more secure and the physical setting for normal
family living was improved through the housing projects subsidized
by the federal government. Before the outbreak of World War II,
Negro families with low incomes had been the chief beneficiaries of
the low-rent housing programs. Although Negro families did not
fare so well in regard to the war-housing projects, their share in
these projects helped to make normal family living possible for
Negroes drawn into defense areas.

One of the most important consequences of the urbanization of
the Negro has been the rapid occupational differentiation of the
population. A Negro middle class has come into existence as the
result of new opportunities and greater freedom as well as the new
demands of the awakened Negro communities for all kinds of
services. This change in the structure of Negro life has been rapid
and has not had time to solidify. The old established families,
generally of mulatto origin, have looked with contempt upon the
new middle class which has come into prominence as the result of
successful competition in the new environment. With some truth
on their side, they have complained that these newcomers lack the
culture, stability in family life, and purity of morals which characterized their own class when it graced the social pyramid. In fact, there
has not been sufficient time for these new strata to form definite
patterns of family life. Consequently, there is much confusion and
conflict in ideals and aims and patterns of behavior which have been
taken over as the result of the various types of suggestion and
imitation in the urban environment. This confusion has been increased by the fact that the middle class has been affected with an

upper class outlook because of the segregation of the Negro. With incomes derived from occupations which would normally give them a middle class status, many families are influenced by extraneous values and attempt to maintain a style of life of a leisured upper class. But with the increase in the size of the middle class as the result of World War II, the upper class fringe is becoming more sharply differentiated from the middle class proper which is developing its own pattern of family life.

The most significant element in the new social structure of Negro life is the black industrial proletariat that has been emerging since the Negro was introduced into Western civilization. Its position in industry in the North was insecure and of small consequence until, with the cessation of foreign immigration during the first World War, it became a permanent part of the industrial proletariat. This development has affected tremendously the whole outlook on life and the values of the masses of Negroes. Heretofore, the Negro was chiefly a worker in domestic and personal services, and his ideals of family and other aspects of life were a crude imitation of the middle-class standards which he saw. Very often in the hotel or club he saw the white man during his leisure and recreation and therefore acquired leisure-class ideals which have probably been responsible for the "sporting complex" and the thriftlessness which are widespread among Negroes. But thousands of Negroes are becoming accustomed to the discipline of modern industry and are developing habits of consumption consonant with their new role. As the Negro has become an industrial worker and received adequate compensation, the father has become the chief breadwinner and assumed a responsible place in his family. Although World War II did not offer the same opportunities for large masses of unskilled Negro laborers as did the first World War, the black worker's position in industry was improved. Since the cessation of the War, the black worker has lost some of his gains but he has not lost his foothold in American industry.

As the result of the drafting of large numbers of Negro men into the armed forces, the lower strata of the Negro population developed a new attitude toward legal marriage. The legal and institutional meaning of marital relations became meaningful for thousands of Negro men for the first time when they were faced with the problem of making allowances for their wives and children. During the early years of the War there was among Negroes as among whites an increase in the birthrate. Following the War there was an increase in the illegitimacy rate at least in some cities. At the same time there has been a growing interest among Negroes in the program of planned parenthood. In various parts of the country Negro college and high school students are becoming interested in the question of planning for family life. Moreover, where clinics have been set up, working class Negro mothers are responding in ever increasing numbers to the advice provided concerning birth control.

When one views in retrospect the waste of human life, the immorality, delinquency, desertions, and broken homes which have been involved in the development of Negro family life in the United States, they appear to have been the inevitable consequences of the attempt of a preliterate people, stripped of their cultural heritage, to adjust themselves to civilization. The very fact that the Negro has succeeded in adopting habits of living that have enabled him to survive in a civilization based upon laissez faire and competition, itself bespeaks a degree of success in taking on the folkways and mores of the white race. That the Negro has found within the patterns of the white man's culture a purpose in life and a significance for his strivings which have involved sacrifices for his children and the curbing of individual desires and impulses indicates that he has become assimilated to a new mode of life.

However, when one undertakes to envisage the probable course of development of the Negro family in the future, it appears that the travail of civilization is not yet ended. First it appears that the family which evolved within the isolated world of the Negro folk will become increasingly disorganized. Modern means of communication will break down the isolation of the world of black folk, and, as long as the bankrupt system of southern agriculture exists, Negro families will continue to seek a living in the towns and cities of the country. They will crowd the slum areas of southern cities or make their way to northern cities where their family life will become disrupted and their poverty will force them to depend upon charity. Of course, the ordeal of civilization will be less severe if there is a general improvement in the standard of living and racial barriers to employment are broken down. Moreover, the chances for normal family life will be increased if large scale modern housing facilities are made available for the masses of the Negro population in cities. Nevertheless, those families which possess some heritage of family traditions and education will resist the destructive forces of urban life more successfully than the illiterate Negro folk and in either case their family life will adapt itself to the secular and rational organization of urban life. Undoubtedly, there will be a limitation of offspring; and men and women who associate in marriage will use it as a means for individual development.

The process of assimilation and acculturation in a highly mobile and urbanized society will proceed on a different basis from that in the past. There are evidences at present that in the urban environment, where caste prescriptions lose their force, Negroes and whites in the same occupational classes are being drawn into closer association than in the past. Such associations, to be sure, are facilitating the assimilation of only the more formal aspects of white civilization; but there are signs that intermarriage in the future will bring about a fundamental type of assimilation. Although there is no reliable measure of the extent of intermarriage at present, it appears that with the increasing mobility of the Negro intermarriage is slowly increasing. But, in the final analysis, the process of assimilation and acculturation will be limited by the extent to which the Negro becomes integrated into the economic organization and participates in the life of the community. The gains in civilization which result from participation in the white world will in the future as in the past be transmitted to future generations through the family.

INDEX

Africa, Negro mothers in, 33-34, 37
African survivals, 3 *ff*.
Alexander, Charles, 28, 46
Anderson, Robert, 26, 28, 46

Ball, Charles, 7, 8, 44, 49
Bassett, John S., 160
Batchelor, Carey, 342
Bernard, L. L., 37
Bibb, Henry, 47
Botume, Elizabeth H., 77, 80, 116
Brackett, Jeffrey R., 148
Bradford, Sarah E. H., 20
Breckinridge, Sophonisba P., 278
Brown, John, 8, 20, 54
Brown, Sterling A., 212
Bruce, Phillip A., 79, 89
Burgess, Ernest W., 232

Calhoun, Arthur W., 36, 51-52, 115, 155
Caliver, Ambrose, 321, 337
Castendyck, Elsa, 268
Catterall, Helen T., 43, 59, 60, 63, 135
Cayton, Horace R., 254
Child, L. Maria, 115
Childs, Benjamin G., 340
Clarke, Lewis, 26, 38, 64
Clarke, Milton, 26
Colcord, Joanna C., 245
Colson, Myra H., 353
Communities, Negro, in northern cities, 232-233; in Chicago, 233; social selection in, 234-236, 237-239; in Harlem, 236-239
Coppin, Levi J., 22, 106
Corey, Lewis, 319
Corruthers, James D., 150
Cullen, Countee, 16

Daniels, John, 148
Davis, Noah, 135-139
Delany, Martin, 9-10
Delinquency. *See* Juvenile delinquency.
Desdunes, R. L., 156, 203
Desertion. *See* Family Desertion.
Differentiation. *See* Social differentiation.

Divorces, among whites and Negroes, 281-282; among whites and Negroes in Mississippi, 282-283; effect of urbanization on, 283-284; among whites and Negroes in Virginia, 285; and desertions, 285-286; in cities, 287; in the middle class, 299-290
Dodge, David, 150
Domestic workers, social position of, 336; in District of Columbia, 337; family desertion among, 343
Donnan, Elizabeth, 34
Douglass, Frederick, 9, 22-23, 27, 41, 46, 115
Drake, St. Clair, 254
DuBois, W. E. B., 11-12, 83, 296, 302

Edwards, Bryan, 4-5
Edwards, W. J., 11
Emancipation, effect of, on race relations, 74-77, 79; on slave family, 77-79; on sex relations, 79-81; on marital relations, 80-82; on economic status, 83; on women, 102; on role of father, 127-128
Emery, E. B., 256
Eubank, Earl E., 246

Family desertion, and urbanization, 245-246; in Birmingham, Ala., 249-250; in Harlem, 250-251; in Chicago, 252-253; in relation to organization of community, 253-254; and divorces, 285-286; among domestic workers, 343
Family disorganization, and westward movement, 364-365. *See also* Family desertion.
Father, during slavery, 48; after Emancipation, 127-128; authority of, and economic factors, 128-131; effect of church on position of, 131-132, 134; purchase of wife and children by, 134-139; interest in family and economic factors, 140

369

Fisher, Myles M., 75, 87

Florida Plantation Records, 128, 129, 130

Folk, Negro, isolation of, 91-92; new contacts of, 92; illegitimacy among, 93; family mores of, 93-96; marriage among, 95-97; conflicting moral ideas among, 100; family disorganization among, 101

Frazier, E. Franklin, 235, 252

Frederick, Francis, 25

Free Negroes, origin of, 143; increase in, 143-144; and economic conditions, 144; distribution of, 144-145; concentration in cities, 145; prominence of mulattoes among, 145-146; education of, 146-147; institutions among, 148; economic status of, 148-149; in North, 151-152; family traditions of, 153-154, 156; in Charleston 154-156; in New Orleans, 155-159; in North Carolina, 159; in Petersburg, Va., 162-163

Gaines, W. J., 47, 82

Goodell, William, 64

Grandmother, during slavery, 114-116; as midwife, 119-120; and younger generation, 122-123; in the city, 123-124

Grandy, Moses, 36

"Granny." *See* Grandmother.

Groves, Ernest R., 284

Hare, Maud Cuney, 65

Harris, Abraham L., 318, 334

Haynes, Elizabeth R., 337

Heard, William H., 42-43, 48

Henson, Josiah, 48

Herskovits, Melville J., 328

Higginson, Thomas W., 73, 78, 114

Husband. *See* Father.

Illegitimacy, following Emancipation, 89-90, 257; statistics on, 90, 257-260; in rural areas, 90; in Birth-Registration Area, 90; and race mixture, 97; and Negro church, 98; and syphilis, 97, 100; and family disorganization, 100; and sexual promiscuity, 100-101; in Sommerville, Mass., 258; in Norfolk, Va., 258; in Trenton, N. J., 258; in Chicago, 258, 261; in New York City, 260-261; and family disorganization, 261-263; casual contacts in city and, 264; frequency of, 265; and personal disorganization, 266; and moral conflicts, 266-267. *See also* Women heads of families.

Industrial workers, sacrifices of, for children's education, 254; increase in, 335-336; outlook of, 338-340; housing of, 340-342; income of, 343; employment of wives of, 343-344; and color conflict, 344-346; family life of, 347-354; children in families of, 349-350; family income of, 355

Irving, Washington, 41, 134

Jackson, Andrew, 18

Jackson, Luther P., 163

Johnson, Andrew, 64

Johnson, James, W., 297

Juvenile delinquency, excess of, among Negroes, 268-269; in District of Columbia, 269; in Nashville, Tenn., 269-276; in New York City, 269-270, 276-277; in Chicago, 277-278; in relation to organization of urban community, 277-279

Kemble, Frances A., 38

King, Grace, 157

Kiser, Clyde V., 236, 241, 349

Lane, Lunsford, 28

Langston, John M., 66-69

Laws, J. Bradford, 89

Lewis, J. Vance, 74, 79, 87

Lichtenberger, J. P., 281

Locke, Alain, 219, 226

Loguen, J. W., 56

Lyell, Charles, 24

Males, excess of, 17-18

Marital relations, effect of northern missionaries on, 80-82; stabilization of, after Emancipation, 81-83; effect of landownership on, 87, marital statistics and, 104; marital status and, 104-106

Maternal family. *See* Maternal households.

Maternal households, in plantation South, 104; extent of, 103-104; in

Macon County, Ga., 110; economic status of, 110-111; social bonds of, 110-112; children in, 112-113; position of grandmother in, 114-119

McCord, Charles H., 263

McKay, Henry D., 278

Middle class, emergence of, 317; composition of, 318; in cities, 318-319; diverse cultural backgrounds of, 319-321; prominence of mulattoes in, 319-321; standards of consumption of, 322-325; conservatism of, in South, 325 ff; family organization of, 327 ff; attitudes and values of, 326-328; children in family of, 330-333; increase in size of, during World War II, 336

Middle Passage, 35

Migrants, letters of, 226-228; disillusionment of, 228-229. See also Urbanization.

Mixed-bloods, isolated communities of, 164 ff; with Indian ancestry, 165; family of, in Tennessee, 165-166; family traditions of, 167-172; patriarchal family traditions among, 168-173, 188; famiiles of, in Ohio, 169-170; families of, in New York, 173-175; in Delaware, 176-177; in New Jersey, 177-180; in North Carolina, 180-182; in Alabama, 182-184; in Virginia, 185-186; and breakdown of caste, 202. See also Race mixture.

Mobility of population, 209; and sex relations, 211 ff.; and romantic complex, 216-217; and sophistication, 217; and demoralization, 222-223. See also Family desertions and Family disorganization.

Morgan, A. T., 102, 129

Mothers, Negro, as foster mothers, 33, 39-40; as breeders, 35; devotion of, 43; as heads of slave cabins, 47. See also Maternal households, Women heads of families, and Illegitimacy.

Moton, Robert R., 11

Mulattoes. See Race mixture, Mixed-bloods, and Social differentiation.

Odum, Howard W., 212, 214

Ogburn, William F., 284

Old families, See Social differentiation.

Page, Thomas N., 115

Park, Mungo, 3, 4, 34

Park, Robert E., 6, 23, 232, 233

Pearson, Elizabeth, 77, 82, 84

Pennington, J. W. C., 30

Phillips, Charles H., 131, 134

Phillips, Ulrich B., 19, 37, 144

Pickard, Kate E. R., 58

Plummer, Nellie A., 29, 133

Puckett, Newbell N., 17

Race mixture, admonition to planters against, 50-51; result of relations of indentured whites and Negroes, 51-52; result of sexual association in cities, 52; result of prostitution, 52; result of relations of masters and slaves, 53; result of compulsion, 53-54; result of acquiescence on part of Negro woman, 54-55; result of mutual attraction, 55-56; and jealously on part of white women, 56-57; resentment of white women toward offspring of, 58-59; legal cases involving, 60-61; all classes involved in, 63; Andrew Johnson on, 64; and mulatto families, 65-69; in Hertford County, N. C., 107; in Issaquena County, Miss., 107; in Macon, Ga., and Ala., 107; and maternal family, 107-109, 121-122. See also Mixed-bloods, Social differentiation.

Reed, Ruth, 258, 259, 260

Reuter, Edward B., 321

Robertson, James, A., 155

Robison, Sophia, 268

Rollin, Frank A., 10

Russell, John H., 142

Sanders, Willy B., 90

Schoolcraft, H. B., 39

Shannon, A. H., 259, 303

Shaw, Clifford, 278

Slave trade, in District of Columbia, 43-44

Slaves, mating of, 18-20; influence of masters on mating of, 20, 29; courtship among, 21; social distinctions among, 22-23; division of labor among, 22-23; religion among, 23-24; as house servants, 24-25; nature of contacts with whites, 25-28; permanence of family relations among, 30; maternal feeling among, 34-43, 40

Smedes, Susan, 33, 80

Social differentiation, determined by family morals, 190; and landowner-ship, 191, 195; and family heritage, 194; and skin color, 198-199, 298-301; and sex morality, 200-201; and conflict of traditions, 203-204; early forms of, 296-298; in District of Columbia, 299-300; role of mulattoes in, 299-307; and caste feeling, 306-308; influence of white contacts on, 309-311; effect of occupational changes on, 313-315. *See also* Mixed-bloods, Old families, *and* Race mixture.

Social stratification. *See* Social differentiation

Spero, Sterling D., 334

Steward, Austin, 8-9, 25, 48

Steward, Theophilus, 81, 177

Steward, William, 177

Sullenger, T. Earl, 285

Sumner, William G., 261

Sutherland, Edwin H., 219

Sydnor, Charles S., 145

Thomas, William H., 259

Thompson, Warren S., 240

Turner, Edward R., 145

Urbanization, of Negro in South, 210; and romantic complex, 215-216; and sexual exploitation, 220-221; as a mass movement, 225; during and following First World War; 255 *ff.*; stimulation of, by Negro newspapers, 226 *ff.*; and effect on social control, 229; and sophistication, 230-231; and family desertion, 245-246

Washington, Booker T., 41, 62, 75-76, 161

Wembridge, Eleanor R., 124

West Indies, polygamy in, 5

Whelpton, P. K., 240

Wilcox, Walter F., 282

Women heads of families, in cities, 246-247; marital status of, 247-248. *See* Illegitimacy *and* Mothers.

Woodson, Carter G., 139, 143, 165, 321

Woofter, T. J., 120

PHOENIX BOOKS
Sociology, Anthropology, and Archeology

P 2   *Edward Chiera:* They Wrote on Clay
P 7   *Louis Wirth:* The Ghetto
P 10   *Edwin H. Sutherland,* EDITOR: The Professional Thief, by a professional thief
P 11   *John A. Wilson:* The Culture of Ancient Egypt
P 20   *Kenneth P. Oakley:* Man the Tool-maker
P 21   *W. E. LeGros Clark:* History of the Primates
P 24   *B. A. Botkin,* EDITOR: Lay My Burden Down: A Folk History of Slavery
P 28   *David M. Potter:* People of Plenty: Economic Abundance and the American Character
P 31   *Peter H. Buck:* Vikings of the Pacific
P 32   *Diamond Jenness:* The People of the Twilight
P 45   *Weston La Barre:* The Human Animal
P 53   *Robert Redfield:* The Little Community *and* Peasant Society and Culture
P 55   *Julian A. Pitt-Rivers:* People of the Sierra
P 64   *Arnold van Gennep:* The Rites of Passage
P 71   *Nels Anderson:* The Hobo: The Sociology of the Homeless Man
P 82   *W. Lloyd Warner:* American Life: Dream and Reality
P 85   *William R. Bascom and Melville J. Herskovits,* EDITORS: Continuity and Change in African Cultures
P 86   *Robert Redfield and Alfonso Villa Rojas:* Chan Kom: A Maya Village
P 87   *Robert Redfield:* A Village That Chose Progress: Chan Kom Revisited
P 88   *Gordon R. Willey and Philip Phillips:* Method and Theory in American Archaeology
P 90   *Eric Wolf:* Sons of the Shaking Earth
P 92   *Joachim Wach:* Sociology of Religion
P 105   *Sol Tax,* EDITOR: Anthropology Today: Selections
P 108   *Horace Miner:* St. Denis: A French-Canadian Parish
P 117   *Herbert A. Thelen:* Dynamics of Groups at Work
P 124   *Margaret Mead and Martha Wolfenstein,* EDITORS: Childhood in Contemporary Cultures
P 125   *George Steindorff and Keith C. Seele:* When Egypt Ruled the East
P 129   *John P. Dean and Alex Rosen:* A Manual of Intergroup Relations
P 133   *Alexander Heidel:* The Babylonian Genesis
P 136   *Alexander Heidel:* The Gilgamesh Epic and Old Testament Parallels
P 138   *Frederic M. Thrasher:* The Gang: A Study of 1,313 Gangs in Chicago (Abridged)
P 139   *Everett C. Hughes:* French Canada in Transition
P 162   *Thomas F. O'Dea:* The Mormons
P 170   *Anselm Strauss,* EDITOR: George Herbert Mead on Social Psychology
P 171   *Otis Dudley Duncan,* EDITOR: William F. Ogburn on Culture and Social Change
P 172   *Albert J. Reiss, Jr.,* EDITOR: Louis Wirth on Cities and Social Life
P 173   *John F. Embree:* Suye Mura: A Japanese Village
P 174   *Morris Janowitz:* The Military in the Political Development of New Nations
P 175   *Edward B. Tylor:* Researches into the Early History of Mankind and the Development of Civilization
P 176   *James Mooney:* The Ghost-Dance Religion and the Sioux Outbreak of 1890

PHOENIX BOOKS
in History

P 2   *Edward Chiera:* They Wrote on Clay

P 11   *John A. Wilson:* The Culture of Ancient Egypt

P 13   *Ernest Staples Osgood:* The Day of the Cattleman

P 16   *Karl Löwith:* Meaning in History: The Theological Implications of the Philosophy of History

P 22   *Euclides da Cunha:* Rebellion in the Backlands

P 27   *Daniel J. Boorstin:* The Genius of American Politics

P 28   *David M. Potter:* People of Plenty: Economic Abundance and the American Character

P 29   *Eleanor Shipley Duckett:* Alfred the Great: The King and His England

P 36   *A. T. Olmstead:* History of the Persian Empire

P 40   *Giorgio de Santillana:* The Crime of Galileo

P 61   *Warren S. Tryon:* My Native Land: Life in America, 1790–1870

P 66   *Alan Simpson:* Puritanism in Old and New England

P 69   *Gustave E. von Grunebaum:* Medieval Islam

P 70   *Oscar Jászi:* Dissolution of the Habsburg Monarchy

P 73   *Howard H. Peckham:* Pontiac and the Indian Uprising

P 80   *Carl Bridenbaugh:* The Colonial Craftsman

P 125   *George Steindorff and Keith C. Seele:* When Egypt Ruled the East

P 144   *Forrest McDonald:* We the People: The Economic Origins of the Constitution

P 147   *Donald Culross Peattie:* Venice: Immortal Village

P 150   *Kenneth Stampp:* And the War Came: The North and the Secession Crisis, 1860–61

P 153   *Eric L. McKitrick:* Andrew Johnson and Reconstruction

P 156–157   *Marc Bloch:* Feudal Society, *Vols I and II*

P 161   *Richard C. Wade:* The Urban Frontier: Pioneer Life in Early Pittsburgh, Cincinnati, Lexington, Louisville, and St. Louis

P 163   *Ernest K. Bramsted:* Aristocracy and the Middle-Classes in Germany

P 165   *Almont Lindsey:* The Pullman Strike

P 166   *William H. McNeill:* Past and Future

P 167   *Muhsin Mahdi:* Ibn Khaldûn's Philosophy of History

P 168   *Henry Bamford Parkes:* Marxism: An Autopsy

P 179   *Leon F. Litwack:* North of Slavery

P 181   *Karl Lehmann:* Thomas Jefferson

P 186   *Frederick B. Artz:* From the Renaissance to Romanticism

P 193   *Herbert J. Muller:* Religion and Freedom in the Modern World

P 194   *M. M. Knappen:* Tudor Puritanism

PHOENIX BOOKS
in Political Science and Law

P 4   *F. A. Hayek:* The Road to Serfdom

P 5   *Jacques Maritain:* Man and the State

P 27   *Daniel J. Boorstin:* The Genius of American Politics

P 67   *Yves R. Simon:* Philosophy of Democratic Government

P 84   *Edward H. Levi:* An Introduction to Legal Reasoning

P 97   *Gertrude Himmelfarb:* Lord Acton: A Study in Conscience and Politics

P 111   *Milton Friedman:* Capitalism and Freedom

P 112   *Leo Strauss:* The Political Philosophy of Hobbes: Its Basis and Its Genesis

P 113   *Carl Brent Swisher:* The Growth of Constitutional Power in the United States

P 115   *Robert A. Dahl:* A Preface to Democratic Theory

P 116   *Sebastian de Grazia:* The Political Community: A Study of Anomie

P 120   *F. A. Hayek,* EDITOR: Capitalism and the Historians

P 121   *Bertrand de Jouvenel:* Sovereignty: An Inquiry into the Political Good

P 130   *Walter J. Blum and Harry Kalven, Jr.:* The Uneasy Case for Progressive Taxation

P 135   *Carl Joachim Friedrich:* The Philosophy of Law in Historical Perspective

P 137   *Dallin H. Oaks,* EDITOR: The Wall between Church and State

P 143   *Karl Jaspers:* The Future of Mankind

P 144   *Forrest McDonald:* We the People

P 152   *Allison Dunham and Philip B. Kurland,* EDITORS: Mr. Justice

P 160   *Robert Endicott Osgood:* Ideals and Self-Interest in America's Foreign Relations

P 168   *Henry Bamford Parkes:* Marxism: An Autopsy

P 174   *Morris Janowitz:* The Military in the Political Development of New Nations

P 182   *Ernst Freund:* Standards of American Legislation

P 185   *Quincy Wright:* A Study of War

P 189   *Hans Morgenthau:* Scientific Man vs. Power Politics

P 190   *Karl Loewenstein:* Political Power and the Governmental Process

P 196   *Walter F. Murphy:* Congress and the Court

P 197   *Lloyd A. Fallers:* Bantu Bureaucracy

P 203   *Philip B. Kurland,* EDITOR: The Supreme Court and the Constitution

DATE DUE

GAYLORD   PRINTED IN U.S.A.

and room for a garden in back. There was a good barn in back of the house which could be transformed into a garage. The house was just across the street from where we used to live. Father instantly began to remodel the house, and Mother and I did all we could to help him. He papered, put in new plumbing, and put in the electricity himself. Then he had experts in these fields come and examine his work. In that way it cost us only the price of the fixtures because Father did this in his spare time. Mother and I washed all the windows, woodwork, and floors. I was a senior in High School, but I was not too proud to help my mother. In fact we were so anxious to have our own home that we all worked to the end of our strength to have it. After the house was cleaned and ready for us, we moved all the light articles of furniture and clothing over in my brother's wagon. Then Father had a truck move the heavy things. We had to buy a few more pieces of furniture to make our new home in good living condition.

Then the big thing before us was the getting of the house paid for. The second floor brought in a large rent which Father paid on the house, he paid his rent on the house also. I got a job after school so as to buy my own clothes, and then to save money for college too. I worked on Saturday mornings and saved the money by weekly payments on a Christmas club savings account. For four summers I had a job as a cook and made quite a large sum of money during the vacation. Father changed the barn into a two car garage and rented both of them out, because then we could not afford a car. During all this hard struggle we never failed to attend church on Sunday, and Father even went to Prayer meeting as he was a deacon. I was a Sunday School teacher and went to both Sunday School and morning church. The entire family went to church on the first Sunday night service so as to take our communion. We always had Sunday clothes even if our neighbors did wonder how we managed.

I graduated from High School the second year we had the house. Father didn't see how he could send me to college with the house to be paid for, but since I had saved five hundred dollars for college he would send me. The year I started in college my little brother started in first grade. Father paid my train fare to college and my savings account paid my first quarter's expenses. The next quarter I made my tuition by working, and my family paid my room and board in the dormitory. Father managed my bank account so that it paid my room and board for two years while I was in college. He paid my train expenses and bought my clothes and I worked for my tuition. At first I wrote my family twice a week and sent telegrams often. Then later, I wrote once a week.

The only time Father and I clashed over ideas was when I started to dance, and wanted to attend dances. Mother and I tried to show him that there was no harm in dancing, but he insisted that Christians should not dance or attend them. I dance and play cards even if my father objects. It makes me happy to know that my family has paid for our home, and that they are now able to enjoy life after the hard struggle which they have put forth to have a few of the necessary things.

In many of the workers' families, the parents, especially the mother, make tremendous sacrifices to give their children an education. A college student, whose father was a stationary fireman, wrote as follows of the sacrifices which were made for her education:

Both my parents did their part in their efforts to give me an education. However, most of the sacrifices were made by my mother when I needed things. Dad was more of an outside show than an executioner. He did a lot of talk about what he was doing but at the root of all his doing was mother's influence.

One can get some idea of the extent of these sacrifices by considering some facts brought out in a study by the Committee on Scholarships and Student Aid at Howard University in 1931. This study revealed that, during the academic year 1929-30, students from families supported by domestic and personal service and skilled and unskilled occupations, received on the average $290.36 and $379.93, respectively, and that Freshmen entering in 1930 from both of these occupational classes expected on the average over $500 from their parents. Yet the average income of the persons in domestic and personal service was only $1,000 and that of the parents in skilled and unskilled labor $1,200. Ordinarily, these children of the workers would have looked forward with certainty to entering middle-class occupations, which would have afforded a relatively comfortable and secure position in the Negro community. However, the depression had not only made impossible such sacrifices on the part of their parents but had made the sons and daughters in workers' families more conscious of the insecurity of the Negro middle class and their dependence upon the workers.

The condition of the black worker is determined by the same